To Secretary of Defense
Mr. Leon E. Paneta

A Book on one p___ ___ ___ ___ hul
active defence, u ___ ___ ___ 's not
meld another.

___ ___ yours

Shlomo Nakdimon

22.02.2012

The Exclusive Story
of How Israel
Foiled Iraq's Attempt
to Get the Bomb

TRANSLATED BY
PERETZ KIDRON

FIRST STRIKE

Shlomo Nakdimon

SUMMIT BOOKS • NEW YORK

COPYRIGHT © 1987 BY SHLOMO NAKDIMON
ENGLISH LANGUAGE TRANSLATION COPYRIGHT © 1987 BY SUMMIT BOOKS,
A DIVISION OF SIMON & SCHUSTER, INC.
ALL RIGHTS RESERVED
INCLUDING THE RIGHT OF REPRODUCTION
IN WHOLE OR IN PART IN ANY FORM
PUBLISHED BY SUMMIT BOOKS
A DIVISION OF SIMON & SCHUSTER, INC.
SIMON & SCHUSTER BUILDING
1230 AVENUE OF THE AMERICAS
NEW YORK, NEW YORK 10020
SUMMIT BOOKS AND COLOPHON ARE TRADEMARKS OF
SIMON & SCHUSTER, INC.
DESIGNED BY EVE METZ
MANUFACTURED IN THE UNITED STATES OF AMERICA

10   9   8   7   6   5   4   3   2   1

LIBRARY OF CONGRESS CATALOGING IN PUBLICATION DATA
NAKDIMON, SHLOMO
  FIRST STRIKE.

    1.JEWISH-ARAB RELATIONS—1973-.   2.BAGHDAD
(IRAQ)—HISTORY—BOMBARDMENT, 1981.   3.NUCLEAR
POWER PLANTS—IRAQ.   I.TITLE.
DS119.7.N292   1987   956.7'043   87-10016
ISBN 0-671-63871-8

TO ZAHAVA, YISGAV AND YANIV;
THEY TOO WERE ON SADDAM HUSSAIN'S LIST.

Contents

Preface

Tammuz 17: that was Iraq's name for the nuclear reactor it purchased from France. Tammuz 17 is July 17, the date the Ba'ath Party achieved full and absolute power in Iraq.

As coincidence would have it, the date is equally significant in Jewish history, where, however, its connotations are painfully tragic: on the seventeenth day of Tammuz in the year 586 B.C. the armies of Nebuchadnezzar, King of Babylonia, battered their way through the walls of Jerusalem, thereby initiating the final phase in the destruction of the First Temple.

Nebuchadnezzar has always been a hero to Saddam Hussain, Iraq's modern ruler. Time and time again, he has exhorted his people to regard Nebucadnezzar as one of the three great forebears in whose footsteps Iraq should advance. In Hussain's view, Iraq is the successor of the Babylonians who once dominated the entire Middle East.

Simultaneously, Hussain also regards himself as scion and heir to the seventh- and eighth-century Moslem conquerors who thundered westward, prosecuting their jihad with the war cry "Mohammed's law is the sword." But as a man of the twentieth century, Hussain uses a slightly modified watchword: "Saddam's law is the atom." That this is his purpose is clearly testified by the course of action he adopted, and by the project he designed and constructed at al-Tuweitha, near Baghdad.

The Israeli Air Force deferred implementation of Hussain's pitiless dreams when it hammered Tammuz into a flaming ruin. The story of how that was accomplished is presented in these pages.

A few words of thanks are called for.

The idea of composing this work arose from a conversation with friend and book lover Yehuda Shiff.

Prime Minister Menahem Begin gave his blessing to the idea.

Colonel Azriel Nevo, who was his military aide, lent a helping hand.

Certain persons connected with the matter thought differently, and some of the material consequently took considerable time and effort to assemble.

Yitzhak Shamir, who succeeded Begin as prime minister, added his recommendations, thereby opening up some doors hitherto locked.

The manuscript was studied by four persons: General (Res.) David Ivry, former commander of the Air Force and the man in direct command of the operation that destroyed the Iraqi reactor; the writer, whose professional competence lies in quite different fields, benefited from Ivry's guidance and assistance far beyond what is customary. Knesset member Professor Yuval Ne'eman commented on the scientific passages and displayed great patience in simplifying complexities. Knesset member Abba Eban read the manuscript from the vantage point of a politician rich in experience who is himself a writer of renown; his comments far transcended the profit-and-loss bookkeeping prevalent in everyday Israeli politics. Aryeh Naor, who was Cabinet secretary at the time of the operation, proffered the counsel of his rich experience.

Three persons assisted in writing this book: Ya'akov Etlinger, a young student with a superb instinct for research, toiled to collate the material from libraries and research institutes. My colleague Rami Tal, an efficient translator and editor, gave the draft manuscript the polish necessary to make it accessible to all. Dr. Amos Carmel, scientist, writer and editor whose mastery of the intricacies of the Hebrew language is one of his outstanding traits, gave the product its final shape, and its title. Carmel and Tal enriched me with their fertile minds and good counsel, and by their endeavor to put themselves in the reader's shoes.

Peretz Kidron, in addition to proving himself as a translator of the first order, surpassed himself in imbuing the text with the spirit of the Hebrew original.

It goes without saying that responsibility for the text is entirely mine.

Finally, as I submit this book to the reader's judgment, I cherish in my heart the memory of Michael Albin, who contributed so greatly to heightening the Israeli business community's awareness of cultural matters and encouraged the research which preceded the writing of this book.

September 1986   SHLOMO NAKDIMON

Thus says the Lord of hosts;
The broad wall of Babylon
shall be leveled to the ground
and her high gates
shall be burned with fire.
The peoples labor for naught,
and the nations weary themselves
only for fire.

—JEREMIAH 51:58

Translator's Note

Sections of this book refer to conversations, declarations or documents which, while originally in other languages, came into the author's possession in a Hebrew version. As a result of their translation and retranslation, minor verbal inaccuracies may have crept in, although every effort has been made to provide an English rendering faithful in substance and spirit to the original.

With regard to certain persons and military code names mentioned in the text, true names are classified information; they have accordingly been given fictitious substitutes which, at their first mention, are so identified in footnotes.

PERETZ KIDRON

1 "Tel Aviv has been wiped off the face of the earth."

Nine o'clock in the morning of Sunday, November 3, 1985: The conference chamber at the Prime Minister's office in Jerusalem. The Israeli Cabinet is convening for its final session before the impending Eleventh Knesset elections. The seat at the head of the table is occupied by Prime Minister Menahem Begin, bespectacled and ascetic, wearing his customary business suit.

Begin opens the proceedings. "My friends," he says, "we are gathered to summarize more than four years of fruitful endeavor. We have achieved numerous successes, and we have also had our setbacks. When the historian comes to record the annals of this period, I hope he will judge us fairly and pronounce our deeds and decisions to have been directed towards promoting the welfare of Israel and its people. As you are aware, this is the last time I shall be presiding over a Cabinet meeting. It has long been my wish to retire, but numerous requests and entreaties persuaded me to defer—"

The Cabinet secretary, Dan Meridom, a handsome young man of great promise, glances up impatiently as the Prime Minister's military aide, Colonel Azriel Nevo, hastens into the conference room. "What the hell does he want?" the secretary growls.

Nevo, his goatee carefully trimmed, approaches Begin. "The Commander in Chief is on the line," he flusters. "It's urgent, he says."

Begin rises and strides to the neighboring room, where he picks up the phone. On the other end, the familiar voice of Major General Moshe Levy is edgy in spite of an evident effort to conceal his nervousness. "Prime Minister," he mutters, "we have a problem. An unidentified Boeing 727 is approaching Tel Aviv from the sea. We sent up interceptors who have signaled the pilot to follow them, but he isn't responding. I request permission to shoot him down. We can't afford to take any risks."

Begin hesitates, recalling the tragic results of the 1972 downing of a Libyan airliner in Sinai. "Is there no other option?" he demands.

"I'm afraid not, sir. I'm told that the plane—"

Abruptly, the receiver in the Prime Minister's hand falls silent. The call has been cut off. "Hello!" Begin calls. "Moshe!" But there is no reply.

"Strange," Begin mumbles. He feels a sudden stab of acute anxiety. Turning to Nevo, who is standing beside him, he snaps, "Get him on another line!" In the meantime, he returns to the conference room to apologise to the ministers.

High over Tel Aviv, two F-15 pilots make strenuous efforts to convince the captain of the Boeing to follow them without further delay. There is no response from the airliner. Transmitting on the international frequency, lead pilot Major Yaakov Tzur* spells out his final warning: "We are opening fire!"

At that precise moment, a large dark object suddenly tumbles from the belly of the Boeing. "It's a bomb!" cries Tzur, simultaneously blazing away with his cannon. His shooting is accurate: the airliner bursts into flames. The air-to-air missile dispatched by Tzur's partner has been fired needlessly.

The dark object continues its plunge.

Colonel Nevo persists in his efforts to renew the direct phone link, but without success. Suddenly, a dull thunderous rumble is heard, coming from a westerly direction. The men in the conference room stare at one another in perplexity. It is a fine clear day, without a trace of cloud in the sky.

9:02 A.M. The whole of Tel Aviv is illuminated by a blinding flash of lightning brighter than a thousand suns. In the Kirya governmental complex, the industrial quarter and the area bordered by Dizengoff Street to the west, Yigal Alon Street to the east, Jabotinsky Street to the north and La Guardia Street to the south, seventy thousand persons die within one millionth of a second. Along with the buildings, cars and trees about them, they dissolve into a gaseous mass whose initial temperature soars to several hundred thousand degrees Centigrade.

9:04 A.M. The conference room.

His eyes glassy, Nevo stares at the telephone. "You . . . you can't mean it . . ." he whispers. He lays down the phone and, his step faltering, stumbles toward the Prime Minister. "Sir," he mutters. "The Commander in Chief has asked me to notify you that an atom bomb fell on Tel Aviv two minutes ago."

*Fictitious name.

• • •

Twenty-five seconds after the detonation, the blast hits the Hatikva quarter, Givat Rambam and north Tel Aviv. Hundreds of buildings collapse like cards. A further twenty-five thousand persons are killed instantaneously.

Over the coming weeks, an additional forty thousand will die from exposure to radiation.

Tel Aviv, Israel's largest city and the nerve center of the Jewish state, has been reduced to a pile of smoking ashes.

9:45 A.M. The conference room. All present stare, pale and speechless, at the radio. A few minutes earlier, Iraqi President Saddam Hussain let it be known that he is about to make a declaration of world-shattering significance. The announcement will be broadcast in Arabic initially, and then in English and Hebrew translation.

The radio, tuned to Baghdad, emits cheerful military marches. Suddenly the music fades and the announcer's voice proclaims: "The declaration of the President of the Republic of Iraq, Field Marshal Saddam Hussain."

Since most of the ministers do not understand Arabic, the Prime Minister resolves not to wait for the Iraqi radio to offer its translation. A seat is placed at the table for a senior official of Iraqi origin, who translates the statement as it comes over the airwaves.

"My one hundred twenty million Arab brethren! In the whole of Arab history, this is the greatest day since the battle of Karnei Hittin eight hundred years ago, when Saladin defeated the Crusader invaders and drove them out of Palestine. Today, Iraq has devastated Tel Aviv—the bastion of the Zionist canker which has lodged for a century within the body of the Arab nation, devouring it from within. Tel Aviv has been wiped off the face of the earth.

"Over the past four years, working in the utmost secrecy, we have developed atomic weapons which our foes did not believe us capable of acquiring. Aided by France and Italy, our Tammuz-17 reactor has enabled us to build up an arsenal of nuclear arms adequate for the utter destruction of Israel—and that is what we shall achieve, if necessary.

"We demand of Israel a declaration, given freely and voluntarily, that she has now ceased to exist as a Zionist entity. An Arab committee over which I shall preside will pronounce upon the fate of the Jewish inhabitants of the former state of Israel. If the Jews reject our terms, we shall annihilate them, leaving no surviving remnant. This is a sacred cause, in pursuit of which we are prepared for any sacrifice.

"The law of Mohammed is the sword."

• • •

10:00 A.M. The conference room.

Begin's voice is soft, but there is something in his tone which makes his listeners' blood run cold. "Gentlemen, we have much to do today, and we will disperse shortly. Saddam Hussain will pay, of that there can be no doubt. But first there is something I must say.

"I take upon myself full responsibility for this new Holocaust which has overtaken our people forty years after the Nazi massacres in Europe. I am to blame! Five years ago, we possessed the military means to destroy the Iraqi nuclear reactor before it ever went into operation. Several of you who served under me at that time will recall the prolonged deliberations my Cabinet held to that end. You will remember our doubts and hesitations. Ultimately, out of concern for the diplomatic repercussions, I bowed to the views of the experts and ministers, and we decided against bombing the reactor. But I blame no one! The responsibility rests upon me. I am guilty. Regrettably, I do not see how any mortal being can ever discharge such a staggering culpability."

The Prime Minister terminates his statement and gazes around the table, surveying the faces of his colleagues. Then he bursts into heartrending sobs.

That is a scenario which might have been. But the train of events unfolded differently. More than four years earlier, during the afternoon hours of June 7, 1981, Israeli Air Force planes bombed the Iraqi nuclear reactor, reducing it to rubble and bringing Baghdad's nuclear program to a resounding halt.

That bombing raid, and the long months of debate and soul-searching that preceded it, constitute the subject of this book.

2 "...Hussain is ...more vicious than Qaddafi."

The sole Arab ruler to sight the Israeli planes en route to their target was King Hussein. The Jordanian monarch spent that Sunday, June 7, 1981, at sea, on board his private yacht, named *Nur* for his fourth wife, Nur al-Hussein.

The sun was sinking into the sea, but the Gulf of Aqaba was still aflame. Like Gothic castles hemming in the gulf from all sides, the surrounding range of pink-tinged hills exuded airy ripples as they released the fiery heat they had stored since sunrise. The turquoise sea swelled gently, with sparkling wavelets dancing in all directions.

As always, forty-seven-year-old Hussein ibn Talal al-Hashmi felt at peace on board the well-fitted royal yacht. But at this moment, around four in the afternoon, the King's sense of tranquillity was abruptly disturbed by the roar of jets which drew his gaze to the skies. Being an experienced pilot, Hussein found no difficulty in identifying the planes comprising the formation overhead: eight multipurpose F-16s, sheltering beneath an umbrella provided by six F-15s (so the strike force was described by the international media, citing Pentagon sources).

"Though unable to make out their insignia, Hussein could judge from their course that they must have come from the nearby Israeli airbase of Etzion." Such was the account later provided by eminent Jordanian personages when Dr. Amnon Kapeliuk paid the first-ever overt visit by an Israeli journalist to their country.

Having ruled Jordan for some thirty years, Hussein was well versed in the strategic intricacies of Mideastern geography. He consequently found no difficulty in deducing that the Israeli planes were headed for a target in some Arab state. That target could be the major Saudi Arabian base of Tebuk, which poses a direct threat to Israel. Or it might be his own kingdom's sole port, Aqaba, where numerous freighters were unloading military supplies for Iraq to employ in its war with Iran. Equally conceivable, the planes could be on some intelligence mission.

However, for a variety of reasons, none of these hypotheses stood up to the most elementary analysis. Hussein was troubled and uneasy. How did he react? Did he alert his military commanders? Did he try to reach his fellow monarch, the King of Saudi Arabia? Dr. Kapeliuk heard that Hussein "tried to warn the Iraqis."

The yacht's sophisticated radio should have enabled the King to contact anyone he chose, anywhere in the region. However, the Jordanians concluded sorrowfully, Hussein "did not have time" to alert Baghdad.

While Hussein continued to ponder over the puzzle, and the Israeli planes continued on their flight course, the Israeli Cabinet assembled at the Prime Minister's official residence in Jerusalem's Talbia quarter.

June 7, 1981, fell on the fifth day of the month of Sivan, which the Hebrew calendar designates as the eve of the Jewish festival of Shavuoth. The previous week, several ministers had asked for that Sunday's regular Cabinet meeting to be postponed, so as to draw out the weekend till the Tuesday after the festival, thereby giving them a much-needed rest before the conclusive phase of the Knesset election campaign, then in full swing.

But the Prime Minister rejected their requests. Cabinet secretary Aryeh Naor, who was privy to every state secret, whether military or political, was instructed by Begin to call the Cabinet meeting for nine o'clock Sunday morning. Convening as "the Ministerial Committee for Defense"—a device which precludes Israeli media coverage and other leaks—the Cabinet heard the Prime Minister report on his talks with Egyptian President Anwar as-Sadat at Sharm al-Sheikh three days earlier.

After the meeting, Naor and military aide Brigadier Ephraim Poran, acting on a hint from Begin, made a personal call to each member of the Cabinet. "The Prime Minister wants to see you at his residence at five this afternoon," they told each minister, taking great care to keep him from learning that his colleagues were the recipients of a similar summons. "Notify no one, not even your personal staff."

Having undertaken to contact religious ministers who lived outside Jerusalem, Poran advised them not to worry about desecrating the impending holy day due to the late hour of their meeting with Begin. The experienced Poran was renowned for his expertise in dealing with "VIP logistics"; rare indeed the technical problems that left him baffled, and this was not one of them. He arranged for helicopters to stand by to ferry the Orthodox ministers to their homes in good time before the onset of the festival.

The late Simha Ehrlich, at that time one of two deputy prime ministers— did not stay till the end of the Cabinet's morning meeting. "That morning I didn't know there was anything on," Ehrlich recalled later. But evidently alerted by his famous "sense of smell," he noted the tension in the air. "I asked a friend in the Prime Minister's office what was going on. He smiled and said, 'Ask the Prime Minister.' I said, 'I don't like to ask if he doesn't tell me.' Then the official said, 'Today is the day.'

"I had to leave for Tel Aviv before the end of the meeting. When I got home, I found a message that I was to come to the Prime Minister's residence that afternoon. My wife, Tzilla, couldn't understand what was up. Why an emergency meeting on the eve of the festival, of all times? I told her there must be some urgent business."

Close on five, when the ministers' cars reached Talbia, they found security men awaiting them three blocks from the official residence. The ministers were requested to cover the rest of the way on foot, while their drivers were sent to park their vehicles in side streets. The aim was, of course, to avoid attracting the attention of the journalists and idlers who perpetually gather around the Prime Minister's home.

Entering the residence, each minister was surprised to find his colleagues present—indicating that, contrary to what he had been led to believe, he was not coming to a private meeting with the Prime Minister. But none of the Cabinet members divined the purpose of the gathering. Only Finance Minister Yoram Aridor—a man with no military expertise to boast of— stared Naor straight in the eye and, in a tone with more affirmation than inquiry, said, "The reactor."

The towering Finance Minister was not mistaken. At that precise moment, the fourteen-plane assault force was approaching al-Tuweitha, near Baghdad. According to the account of Egyptian journalist Anis Mansour in the weekly *October*, the planes bypassed seven military airfields and numerous radar networks. Mansour, who gets his information directly from Egyptian presidential circles, wrote that the Israelis chose a flight path not covered by their enemies' radar.

On various occasions, Prime Minister Begin was to point out that the planes were easy to identify: bearing no camouflage, they openly displayed their Israeli Air Force insignia. It is therefore probable that they were identified successively by the Jordanians, the Saudis and the Iraqis. Only when King Hussein sighted them again as, homeward bound, they crossed his country's airspace on their way to land at Etzion, could he deduce that their objective must have been much farther removed than Saudi Arabia.

News of the attack on al-Tuweitha was relatively late in reaching the Iraqi President. It emerged later that King Hussein had failed to locate Field Marshal Saddam Hussain, who was touring the Iranian battlefront that day.

It transpired further why Hussein had been equally unsuccessful in his attempts to contact the Saudi King: Khalid ibn Abdel-Aziz was at an exclusive Swiss clinic, whence he planned to continue to Britain for a state visit. On learning of the attack, he phoned Crown Prince Fahd, instructing him to stand by Iraq.

The Iraqis, briefed by Jordan about the route taken by the attacking planes, deduced that the raid was the work of the Israelis. Acting in coordination, Jordan and Saudi Arabia now decided to approach the Americans. Early on June 8, an official Saudi representative visited the U.S. Embassy in Riyadh to complain of Israeli warplanes overflying his country on their way to attack objectives in Iraq. The Saudis also contacted the stunned Iraqis for the purpose of taking action against Israel.

Radio Amman later reported that King Hussein had finally succeeded in establishing telephone contact with Saddam Hussain. The Jordanian monarch assured Iraq's President of his support "to the hilt" for the "just war" he and his country were waging on two fronts: against Iran and against Israel. Iraq, the King affirmed, would always constitute the strategic depth of the entire Arab nation; whoever failed to take Iraq's side supported Israel in effect.

However, King Hussein was too experienced to retain much trust in the resolve of his Arab fellow rulers. Intent on spurring them into effective action, he directed his Prime Minister, Mudar Badran, to issue a public statement. Thus it came about that at two in the afternoon of June 8, Radio Amman, citing Badran, announced that Israeli aircraft had repeatedly bombed vital targets in Iraq.

"They can be understood to refer to the bombing of the reactor," commented Prime Minister Begin when his military aide hastened to tell him of the Jordanian announcement, which appeared to be the first public reference to the raid to come from Arab sources.

The official Israeli communiqué lay ready on the Prime Minister's desk. Its release had been delayed so that Israel would not be the first to make the raid public. Now that Jordan had taken the lead, Begin ordered publication of the Israeli response. Later, when critics complained that Amman had not specified the reactor as the target of the raid, Begin would respond, "Was it necessary to 'poke a finger into the mouth' [make them spell it out] to know that such was their meaning? . . . Should we have allowed Iraq to get in first . . . ? What are we, thieves in the night?"

Three days prior to the raid, on June 4, Begin had met with Egyptian President Anwar as-Sadat at Sharm al-Sheikh. The two leaders discussed various aspects of bilateral relations, and broader Mideastern issues. In the course of their conversations, Iraq was mentioned only once, and that was at Sadat's initiative. "Saddam Hussain," said the Egyptian President "is even more vicious than [Libyan ruler] Qaddafi."

Indeed, Begin mused, who could equal Sadat's close acquaintance with his fellow Arab rulers?

So he thought as he committed Sadat's characterization to memory.

3 "The Butcher of Baghdad"

The publicized portions of Saddam Hussain's biography depict a tortuous path. With regard to numerous details, the full truth has never emerged, and others are the subject of controversy. In typical Arab fashion, his official biography has undergone frequent rewrites, aimed at depicting him as a courageous warrior fully aware from an early age of the course that was to take him to preeminence.

Beyond dispute is the fact that Hussain was born in April 1937, in a small village on the banks of the Tigris River, near the town of Takrit. His peasant father having departed this world, Saddam spent his childhood in the homes of various uncles, beginning his schooling at a relatively late age. Those who remember him from high school describe him as weak and gangling, earning him the nickname of "Hunchback" from jeering classmates. Even if his defects were not a deliberate fabrication designed to present him as an antihero, they did not stand in the way of his political ambitions. While still a high-school student, Hussain enrolled in the then minuscule Ba'ath (Resurrection) Party.

Founded in Syria during the forties, the Ba'ath is a pan-Arab socialist party. It adopts hard-line policies which are simultaneously anticapitalist, anti-imperialist and anti-Zionist. Right from the start it bitterly opposed any dealings with Israel, which the Ba'athists perceive as the greatest menace to pan-Arabism. While the various Arab regimes went in fear of Ba'ath extremism, the party gained adherents among junior officers still smarting over their defeat by Israel in 1948.

On July 14, 1958, an officers' coup overthrew the Iraqi monarchy; the King and his ministers were brutally murdered. Power fell to the leader of the plot, Brigadier Abdel-Karim Kassem, who had commanded a battalion in the Iraqi expeditionary force sent to fight in Palestine in 1948. Kassem soon found himself embroiled in factional infighting, and the Ba'ath leaders planned a further coup to depose him. Saddam Hussain was given the key assignment of assassinating Kassem; however, the prospective victim escaped harm, while Hussain got a bullet in the leg, apparently from one of his fellow conspirators. Years later, the story was rehashed to present Hussain as an unflinching hero: it was related that he used his commando knife to dislodge the bullet from his leg. Whether true or a fabrication authored by Hussain himself, the story appears in all his biographies as well as in various works of research.

Hitherto a freshman at the college of Baghdad, Hussain now found himself one of the most wanted men in Iraq. Disguised as a Bedouin, he fled to a remote province, while a Baghdad military court sentenced him to death in absentia. However, by the time the verdict had been handed down, Hussain was in Syria, which was then unified with Egypt in the United Arab Republic, headed by Gamal Abdel Nasser. The reputation of the fugitive Iraqi conspirator soon reached Nasser, who took an interest in young revolutionaries from all parts of the Arab world, regarding them as the cadres who would help achieve his life's ambition of uniting the Arab world under Egypt's leadership.

Nasser had Hussain brought to Egypt, where he graduated from college and went on to enroll at Cairo University's law school. Most of his time was spent in activity among the political emigrés Nasser was organizing to promote his plans for pan-Arab revolution.

In 1962 Hussain returned to Syria. In February 1963, the Iraqi Ba'ath Party succeeded in carrying through its long-awaited coup. Kassem was assassinated and was replaced by Colonel Abdel Salam Muhammed Arif, likewise a veteran of the 1948 Palestine campaign, who had been Kassem's principal associate in the antimonarchial conspiracy. Later the two men drifted apart, until Arif was sentenced to death for plotting to murder Kassem. But the latter pardoned his old friend—a mistake for which he would soon pay with his life.

The latest revolution soon set off conflicts among various Ba'athist factions, and Hussain was arrested, though his detention left him some freedom of action. Furthermore, events unfolded swiftly: Arif was killed in a mysterious airplane accident and was succeeded by his brother Abdel Rahman Arif, who managed to cling to power till July 17, 1968, when he was overthrown by a junta of officers who did not adhere to the Ba'ath, but whose coup nevertheless restored the party to power.

Iraq was now ruled by a revolutionary council under General Ahmed Hassan al-Bakr, a member of the Free Officers group which had toppled the monarchy and the first prime minister appointed by Arif, though he was soon dismissed. While not a Ba'athist, Bakr sympathized with the party's more moderate right wing. His emergence marked the onset of "Takritization," monopolization of power by natives of the town of Takrit and its vicinity, his takeover being backed by several generals likewise originating in that region. Like most of the Moslems in the Mideast, the people of Takrit are Sunnis, and the new regime soon turned against the country's Shi'ite Moslem majority, which was reduced to the status of a powerless minority. The Bakr-Ba'athist coalition also took swift and drastic action against survivors of the previous regimes, showing no hesitation in killing off officers and civilians who had helped them in their rise to power. The list of those executed represented a who's who of all classes of Iraqi society, with thousands more unwittingly in line for the firing squad.

In the tradition of all totalitarian regimes, the new government placed its followers in key posts throughout the administrative apparatus. The most important of these was, of course, the Army: civilians who had never donned uniforms were given senior military commissions to serve as political commissars supervising the armed forces. The new regime learned from the experience of its predecessors, which were all overthrown by officers' coups. Bakr and his colleagues were determined not to risk a similar fate.

This state of affairs was highly beneficial to Saddam Hussain. He was a first cousin of fellow-Takritite Bakr, and no one was surprised when he was given general's rank along with a wealth of titles, including the important ones of deputy secretary general of the Iraqi Ba'ath and deputy chairman of the Revolutionary Command Council (RCC). These titles placed the youthful Hussain second only to Bakr, who held five titles: state president, Ba'ath general secretary, chairman of the RCC, prime minister and minister of defense.

As number two in the political hierarchy, Hussain undertook to "complete" his formal education, to which end he was not required to invest much effort. One day he appeared in the examination hall of Baghdad's law faculty escorted by four armed bodyguards. He had two pistols stuffed into his belt, while his guards brandished assault rifles. The point was taken. That same day Hussain was awarded his law degree.

One of Hussain's first achievements was the 1970 agreement with Iraq's Kurdish minority, which put an end to the Kurds' twenty-five-year rebellion against the Baghdad authorities. In return, Kurd leader Mullah Mustafa Barazani got a written undertaking which guaranteed his people full autonomy within four years. But Hussain had not the slightest intention of keeping his pledge, and the Kurds, realizing they had been duped, took up arms once again.

However, Hussain had a further trump up his sleeve. Before his agreement with the Kurds reached its term, he approached Iran's Shah Mohammed Reza Pahlavi, who was providing the Kurds with financial and military aid, and proposed an agreement on navigation rights in the Shatt-al-Arab waterway. Lying on the Iran-Iraq border, the estuary is the outlet from the Tigris and Euphrates rivers to the Persian Gulf; Iran had always complained of getting the raw end of the allocation of navigation rights in the waterway. Falling for Hussain's ruse, the Shah cut off his support to the Kurds; the "rewards" fell to his successors when Hussain launched his September 1980 invasion of Iran.

Unfulfilled promises, concessions pledged and later denied: these were Saddam Hussain's favorite devices.

In September 1970, Bakr announced his resignation, disappointed by Iraq's inaction during the "Black September" when King Hussein of Jordan massacred Palestinian guerrillas while the Iraqi division stationed at Mafrak in Jordan stood by.

This looked like a golden opportunity for Hussain to succeed his aging cousin. But Hussain was in no hurry. He realized that taking power at the age of thirty-three, with no military career behind him, was liable to bring about his rapid demise. Requiring additional time to prepare his final takeover, he resolved to foil Bakr's resignation. He went about it in the following manner:

Pointing his pistol at the President, he commanded, Withdraw your resignation immediately and return to the presidential palace. Your resignation does not release you from the responsibility you bear. Our response will be unequivocal.

Bakr: You want to keep me at the Palace of the Republic by force?

Hussain: We demand your return. We shall not accept your resignation. We do not agree that you withdraw now. You are responsible just as we are for what happened in Jordan. You must stay with us till the end of the road.

Bakr returned to his presidential duties—until Hussain decided that the time was ripe for his removal. Hussain's manner of handling the episode may have been inspired by his mentor, Gamal Abdel Nasser, who made similar use of the aging general Muhammed Naguib until he was strong enough to get rid of him.

When Hussain decided that it was time for the final takeover, he proved himself to be of very tough fiber. "Power-hungry to the point of insanity" was the characterization he earned from the sharp-eyed Mullah Mustafa Barazani. Of all the descriptions of Hussain, the Kurdish leader's was probably the most apt. The Revolutionary Command Council took over all constitutional authority, and the power apparatus, civilian and military, was packed with party members. It goes without saying that all RCC members were of Hussain's faction of the Ba'ath, as were most Cabinet ministers; the others, holding lesser portfolios of a technical nature, lacked real authority or political power.

Having once attempted to assassinate Kassem, Hussain was well aware that few of the rulers of modern Iraq had died quietly in their beds. It was therefore of supreme importance to guarantee his personal safety, which he equated with the security of the regime. To this end, he constructed an all-powerful security apparatus, similar to those maintained by Communist regimes. Its agents—party loyalists to a man—supervised everything that went on in the Army and the police, in trade and industry, in schools and universities; they even kept a close watch on the party itself. A special section engaged in operations beyond Iraq's borders, in Arab states and elsewhere.

Characteristic equally of this covert apparatus and its master, Saddam Hussain, was its vicious mode of operation. Any individual or group suspected of subversive activity was simply liquidated, "subversive activity" embracing everything from underground acts aimed at toppling the regime to mild criticism voiced among friends. Hussain's agents also engaged in kidnappings and arrests, without, of course, troubling to apply for court orders, even though it may be assumed that such formalities would have been provided automatically if requested. Most of the victims came from the top rungs of society—politicians, officers, scientists, lecturers and prominent businessmen—but the security apparatus was not averse to laying hands on ordinary citizens who showed any reluctance in dancing to the official tune.

Detainees were kept in special cells at secret police facilities, where they suffered barbaric torture. Here are a few isolated instances:

Dr. Talib al-Baghdadi, a Baghdad University lecturer on economics, disappeared in 1976 shortly after a lecture in which he pointed out defects of economic policy. His fate was relatively mild: he got a three-year jail sentence for agitation.

The leniency of Baghdadi's treatment is highlighted by the account of a Christian Assyrian who fled to Europe to report on his experiences: after rejecting attempts to recruit him as an informer, he had been confined to the secret-police dungeons, where his ordeal included whippings over the head, back and belly and the ubiquitous electric-shock treatment.

Maaruf Abdallah Fath, a twenty-nine-year-old Kurdish teacher from Zawita, came under suspicion of attempting to form a cell of the outlawed Kurdish Democratic Party. His interrogators stuffed his head into a sack filled with ants, beetles and maggots, which naturally crawled into all his orifices. He lost his sanity, and it was in this state that he was restored to his family.

The security police did not rest content with clubs, rubber truncheons, whips and electric shocks: Amnesty International reports also refer to rapes of detainees by homosexual interrogators.

The Soviet Union provided most of the Bakr-Hussain regime's support during the early years, but that did not inhibit the savage campaign against Iraqi Communists. Hundreds of Communist Party leaders and activisits— almost the entire leadership—were murdered summarily, or sentenced to death by "revolutionary tribunals." The Soviets proffered feeble protests.

However, Hussain's principal efforts were directed at the top rungs of the Iraqi administration. The victims included officers, politicians and Ba'athists who showed the slightest sign of independent thinking or were regarded as potential candidates for an alternative leadership. Many managed to flee the country, but "the butcher of Baghdad" had a long reach to pursue them in their places of asylum. Like a murderous octopus, Hussain extended his tentacles far beyond Iraq's borders to Egypt, Syria, Britain, France and other countries which offered refuge to Iraqi exiles. Enormous oil revenues paid the hire of professional killers and financed links with international terrorism. Hussain provided arms and cash to the notorious Carlos, as well as to the Irish Republican Army and other terrorist organizations. Initially, he also granted unstinted aid to Palestine Liberation Organization leader Yassir Arafat, but when Arafat rebelled against his role as Hussain's stooge the Iraqi President launched a merciless campaign against him. Several prominent Arafat followers in Western Europe were killed by Hussain's gunmen, some operating under diplomatic guise with scant respect for the sovereignty of their host countries. Hussain backed Arafat rival Tzabry al-Banah, a.k.a. Abu Nidal—one of the most ruthless killers in the Arab world. Enjoying unlimited Iraqi support to this day, Abu Nidal has largely directed his operations against any PLO member who ventured to consider coexistence with Israel. His victims include Said Hamami, PLO representative in London, and Issam Sartawi, a member of the PLO Executive, both men having held frequent meetings with Israelis.

The Bakr-Hussain regime engaged in large-scale atrocities which are documented in Amnesty International reports. There was the 1975–76 massacre of the Kurds, when numerous villages were razed and the survivors exiled for the purpose of creating a twelve-mile-wide "security zone" along Iraq's borders with Iran and Turkey. The Iraqi Air Force played its part in the operation by indiscriminate bombing of villages beyond the border so as to deny any possible aid to the beleaguered Kurds. Shi'ite dignitaries who had the effrontery to criticize the treatment of the Kurds were arrested; some were executed.

Saddam Hussain never made any effort to play down his reputation for merciless cruelty. On the contrary: he regarded it as a useful means of intimidating his adversaries and thus promoting his own aims. He has never denied persistent rumors that as a young man he killed two persons with his own hands in the course of a family feud. It is also rumored that while in exile in Cairo he uttered death threats against an Egyptian citizen, for which he was imprisoned until Nasser intervened on his behalf.

By the midseventies, it was obvious to all, inside Iraq and abroad, that Hussain was the country's effective ruler. But it was only on July 16, 1979, the eve of the eleventh anniversary of the Ba'ath regime, that Bakr resigned all his duties, "naturally" transferring the leadership to Hussain. Bakr claimed poor health as the reason for his resignation, but that was of little importance: for years, he had been little more than a dummy, with the strings being manipulated by his ferocious cousin.

Israeli Labor Party leader Shimon Peres visited Egypt some ten days after the bloodless coup in Baghdad. Egyptian President Sadat, having been briefed by his own intelligence services, told Peres that the "peaceful" nature of the coup was illusory. "Bakr was forced out by threats and intimidation," Sadat related. "Hussain wanted the presidency without delay, and Bakr, realizing that his deputy was getting impatient, was left with no choice. After having Hussain at his side for ten years, Bakr knew him to be capable of carrying out all his threats." Brandishing a cautionary finger, Sadat added, "That man will stop at nothing to achieve his ends," and stressed that Hussain does not follow the rules of civilized behavior.

Sadat knew what he was talking about. Within days of his appointment as chairman of the RCC, president and Ba'ath secretary-general, Hussain launched an extensive purge. Fifty-five leading officials—some appointed only a month earlier by Hussain himself—were indicted on the traditional charge of "conspiring against the regime"; twenty-one were sentenced to death. It recalled the conduct of princes of old who, on succeeding their fathers to the throne, secured their own hold on power by killing off their brothers and other potential rivals. However, Saddam Hussain added his own personal touch of sadism: the executions were carried out in public, the firing squads being composed of senior officers and Ba'ath leaders. Since most of the latter possessed neither military skills nor experience in executions, some of the condemned men were merely wounded and had to be shot repeatedly to finish them off.

Now in supreme office, Hussain gave free rein to his brutal nature. Iraqi citizens of Iranian origin were deported, being sent back to their ancestral homeland in their tens of thousands. Torture chambers were installed at the Defense Ministry in Baghdad and at secret-police headquarters in various cities. Amnesty International reports depict a whole army of sadists exercising all their ingenuity in inventing new methods of torture.

Burhan al-Shawi, a twenty-five-year-old journalist, made his escape to Europe after enduring two years of torment in Iraq. He related how he had been taken to Baghdad security police headquarters, where he was blindfolded and "beaten on various parts of my body with hard blows, by sticks, by rubber tubes and by severe kicks. I was thrown about from one corner to another, hitting the walls and crashing down on my face or back, for the hard beating to commence now on my face and back, on the sensitive parts of my body such as the kidneys, the neck, the sex organs, and the elbow. I was also caned and flailed until my feet were swollen." A Danish hospital team examined Shawi and confirmed his account, which included thirty-five burns on different parts of his body.

Another prisoner was stripped naked and placed in a small cell, where the temperature was swiftly switched back and forth between icy cold and frizzling heat. Yet another prisoner had water forced up his nostrils until he suffocated. Civilians summoned for interrogation were offered cool drinks before their release. Arriving home, they came down with debilitating ailments: the drinks turned out to have been laced with thalium, a heavy metal used in manufacturing rat poison.

On one occasion, an official Iraqi statement denied Amnesty charges, but it failed to refute a single allegation.

In its war with Iran, Hussain's Iraq has likewise flouted all international conventions, including the 1922 ban on gas warfare, which was observed even when World War Two was at its height. Egypt (in the Yemen campaign of 1960) and the Soviet Union (in Afghanistan, 1980–83) have been accused of employing chemical weaponry, but even if the charge was true, both countries denied it vigorously. Iraq remains the sole country since World War One to employ gas openly and brazenly.

Furthermore, Iraqi forces were undiscriminating in their choice of targets. Dozens of Iranian hospitals, schools and other civilian installations were bombed from the air or ravaged by artillery and missiles. Early military successes allowed the Iraqis to occupy extensive areas in Iran, where they committed horrifying atrocities. Men were executed out of hand, women and children were raped and later murdered. Numerous western-Iranian villages and townships were depopulated.

Saddam Hussain is unabashed in vindicating his cruelty: "Whoever tries to lay a hand on this regime, directly or indirectly, we shall cut off his hand, he shall be struck down, because that is our right to self-defense. Enemies of the regime, at home or abroad, will be destroyed by all the means at Iraq's disposal, because defense of our existence is more important than human life."

Several of the world's intelligence agencies are of the opinion that since he became president, Hussain's incipient megalomania, always present, has come out into the open; in consequence, he has lost his grip on reality and his capacity for a realistic evaluation of his own strength. This may explain his massive onslaught upon Iran, a country which, in spite of being enfeebled by the rise of Khomeini, is still several times larger than Iraq and consequently possesses far greater resilience and powers of resistance.

Academics attempting to analyze the ideology guiding Hussain have run into considerable difficulty, for his political lore is unstructured. Unlike other Arab leaders, Nasser in particular, Hussain has published almost no theoretical writings. However, his speeches do reflect his guiding principles.

All intelligence reports are unanimous on one point: Hussain hopes to make Iraq into a major power—in diplomatic, military, industrial and economic terms. He appears to believe that the present-day global balance of forces, with its three superpowers, leaves scope for a "multipolar" world where large regional powers will control extensive subcontinents, to expand into superpowers in their own right. Iraq's strategic position at the heart of the world's richest oilfields makes that country—in the view of its President—a potential candidate for such a role.

An important thread in Hussain's ideology is his attempt to link modern Iraq with ancient Babylon. Addressing an audience of young Iraqis, he declared, "Nebuchadnezzar, Sargon and Hammurabi are our grandfathers." The message was clear: Iraq is the direct heir and successor of the Babylonians, who ruled the entire civilized world of ancient times.

But while dwelling upon the splendors of ancient Babylon, Hussain makes no attempt to deny that his modus operandi derives from a modern regime: that of Stalin. "We are now in our Stalinist era," he said on one occasion. "We shall strike with an iron fist against the slightest deviation or backsliding, beginning with the Ba'athists themselves." There are personal parallels too: Recalling Stalin, the unemotional Hussain is no overwhelmingly charismatic leader—which may explain his fear of more attractive figures, whether in the Army or in the Ba'ath. He is an uninspired conversationalist, with a poor mastery of foreign languages; his contacts with foreigners are abrupt and businesslike, with few of the conventional flourishes of courtesy and friendship. Like Stalin, he reads his speeches. Possibly due to his stocky stature (a trait which likewise troubled Stalin), Hussain appears to lack self-confidence—a possible reason for his recurrent temper tantrums.

Hussain's dream of making his country into a regional power—and a potential rival of the superpowers—inevitably led him to a conclusion which rapidly expanded into an *idée fixe*: Iraq needs nuclear weapons. A comprehensive American report affirms that Hussain attributes supreme importance to nuclear power. If he is to become the leader of the Arab world, Hussain is convinced, he must annihilate Israel or, at least, reduce the Jewish state from its present status as the region's strongest military power to humiliated helplessness. To subject Israel to the fate of the Crusader state of medieval times, the essential precondition for the Arabs is acquisition of nuclear arms.

The Arab crusade against Israel was long spearheaded by Egypt. By dint of its population, and its cultural and scientific progress, Egypt was the well-nigh automatic leader of the Arab world, and it instigated the periodic Arab–Israeli battlefield confrontations, for which it also provided the bulk of the Arab manpower.

But that state of affairs changed radically in November 1977, when Anwar as-Sadat made his historic journey to Jerusalem. Two years later Egypt deserted the anti-Israel camp when it concluded a peace treaty with its former enemy. Saddam Hussain, having organized the 1978 Baghdad summit meeting where the entire Arab world resolved to sever its ties with Egypt, seized this golden opportunity to present his candidacy for undisputed leader of the Arabs. Consequently, he regarded nuclear arms as his most pressing requirement. First steps to that end had already been taken a few years previously. He now decided to accelerate the process and bring closer the day when the mushroom cloud would cast its menacing shadow over Israel.

Later, Israeli Commander-in-Chief Major General Raphael Eytan would summarize the matter in simple terms. The Iraqis, he said, chose the nuclear option because all previous Arab attempts to defeat Israel had been foiled; in consequence, they adopted a new concept: "acquisition of a weapon against which there is no defense."

4 "Worse than Pharaoh"

The attack on the Iraqi reactor was not the first historical occasion when fate linked Israel and Iraq.

The latter country, known in Hebrew as Aram Naharaiim ("Aram of the Two Rivers"), lies on the mighty Tigris and Euphrates rivers, which brought forth some of the greatest cultures of antiquity. Iraq is at the eastern extremity of the Mideastern Fertile Crescent, while Israel is at the opposite, western extremity. It is well known that opposing poles exercise both attraction and antagonism.

Every Jewish child studying the history of his people encounters the name of Babylonia at the very outset. The Euphrates delta was the site of Ur, birthplace of the patriarch Abraham, the forefather of the Hebrew nation. Farther to the north, in ancient Haran, dwelt Abraham's relatives, with whom he conducted an intensive love-hate relationship. Abraham's son Isaac and his grandson Jacob were commanded to take wives from among the daughters of the family in Haran. However, these Haranian relatives, headed by Laban the Aramite, repeatedly bullied the young Jacob whose grandfather had abandoned Aram Naharaiim for another land. The enmity and fear entertained toward those distant Haranian relatives find powerful expression in the Passover Haggada, which recalls that Laban the Aramite ("Iraqi") was worse than Egypt's Pharaoh, for the latter sought only to kill the Hebrews' male offspring, whereas Laban wished to annihilate them all, male and female alike.

The Jewish people's links with Babylonia and Assyria persisted far beyond the patriarchal era. In the ninth century B.C., the warlike Assyrians overran the ancient kingdom of Israel, seizing control of large portions before finally destroying it and sending its inhabitants into exile in the remote regions of their empire. They also attempted to conquer the other Jewish kingdom, Judah, but their campaign, marked by violent cruelty, ended with the surprise defeat of King Sennaherib at the gates of Jerusalem.

The Assyrian capital of Nineveh, lying on the banks of the upper Tigris, was one of the greatest cities of the ancient world. It was the scene of one of the most striking Biblical tales, which recounted how the prophet Jonah, having been swallowed by the whale, was thrown upon the shore and instructed by the Almighty to go to Nineveh and warn its people of their impending destruction.

Over a century after the destruction of the kingdom of Israel, it was the turn of Judah. Assyria had been overthrown by Babylonia, whose King Nebuchadnezzar conquered Jerusalem, burning the First Temple and sending the people of Judah in their tens of thousands into exile in Babylonia. But unlike the ten tribes of Israel, who assimilated and vanished from the stage of history, the exiles of Judah—henceforth known as Jews for their ancestral home—maintained their separate identity; seventy years later, when King Cyrus of Persia conquered Babylonia, some of them returned to their former homeland to construct the Second Temple.

With that, many of the exiles remained in Babylonia, whose flourishing Jewish community in time achieved numerical and cultural supremacy over their brethren in Palestine. After the destruction of the Second Temple, Babylonia remained the undisputed center of Jewish culture. Its renowned centers of learning at Sura, Naharda and Pumbadita brought forth the Babylonian Talmud.

After the European Holocaust of World War Two, when the Jewish people sought to rebuild a state of its own in its historical homeland, one of its bitterest foes was the modern successor of ancient Babylonia and Assyria: Iraq.

In October 1947, one month before the United Nations General Assembly resolution advocating the establishment of a Jewish state in Palestine, the Arab League set up an inter-Arab command whose sole purpose was to wage war against the Jewish state, should the latter indeed come into being. The command was headed by an Iraqi general, Ismail Saffoth. The League also organized the "Army of Salvation" under the command of Fawzi Kawkji, a notorious gang leader from Lebanon who had gained renown for his pro-Nazi leanings. Kawkji's biography includes a period as lecturer at Baghdad's military academy; not fortuitously, his forces were largely made up of Iraqi recruits. Later, in anticipation of the proclamation of the Jewish state, the Arab states sent their armies to stifle it at birth, under the overall command of Iraqi general Nur-a-Din Mahmoud.

On May 14, 1948, the day David Ben Gurion proclaimed the establishment of Israel, an Iraqi brigade was already in action against Israeli forces. The Iraqi expeditionary force took part in battles in the Jordan Valley, in

Samaria and in Sharon; by the time hostilities ended, the Iraqis, with some sixteen thousand men, were the largest Arab contingent in Palestine.

As will be recalled, that war ended with a brilliant Israeli victory. The neighboring "front-line" states, Egypt, Lebanon, Jordan and Syria, entered into armistice negotiations with Israel, but nothing would induce the Iraqis to negotiate with "the Zionist canker." Rather than deal with the Israelis, they preferred to surrender all their military gains and hand over the areas they controlled to the Jordanian Arab Legion.

The Iraqi forces returned home, but eight years later, during the 1956 Sinai campaign, they reappeared on Israel's borders; they did the same in June 1967, prior to the outbreak of the Six-Day War, and again in the 1973 Yom Kippur War.

In spite of its resounding setbacks in the war against Israel, Iraq could claim numerous "triumphs" in the campaign against its own Jewish citizens. The latter were the victims of recurrent bloody pogroms inspired and encouraged by the Baghdad authorities. That went back to 1941, when Iraq was shaken by the anti-British, pro-Nazi "colonels' revolt." Having gained independence of Britain in 1932, Iraq remained in effect a British protectorate; the conspirators now hoped to deny Britain their country's support in the war against Nazi Germany. British troops were sent to put down the revolt, but they did not prevent Iraqi mobs from taking out their fury on the Jews of Baghdad in the notorious "Farhoud." A further Farhoud threatened in the spring of 1948, when the Arab armies invaded Israel. Proclaiming a military emergency, the Iraqi government forbade its Jewish citizens to leave the country and decreed the death penalty for Zionist activity. The hint was taken up by the street mobs, who reduced the Jewish community to a state of chronic insecurity.

In 1950, the Iraqi government decided to permit the Jews to leave. Some 125,000 emigrated to Israel, and about 12,000 headed for other lands. The departing Jews left behind assets worth billions. Only some 2,500 Jews remained in Iraq, mainly out of reluctance to abandon their property. Their plight was precarious. The Iraqi authorities regarded them as subversives, subjecting them to continual persecution. With the rise of Colonel Abdel Salam Arif in 1963, numerous Jews were arrested and their businesses confiscated. Matters reached a tragic head in 1969 when, after a show trial which convicted them of spying for Israel, nine Jews were hanged in Baghdad's central street before the eyes of a tumultuous mob.

Iraq's rulers nevertheless regarded persecution of their Jewish citizens as little more than a prelude to the destruction of Israel, or, as they preferred to say, "the Zionist entity." Attempts to rout Israel on the field of battle were all defeated. Indeed, the passage of the years brought a growing disparity between Israel's military might and that of the Arabs. To crush Israel, it was vital to acquire an "ultimate weapon" whose mere possession by Iraq would bring the Jewish state to its knees. The man who sought to endow Iraq with such a weapon was Saddam Hussain—an individual depicted by friend and foe alike as lacking any inhibitions.

Ba'ath ideology is modernist to the highest degree, its principal components comprising socialism and nationalism. However, Saddam Hussain was acutely aware of the importance of religion in all his undertakings, his crusade against Israel and Zionism in particular. Though never having taken any interest in religion, he now proceeded to don the theological mantle, proclaiming anti-Zionism as a basic tenet of Islam.

In truth, his affirmation had strong historical foundations. When the Jewish tribes of the Arabian Peninsula refused to give up their religion or replace the traditional "Hear O Israel, the Lord is our God, the Lord is One" with "There is no God but Allah, and Mohammed is the emissary of Allah," the Prophet did not hesitate to put them to the sword. His spiritual and political heirs, the caliphs, likewise subjected the Jews to various degrees of maltreatment. It was three hundred years after the death of Mohammed before a modus vivendi was achieved between Moslems and Jews, fleetingly bringing its benefits to both sides. But it was not long before the Moslems renewed their persecution of the Jews.

As Saddam Hussain laid plans for his war of annihilation against Israel, he endeavoured to link his own regime with the founders of Islam: "We, the offspring of those magnificent figures, bear the responsibility for the jihad [holy war] of the modern epoch, on behalf of the selfsame principles for which our forefathers fought."

He continued to harp on the religious theme when he addressed the conference of Moslem foreign ministers which convened in Baghdad on May 2, 1981: "Jerusalem is presently under the hateful Zionist conquest . . . that is also the condition of the whole of the land of Palestine."

"Mohammed's law is the sword!" was the slogan of the seventh- and eighth-century Moslem conquerors as they swarmed like locusts across the breadth of the Mideast, North Africa and southern Europe. Inhabitants of those regions who adhered to other faiths were given the choice of death by the sword or conversion to Islam. The Iraqi prophet of the modern jihad expounded a new dogma: "Saddam's law is the atom." Saddam Hussain was convinced that acquisition of nuclear weapons would put him in a position to confront Israel with a choice similar to that the Moslem conquerors offered their vanquished foes: surrender or annihilation.

5 Moscow said *"Nyet!"*

It was not Saddam Hussain who initially conceived the idea of a nuclear Iraq. That evolved in a lengthy and complex process which appears to have commenced under the monarchy. But Iraq's nuclear program got its primary impetus in 1959, shortly after the Kassem coup.

After heading the antimonarchial conspiracy, Colonel Abdel Karim Kassem had to fight hard to establish himself in power. In these tussles, he allied himself with the Iraqi Communists—a fact which helped him in his contacts with Moscow.

In March 1959, Soviet-Iraqi contacts sprouted agreements in various spheres. One of these was nuclear cooperation: the Soviets undertook to construct a nuclear reactor, to supply enriched uranium of a submilitary grade for its operation, and to train Iraqi scientists, engineers and technicians in the various fields of nuclear technology; they also agreed to conduct geological surveys in Iraq, in quest of uranium deposits.

These agreements with Moscow must have encouraged the local Communists, whose adherents in the Army attempted to take control of the country. Kassem reacted ruthlessly, putting down the Communists with an iron fist. In retribution, the Russians halted their aid. Kassem now resolved to prove that Iraq would proceed with its nuclear development whether Moscow liked it or not. Recalling the ten Iraqi scientists and engineers who were studying in the Soviet Union, he sent them off to research centers in West Germany, Egypt, Britain and the United States.

The Iraqi Communists realized that they had overreached themselves. Apparently on instructions from Moscow, they moderated their conduct, whereupon relations between the two countries began to return to normal.

In August 1959 an Iraqi delegation left for Moscow, headed by Planning Minister Dr. Talaat Tubani. Tubani was chairman of Iraq's Atomic Energy Commission, which had been established three years earlier. The commission enlarged the number of study grants available to Iraqis training at Soviet nuclear centers. In December of that year, its Soviet counterpart approved four-year bursaries for ten Iraqi students. A year later, the two countries signed an agreement for the construction of a nuclear research reactor in Iraq.

The site chosen was al-Tuweitha, on the banks of the Tigris about twelve miles southeast of Baghdad. The Iraqi government set aside a three-hundred-acre stretch for the project, and the once desolate site was soon a hive of activity. Kassem in person had the honor of laying the foundation stone.

The two Iraqi engineers appointed to direct the reactor's construction paid sporadic visits to Moscow for talks and further study, but the Russians were in no hurry to implement the agreement. Their principal aim in Iraq was to expand their influence—and that was largely attained by the mere act of signing agreements. Moreover, at that time the Soviet Union was busy with extensive nuclear projects of its own. Nikita Khrushchev proclaimed the aim of overtaking the West in the development of nuclear weapons. He also demanded increased efforts to step up the Soviet Union's nuclear power capacity. In view of these endeavors, the Soviets did not have an abundance of nuclear experts. Moscow soon told the Iraqis in plain terms that construction of the reactor would not commence before an adequate number of their scientists had undergone the necessary training.

Finally, on May 18, 1961, the construction contract was signed. Supervision of the project was delegated to Industry Minister General Muhi-a-Din Abdul Majid, who was also appointed to head the Atomic Energy Commission, thereby acquiring the necessary authority for allotting the required manpower and resources. On Majid's instructions, his ministry worked out a five-year plan for scientific development, which allotted £2 million for construction of the al-Tuweitha nuclear-research center; it also paid for three additional Iraqi engineers to study reactor engineering in preparation for work alongside three Soviet engineers who were preparing a survey on the requisites for the reactor's operation.

In October 1962, four Soviet freight ships entered the Iraqi port of Basra, where they unloaded the first shipments of material for the construction of the reactor. Some time later, early in 1963, Soviet experts arrived to launch the project.

The reactor to be built would be of the small IRT-2000 research type, generating no more than two megawatts of heat. It would be fueled by uranium enriched to a grade of 10 percent, which is unsuitable for military use. The IRT-2000 was designed during the fifties, principally for the use of physicists conducting research into nuclear processes. It was also capable of producing radioactive isotopes for medical use and other scientific purposes; it was invaluable in training nuclear technicians. But as long as it is fueled by 10-percent-grade uranium and lacks facilities for plutonium extraction, it has no military use, nor can it ever be adapted to such a purpose.

Now is the opportunity to recall that uranium is a metallic element, one of ninety-two to be found in nature. In natural deposits, most of the metal (99.3 percent) consists of the uranium-238 isotope, whose atomic nuclei hold 92 protons and 146 neutrons; the remnant (0.7 percent) is the 235 isotope, whose nuclei likewise comprise 92 protons, but have only 143 neutrons. It is the number of protons that fixes the chemical properties, which is why both these nuclei are uranium nuclei. The uranium-235 nucleus is marked by its unusual characteristic of fissionability: when struck by a slow-moving neutron, it disintegrates into two more or less equal halves, extruding two or three neutrons and liberating enormous amounts of energy—nuclear energy. The neutrons released by fission can go on to bombard the nuclei of other uranium-235 atoms, releasing further nuclear energy and liberating additional neutrons, which in their turn strike further atoms, and so on. This process is the chain reaction which underlies nuclear power. If uncontrolled, the chain reaction takes place in a brief instant, of the order of millionths of a second; the result is a bomb which releases all the nuclear energy in a single devastating blast. If the chain reaction is kept under control, the selfsame quantity of nuclear energy (which is in direct proportion to the quantity of fissionable uranium 235) is released at a moderate rate, making it suitable for peaceful purposes. In effect, a nuclear reactor is designed for a controlled chain reaction.

Research in the forties which paved the way for the first atomic bomb also discovered that the nonfissionable uranium 238 can absorb a neutron in its nucleus; two of its $46 + 1 = 47$ neutrons then spontaneously emit electrons* and turn into protons. A new "artificial" (i.e., not present in nature) fissionable element is thus created. This is plutonium 239, with 94 protons and 145 neutrons.

The discovery was of enormous significance. Separation of uranium 235 from its 238 isotope is a complex and costly process. The chemical properties are the same, both being nuclei of uranium, with the same number of protons. To separate them, one has to make use of the difference in weight, due to the different number of neutrons. It is done, for instance, by causing the mixture to flow, as a gas, through thousands of miles of thin pipes and membrane pores, giving the lighter nuclei the chance of running faster. On the other hand, the separation of plutonium-239 quantities from bars of uranium 238 on which they have been "bred" is an ordinary chemical oper-

---

*Accompanied by an additional type of radiation, "antineutrinos," that play no further role in this process.

The succession of bloody coups which overtook Iraq did not prejudice that country's nuclear program: on the contrary, each new junta turned to Moscow for continued aid in this sphere. Iraq urged the Soviets to speed up completion of the reactor, mentioning the ninth anniversary of the Ba'athist revolution—July 14, 1967—as a suitable date for the inauguration. But the Kremlin was in no haste to accede to Iraq's pleas. Resolving to wait no longer for Moscow's reply, Baghdad consequently made it known that by late 1967 an Iraqi reactor would be producing nuclear energy for peaceful purposes.

The reactor was ultimately inaugurated on January 6, 1968—Iraq's Army Day—the ceremony being attended by every personage of prominence in the Baghdad government. The guest of honor was, of course, the Soviet ambassador, Vassily Nikolayev, who expressed confidence in the growth of cooperation between the two countries.

It should be recalled that this was now the post-1967 period following Israel's crushing Six-Day War victory over the Arabs. Prior to that war, Arab media frequently debated whether or not Israel possessed nuclear arms or the means of manufacturing them; after the war, the Arabs were convinced that if Israel had yet to acquire atomic weapons, it soon would.

Iraqi Atomic Energy Commission Director Dr. Haari Awad drew the necessary conclusions, undertaking frequent trips to Moscow and Vienna in a bid to drum up aid for Iraq's nuclear program. He voiced harsh criticism of the richer Arab governments, whose failure to foresee the trend made them tightfisted. "We are dutybound," he declared, "to mobilize our finest scientific and technical resources and provide good working conditions, so as to take the Arabs into the atomic era. As long as we do not construct atomic reactors or produce atomic fuel, we shall be unable to declare, 'Indeed, we have entered the atomic era.'"

The Iraqi journal *Economic World* advocated the slogan "The atom for life"; it called for resort to the international media to create "an all-embracing Arab atomic program" directed, it goes without saying, against Israel. East Germany provided the so-called "vindication": a joint statement issued by Iraq and the German Democratic Republic claimed to have uncovered military nuclear cooperation between West Germany and Israel.

In the meantime, Iraq's ties with the Soviet Union were growing closer. The two states concluded an increasing number of agreements in a variety of fields. In December 1971, Soviet Defense Minister Marshal Andrey Grechko visited Iraq, where he met with President Bakr. The highlight of the visit was the conclusion on December 19 of an agreement on nuclear-energy cooperation, whereby the Soviets undertook to boost the output of the Iraqi reactor from two to five megawatts; this portion of the agreement was kept confidential.

ation, since these are two different chemical elements. No wonde
nuclear weapons—95 percent of existing arsenals—are plutoniur

Furthermore, a plutonium bomb can be smaller than the ur
type. Construction of the former requires no more than eight kil
nuclear explosive, while the latter calls for twenty to twenty-five
of expensive material. On the other hand, a uranium-235 bomb is
simple to construct, unlike the plutonium-based weapons, which
advanced technological and engineering infrastructure.

Operating a nuclear reactor does not call for pure uranium 235.
aim is a controlled chain reaction (which requires the uranium-23:
be kept at a distance from one another), use can be made of na
nium, where isolated uranium-235 atoms swim in a veritable oce
nium 238. Reactors frequently employ enriched uranium, whei
processes have produced a larger-than-normal concentration of
235.

Arising from the foregoing description—and endorsed by exp
the neutron bombardment of uranium has a dual result: in additi
fission of uranium 235, uranium 238 absorbs neutrons and is tra
into plutonium 239. The latter material accumulates within the
nuclear waste, from which it can be extracted if the appropriate fac
available. Moreover, one may lay within a reactor large quantities
uranium (or uranium 238) just to be neutron-irradiated and thus
plutonium. This "passive" uranium (it does not take part in the
chain reaction) is known as a "blanket." The amount of plutonium
produces depends upon a number of factors, including the flow of
within it. However, since the fission of uranium-235 atoms frees
(which, it will be recalled, extend the chain reaction), the greater t
tity of fissionable atoms the reactor contains, the more neutrons it
and the more plutonium it can produce in the blanket, for instance.

In other words, if a country possesses a nuclear reactor fuelled by
uranium 235, and it is not inhibited by international supervision
easily accumulate quantities of plutonium adequate for the manufac
"primitive" bomb.

Iraq continued to dispatch gifted students to the Soviet Union
West, with the aim of training the skilled manpower required to pro
nuclear program. In addition to the Soviet advisers permanently stati
al-Tuweitha, Iraq invited guest scientists and engineers from India,
Brazil, Italy and other Western countries. Experts from Poland, Cze
vakia, Hungary and East Germany also put in an appearance. It
rumored that subsequent stages of nuclear research at al-Tuweitha v
tended by Palestinian scientists sent by the PLO.

However, in spite of the visits exchanged by leaders of the two countries, in spite of pacts of friendship which included particularly ferocious attacks on Zionism, and in spite of Soviet support for Iraqi ambitions in the Persian Gulf—from which Moscow hoped for some gains of its own—the Soviets were in no hurry to fulfill their explicit promises.

Nine years elapsed from signature of the agreement until the long-awaited upgrading of the reactor. Its core was replaced, and it operated henceforth on a higher grade of fuel: uranium enriched to 80 percent.

Some believe that, had the enlarged reactor functioned without interruption or external supervision for ten years, up to 1991, it would have produced sufficient plutonium for a "mini" atom bomb. But such an eventuality was hardly feasible in view of strict Soviet control.

It began to dawn upon the Iraqis that if they were to develop a military nuclear potential, they could hardly pin their hopes upon the Soviet Union. Now that Iraq had nuclear experts of its own—graduates of Soviet academies and Western research centers—they were available to advise the Baghdad authorities on the prospects of Soviet aid for a military nuclear program. What the Iraqi experts had to say was most disheartening. The Soviet Union exceeded any other nuclear power in its near-fanatical refusal to export any nuclear knowhow or technology suitable for military application. The sole departure from that principle occurred during the midfifties, when Soviet experts aided the Chinese in their first steps toward a military nuclear capability. However, soon regretting this rashness, the Kremlin cut off its nuclear aid, thereby helping to precipitate the Sino–Soviet rift of 1959.

Thus it came about that the early sixties found the Iraqis casting their eyes to the West in the hope of acquiring the nuclear technology they required for an atom bomb of their own. The Iraqi scientists and engineers who received their training in the West were reportedly critical of Soviet nuclear technology, which they dismissed as clumsy and unreliable; by contrast, they showered praise upon Western techniques. This may have been the case, but it was not the decisive factor in guiding the Baghdad authorities. What finally convinced them to turn to the West was their conviction that the Soviet Union would not provide nuclear aid for military purposes.

6 France and Iraq: "Equal Relations"

In its courtship of the West, Iraq had plenty to offer: plenty of oil. Iraq occupied an increasingly prominent role as an oil exporter to the West, where economic growth in the late sixties and early seventies boosted demand by a significant percentage each year.

Iraq's proven oil reserves are estimated at 41 billion barrels, placing that country in sixth place in the global table (for comparison: Saudi Arabia heads the list with reserves of 162 billion barrels). Realizing that oil was the most effective weapon the Arabs possessed, Saddam Hussain was one of the architects of the 1973 oil embargo applied in retribution for the West's assistance to Israel in the Yom Kippur War. The embargo marked the high point in a carefully planned campaign to boost Arab oil revenues threefold or more. Hussain, who personally supervised his country's oil deals, could pat himself on the back for his achievements: from $2.5 billion in 1967, Iraq's oil income had soared to no less than $20 billion in 1979.

This enormous wealth permitted Iraq's rulers to pursue their great dream: hegemony in the Persian Gulf, among the Arab states and in the Third World as a whole. Believing nuclear weapons to be a prerequisite, and having given up hope of effective aid from the Soviet Union, they decided to force an utterly oil-dependent West to pay for the "black gold" by helping Iraq to develop its nuclear potential.

No undue pressure was called for. The Arab oil exporters had accumulated hundreds of billions of petrodollars, sums which the West could not regain unless it managed to sell its manufactured products to the oil states. This realization flung the industrial countries into fierce competition over penetration of the world's most lucrative market.

The Iraqis worked fast, as indicated in the few days between December 17 and 20, 1973, when they hosted no fewer than three delegations from industralized countries, East Germany, Japan and France, all arrived to discuss trade, technical assistance and oil deals (Iraq already had an agreement with East Germany for the annual delivery of 500,000 tons of crude oil).

The countries Iraq picked out for the acquisition of nuclear technology were, first and foremost, France and Italy, and to a lesser extent, Brazil, West Germany and Japan.

France, possessing no oil reserves of its own, imports most of its requirements from OPEC (Organization of Petroleum Exporting Countries). In 1973, France's imports of Iraqi oil came to 357,000 (some 15 percent of French purchases from OPEC); by 1979, Iraqi supplies were up to 489,000 barrels a day (21 percent of France's purchases from OPEC). At the same time, France had built up one of the world's foremost nuclear industries. In the late fifties, when President Charles de Gaulle, declining to settle for a status similar to that of Britain, ordered the creation of an independent French nuclear deterrent, it gave an enormous boost to his country's nuclear progress. The efficiency of French nuclear-power stations made them a hit on the world market; there were similar advances in France's development of military reactors designed principally for the production of plutonium.

Italy is equally deficient in energy sources. In 1973, Italy imported Iraqi oil at a rate of 383,000 barrels a day (17 percent of Italy's OPEC imports); by 1979, that had risen to 447,000 barrels a day (24 percent of OPEC imports). Italy possesses no nuclear deterrent of its own, though it would have experienced little difficulty in evolving one had it so desired. A number of Italian companies have specialized in manufacturing the supplementary systems required by nuclear technology—systems in which Iraqi displayed great interest.

Brazil possesses no oil, but it does have large uranium deposits. It was consequently natural for the Brazilian government to sign an agreement with West Germany, whose nuclear industry is one of the most advanced in the world. The agreement called for the Federal Republic to provide Brazil with nuclear-power stations, to be paid for by Brazilian uranium.

Iraq's rulers soon saw that cooperation with Italy, Brazil and France—the latter in particular—would permit a rapid advance toward their cherished dream of a military nuclear capacity.

No Arab state would ever have imagined French aid on such a scale in the not-so-distant past when France and Israel maintained an unwritten alliance reinforced by a profound friendship. However, that special relationship collapsed at the outbreak of the 1967 Six-Day War when Israel, rejecting de Gaulle's advice, acted to smash the Arab encirclement. The freeze on relations with Israel imposed by an infuriated de Gaulle soon turned out to be part of a well-laid plan to restore France to its earlier preeminence in the

Arab world. De Gaulle's successors Georges Pompidou and Valéry Giscard d'Estaing reduced France's ties with Israel to an all-time low; Israeli diplomats in Paris looked on helplessly as France groveled before the kaffiah-clad Arab oil princes. Laying aside the banner of Liberty, Equality, Fraternity, France sold its lofty principles for oil and cash.

Arab pronouncements of the most aggressive nature no longer evoked the slightest French response. When Iraqi Oil Minister al-Baqi al-Haditi told a Greek journalist on January 23, 1973, that "Israel must be eliminated . . . by armed struggle and threats against the imperialist powers that protect Israel," official Paris reacted with nothing more than a shrug.

When the 1973 Yom Kippur War ended in a resounding Israeli battlefield victory, it transpired nevertheless that the current energy crisis had boosted the economic and diplomatic muscle of the Arabs—the oil exporters in particular. Preceding other Western leaders in comprehending the inherent threat, French President Pompidou hastened to appoint his loyal confidant Michel Jobert to the post of foreign minister, instructing him above all to cultivate France's ties with the Arab world.

Late in January 1974, Jobert—referred to by his countrymen as "the French Kissinger"—set off for the Mideastern oil states. On February 6 he stopped over in Istanbul, where he told journalists that he was going to Baghdad to "develop good relations" with Iraq. Iraq, he added with commendable candor, was second only to Saudi Arabi in its oil sales to France. Arriving in Baghdad the following day, Jobert was equally direct in his talks with his hosts: in exchange for enlarged deliveries of Iraqi oil, France would provide anything Iraq needed for the construction of a scientific, technological and industrial infrastructure.

The Iraqis smiled: "Now you're talking!"

Details were delegated to experts from both sides. Before leaving Iraq, Jobert addressed a press conference saying, "I am happy to be with you and in your great country, which now possesses the means to enable it to restore the voice of the past and glory. . ."

Within a week, a delegation of French experts arrived in Baghdad. Less than a month later, a comprehensive trade treaty had been concluded, providing for French credits totaling half a billion dollars to finance various projects to be erected in Iraq by French companies.

Pompidou's health deteriorated rapidly. He died in April 1974, to be succeeded by Valéry Giscard d'Estaing. Nicknamed by friend and foe alike *"l'aristocrat,"* Giscard was a cold man, with an air of pronounced superiority. His elevation to office came as a profound disappointment to Israel, which would have preferred to see the Élysée Palace occupied by one of his rivals—Jacques Chaban Delmas or François Mitterrand. Jerusalem foresaw that Giscard would go even further in courting the Arabs.

During the frenzied election campaign, the most prominent figure alongside Giscard was Jacques Chirac, a tough and gifted young Gaullist. Pompidou had nicknamed Chirac "the Bulldozer," evidently considering him a potential president. But at the age of forty-one he had to settle for the number-two slot. On May 27, 1974, he took up his duties as premier. Six months later, on December 1, 1974, he set off for a visit to Iraq, at the invitation of Vice-President Saddam Hussain.

On his arrival at Baghdad airport, the guest was greeted by the entire Iraqi leadership, headed by President Bakr. Chirac and his companions were treated with lavish Eastern hospitality, both sides going out of their way to highlight their friendship.

Hussain soon won the heart of the French Premier. The Bulldozer was much taken with Iraq's strongman, who impressed Chirac as an imposing leader with a good grasp of his country's problems and clear ideas on how to solve them. In spite of having read intelligence reports detailing the savagery of Hussain's policies, Chirac did not appear overperturbed thereby; on the contrary, rumors in the Parisian diplomatic community related that on returning home Chirac began to take Arabic lessons so as to be able to converse with his new friend directly, with no need of interpreters.

Chirac himself depicted his efforts in the following terms: "I cultivated ties with Iraq within the framework of the policy laid down by the President of the Republic . . . it was in no one's interest to leave [Iraq] in the exclusive orbit of the Soviet Union. . . . In that regard, the action taken was effective . . ." That was not an accurate presentation. It will be recalled that, irrespective of external blandishments, Baghdad itself sought ways of terminating an alliance with a Moscow reluctant to meet Iraqi expectations.

Be that as it may, Chirac outdid his President in the earnestness of his efforts toward fostering relations with Iraq. He personally took a hand in wording the joint statement which affirmed that his talks with the Iraqis "were held in an atmosphere of profound friendship and confidence."

Hussain could pat himself on the back over his success in inducing the French Premier to sign a statement which included a call to Israel to withdraw from all the occupied territories. "The Iraqi side appreciated the French attitude toward the Palestinian problem and toward all the Arab issues," the statement said. The two leaders expressed gratification over "the development of the economic, industrial and technical relations between their two countries." The statement concluded: "Jacques Chirac and the delegation expressed their satisfaction and extreme pleasure for the warm welcome accorded them."

At a joint press conference with his guest, Hussain spoke of "equal relations between France and Iraq . . . for the sake of the two countries' independence." Chirac, going all out to flatter his host, referred to Hussain as "the great statesman who enjoys the qualities of willpower and competence to lead the people toward progress and national prosperity."

Iraq now called for a PLO observer to attend the Arab-European dialogue currently in preparation. That was "a procedural matter," responded Chirac, evidently convinced that such a triviality should prove no obstacle to the Paris-Baghdad alliance.

One of the principal provisions in the Franco-Iraqi framework agreement called for long-term cooperation in the energy sphere, "including the employment of nuclear energy for peaceful purposes."

"During my visit to Iraq," Chirac would recall later, "I laid the foundations for nuclear cooperation—and I stress—*for peaceful purposes.*"

How did Iraq convince France to assist in its nuclear development? Shortly after the Israeli attack on the reactor, Giscard was to state, "The argument that convinced the French delegation initially was this: Iraq estimated that, at some time in the future, her oil reserves would run out, and she was therefore bound to prepare for such a situation by acquiring basic knowhow in the field of nuclear energy." Events would prove this reasoning to be baseless, even though the French, claiming to be convinced, provided aid which extended far beyond "basic knowhow." Iraq exploited its oil reserves as though they were inexhaustible, displaying no apparent concern about the wells running dry.

Chirac pointed out that Iraq was now France's chief oil supplier—a fact of profound political significance which "conformed with the basic interests of both countries." Iraq had adopted an unswerving policy of national independence and regarded its links with France as "a model for its international relations."

France now invited Iraq to conclude a new oil agreement, much broader in sweep than the existing multiannual agreement. In exchange for oil, France promised industrial goods, arms, and scientific and technological aid.

This was precisely what the Iraqis had been waiting for. But, after the manner of bazaar traders, they were in no hurry to clinch the deal. They indicated that nuclear development—"for peaceful purposes," of course— was now the subject of negotiations with other countries. The hint was plain: it was up to France to make an offer Baghdad could not refuse. From their point of view, the Iraqis were quite right. In the desperate quest after ever-growing quantities of oil, the Western countries were now engaged in a gloves-off scramble for the favors of the Arab oil states, and Iraq made the most of its advantage. The "other countries" negotiating a nuclear deal with Iraq turned out to be—Canada.

The United States's northern neighbor had earlier sold a CANDU (Canadian Deuterium Uranium) reactor to India. That country used it to produce the plutonium for the nuclear device which, when detonated in May 1974, made it the sixth member of the global nuclear club.

Initially designed as a nuclear-power station, CANDU had as its most attractive feature its use of natural uranium rather than the enriched variety; among other advantages, this allowed for refueling without halting the reactor's operation—unlike facilities employing enriched uranium. However, Iraq's interest in CANDU stemmed not from its operational advantages, but from the fact that, in addition to generating power, it also gave off large amounts of plutonium—the cheapest nuclear explosive.

This was precisely how India proceeded. Its scientists, having mastered the technique of extracting plutonium from the reactor's nuclear waste, accumulated a sufficient amount of the metal to construct their nuclear device. Western intelligence reports did not dignify the Indian device with the title of "bomb": weighing several dozen tons, it could hardly be used for military purposes. But the leap from such a device to an operational bomb is a straightforward engineering problem well within the capabilities of a government which allots the manpower and resources required for its solution.

For reasons unknown, Iraq did not ultimately buy the Canadian reactor. However, that does not affect the fundamental question which calls for an answer: How could Western countries claiming to be advanced and civilized envisage the sale of a plutogenic (plutonium-producing) reactor to a state like Iraq? It should be recalled that Canada continued to negotiate the CANDU sale with Iraq even after India had detonated its device built with the aid of a similar reactor.

Canada and France both sought refuge in formal arguments whose hollowness must have been obvious: Iraq, they argued, was a signatory to the Non-Proliferation of Nuclear Weapons Treaty (NPT) and had placed its nuclear facilities under the supervision of the International Atomic Energy Agency (IAEA). Consequently, it was assumed that Iraq would gain no military benefits from the nuclear plant, the technology and the materials it purchased.

Even if factually correct, this defense bore not the slightest relation to practical realities, as must have been plain to anyone acquainted with nuclear development.

The IAEA, with permanent headquarters in Vienna, was created in 1956 at the initiative of President Eisenhower, and has functioned since under UN auspices. At the time of the agency's establishment, there were widespread hopes for peaceful use of nuclear energy; it was generally foreseen that all power stations would soon be nuclear. The IAEA charter stresses that one of the agency's most important aims is to provide developing nations with knowhow and training in use of nuclear energy for generating electricity and for medicine, agriculture and industry. However, like other UN-controlled agencies, the IAEA soon became less a scientific clearinghouse and more a political arena, a hotbed of power struggles, intrigue and espionage.

Iraq was swift to grasp the advantages arising from adherence to the IAEA. It applied for membership in 1959, and in 1961–62, before the first Iraqi students completed their studies in Moscow, an Iraqi representative was on the agency's board of directors, even serving as chairman for a time.

In 1961, discussions commenced on an international convention to prevent proliferation of nuclear weapons. Talks went on for seven years, until 1968, when a draft text, drawn up by American and Soviet experts, was approved by the UN General Assembly, which called upon all countries to adhere to it; on March 5, 1970, the Non-Proliferation of Nuclear Weapons Treaty came into effect.

Several months earlier, in October 1969, Iraq signed the treaty, going on to sign, on February 29, 1972, a specific undertaking to subject all its nuclear facilities to IAEA supervision.

In signing the NPT, a country committed itself to refrain from joining the "club" of military nuclear powers—if, at the time of its adherence, it possessed no nuclear weapons. In fact, however, the treaty contained no effective provision to enforce that undertaking. Article 10 grants each signatory "the right to withdraw from the Treaty if it decides that extraordinary events, related to the subject matter of this Treaty, have jeopardized the supreme interests of its country. It shall give notice of such withdrawal . . . three months in advance." In other words, a signatory could withdraw from its undertakings without being required to render account to other states or to any authorized international body.

Further, as international-law experts have pointed out, the treaty's Article 2, while banning manufacture or acquisition of nuclear weapons or explosives, does not preclude the preliminary steps necessary for the production of nuclear arms. Consequently, a party to the treaty could, without violating its terms, complete all preparations for the manufacture of nuclear arms with the exception of their final assembly.

In brief, a state could develop a nuclear option and make all preparations for taking it up; on completion of those preparations, it could announce that, in pursuit of its "supreme interests," it would terminate its obligations in three months' time. Such a course would in no way violate the treaty.

Why did Iraq ever go to the trouble of entering into commitments to the NPT and the IAEA? After all, Baghdad could have emulated some of the most respected members of the international community which have refused to sign.

A possible solution to that riddle may be found in a report by the Swedish International Peace Research Institute (SIPRI); dating from 1972, the report analyzes the motives of various states in deciding whether or not to sign the NPT. The institute's researchers held that some of the nonadherents plan, at some stage, to join the military nuclear club, or, even without such specific intention, are reluctant to forfeit their options. Such countries possess an advanced scientific and technological infrastructure which, given the necessary effort, could facilitate the creation of a military nuclear capability. Nations listed in this category include India (the report was completed two years before India detonated its nuclear device—a reflection of the accuracy of its assessments), Pakistan, Israel, Argentina, Brazil, South Africa and others.

However, SIPRI researchers held that a country which lacks such an advanced infrastructure but which nevertheless wishes to attain a nuclear capability is well advised to join the NPT and submit to IAEA supervision. This seems like a paradox, but it contains a considerable measure of truth. As the SIPRI report sees it, the mere existence of the NPT has wrought a fundamental change in international nuclear traffic. Members of the nuclear club which signed the treaty are forbidden by its Article 1 to transfer nuclear arms to another state or to assist another state in the acquisition or development of such weapons. However, general nuclear aid is denied only to states which decline to sign the treaty; those which do adhere are free to receive fissionable materials, reactors, and training for their nuclear personnel. They need only point to their signature on the treaty to prove that they are "kosher."

Of course, not every country which signed the treaty entertained such nefarious designs. But the wily Saddam Hussain did exploit Iraq's adherence to the NPT as camouflage for his true intentions. While denying any intention of producing nuclear arms, Iraq's leaders harnessed their practical policies to that precise end.

On commencing their talks with France, the Iraqis expressed an interest in buying an electric-power reactor of the gas-graphite type. Of British design, the first such reactor went into operation at the British nuclear center of Calder Hill in 1956. French scientists were quick to note its plutogenic traits; consequently, when France created its Force de Frappé independent nuclear deterrent, nuclear plants at Marcoule began manufacturing gas-graphite reactors which were to provide most of the plutonium for the French nuclear stockpile. However, while it is an efficient source of plutonium, the gas-graphite reactor is much less effective in generating electricity. In the early seventies, the French therefore halted production of this type, going over to American-designed pressurized water reactors (PWRs).

But the Iraqis were not interested in generating electricity; they chose the gas-graphite reactor for the plutonium it could produce. Moreover, it uses natural uranium, which is readily available on the international market, unlike the enriched variety. Had they acquired the gas-graphite reactor they sought, the Iraqis would have been able to produce plutonium in enormous quantities. According to reports by the U.S. Congressional Research Service and by French scientists, the amounts produced would have sufficed for the construction of from five to eight bombs per annum.

Chirac's reaction to the Iraqi request remains unclear to this day. Some claim that his initial response was favorable. Others say that he declined to commit himself. Chirac himself has refused to respond directly. Be that as it may, the French Premier could hardly have failed to comprehend the significance of the Iraqi choice: his delegation included Dr. Yves Girard, a special adviser to France's Atomic Energy Commission, who, being well acquainted with the unique traits of the gas-graphite reactor, would have been able to instruct Chirac on the subject. Further consultations with French experts on his return home must have established that the Iraqis were intent solely on producing plutonium. But Chirac refused to be deterred.

However, even if the ambitious Premier was bent on meeting Iraqi wishes, it was beyond his power to do so, for the simple reason that the French reactor manufacturers, Framatome, had discontinued production of gas-graphite reactors several years previously. Dr. Bertrand Goldschmidt of France's Atomic Energy Commission claims that there were discussions about the advisability of meeting the Iraqi request, but that the matter was dismissed "for reasons that had nothing to do with nuclear proliferation"—i.e., by virtue of France's inability to supply the type of reactor the Iraqis wanted.

Had the Iraqis indeed desired an electric-power reactor—as they claimed when requesting a gas-graphite installation—they could have applied for one of the newer American-designed models the French were now manufacturing. But on learning that a gas-graphite reactor could not be supplied, the Iraqis, temporarily at least, showed no further interest in any French-built reactor.

In January 1975, Chirac paid an official visit to India; on his way home, he made a stopover in Baghdad. As on his previous visit, he was again accompanied by an entourage of senior officials, including Foreign Trade Minister Raymond Barre, who was soon to replace him as premier. But Chirac's companions took no part in his talks with Hussain.

The Iraqi President refused to give up hope of acquiring a gas-graphite reactor. Under pressure from his host, Chirac promised to review the matter.

But on his return to Paris the French Premier realized that it was out of the question. Even had he managed to convince Framatome to restore the dismantled production line and renew production of a gas-graphite reactor, he would still have had to contend with powerful domestic opposition, as numerous Frenchmen raised their voices in protest against the delivery to Iraq of a reactor similar to those which France had used in building up its own nuclear arsenal.

Chirac consequently notified Hussain that he must relinquish hope of getting the reactor of his choice. With that, the French Premier promised to provide a suitable substitute. That pledge would be honored, by Chirac himself and by his successors in the French government.

7 "The God of Hell and Death"

Briefly, it appeared that Iraq would relinquish the French option and buy a Canadian-built CANDU, which had proved so helpful to India. But Jacques Chirac did not give up so easily; he had put in too great an effort to guarantee his country its supplies of Iraqi oil and the lucrative commercial contracts included in the deal. Chirac and his supporters could argue that France would soon become Iraq's foremost trading partner: the two countries had long-term contracts for the sale of industrial products and technology, and in 1974 Iraq bought French industrial equipment to a value of $1.4 billion.

On March 3, 1975, Saddam Hussain paid a return visit to Paris, bringing a valuable gift for Chirac: an ancient musket. However, it was not that venerable piece of military hardware which set off the alarm bells at Israel's Paris embassy. Hussain's visit was adequate indication of Iraq's continued efforts to elicit French aid for its nuclear program. The conclusions were alarmingly clear. Saddam Hussain missed no opportunity to reiterate his intention of annihilating Israel. It began to look as though he would be helped toward his goal by the power Israel had once regarded as its ally and friend. Israel's intelligence community began to calculate the odds.

One of the bodies alerted was the Mossad, or, by its full name, the Institution for Intelligence and Special Tasks. The Mossad handles clandestine operations beyond Israel's borders. It gathers information on military and diplomatic matters and on any subject pertaining to Israel's national security. In its worldwide operations, the Mossad discards its veil of secrecy only on the rarest of occasions (as when its agents kidnapped Nazi mass murderer Adolf Eichmann and brought him to Israel to stand trial). The Mossad is regarded as one of the world's finest intelligence services, and numerous legends surround its exploits.

At that time, the Mossad was headed by General (Res.) Yitzhak Hoffy, "Hakka" to his friends. Born in 1927, Hoffy completed twenty-six years of military service which included a variety of field and staff posts. After heading Northern Command during the Yom Kippur War, he terminated his military career in 1974 as head of operations and deputy commander in chief. From there he went on to head the Mossad.

Military Intelligence also entered the picture. General Shlomo Gazit, then its director, recalled, "We were not worried about the Russian reactor operating in Iraq. We knew that the Soviet Union would not permit its exploitation for the production of nuclear arms." However, like the Mossad, Military Intelligence was concerned about the frequent contacts between France and Iraq, the constant to-and-fro of leaders of both countries on the Paris–Baghdad line, and, of course, about their nuclear cooperation treaty.

Gazit added, "We issued a comprehensive survey which analyzed the signficiance of Franco–Iraqi contacts and the threats posed thereby to Israel. This survey was disseminated to all echelons required to know thereof, military and political." After thirty-one years of military service, Gazit had reached his present post at a crucial juncture, following the dismissal of his predecessor, who was held responsible for the breakdown of intelligence in the runup to the Yom Kippur War. Gazit was charged with rehabilitating Military Intelligence, and his eagerness to succeed made him doubly alert and anxious. "We prodded the Foreign Ministry to take a hand in the matter," Gazit recalled. "I was in continuous contact with senior officials directly responsible to the Minister."

The Foreign Minister at that time was another reserve general: Yigal Alon, one of the heroes of the 1948 War of Independence. Having grasped the gravity of the matter, Alon paid a working visit to Paris on April 29–30, 1975, as the draft Franco–Iraqi agreement reached its final stages of completion.

Alon was given a friendly welcome. On arrival at the Élysée Palace, he was greeted by an honor parade of the presidential guard, in high boots and plumed helmets, grasping drawn swords. Alon's hosts smiled while the press cameras whirred and clicked. But smiles were all he got.

In his talks with the three main pillars of the French administration, President Giscard, Premier Chirac and Foreign Minister Jean Sauvagnargues, Alon conveyed Israel's concern over the possibility of Iraq's misuse of the nuclear technology and fuels whose purchase it was negotiating with France. Anxious to fend off an international outcry, the French leaders endeavored to reassure their Israeli guest. Sauvagnargues, a tough and chilly diplomat, expressed the official French position: though not a party to the NPT, France would continue to behave as though its signature were appended to the treaty. He was referring, of course, to Article 1, which forbids any country possessing nuclear weapons to transfer them or the knowhow for their production to any other country. The Foreign Minister promised his guest that France would keep an eye on developments in Baghdad.

Alon refused to buy the French story; disappointed, he took his leave.

While pursuing their contacts with France, the Iraqis also cultivated ties with the international scientific community. Between April 7 and 12, 1975, Baghdad hosted an international scientific conference on atomic energy, attended by 140 scientists from Europe and the United States. The hosts paid particular attention to the French and Italian participants.

Finding itself unable to supply a gas-graphite reactor, the French government now offered Iraq two alternatives. The first was an American-designed PWR reactor, which generates electricity and is cooled by ordinary water under high pressure. The PWR requires large amounts of enriched uranium, but, its grade (uranium-235 content) being 2–3 percent, it is unsuitable for direct military use, which requires a much higher grade. Small wonder that the Iraqis showed no interest in the PWR.

The second alternative was an Osiris research reactor—an advanced all-French design whose prototype was inaugurated at the Saclay nuclear center near Paris in 1964. A material-test reactor (MTR), Osiris is designed for research into the behavior of materials in a radioactive environment, for production of radioisotopes for research and medical purposes, and similar uses. Osiris was supplemented by Isis, a small research reactor developed initially as an experimental prototype of Osiris. When Osiris went into operation, the French decided to employ both reactors in conjunction, using Isis to train technicians.

When the French offered the Osiris-Isis combination, the Iraqis agreed—on one condition: of the two types of Osiris, they demanded the larger 70-megawatt model. Anyone with rudimentary nuclear knowhow is aware that a reactor's plutonium-producing capacity is proportionate to its output. But the French turned a blind eye to this fact, and to the light it shed upon Iraqi intentions. Moreover, the level of Iraq's nuclear research at that time could not justify the acquisition of an Osiris reactor. The Iraqis had barely begun to take advantage of the research possibilities offered by their Soviet reactor. Their interest in Osiris obviously stemmed exclusively from its plutogenic traits.

Osiris, the ancient Egyptian god of hell and death—and the consort of the goddess Isis—headed a divine tribunal which decreed the fate of deceased mortals: either eternal life or delivery to the fangs of fearful monsters. We do not know why these particular names were chosen for the reactors, but they certainly symbolized the ambitions of Saddam Hussain: eternal life for the Arabs, while Israel was delivered to the fangs of the nuclear monster.

Now that the sale of Osiris had been agreed, French and Iraqi began wording a framework agreement. To ward off possible criticism, the French took the precaution of letting it be known that the agreement was nothing more than "a practical program for the use of nuclear energy for peaceful purposes."

On September 10, 1975, Saddam Hussain arrived in France for a further official visit. He was accompanied by several senior aides, including RCC member Sa'dun Ghaydon and Ednan al-Hamdani, an acting foreign minister, a member of the Ba'ath council and secretary general of the committee for oil and international agreements. The highpoint of the visit was a "working tour" of the Cadarache atomic-research center in southern France. Hussain held a three-hour meeting with President Giscard and spent an eventful weekend at a country house as the guest of Chirac. There can be little doubt that this visit marked final agreement on the guidelines for nuclear cooperation between the two countries.

Following the talks Chirac declared, "Iraq is now building its own nuclear program, and France desires to take part in this endeavor."

One might have imagined that, as long as talks were in progress, Hussain would have made an effort to conceal his intentions. But the wily Iraqi leader could see that the whiff of oil had turned French heads, robbing them of any willingness to pick up warning signals. In a September 8 press interview, on the eve of his departure for France, he therefore felt free to declare, "The search for technology with military potential was a reaction to Israel's nuclear armament, and the [Franco-Iraqi] agreement was the first actual step in the production of an Arab atomic weapon, despite the fact that the declared purpose for the establishment of the reactor is not the production of atomic weapons."

The French response was feeble. "Our policy is dictated not merely by interests, but also by the imperatives of the heart," Chirac told journalists.

It was shortly after the Yom Kippur War, and Israel was engaged in negotiations with Egypt for an interim disengagement agreement. Nevertheless, Jerusalem could not overlook the Iraqi menace. Prime Minister Yitzhak Rabin, having been briefed by his foreign minister, Yigal Alon, and by the heads of the Mossad and Military Intelligence, broached the subject with U.S. Secretary of State Henry A. Kissinger, who was shuttling about the region in pursuit of diplomatic understandings between Israel and its neighbors. Rabin urged Kissinger to approach the French leaders, and the Secretary of State reported later that he had acted upon the Israeli request; his efforts, however, turned out to have been fruitless.

"At that time," Rabin would recall later, "the reactor was still a kind of fetus, and that was how we related to it." Military Intelligence chief Shlomo

Gazit likewise saw the reactor as no immediate threat. Israeli policymakers were convinced that many years would elapse before the threat became real, but all agreed that it would make sense to abort the fetus before it could grow. It is, after all, well known that a fetus developing in a radioactive environment is liable to emerge as a monster. The aim, as Gazit recalls, was to induce France to withhold delivery of the reactor, or at least to refrain from supplying enriched uranium which could serve either to produce plutonium or directly as a nuclear explosive.

On October 28, 1975, Hussain held a lengthy meeting with Iraq's Atomic Energy Commission, whose members told him that, Osiris not being ideal for the production of plutonium, the Canadian reactor would be preferable. Having listened intently, Hussain contacted his French friends to make inquiries. A week later, on November 5, he reported back to the commission with details of his talks. In effect, he declared that he had reached agreement with France. Presented with a fait accompli, the scientists could only make the most of the situation. Hussain's well-honed senses detected that France was prepared to pay any price for closer relations with Iraq. His advisers must have told him that designing a bomb and constructing it would take several years—in the course of which Osiris would turn out sufficient plutonium for twenty nuclear bombs. That was quite enough to set his mind at rest.

Events now unfolded rapidly. On November 17, French Industry Minister Michel d'Ornano arrived in Baghdad. The following day, after comprehensive talks with Hussain, he signed an agreement for "cooperation . . . in employment of nuclear energy for peaceful purposes" whose wording had been agreed on during Hussain's visit to France. Ornano's signature on behalf of France was matched for Iraq by Hussain confidant Hamdani. Under the agreement, France would supply Iraq with an MTR reactor, to be constructed by the Technikatome company, which had built the Osiris reactor at Saclay. France also undertook to supply enriched uranium and to train an Iraqi team of nuclear physicists, engineers and technicians.

Overnight, the budget allotted to Iraq's Atomic Energy Commission was boosted thirteenfold, from 1.5 million dinars to 20 million. The "nuclearization" of Iraq was in train.

In Paris, Giscard, Chirac and d'Ornano embarked upon implementation of the agreement with all the care and discretion called for by a matter of such delicacy. Six years later, when Israel bombed the reactor, each of the three French leaders would attempt to pass the buck to the others regarding responsibility for its construction.

8 "Who knows where a new Hitler will emerge?"

Details of the Franco-Iraqi agreement, and of the concomitant technical negotiations, were a closely guarded secret; the French government knew well that any publicity was liable to spark an international scandal.

The agreement was without precedent in the annals of nuclear development. The two founder members of the global nuclear club, the United States and the Soviet Union, attained their military nuclear capacity unaided. Britain's nuclear program benefited from massive U.S. aid, but that was at a time when Britain was still regarded as a first-class power; furthermore, Britain consented to a near-total U.S. veto over use of its nuclear-arsenal. China's early steps into the nuclear field leaned on Soviet aid; but when that aid was cut off, the Chinese were obliged to complete their nuclear-weapons program with their own resources. France developed its nuclear capability almost without outside help, as did India, which evaded international supervision to do so.

But while these large and powerful countries boasted stable and responsible regimes, Iraq was universally regarded as irresponsible and aggressive. Saddam Hussain and his associates were unabashedly on the lookout for an opportune moment to seize the Persian Gulf emirates and large portions of Iran and Turkey. Day and night, they proclaimed their intention of annihilating Israel and boasted of their assistance to international terrorist groups, from the PLO to the IRA.

The French authorities were consequently well aware that their nuclear aid to such a regime was liable to arouse enormous indignation, domestic and foreign; they therefore did everything in their power to keep the matter confidential. On November 17, when the Élysée spokesman was asked whether France had signed a nuclear-cooperation agreement with Iraq, he responded with a shrug. Was his evasiveness the result of a presidential directive, or did he understand what was expected of him without explicit instructions?

The agreement was not submitted for ratification by the French parliament. At the time of its signing, in November 1975, the principal French papers published no more than partial details. Its full text has been kept secret to this day. It was only in mid-1977, after public pressure, that the French official gazette printed the exchange of letters appended to the agreement, relating to supervision of its provisions.

The Iraqis, by contrast, faced an entirely different dilemma. On the one hand, they wished to pose as the trailblazers leading the Arab world into the nuclear era, incidentally endeavoring to overawe their neighbors. But they were also aware that publicity could imperil implementation of the agreement. Accordingly, they adopted a sophisticated compromise: while declining to confirm reports of their efforts to develop a military nuclear capability, they gave overt and covert encouragement to reports of their interest in nuclear development.

Addressing an OPEC convention in November 1976, Iraqi Oil Minister Tayih Abed al-Karim withheld comment on reports that Iraq would be the first Arab country to possess a nuclear bomb; but he did confirm that his country intended to employ nuclear energy for peaceful purposes.

After concluding their agreement with Iraq, the French renamed the Osiris reactor destined for that country "Osirak." Semi-earnestly David Renen, scientific adviser to Israel's Paris embassy, suggested that, in deference to the key role played in the deal by Jacques Chirac, the name should be "Ochirac." This name was swiftly adopted by the diplomatic community in Paris.

Hussain himself was taken neither by "Osiris" nor by "Osirak"; he preferred an authentic Iraqi name. He recalled that the Egyptian god Osiris had a counterpart in Babylonian mythology, in the form of Tammuz, the god who dies every summer only to be resurrected in winter. Further, the Babylonian calendar (with a close resemblance to its Hebrew counterpart) features the month of Tammuz, which parallels July; July 17 marks the anniversary of the Ba'ath's seizure of power. Consequently, the Iraqis began to refer to Osiris-Osirak by the name Tammuz 1, while Isis was renamed Tammuz 2; the overall code name for the nuclear project was Tammuz 17. For Jews and Israelis, that latter date bore an ominous symbolism: on the seventeenth day of Tammuz in 586 B.C., the armies of Babylonian King Nebuchadnezzar broke through the walls of Jerusalem, initiating the final phase of the battle which ended with the destruction of the First Temple.

Whatever its name, the reactor was of the open-core type, cooled by ordinary water—hence its appellation "swimming-pool reactor" in physicists' jargon. The reactor fuel is uranium enriched to a grade of 93 percent.

The reactor core contains an amalgam of aluminum with 13.9 kilograms of metallic uranium, 12.9 kilograms of that being the 235 isotope. When operating at its full output of 70 megawatts, the reactor uses up three to five such loads of fuel per annum. Along with the reactor itself, the French undertook to deliver 80 kilograms of enriched uranium. Verbal agreement provided for further French deliveries of enriched uranium when the initial stock was exhausted.

It goes without saying that these facts were all contained behind a thick veil of secrecy. Nevertheless, concealment was less than total, and some data leaked out. On January 10, 1976, the *London Daily Mail* wrote: "Iraq is soon liable to achieve a capacity for producing nuclear weapons." The paper went on to note that the reactor to be supplied to Iraq—"one of the most unstable states in the Arab world"—would be the largest and most advanced in the Middle East. The paper added that France would be powerless to impose effective control over the use to which the Iraqis would put it.

On January 13, 1976, Yigal Alon sent his ministry's deputy director-general for West European affairs to meet French Ambassador Jean Herly and request clarifications regarding his country's current contacts with Iraq. Herly explained that the November 1975 agreement called for cooperation in the peaceful use of nuclear energy, adding that it would be supplemented by a tripartite accord between the two countries and the IAEA. The main topic being discussed by France and Iraq, Herly said, was delivery of a light-water reactor for generation of electricity, with an output of 600–900 megawatts, to be manufactured by Framatome. Another company, Technikatome, would supply a research reactor.

The French ambassador's account was a classic blend of truths, half-truths and arguable untruths, woven together in a manner which obscured the facts. Iraq had never shown any interest in a reactor for generating electricity, being intent solely on acquiring one for the production of plutonium. Was Herly aware of having been misinformed, or did he convey his replies in good faith? That is a riddle to which we can proffer no answer.

In the meantime, the Iraqis faced up to their final major problem: facilities for reprocessing the reactor's spent fuel rods to extract the plutonium needed for nuclear weapons. The obvious step should have been to seek the equipment in France. But the Iraqis did not want the French engineers and technicians employed at the reactor to take a hand in supervising the extraction facilities. Accordingly, they sought a different source.

It was rumored that the Iraqis did try to acquire the extraction facilities in France. The German *Frankfurter Allgemeine Zeitung* reported that Iraq had also applied to Bonn for a "hot cell"—scientific jargon for a laboratory for the separation of radioactive materials—but that the request was turned down. However, as the Franco-Iraqi agreement was concluded, Baghdad was already at an advanced stage of confidential negotiations with Italian manufacturers of hot cells. It is even alleged that these talks were conducted with the covert blessing, or at least tacit consent, of Paris.

Iraq's nuclear courtship of Italy had likewise commenced with an economic-cooperation agreement signed in July 1975 by the two foreign ministers, Charles Tak'a for Iraq and Aldo Moro for Italy. The agreement guaranteed the Italians regular deliveries of oil, in return for which they undertook various projects pertaining to Iraq's national-development plan. Next, a delegation of Italian scientists and officials, headed by Professor Enzio Clementali, chairman of Italy's Atomic Energy Commission, arrived in Baghdad on January 13, 1976. Two days later the delegation concluded a ten-year agreement for "the peaceful uses of nuclear energy." The crux of the agreement was Italy's undertaking to supply Iraq with a radiochemical laboratory comprising three lead-encased hot cells for handling dangerous radioactive materials.

From here on, there was no call for secret investigations by sophisticated intelligence services; it was now plain for all to see precisely where Iraq was headed. Once a highly guarded secret, the production of a nuclear bomb had, over the years, become common knowledge to an extent which placed it within the scope of any average physicist. For those with a hankering after nuclear weaponry, the principal problem was acquisition of the necessary explosive—preferably plutonium, though uranium 235 would do at a pinch. As soon as the French consented to deliver the larger model of Osiris, and the Italians contributed their hot cells, the Iraqis had solved their problem—and, simultaneously, made it perfectly obvious to any person of intelligence just what they were up to.

As far back as December 1975, researchers at the prestigious Hudson Institute in Croton, New York, predicted that the French reactor would give Iraq sufficient plutonium to build "two nuclear devices per annum." These findings, published in the December 1975 issue of *Middle East Enterprise*, cited senior sources in the U.S. Energy Research and Development Administration (the new title of the Atomic Energy Commission). The periodical added that Iraq's key to nuclear weapons lay in "being able to build a reprocessing capability" to extract plutonium from the reactor's spent fuel rods. The complex process calls for advanced technology, but the writer believed the Iraqis capable of surmounting the difficulty. So they were—with Italian aid.

Furthermore, one salient feature of Osiris which attracted the Iraqis was its use of uranium enriched to a 93 percent grade. The moment they received the first shipment of enriched uranium—20 kilograms would suffice—they would be able to build a "primitive" atom bomb. The mere possession of the nuclear explosive would make Iraq a potential nuclear power, with only a short distance to traverse before realizing that potential.

This was well known to Saddam Hussain when he opted for Osiris rather than the Canadian CANDU reactor, which, while far more efficient in its production of plutonium, operates on natural uranium rather than the enriched variety. Relying exclusively on the production of plutonium could entail failure should Iraq's designs emerge, whereas Osiris granted the Iraqis the best of both worlds: by means of the Italian hot cells, they could try to extract plutonium and use it for the secret construction of nuclear weapons; in the event of their plan's leaking out and causing an international outcry, they could seize the dozens of kilograms of uranium in use at the reactor or ready for insertion, and employ the fuel for the construction of two or three uranium-235 bombs.

Iraq's insistence on high-grade uranium was camouflaged by "scientific" arguments, principally the claim that it would permit of experiments of a far more complex nature than lower-grade uranium. But only wide-eyed innocence—or self-deception—could induce anyone to believe Iraqi scientists capable of mounting such advanced scientific research.

On January 26, 1976, France was the sole Western country to support an anti-Israel resolution presented to the UN Security Council by the Arab states. It was a clear indication that France's courtship of Iraq—at Israel's expense—was now in full swing.

Forty-eight hours later, Premier Chirac arrived in Iraq for a further visit. This time, he had the benefit of a firsthand account of his hosts' nuclear progress, from the nuclear attaché now posted to the French Embassy in Baghdad. Chirac personally toured al-Tuweitha for a close inspection of the site picked for the French nuclear complex. The tour provided an opportunity for a flow of flowery rhetoric. Relations between the two countries, Chirac boasted, presented "an example that should be followed in establishing relations between a big independent European country and a big independent Arab country."

The French Premier now issued specific directives to remove any administrative obstacle hindering the swift and flawless implementation of the contract. Dozens of French engineers and technicians arrived in Iraq to plan work on the infrastructure, while numerous Iraqis were sent to study at nuclear-research centers in France.

Chirac's visit to Iraq came after Iraq had concluded its agreement with

Italy. The French Premier was therefore fully aware that Iraq was acquiring hot cells for the extraction of plutonium, and he could thus gauge precisely where the Iraqis were headed. If there was any lingering doubt, Hussain removed it when he declared in a February 17 radio broadcast, "Politics was involved in all, and science and scientific research were useless if they were separated from the strategic political concepts of the revolution." In view of Iraq's nuclear efforts, such an utterance was open only to one interpretation. But France and Italy reflected the Biblical characterisation "They have eyes but do not see, they have ears but do not hear."

On February 15, a delegation from the French National Institute for National Defense Research, headed by a respected general, arrived in Iraq. On April 3, the framework agreement was ratified by both countries. On May 5, French Foreign Minister Jean François-Poncet arrived in Baghdad. Three weeks later, he was followed by Foreign Trade Minister Raymond Barre, who was soon to succeed Chirac as premier. Barre held four days of confidential talks, the principal topic being a straight quid pro quo: enlarged shipments of Iraqi oil to France in exchange for a speedup in the delivery of Osiris.

It goes without saying that Israel's intelligence community was in no position to air its assessments and concerns about developments in Iraq, but a number of members of Israel's Knesset decided to alert public opinion. On January 27, 1976, a few days after conclusion of the Franco-Iraqi agreement, four Knesset members, drawn from the government coalition and the opposition, submitted urgent motions to the agenda relating to Iraq's nuclear program. The principal disclosure came from Dr. Yehuda Ben Meir, of the legislature's Foreign Affairs and Defense Committee: he reported that a nuclear attaché had been posted at France's embassy in Iraq, for the exclusive purpose of furthering that country's nuclear program. Ben Meir and his colleagues derided the French contention about the feasibility of effective control over the reactors. They cited Libyan dictator Muammar al-Qaddafi: "In future, the might of a nation will be gauged by the number of atom bombs it possesses." They pointed out that, in spite of Soviet enmity toward Israel, Moscow had refused to supply Iraq with weapons-grade uranium whereas France had shown no such inhibitions. Where, they demanded, was the France of the Revolution, of Liberty, Equality, Fraternity, of Émile Zola?

Responding to the agitated Knesset members, Foreign Minister Alon declared publicly that the Israeli government was following with lively concern the cooperation being forged between the Arab states and countries possessing advanced nuclear technology; he warned against the grant of such technology to Mideast states liable to misuse it. "We act to the best of our ability whenever such dangers are revealed," he affirmed, without, of course, being able to elaborate.

A short time later, Alon held a further meeting with the French ambassador, requesting the latter to convey to his superiors the anxiety expressed in the Knesset. "Providing a nuclear capability to irresponsible Mideastern states is a perilous act," Alon warned, reiterating Israel's concern over France's nuclear ties with Iraq.

However, Alon's appeal fell on deaf ears. Paris, overjoyed at its success in concluding a deal which guaranteed oil supplies and lucrative commercial contracts, paid no heed.

By contrast, there was profound anxiety in Washington. Israel may be assumed to have warned the Americans of what was in train between Paris and Baghdad, and the Americans were unable to overlook the danger. The U.S. government requested clarifications from France. Washington's concern focused on the weapons-grade uranium that France was supplying to Iraq, which, either directly or by conversion into plutonium, could be used to produce nuclear arms. What irritated the Americans in particular was the fact that all the enriched uranium used by France for civilian purposes— whether in power or research reactors—came from U.S. sources. (In fact, only the uranium used in France's nuclear arsenal was locally produced.) This state of affairs enabled the Americans to make it plain that they wanted no part, direct or indirect, in supplying Iraq with nuclear fuel.

While the U.S. Administration pursued diplomatic paths, four senior American nuclear physicists launched an international campaign to spotlight the perils of selling nuclear technology to states known for their lunatic irresponsibility. In a special program broadcast by Britain's independent Granada network, Professor George Ratgens, a former chief scientist at the U.S. Defense Department, declared, "Only thirty years ago, Germany was led by Adolf Hitler. Who knows where a new Hitler will emerge? A crazy leader like Qaddafi, who has no nuclear arms, is liable to try and get them by any means available. He could employ mercenaries to get him black-market plutonium and build a do-it-yourself bomb. Leaders like Qadaffi or [Uganda's] Idi Amin are liable to endanger world peace if they get their hands on nuclear weapons."

Ratgens' colleague Professor Bernard Feld, a member of the scientific team which designed the first atom bomb, and currently head of Boston University's nuclear-physics department, told of a nightmare which haunted him incessantly: In the middle of the night, he is awakened by the mayor of Boston, who tells him that a group of terrorists have announced that they have laid an atom bomb somewhere in the city's downtown. A check reveals that the U.S. government's plutonium stockpile is short by 10 kilograms—more than the amount needed for a "small" bomb. In his dream, Feld advises the terrified mayor to capitulate to the terrorists' demands, to save Boston's two and a half million inhabitants from destruction.

Feld concluded his words with a warning: "The world is now at a crossroads. If the powers persist in trading in nuclear reactors, my nightmare will become reality."

The four scientists illustrated their reference to "lunatic leaders" by naming the since-deposed Idi Amin, and Libya's Qaddafi, who still persists in his efforts to acquire nuclear weapons. For some reason, they inadvertently failed to mention Saddam Hussain—evidently unaware that the Iraqi strongman had far outstripped his crazy colleagues in the race for a nuclear bomb. Even though the four scientists made a considerable impact on international opinion with their campaign, Hussain himself was unperturbed by it. While the foursome continued their European tour, Iraq approached the IAEA to propose the posting of permanent PLO observers at the agency's Vienna headquarters. Such a move would obviously grant the terrorist organization access to information about nuclear reactors and fuel and the safeguards taken for their protection. But Hussain's outrageous proposal stemmed from an evident sense of strength and self-confidence. Small wonder: less than four months after the four American scientists' tour of Europe, France and Iraq concluded a comprehensive commercial agreement; linked to their earlier nuclear pact, it defined the terms for the delivery of the reactors to Iraq.

The new agreement was signed on August 26, 1976—just one day after the resignation of Premier Jacques Chirac. The timing was an encouraging sign for the Iraqis: the bitter differences with President Giscard which had induced Chirac to step down did nothing to prejudice Franco–Iraqi nuclear links. Even after Chirac's departure, bilateral cooperation would continue to flourish with the blessing of Giscard.

In June 1981, following Israel's destruction of the reactor, Giscard and Chirac would trade charges about responsibility for its construction; the dispute also dragged in Chirac's successor, Raymond Barre.

Chirac claimed to have insisted on full Iraqi guarantees against misuse of the reactor. Anyway, the agreement was incomplete at the time of his resignation. It was signed, he said, by his successor as premier, Raymond Barre. As for safeguards, Chirac was unsure about the "definitive decisions taken after my departure, under the authority of the President of the Republic, by the Premier." By this roundabout wording, Chirac sought to kill two birds with the single stone he directed at both his rival Giscard and his successor Barre—while simultaneously insisting that he himself had acted properly as premier.

Chirac's defense was upheld by his intimate, former Commander in Chief

General Guy Méry, who had served on France's Atomic Energy Commission during the seventies: according to Méry, it was Barre who made the decisive steps.

For his part, Raymond Barre played down the significance of the August 1976 agreement, which he depicted as of "limited importance in comparison with other agreements signed by France and Iraq." He offered no clue as to whether these other agreements likewise contain provisions liable to cause concern to Israel.

In the meantime, the Iraqis were urging the French to modify the original reactor design. Having successfully pressed their demand for the larger 70-megawatt design, they now argued—justly, in technical and scientific terms—that the reactor required supplementary cooling systems.

However, this demand again highlighted Iraq's quest for large-scale production of plutonium. The most common method of production—that employed by India, for example—encompasses the reactor core with a ring ("blanket") of uranium oxide. But while facilitating production of large amounts of plutonium, the "blanket" gives off enormous heat. Anyone wishing to use a reactor principally for plutonium production is therefore required to install a cooling system larger and more effective than the normal design. The French were well acquainted with these details, but they nevertheless acceded to the Iraqi request without blinking an eyelid. Later, they would claim that research requirements justified a larger output, since this would enable scientists to test the thermal and mechanical qualities of materials within an environment similar to that of a "true" reactor (i.e., a power reactor or one designed from the outset for the production of plutonium). But the rudimentary level of Iraq's nuclear research presents this claim in a ludicrous light. Under the circumstances, Iraq's insistence on enlarged output could have only one explanation: an interest in boosting plutonium production. IAEA Deputy Director-General Hans Grümm has estimated that "the uranium blanket" at Osirak could yield enough plutonium for one to two bombs per year."

Still not satisfied, the Iraqis came up with a further demand whose purpose likewise must have been obvious to anyone with eyes in his head: they requested to have Osiris fitted with a tank of heavy water. Though such a tank is attached to French research reactors, it has nothing to do with the normal functioning of an Osiris-type reactor, its principal use being in highly advanced experiments with neutron rays.

There can be no doubt as to Iraq's inability to contemplate serious scientific experiments with neutron rays. Harvard physics department head Richard Wilson, who visited al-Tuweitha at the invitation of the Iraqis following Israel's attack, affirms that, despite Iraqi explanations, he failed to discover any link between neutron-ray experiments and the nuclear-research program Iraq claimed to be conducting.

On September 11, 1976, some two weeks after concluding their agreement, the governments of Iraq and France exchanged letters relating to supervision procedures. The substance of the letters was kept secret for several months, but they affirmed that, in relation to Osirak, France would rest content with the safeguards recommended by the IAEA. French experts must have known that IAEA supervision is ineffective against a government intent on acquiring nuclear weapons; but the French authorities, sheltering behind the broad back of "international control," preferred to shut their eyes to that fact.

In later years, the French were to argue that IAEA inspection was merely an additional prrecaution, to supplement the presence of French technicians and engineers at the reactor. However, this claim does not hold water. The bilateral agreement specified that the reactors were the exclusive property of the Iraqi government, which was therefore free at any time to dismiss the French technicians. Furthermore, all that the Iraqis needed to do was bribe a number of technicians—or subject them to blackmail or intimidation—to achieve full freedom of action.

The provision for a tripartite agreement among France, Iraq and the IAEA, to be concluded should Iraq terminate its agreement with the IAEA, is a masterpiece of sleight of hand. In such an event, what could induce Iraq to sign an unparalleled "tripartite" agreement? This provision, apparently appended to reassure opponents and critics, was in effect worthless.

9 "Thieves in the Night"

Early in 1977, Saddam Hussain began preparations for the ouster of aging President Bakr. No longer content with the status of strongman, Hussain now wanted the formal title for himself. As though at the wave of a wand, rumors began to circulate, in Iraq and abroad, about the grave ailment afflicting Bakr. A number of officials and officers were removed from sensitive posts, to be replaced by Hussain loyalists. The authorities stepped up measures against surviving remnants of the opposition. Unexpectedly, bombs were discovered in the towns of Najf and Karbela, but the security services defused them before they could go off. The whole story reeked of provocation; however, it gave the government a pretext to arrest so-called subversive elements.

Domestic developments within Iraq naturally evoked disquiet in neighboring Iran. It was not long since Hussain had concluded the agreement with Iran which, it will be recalled, recognized that country's navigation rights in the Shatt-al-Arab waterway. But the Shah knew whom he was dealing with; he declined to trust Hussain, foreseeing that Iraq would seize upon the first available opportunity to violate the agreement.

By now, the Kurds, realizing they had been duped by Hussain, had renewed their uprising in northern Iraq. Iraq, learning that Iran was secretly aiding the rebels, started mouthing threats, whereupon Teheran sent a high-ranking emissary to placate its angry neighbors.

Observing these developments, Israel saw that its own anxiety about Iraq's nuclear program was probably shared by Iran. In view of the long border between the two countries, and Iraq's undisguised territorial designs, Iran probably had even more cause to fear Hussain's intentions.

It is now common knowledge that the Shah's Iran, while having no formal diplomatic ties with Israel, nevertheless maintained ramified links and bilateral cooperation in numerous spheres, with frequent exchanges of visits by prominent leaders on both sides. It was therefore no unusual occurrence when, in February 1977, Israeli Foreign Minister Yigal Alon met with Assadulla Amini,* a top-ranking Iranian who served as his country's principal liaison with the Israelis. But there was nothing routine about the topic the two men discussed: Iraq's nuclear program.

If Alon expected the Iranian official to come right out with unhesitating concurrence with Israel's concerns, he was disappointed. Alon could sense that the Iranians mistrusted Iraq, but Amini was not prepared to say anything explicit. His reticence may have been intentional: at the time, the Shah's ever-soaring imagination was toying with the construction of a network of nuclear-power stations in his own country. Consequently, action to alert the international community against nuclear aid to Iraq was liable to boomerang against Iran's own plans. The gist of the Alon–Amini dialogue on this topic was as follows:

Alon: "Are the Iraqis attempting to produce nuclear weapons with French assistance?"

Amini: "They are."

Alon: "Will France assist them?"

Amini: "Only [in construction of] an atomic [research] center."

Alon: "But for military purposes."

Amini did not respond. His taciturnity set off yet one more alarm bell.

Disappointed in Iran, Israel now pinned its hopes principally upon the United Sates, which had, since 1975, conducted a most vigorous campaign against dissemination of military nuclear technology. The campaign began with pressure by President Gerald R. Ford upon Pakistan to forgo the plutonium-extraction plant it had purchased from France in response to India's 1974 nuclear explosion. The Americans also took steps to block nuclear initiatives by Libya, and by Brazil and Argentina.

Washington intelligence files were bursting with information about Libya's contacts with countries including China, the Soviet Union, Pakistan, India, France and West Germany, in pursuit of a "civilian" nuclear capability of which Libya had not the slightest need. When Libya concluded a treaty of friendship with Argentina in 1974, U.S. intelligence agencies learned that it contained a secret codicil with a specific Argentinian pledge to give Libya a share in its own nuclear-development program. Argentina was reportedly making earnest efforts to attain a capacity for uranium enrichment, therevy unfolding an alarming scenario according to which Qaddafi's Libya received Argentinian fissionable material of a military grade. The Americans also discovered that Libya had offered lavish financial aid to Pakistan in return for plutonium from its reactors—a request Pakistan turned down.

*Fictitious name.

Washington learned further that Argentina's nuclear program was causing disquiet in Brazil. That enormous country, which had almost no oil reserves, was interested in developing its nuclear-power capacity—along with a concomitant military capability. The United States foresaw disastrous results to a nuclear-arms race between the two Latin-American giants. This concern prompted U.S. officials to approach Brazil and West Germany in a bid to modify their nuclear-cooperation agreement whereby the Federal Republic was to supply Brazil with an installation for reprocessing irradiated nuclear fuel.

In view of this vigorous antiproliferation campaign, it was only natural for the United States to attempt to talk Paris into renegotiating its agreement with Iraq. While details of that agreement remained confidential, the Americans were keenly aware that a reactor of the size of Osiris, which consumed dozens of kilograms of enriched uranium each year, was liable to pave the way for Iraq to manufacture nuclear arms. But, equally aware that France would be reluctant to forfeit the enormous profits arising from its deal with Iraq, they suggested that France could, without giving Iraq a military nuclear capability, meet is commitments by fueling the reactor with uranium enriched to no more than a 20–25 percent grade. The French government promised to study the American proposal, but in the meantime it maintained a feverish pace in discharging its obligations to Iraq.

Briefly, it looked as though the Americans would take vigorous action to dissuade their European allies from trading nuclear technology for oil and raw materials. The first indication was a slowdown in American deliveries of enriched uranium to Western European power and research reactors. The delay was depicted as bureaucratic, but the U.S. government is renowned for its skill in removing such obstacles or causing their appearance, as circumstances require. In the general view, the slowdown represented U.S. pressure on America's two largest customers for enriched uranium, France and Germany, in relation to their deals with Brazil, Pakistan and Iraq.

In November 1976, Jimmy Carter was elected the thirty-ninth President of the United States. The former governor of Georgia lacked experience in international diplomacy, but he had an impressive mastery of nuclear subjects, his service with the U.S. Navy having been spent on board a nuclear submarine. Moreover, his studies at the U.S. Naval Academy, hingeing upon nuclear physics and reactor technology, had endowed him with considerable expertise in the technical aspects of nuclear systems. In the course of his election campaign, Carter stressed the threat posed by dissemination of nuclear technology; he pledged that, if elected, he would take sweeping international action against agreements which exacerbated such dangers.

France was almost totally dependent upon U.S. supplies of enriched uranium—a dependency which could only grow, in view of French hopes that the coming decade would see half of France's electricity generated by nuclear reactors. Israel consequently had grounds for expecting to see France bow to Washington's will by withholding the weapons-grade uranium promised to Iraq. But those expectations were not borne out by events.

In March 1977, French Industry Minister Michel d'Ornano was forced to admit the existence of a nuclear-cooperation agreement with Iraq, but he stubbornly refused to reveal its substance.

At about the same time, Iraqi Deputy Prime Minister Tarik Aziz declared, "It is necessary to overcome the Israeli Army's qualitative edge and resourcefulness by employing the quantitive advantages of the Arabs: population, geographical size and oil. If these resources are employed in a sophisticated manner, the world will treat the Arabs with respect, and the Arabs will be able to tilt the balance of force in their favor, permitting them to withstand a long and arduous war till victory. War with Israel is inevitable . . ." In conventional confrontations, Israel's Army had repeatedly demonstrated its prowess, even when, as in 1973, the Arabs enjoyed the advantage of surprise. According to the thinking of Aziz, it was now up to the Arabs to employ their resources in a "sophisticated" manner. In view of Iraq's nuclear agreement with France, and the contract for the purchase of the Italian hot cells, his words could mean only one thing: Iraq was taking the nuclear warpath.

For France, it was the moment of truth. And, as fate would have it, this precise period witnessed a development which helped highlight Iraqi intentions beyond any shadow of doubt.

After years of effort, a team of French scientists at the Saclay nuclear center succeeded in developing a new type of nuclear fuel. Named "Caramel" for its resemblance to the candy relished by millions of connoisseurs, it was designed especially for research reactors. With a uranium-235 content not exceeding 20–25 percent, its unusual composition nevertheless permitted its use in advanced scientific experiments hitherto feasible only with military-grade uranium. The discovery thus killed two birds with the same stone: while reducing the need for large amounts of rare and costly uranium 235, it also reduced the danger of weapons-grade fuel falling into the wrong hands.

Had the Iraqis indeed wished to use Osiris for research purposes, they should have been overjoyed at the breakthrough: Caramel would have cut their reactor's operating costs to a marked degree. But when the French had the temerity to advise use of the new fuel in place of weapons-grade uranium, they encountered a veritable storm of protests and threats whose shrillness clearly showed up Iraq's true intentions.

At this stage Caramel was being produced on a laboratory scale, and three or four years would elapse before it was available in industrial quantities. The French government was racked by internal debates about whether to honor the original terms of the agreement with the Iraqis or to try and talk them into accepting Caramel. This debate soon merged into the overall "reassessment" of France's nuclear-export policies, instigated after the resignation of Chirac. While the latter had no reservations, either moral or political, about supplying French nuclear technology to anyone prepared to pay hard cash, some of his fellow countrymen sensed the heavy burden of responsibility imposed by such a course. At least for a time, this group included President Giscard, who ordered the "reassessment": his directive led to France's reneging on its undertaking to help Pakistan in constructing a reprocessing plant for irradiated fuel.

But the most pressing issue, the Iraqi agreement, remained open.

The ever suspicious French administration made sure that its inner disagreements would not become public knowledge. However, it is now generally thought to have been the Foreign Ministry which wanted the agreement with Iraq modified so as to permit the use of Caramel, while France's Atomic Energy Commision (CEA) insisted on honoring the original terms. In all probability, the Quai d'Orsay was apprehensive about unfavorable international repercussions when it became known that France was effectively assisting Iraq in acquiring a military nuclear capability. France's diplomats may also have balked at a sharp confrontation with President Carter, who was known for his out-and-out opposition to dissemination of sensitive nuclear technology. By contrast, the CEA represented the financial and commercial interests of France's nuclear industry, which refused to let anything impede punctilious fulfillment of the agreement with Iraq, and the enormous benefits it would gain thereby.

France's mixed feelings at this time (late 1976 and early 1977) were reflected in the visit to Israel of the new Foreign Minister, Louis de Guiringaud, on March 30–31, 1977.

Several weeks earlier, Franco–Israeli relations had plunged into a severe disagreement when a Parisian court ordered the release from custody of Muhammed Daud Udah, known as Abu Daud, a senior officer of "Black September," the most murderous section of al-Fatah, a major component of the PLO.

Entering France on a forged Norwegian passport, Abu Daud had arrived in January 1977 to investigate the circumstances surrounding the murder in Paris of PLO official Mahmoud Sulh. A few days aftrer his arrival, Abu Daud was detained by French security agents. News of his arrest prompted both Israel and West Germany to request his extradition. At the time of the

1972 Olympic Games in Munich, Abu Daud had been among the planners of the terrorist attack which ended in the deaths of eleven Israeli athletes. He was also implicated in planning numerous attacks and acts of sabotage against Israeli installations at various places around the world. Nevertheless, before the Israeli extradition request could pass through the customary procedures, a French court ordered him released and deported. The verdict was blatantly political, the judge having come under massive official pressure.

Learning of the ruling from an Israel radio newscast which cited the French news agency, Foreign Minister Alon called his ambassador in Paris, Mordachai Gazit, fuming over the latter's failure to notify him. But Gazit turned out to be as surprised as his superior.

In protest over the release of Abu Daud, Israel recalled Gazit for consultations. Though he considered the directive misjudged, the ambassador naturally complied, but before leaving he was warned by French Foreign Ministry director general Jean-Marie Soutou, "We did not request your recall to Israel, and it will be difficult to find a pretext for your return to Paris." Acting on his own initiative, Gazit met with Elysée Palace Director-General Jean François-Poncet.

"The President knows you are here," François-Poncet told Gazit.

"I'm on my way home," Gazit said, adding, "The Foreign Minister and I learned from the radio of your decision to deport Abu Daud. That is the conduct of thieves in the night. You misled us on this matter, you deceived us, you violated the extradition treaty between Israel and France."

While admitting that France's Foreign Ministry was "not quite in order," the director-general did not hesitate to raise his voice to the ambassador, telling him, "This is not the way to behave in the presidential palace."

"If you desire scandals with Israel, just persist in your present course," Gazit retorted in a tone equally acrimonious.

Gazit departed for Israel, for "consultations" whose duration he could not foresee. He left the embassy in the charge of his assistant, Minister Mordechai Drori. Some ten days after Gazit's departure, Deputy Minister Lionel Stoleru, a former special adviser to the French President who continued to act on the latter's behalf, initiated a meeting with Drori. Assuring the Israeli diplomat that his President was "interested in terminating the affair," Stoleru exhibited testimony in the form of a presidential directive to French ministers to cease their advocacy of a Palestinian state. If the Israeli ambassador returned to Paris without delay, Stoleru promised, he would be rewarded by an extraordinary gesture: President Giscard would immediately receive him, thereby departing from his custom of declining to meet with foreign diplomats accredited to France.

Drori's report of the exchange was laid before Israeli Prime Minister Rabin, Foreign Minister Alon and, of course, the "exiled" Ambassador

Gazit. After study of the report, Drori was instructed to make preparations for the ambassador's return to Paris. The Israeli minister accordingly requested an interview with François-Poncet, to encounter an astounding response.

"What!?" cried the Élysée director-general. "Shall France kneel before Israel? Shall the President of France receive the ambassador? When the ambassador returns, he will meet with me. Should he request to see the President, it may be assumed that Giscard will receive him."

Drori was amazed. Was this a piece of playacting, a coordinated demarche between the President and his director general? Or had Giscard dispatched Stoleru to Drori without the knowledge of the all-powerful François-Poncet?

Whatever the answer to the riddle, Drori took care to avoid any further diplomatic incident. Contacts were resumed, and Gazit's twenty-five-day absence ended with his return to Paris, where he was later received by the President.

Against this backdrop of lingering resentments, Guiringaud came to Jerusalem to meet Alon. In spite of the importance Israel attached to the recent incident and its implications, the principal Israeli concern was the Franco-Iraqi nuclear treaty.

In addressing his Israeli colleague, Guiringaud adopted a tone halfway between discomfort and self-righteousness. The gist of his remarks was that France, being aware of the great danger of nuclear proliferation, would do nothing to grant atomic weapons to any state which did not yet possess them. For example, he argued, France was committed to supplying Pakistan with an extraction plant for spent nuclear fuel; but concern that such a plant could enable Pakistan to manufacture nuclear arms was inducing Paris to try to renege on its undertaking. Could there be better proof of France's firm stand against nuclear proliferation?

It was a convincing presentation, but a closer scrutiny points to certain omissions and inaccuracies. Above all, Guiringaud failed to mention that, France's interests in Pakistan being relatively limited, the contract for construction of the extraction plant was in substance a purely commercial proposition, not the outcome of a high-level decision arising out of overall national policy. By contrast, the treaty with Iraq stemmed from a decision by France's leaders (President Giscard and Premier Chirac), who were guided by the broader aim of making Iraq into France's principal client in the entire Mideast, and thereby guaranteeing Iraqi oil deliveries in large quantities and at moderate prices—considerations which did not bear upon the contract with Pakistan.

Ignoring these salient distinctions, Guiringaud continued to try to reassure his Israeli host. There was "exaggeration" in assessments of the traits and capabilities of the Osirak reactor, he claimed. First, it was not a large reactor. Second, it was designed for research, not for production of plutonium. Third, while there was admittedly some risk in supplying Iraq with 93-percent-grade uranium, France had provided for adequate safeguards and guarantees to eliminate the danger.

Alon did not swallow the bait. He knew that the Osiris, while not large in relation to electric-power reactors, was enormous in comparison with other research reactors. Furthermore, even research reactors produce plutonium; and, above all, Alon was sufficiently experienced to know that neither "safeguards" nor "guarantees" could prevent any state determined to manufacture nuclear arms from doing so if it possessed the necessary means. "That," said Alon, referring to the professed safeguards and guarantees, "does not reassure me at all, because the Iraqis can deceive the French inspectors or expel them."

To which Guiringaud replied, "They are unlikely to do so, because they will need French fuel."

This reply was equally unsatisfactory, but before Alon could say so Guiringaud hastened to divulge what he referred to as "a secret." French scientists, he said, had achieved a highly significant scientific breakthrough, which would soon make it possible to modify the reactor structure to use uranium enriched to a grade of no more than 20–25 percent. This would leave Osiris still capable of almost all the scientific experiments planned, but would preclude use of the nuclear fuel for military purposes. The discovery, he said, would be announced at a scientific convention to be held in June. In any case, Guiringaud stressed, the fuel was not an immediate concern because the reactor would not be completed before 1979 or 1980.

The "secret" was indeed of considerable significance. If France were to supply the new fuel (the reference was, of course, to "Caramel"), the Iraqis would be unable to make weapons out of the fuel, and also less able to exploit it for plutonium production. Nevertheless, they would still retain the option of secretly producing plutonium by operating Osiris on fuel acquired from other sources. The "secret" therefore failed to reassure Alon, who reiterated that acquisition of such a large and advanced reactor would give Iraq extensive opportunities in the nuclear sphere. He recalled that Israel was not alone in its concern, indicating that he possessed information which pointed to similar disquiet in Syria and Saudi Arabia.

Realizing that he had failed to sweeten the pill, Guiringaud concluded the exchange about the reactor by saying, "I would like to think it over."

Did his desire to "think it over" stem from eagerness to get Alon off his back? Fairness requires that his wish be regarded as genuine, stemming from the impact of his visit to the Yad Vashem memorial to the six million Jews who died in the Nazi Holocaust. Guiringaud was profoundly shaken by his tour of the shrine. Wearing a hat, and with his hands clasped behind his back, he entered the memorial, his expression growing somber. Hours after emerging, he remained unsmiling. His inscription in the memorial's visitors' book read: "*Hommage au sacrifice, au courage, à la grandeur du peuple juif* [Homage to the sacrifice, the courage and the greatness of the Jewish people]." Still stunned by that visit, could the French Foreign Minister take a light view of Israel's warnings or its fears of Iraqi preparations for a new holocaust?

On that point, Saddam Hussain made no attempt to deceive his new French allies. "Never," he proclaimed in an interview published in the United States on May 16, 1977, "shall we recognize Israel's right to exist as an independent Zionist state."

Eliyahu Maicy, Paris correspondent for the Israeli daily *Ha'aretz*, had excellent connections with French officialdom. Throughout this period, Maicy published repeated warnings about what was in train in Baghdad. Late in May 1977, he wrote of the "conspiracy of silence" surrounding the reactor sale to Iraq, and added an interesting revelation: a woman scientist employed at Saclay had "left France in disgust." It was her dignified protest as a Jew against the ban on employing Jews in construction of the reactors to be sold to Iraq (the ban embraced work in France). In defiance of the French constitution, the Paris authorities had knuckled under to the Iraqi demand.

Maicy had uncovered no more than the tip of the iceberg, which would be fully revealed three years later by the French Socialist newspaper *Libération*. In October 1980 the paper disclosed that French companies involved in the Iraqi nuclear project had signed a document entitled "Israeli Boycott"— in defiance of a French law adopted on June 7, 1977, to combat the Arab boycott on companies doing business with Israel. According to *Libération*, the companies involved undertook to employ no Jews at the construction site in Iraq, and to comply with all regulations of the anti-Israel boycott.

Libération substantiated its charges with a confidential Technikatome memorandum dated September 4, 1979, and giving details of the company's contract with Iraq. According to the newspaper, the French were coaxed into signing by stages. "The Iraqis did not proclaim the restrictive clauses right away. Initially, they expressed overall agreement with all the demands of the French companies. Then they organized a great banquet for the signing of the agreement. Then they proclaimed: 'No Jews in Iraq!' "

This episode came to light after Raymond Barre had succeeded Chirac as premier. Chirac himself would boast, "Never did the French government which I headed accept, for itself or on behalf of any public or private company participating in these projects, a demand tending to impede Frenchmen of the Israelite confession from participating in the execution of the Osirak project."

Be that as it may, the fact remians that during Raymond Barre's term of office the French government, with the full knowledge of President Giscard, capitulated to the Iraqi diktat by excluding Jews.

10 "Using All Available Means"

On May 17, 1977, the citizens of Israel went to the polls to elect the Ninth Knesset. The outcome was a political landslide which terminated twenty-nine years of continuous rule by the labor movement, whose greatest adversary, Menahem Begin, now took the helm.

Menahem Begin was born August 13, 1913, in the city of Brest-Litovsk, Poland. His father, Zeev Dov Begin, was a proud Jew and a fervent Zionist. At the age of sixteen, Menahem joined the Revisionist movement headed by Zeev Jabotinsky, an eminent Zionist leader and the man who, more than anyone else, shaped Begin's future course. Growing dissension within the Zionist movement, between the labor wing and the followers of Jabotinsky, hinged upon the most fundamental Zionist issue: how and when was a Jewish state to be established in Palestine?

While studying law at Warsaw University, Menahem Begin was intensely active in the Revisionist youth movement, Betar. The pale, emaciated youngster, who displayed imposing oratorical powers, progressively assembled an entourage of loyal admirers, who came to regard him as Jabotinsky's heir and successor.

In March 1939, Begin became head of Betar in Poland. Six months later, World War Two erupted. After the Nazi seizure of Poland, Begin fled to Russian-occupied Vilna, where he was arrested and sent to a Siberian labor camp. Fortunately for him, Joseph Stalin soon concluded an agreement with the Polish Prime Minister in exile, General Wladyslaw Sikorski, whereby Polish citizens who had fled to the Soviet Union were permitted to enlist in a Free Polish army under General Anders. Begin joined the Polish units as they set off in May 1942, by way of Persia and Iraq, to Palestine.

There, one year later, Begin became head of the clandestine Irgun Tzvai Leumi (National Military Organization), or Etzel. In later years he was to declare that no post he had ever held, either previously or subsequently, including the office of Israel's prime minister, could equal his role as commander of the anti-British underground.

But above all, what shaped Begin's course, and his personal philosophy, was the Holocaust—that national calamity in which his own father and mother perished, as did most of his family. Unlike other Israelis, who regard it as a unique, never-to-be-repeated historical catastrophe, Begin believes fervently that the Holocaust must teach the Jewish people to defend itself in its own land, so as to ward off any renewed threat to its existence. Differing sharply with those Israelis who consented to renew their ties with Germany, Begin was vehemently opposed to the German-Israeli reparations agreement, which he regarded as a national disgrace. It may have been fate rather than coincidence that his final resignation as prime minister came just one day before he was due to welcome West German Chancellor Helmut Kohl on his arrival in Jerusalem.

With the establishment of Israel, Begin and his colleagues of the Etzel command formed a new party: Herut (Freedom). Begin soon emerged as the principal adversary of David Ben Gurion, the undisputed leader of the labor movement and Israel's first prime minister. Having been a bitter foe of the mentor, Jabotinsky, Ben Gurion rejected all cooperation with the pupil, Begin.

Within his own party, and outside it, Begin came to be seen as "the eternal loser." After repeated electoral setbacks, there were sporadic attempts to oust him as leader, but Begin survived them all. Ostracized by Ben Gurion's slogan "Without Herut or Maki" which forced his movement into the political wilderness along with the Communists, Begin pulled off an imposing political coup in 1965 when he succeeded in allying Herut with the Liberal Party to create a large centrist bloc. On the eve of the 1967 Six-Day War, when public pressure called for political differences to be shelved, Begin was among the architects of the "National Unity" Cabinet, which he joined as minister without portfolio. It marked the end of the boycott instigated by Ben Gurion, and the two leaders finally met to make their peace. Begin continued to pursue his principal aim: the conquest of political power.

Thus it was that in 1977, after eight unsuccessful election campaigns, the ninth brought sixty-four year-old Begin to office. His great triumph came as a surprise to almost everyone—except himself. Recently recovered from a heart attack, he showed no hesitation in seating himself at the tiller. He took over the post of prime minister with confidence, as though he had long made his preparations for the office.

Begin had always been regarded as a superb parliamentarian—probably the Knesset's best. He regularly served on the legislature's Foreign Affairs and Defense Committee, displaying an extensive interest in its farflung spheres of jurisdiction, his expertise unquestioned even by his critics. In addition, he frequently entertained foreign dignitaries and leaders, who were invariably struck by his knowledgeability, his courtesy, his command of English, his capacity for listening and his gift for presenting his own viewpoint. During his three years in the National Unity coalition, he always came to Cabinet meetings well briefed and brimming over with useful ideas which he articulated brilliantly.

On taking office as prime minister in 1977, Begin undertook a thorough study of the complex subjects delegated to his direct personal supervision. Like his British counterpart, Israel's Prime Minister is responsible for the secret services: the Mossad and the domestic Shabak (General Security Service).

When the new Prime Minister met with Mossad chief Yitzhak Hoffy for a briefing, the Iraqi nuclear reactor was naturally one of the first subjects broached. Begin, with his near-obsessive concern for the future of Israel's children, was profoundly disturbed by Hoffy's report. His sense of dread grew sevenfold on learning that the Franco–Iraqi agreement involved a French undertaking to supply the Iraqi reactor with "tested" fuel; in other words, France was committed to supplying Iraq with weapons-grade fuel from its own nuclear arsenal.

Having made inquiries, Israeli Ambassador to Paris Gazit confirmed on July 15, 1977, that, as François-Poncet had recently told Yigal Alon, the French were making strenuous efforts to produce uranium enriched to a grade of 20–25 percent ("Caramel"). However, the new fuel was still at the experimental stage, making it far from certain that the technical problems would be surmounted by the date the French had undertaken to bring the reactor into operation. Should they fail, the Iraqis would receive the promised weapons-grade fuel.

A senior diplomat and the brother of the current director of Military Intelligence, Gazit had long made a name for himself, and the information and assessments he submitted were accepted without question. After being wounded in the 1948 battle for Jerusalem's Old City, he recovered to serve many years in Israel's intelligence community, from which he went on to the diplomatic service. He soon attained renown as a superb professional, standing out with his analytical mind, his original thinking and his intellectual honesty. When a man of his stature sounded such clear warnings, it was out of the question to ignore them.

In the meantime, there were disturbing developments in Pakistan. It now emerged that even if the United States succeeded in coaxing France into reneging on its contract to supply a reclamation plant (including the hot cell essential for the production of plutonium), that would have almost no effect on Pakistan, which had already acquired adequate French technological knowhow to construct such installations unaided. It goes without saying that this revelation heightened concern over a similar situation occurring in Iraq.

This disquiet redoubled when it transpired that while the French continued to wheel and deal with Iraq, other Arab states were also pinning their nuclear hopes on France. Cairo sought credits for construction of French power reactors. Saudi Arabia and Kuwait likewise showed a keen interest in purchasing French reactors. In brief, French manufacturers of nuclear equipment could foresee a rosy future in the markets of the Middle East. And after being long overshadowed by the United States, Germany and Japan, France was overjoyed at the prospect of regaining its position as an economic power of the first order.

Like his predecessors in office, and for identical reasons, Menahem Begin hoped to cultivate Israel's special relationship with the Shah of Iran. In view of Iran's constant dread of Saddam Hussain, the new Prime Minister naturally wondered how Iraq's nuclear program appeared to Teheran. Thus it came about that on July 7, 1977, Begin's new Foreign Minister, Moshe Dayan, was dispatched to Iran, where, like Alon's, his meetings included a conversation with senior official Amini, the Shah's confidant.

"Aren't you worried about the Iraqis getting nuclear weapons?" Dayan asked his host.

Amini's reply was vague. In future, he predicted, no state capable of acquiring nuclear weapons would refrain from doing so.

Nevertheless, it emerged later that Dayan's talk with Amini had set off alarm signals at the Shah's palace. In 1980 the British 8 Days published a photograph of a letter to the deputy chairman of Iran's Royal Council; classified "Secret," it was dated July 17, 1977, a few days after Dayan's visit. The writer was U.S. Ambassador William Sullivan, and the wording of the letter indicates that the Shah had personally directed his Foreign Minister to approach the United States for any information available about the French reactor shortly to be delivered to Iraq. The information requested was appended to the letter, whose recipient was urged to transmit it directly to the Shah.

Be that as it may, Iran decided, for reasons which remain obscure, to refrain from any cooperation with Israel on this issue, and no hint of Iranian concern reached Jerusalem.

Likewise presuming that Iran should be eager to prevent Iraq from joining the nuclear club, Israeli representative in Teheran Uri Lubrany (who bore the personal rank of ambassador, though, as already mentioned, the two countries had no formal diplomatic ties) decided to check his hypothesis directly. He sought out Teheran's principal authority on the subject, Deputy

Defense Minister General Hassan Tuffenian. But Tuffenian's replies were equally vague and cloudy.

The inconclusive outcome of these feelers reinforced the impression already prevalent in Jerusalem that Iran was itself seeking a military nuclear capability and possibly hoped to emulate Iraq by receiving French aid to that end. If so, the Iranians would be reluctant to place obstacles on their own path by taking resolute action against Iraq's nuclear program.

Iran's nuclear ambitions were no innovation. As far back as the early fifties, the Shah was already resolved that by 1992 one half of his country's electric power would be generated by nuclear reactors. The Shah repeatedly argued that rather than burn up precious oil reserves for the generation of energy, Iran should reserve them as raw material for the petrochemical industry. His program called for the construction of twenty to thirty atomic-power stations in Iran by 1992. The Iranian monarch disclaimed any intention of making his country a nuclear power, but these declarations failed to reassure his neighbors, who were well aware of his dreams of reviving the glories of the great Persian Empire of antiquity. Familiar with the Shah's repeated analogies between modern Iran and the Persia of Xerxes and Darwish, Iraq, Kuwait and Saudi Arabia all expressed concern over the military option Iran would acquire with the construction of its nuclear-power plants.

Be all that as it may, Iran evidently intended to voice no protest against the Iraqi nuclear threat.

The discouraging replies from Iran induced Begin to place the issue of Iraq's nuclear armament at the head of his concern. Following consultations on the subject, he issued an unequivocal directive: under no circumstances would he permit any neighboring state on terms of belligerency with Israel to construct a nuclear reactor which could threaten the survival of the Jewish state.

Begin's directive could not have come to the attention of France and Iraq, which went about "business as usual." On June 25, 1977, French Premier Raymond Barre arrived in Iraq on an official two-day visit. A professor of economics by profession, Barre is a tubby man, deceptively cheerful, but his sharp wits make him a formidable politician who, moreover, boasts of phenomenal reading powers and pursues fifteen-hour working days. Most of his life had been spent in academic pursuits, but he was always intimately connected with France's great industrialists—the selfsame circles which so earnestly desired to promote the agreement with Iraq.

Arriving in Baghdad, Barre declared his government's intention of "using all available means" to foster Franco-Iraqi relations. His airport declaration included another significant passage: "France was one of the first states to point out the importance of the Palestinian reality," to which he added that there will be no peace in the Mideast "as long as there is no response to the legitimate rights of the Palestinian people."

Barre went straight on to meet Saddam Hussain. The Iraqi leader was flanked by Planning Minister Adnan Hussain, Foreign Minister Sa'adun Hammadi, and Iraq's Paris ambassador. The brief statement issued subsequently gave no details of the meeting's substance, but stressed that the sides exchanged views on international problems, including "the Arab–Zionist conflict." This term, replacing the more usual "Arab–Israeli conflict," reflected France's capitulation to the Iraqis.

At the end of Barre's visit, a joint communiqué declared: "Regarding the Middle East conflict, the two sides reaffirmed their traditional known stands that the achievement of a just and durable peace depends on the withdrawal of Zionist forces from the occupied territories and recognition of the legitimate rights of the Palestinian people." There was no mention of Israel's right to exist within secure and recognized borders, as specified in UN Security Council Resolution 242, or of the advisability of Arab–Israeli negotiations.

It stands to reason that nuclear matters were a principal topic in Barre's talks with Hussain, but there is no trace thereof in their joint statement, which declares only: "The two sides affirmed their eagerness and desire to strengthen these relations and to expand cooperation in the economic, scientific, technical and cultural domains."

Bilateral nuclear cooperation was mentioned at Barre's press conference, where he declared that the nuclear project France was constructing in Iraq would be "the biggest center of its kind in the region." In his farewell declaration at Baghdad airport, Barre proclaimed, "France . . . fully realizes the desire of a country like Iraq to protect its independence by every means available to it. Our comprehensive and long-term strategy is a strategy of independence and cooperation."

Saddam Hussain could ask for nothing more.

Less than two weeks later, on July 8, 1977, the well-informed *Le Monde* published a lengthy article entitled "Iraq Will Receive French-designed Military Equipment Worth 7 Billion Francs" (then the equivalent of $2 billion). Citing "a reliable source in Paris," the article related that Barre's visit to Iraq had produced a series of bilateral agreements for the sale of military equipment, including seventy-two Mirage F-1s—planes of the first line in France's own Air Force—complete with advanced electronic systems. Iraq was also promised Puma planes, tanks and AMX armored troop carriers. Regarding maintainance services and spares for Iraq's Soviet-made weaponry, the French were initially reluctant, but they were quick to capitulate when Iraq threatened to purchase Soviet MIG 23s in place of the Mirages.

The article pointed out that the agreement made Iraq into a leading client of France's arms industry. It also recorded that the agreement had been concluded in spite of strenuous pressure from the Soviet Union. In inducing Baghdad to relinquish Soviet arms for the French variety, France had evidently dangled some highly tempting bait before Iraqi noses. That bait appears to have been the nuclear project. The Soviets paid a heavy price for their nuclear prudence.

On mid-October, Iraq's Planning Minister, Adnan Hussain, flew to Paris for a two-week visit, in the course of which he met with President Giscard, Premier Barre and a number of other ministers, for talks about arms contracts and the al-Tuweitha reactor. The Iraqi minister also visited the French nuclear research center and an Air Force base. The statement at the conclusion of his visit said only that his talks had "hinged on Franco–Iraqi cooperation in various spheres." In hindsight, there can be little doubt as to which sphere predominated.

On December 27, 1977, Dayan again visited Teheran, mainly to brief the Shah on the progress of Israel's negotiations with Egypt. But discussions naturally turned to other topics.

"Iraq is preparing for war against Israel," the Shah predicted, though he did not foresee such a step without Soviet consent. This would be forthcoming, the monarch predicted, and the Russians would furthermore urge Syria to lay aside its disagreements with Iraq and join in the fighting so as to wreck any possible U.S.-sponsored peace agreement between Israel and Egypt.

Dayan also held talks with Amini, who cited information in his possession to back his claim that, with Egypt's withdrawal from the anti-Israel camp, Iraq was aiming for leadership of the Arab world—to which end Syria had been approached to permit Iraqi units to take up positions on the Israeli border.

Uri Lubrany related that, in talks with the Iraqi President early in December 1977, the Shah posed a question he himself had heard from Dayan: Why did a country like Iraq require hundreds of combat planes and thousands of tanks? Hussain's reply was, "Don't disturb yourself, the arms are directed against Israel."

Some days earlier, on December 17, 1977, Iraq had sent a memorandum to the Arab League council regarding "the inevitable nuclear-arms proliferation in the Middle East ... resulting from the Arab–Israeli conflict." The memorandum predicted that this proliferation would transcend the Arab–Israeli conflict, to reach "areas not directly connected to the conflict, primarily the Persian Gulf, Africa and the Indian Ocean."

The thinking behind that memorandum found its practical expression when the 1978 budget of Iraq's Atomic Energy Commission was increased fourteenfold, from $5 million to $70 million.

On January 13, 1978, Israeli Ambassador Gazit paid a further visit to Foreign Minister Louis de Guiringaud, at the latter's sumptuous office in the Quai d'Orsay. Anxious to reassure his visitor, Guiringaud declared, "Under no circumstances will we exceed the amount of uranium required for the immediate operation of the reactor. We will not provide Iraq with a stockpile of nuclear fuel. Even if we look forward several years, the Iraqis will not have their own nuclear fuel rods. The rods we shall deliver will be loaded into the reactor and irradiated immediately upon arrival, to prevent their use for other purposes. After irradiation, the spent rods will be returned to France for reprocessing." Furthermore, the Foreign Minister promised, the nuclear fuel would not be shipped before the reactor was on the verge of operation.

However, this sugary coating was designed principally to sweeten a very bitter pill: the fuel would, after all, be 93-percent-grade uranium. But the Foreign Minister hastened to promise that France would continue to seek a substitute for this fuel, whose military value he did not deny.

Gazit attempted to persuade Guiringaud to drag out negotiations with Iraq until completion of experiments on Caramel. But that precisely was the difficulty, the Foreign Minister admitted: France had undertaken to provide Iraq with tested (i.e., military-grade) fuel. Gazit snapped that this would be like supplying meat to lions.

Guiringaud urged Gazit to trust him: if a confrontation with the Iraqis was called for, France would not shirk it.

In spite of these pledges, Gazit could not overlook the term "tested fuel," which implied that there was no further hope of Osirak being fueled with uranium difficult or impossible to use for manufacture of a bomb. Recalling Guiringaud's promise to former Foreign Minister Yigal Alon, Gazit declared that Alon's successor Moshe Dayan insisted on implementation of the French undertaking.

On January 21, 1978, French Defense Minister Yvon Bourgés arrived in Baghdad for a four-day visit, to meet with Saddam Hussain and Iraqi military leaders. The visit concluded with a highly laconic joint statement: the sides had discussed bilateral relations and ways of expanding them.

Along with its links with France, Iraq cultivated ties with Italy, which likewise sought to guarantee long-term supplies of Iraqi oil. On February 8, 1978, Iraq's Atomic Energy Commission concluded an agreement with its Italian counterpart and the Snia Vicosa company. The company, which specialized in nuclear engineering, had developed laboratories for separation of radioactive materials (hot cells) and facilities for reprocessing spent nuclear fuel. The Italian company was to construct what the Iraqis referred to as "the project of July 30," named for the date in 1968 when General Bakr completed the Ba'ath takeover by adopting the titles of Prime Minister and Supreme Military Commander. Complementing "the project of Tammuz 17" whose name commemorated the Ba'ath revolution, the Italian installation would be built within the al-Tuweitha nuclear complex, putting the finishing touches to Iraq's nuclear program. Snia Vicosa signed the contract as prime contractor, while Italy's Atomic Energy Commission undertook an advisory capacity. The Iraqi body which commissioned the project also took a minor role in carrying it through, its share approximating to 5 percent of the $50 million investment.

On February 26, 1978, President Giscard's right-hand man Jean-Pierre Fourcade arrived in Baghdad, where he met with a number of ministers and addressed the opening of a French technical exhibition on "the interests of both France and Iraq."

The nature of those interests was highlighted by the Kuwaiti *a Siasia*, a paper that even Jerusalem regarded as authoritative. On March 24, 1978, the paper published a lengthy article which could be summarized in a single sentence directed at those Arabs who rejected any compromise with Israel, and demanding whether they had any alternative to offer: "The question of Israel's possession of an atomic bomb has turned from being a subject of speculation and varying news reports into one of direct political blackmail of the Arabs through which Israel intends to impose its absolute will and the solutions it wishes."

According to *a Siasia*, an appropriate answer to that question was in preparation in Iraq.

Somewhere between the Euphrates and the Tigris, at a distance of several kilometers from Baghdad, the Iraqi capital, a model village has been built consisting of a large number of villas at the center of which there are swimming pools, playgrounds, public gardens and nightclubs. The model village is surrounded by a wall of barbed wire and on its main iron gate a large sign says: "Entrance absolutely prohibited." The village is guarded by a select force of Iraqi security men. Some 480 French engineers and technicians live in this village with their families.

As for their task, it is to build a nuclear reactor of the "Oziris" type.

Vice-Chairman of Iraqi Revolution Council Command Saddam Hussain had agreed with French President Giscard d'Estaing on building this reactor when he visited France in September 1975. This major project costs $1.45 billion. Construction of the reactor began after the final signing of the agreement in August 1976. The agreement provides that the construction of the reactor should be completed by 1981.

Construction is being carried out by the French "Syriac" consortium in arrangement with the Iraqi and French governments. . . . The reactor operates with 93 percent enriched uranium, which is sufficient to produce an atomic bomb.

It is for this specific reason that the United States opposes the building of this reactor. The United States tried to bring pressure on France to cancel the deal, but Iraq threatened with abrogating all economic, commercial, and oil deals with France. The United States then tried to bring pressure on France so as not to sell enriched uranium to Iraq and to restrict the reactor's operations to tests and scientific research involving the use of only 70 percent enriched uranium. But the Iraqi-French agreement provides for France to supply Iraq with enriched uranium for a period of two years. While France canceled a similar agreement with Pakistan, it honored its agreement with Iraq, just as West Germany honored its agreement with Argentina, Canada with India.

However, Iraq's possession of a nuclear reactor capable of producing a nuclear bomb will have far-reaching political and military repercussions. This is because Israel is trying to have the exclusive possession of nuclear weapons so that it can maintain its military supremacy and therefore be able to dictate its political conditions on all the Arab world.

There is no longer any doubt that Israel possesses at least 15 atomic bombs. This has been confirmed by the CIA and the Soviet KGB intelligence reports.

. . . In order to contain any initiative by the Arab countries to possess an atomic bomb, three secret meetings have been held in London up to this date by countries producing or capable of producing atomic bombs, in order to prevent the export of the atomic bomb or the knowhow of its manufacture to the other countries.

Obviously, the other countries meant here were the Arab countries, foremost of which is Iraq, and this for two reasons:

First, because Iraq is building a nuclear reactor with the help of French technology and because the agreement on building the reactor commits France to providing Iraq with its requirements of enriched uranium;

Second, because Iraq pursues a policy extremely hostile to Israel to the point that it is the only country among the 22 Arab states that rejects the principle of Israel's existence and its right to live within secure and recognized borders in accordance with Security Council Resolution No. 242.

The Iraqis, who are well aware of the true intentions of the Israelis, are taking precautions and are going ahead in building the nuclear reactor and boosting their military forces on the grounds that a political settlement is bound to fail and that war is inevitable.

Iraq's quest for nuclear arms was justified in succinct terms by RCC Deputy Chairman Naim Haddad on March 24, 1978: "If Israel has nuclear weapons, the Arabs too must acquire them. The Arab countries must possess all the means necessary for their defense."

11 "Do Everything to Save Ourselves"

The Cabinet chamber in the Knesset building is a round room with brown wood-paneled walls. Its somewhat somber atmosphere is alleviated by an enormous Galilee landscape, the splendid creation of the painter Reuven Rubin. Outside the windows, with their view of the Judaean hills, blue-uniformed Knesset guards bearing Uzzi submachine guns patrol the surrounding terrace, and the Knesset's flower gardens are guarded by fearsome dogs. Under such watertight security, the secrets bandied about within these walls are safe from any eavesdropper.

Like their predecessors, members of Menahem Begin's Cabinet spent many long hours in this chamber, weighing up a great variety of topics, some prosaic, others of historic significance, such as Israel's peace treaty with Egypt. It was in this chamber, in the afternoon of August 23, 1978, that Begin convened a special meeting of all those privy to the subject of nuclear development in the Arab world at large, and in Iraq in particular.

Some of the participants were figures familiar to television viewers in Israel and the world over. Others were anonymous experts drawn from Israel's renowned intelligence community.

The meeting was dominated by the Prime Minister, whose authority, whether among his own colleagues or with the public at large, far exceeded that of any run-of-the-mill politician. Begin was now at one of the peaks of his career. He would leave shortly for the United States, at the invitation of President Carter, for an effort to achieve an agreed settlement with Egypt. Prospects did not appear particularly bright, but, as a commander of the Etzel underground many years previously, Begin had acquired an indomitable optimism.

Another prominent participant was Deputy Prime Minister Yigael Yadin. After acting as the de-facto commander of Israel's forces in the 1948 War of Independence, Yadin rose to the rank of commander in chief. Founding father David Ben Gurion foresaw a great future for him, and during his years as professor of archaeology at Jerusalem's Hebrew University Yadin became something of a living legend, being credited with great promise. Regrettably, much of that glamor evaporated when he finally took the plunge into politics.

Finance Minister Simha Ehrlich was leader of the Liberal Party, which formed a component of Begin's Likud alliance. Ehrlich lacked military experience, but his wisdom was widely acknowledged, as was his political acumen.

Of those present, the man of greatest worldwide renown was Moshe Dayan—in the past, successively commander in chief and defense minister. Dayan's political career suffered a crushing setback due to the 1973 Yom Kippur War, but Begin, who admired the intelligence and creativity of the man with the famous black eyepatch, had restored Dayan to the center of the political stage by making him his foreign minister.

Another prominent participant was the current Defense Minister, Ezer Weizman. Weizman, a tall, attractive figure who exercised his charms on men and women alike, had spent many years as commander of the Air Force, training it for what was to be its greatest triumph, the lightning strike which destroyed the Arab air forces at the outbreak of the 1967 Six-Day War.

Others present included:

Agriculture Minister Ariel Sharon, widely regarded as Israel's foremost general; a man of great originality and energy, Sharon made no secret of his conviction that the agriculture portfolio was much too trivial an office for his gifts and aptitudes.

National Religious Party leader Dr. Yosef Burg, a veteran politician who had adorned almost every Israeli Cabinet since the fifties and now officiated as minister of the interior and police.

Minister of Industry, Trade and Tourism Yigael Hurwitz, a successful businessman and a redoubtable politician.

Deputy Defense Minister Mordechai Zippori, a brigadier in the reserves, a cautious man of broad military expertise, practical as well as theoretical.

Also at the table was Major General Raphael Eytan, known to one and all as "Rafful," now four months into his term as armed-forces commander in chief. The heavy-tongued farmer had not been briefed on the problem of the Iraqi reactor when he took over from his predecessor, Major General Mordechai Gur (the latter was now a prominent leader of the opposition Labor Party). "Rafful" was accompanied by Military Intelligence Director General Shlomo Gazit and several other senior officers.

Defense Minister Weizman made a brief presentation of the topic under consideration. The problem of nuclear armament was by no means new to him; in fact, it had come up in a direct exchange he conducted with a prominent Arab personage the foregoing November. It was at a banquet given by Begin for his distinguished guest Egyptian President Anwar as-Sadat. Weizman found himself seated alongside Egyptian Prime Minister Mustafa Halil, one of the most brilliant minds in the Egyptian administration. Weizman was holding forth to Halil on Israel's security problems when the Egyptian remarked, "Why are you so worried about your security? After all, you possess an atom bomb."

This conviction, widely prevalent in Egypt, could—in Weizman's view —have been one of the factors which induced Sadat to come to Jerusalem, having come to the conclusion that he could not defeat Israel in a conventional war, nor easily acquire the nuclear weapons Israel was commonly believed to possess.

Later, when Weizman went to Egypt for talks with Sadat and his senior advisers, he also met with War Minister Muhammed Abdel-Aini Jamassy, the architect of the Yom Kippur War. "As we were about to take our leave of each other,'" Weizman recalled later "Jamassy said, 'You have nuclear weapons, or at least a nuclear option. We should think about an agreement for the nonproliferation of such weapons.'"

Weizman answered Jamassy in the same words he had used to Halil: "First discuss it with Libya and Iraq."

Refusing to let Weizman have the last word, Jamassy fired back, "They don't have nuclear weapons." Weizman did not, of course, share his inside information on the subject with the Egyptian War Minister.

"Ever since the matter appeared on Israel's agenda—immediately after the 1956 Sinai war—it has been on my mind," Weizman would recall. "All that time, the question hammering at my brain was: What happens if we ever confront a nuclear reactor beyond our range? How do we deal with such a contingency?"

That contingency had now arisen.

At the Prime Minister's request, nuclear developments in the Arab world were now surveyed by Military Intelligence Director Gazit and one of his aides. Citing scientific experts, the two men discussed the various implications of the Arab world's plunge into the nuclear era.

Begin now opened the topic for discussion.

Ariel Sharon, corpulent and gray-haired, spoke with characteristic decisiveness, advocating that Israel regard any Arab attempt to develop or acquire nuclear weapons as a clear *casus belli* to be met with appropriately forceful means.

Most of the other speakers displayed little enthusiasm for Sharon's line of thought, which they viewed as excessively belligerent. Rejecting the concept of hard-and-fast principles, they advocated close and meticulous surveillance of developments in the Arab states, Iraq in particular, with action to be taken subject to those developments.

To the surprise of all participants, not least of Sharon himself, his sole supporter was Finance Minister Ehrlich, usually considered a moderate, if not an outspoken dove. Having in the past disagreed sharply with Sharon on almost everything, Ehrlich now concurred with him totally. "It was the only instance," Ehrlich recalled later, "that Sharon and I shared the same opinion. . . . In view of the presentations we heard, I felt that we must deny nuclear arms to an Arab state whose leaders were criminals and killers liable to use such weapons against densely populated cities. Consequently, I concluded that we had to do everything to save ourselves. Nineteen sixty-seven taught us the value of guarantees by the powers. . . . I found it self-evident that we could not countenance such a terrible menace to the survival of our people."

Weizman attempted to cool the ardor displayed by Sharon and Ehrlich. There was no urgency about drawing conclusions, he said, nor had any proposal emerged. The consultation had been convened solely to update its participants, not to adopt operational decisions.

Concluding the discussion, Begin proposed action on two planes: Foreign Minister Dayan was directed to raise the matter in his forthcoming talks with his French counterpart, and Weizman was instructed to draw on Mossad assistance in assembling all available information, and to continue regular briefings of all concerned. Terminating the meeting, Begin urged its participants, "Gentlemen, please think. A lot of thought has to be given to the question of how to prevent this."

Everyone was aware that one way "to prevent this" would be to attack the reactor. But not everyone was in favor of such an action. The leading opponent turned out to be Deputy Prime Minister Yigael Yadin. Yadin's mind was firmly set against an attack from the very first moment. His view was endorsed by professionals such as Mossad chief Hoffy and Military Intelligence Director Gazit, who agreed with Yadin that before the reactor became operative, thereby posing an active threat, several years would elapse. At present, they stressed, the reactor contained no radioactive material at all.

Yadin raised a number of objections which he was to reiterate frequently. Among others, he feared that such an action was liable to set off a whole series of preemptive antinuclear strikes by the two superpowers. Furthermore, he argued that an Israeli attack on the Iraqi reactor could grant the Soviet Union a pretext for an attack of its own on Israel. Yadin foresaw the probability of U.S. anger over the use in such an operation of American arms—referring, of course, to the U.S.-built planes upon which the Israeli Air Force depends. Yadin also mentioned the risk of an Israeli pilot falling into captivity in the course of the operation—"and it's obvious what his fate would be." Yadin, in continual receipt of intelligence briefings, argued that there would always be time to decide on a strike against the reactor. Recalling the hoary Jewish joke about the man who promises the lord of the manor to teach his dog to read and write in the wistful hope that, before it emerged that he had failed, the dog's owner would no longer be among the living, Professor Yadin too hoped that "the lord of the manor would die" and the Iraqi project would turn out to pose no threat to Israel.

Another professor held the opposite view. Yuval Ne'eman, who commanded his own sources of information about al-Tuweitha, was in no two minds as to the response called for. A prodigy who commenced his studies at Haifa's prestigious Technion (technical university) at age sixteen, going on to become successively deputy director of Military Intelligence and military attaché in Britain, Ne'eman was a nuclear scientist of renown who served in prominent consultative posts. Ne'eman's hard-line political leadings would in time take him to the Knesset as leader of the far-right Tehiya Party.

With regard to the Iraqi reactor, Ne'eman's frequently reiterated advice to Defense Minister Weizman was unequivocal: Bomb it. But, as Ne'eman recalls, Weizman's reply was invariably negative. "It was like a game of Ping-Pong. I knew Ezer would never adopt the correct decision." "Correct" as interpreted by Ne'eman, of course.

Late in August 1978, the new Iraqi ambassador in Paris, Nuri Ismail al-Ways, sent home an enthusiastic report on his conversation with President Giscard while presenting his accreditation. Later, in a Radio Monte Carlo interview recorded on September 12 by the American Foreign Broadcast Information Service (FBIS), which monitors overt communications in the Middle East, al-Ways referred to Iraq's eagerness "to develop relations with France" and credited President Giscard with "the same eagerness for developing relations with Iraq." The ambassador claimed, "The two countries have the same outlook for a world where nations cooperate on the basis of respecting one another's policies and private choices."

On October 19, Ambassador Gazit held a further meeting with Guiringaud. The French Foreign Minister had recently attacked Israel's intervention in Lebanon, employing terms of unprecedented abrasiveness. His criticism drew unfavorable domestic comment, being deplored as "wild" by Pierre Messmer, who had served repeatedly as France's defense minister. Much of Gazit's talk with Guiringaud was devoted to explaining Israel's actions in Lebanon, but he also had an urgent question on another matter: Did the French government intend to supply Iraq with the weapons-grade uranium, and if so, when?

Guiringaud's reply, confirming reports Israel had received from other sources, left little room for doubt: the first shipment would be sent off early in 1980.

Gazit's expression must have reflected his anxiety, and Guiringaud hastened to reassure him. He was aware of Gazit's concerns, he told the ambassador, and he understood them. In the past, he said, he had pledged officially on behalf of the French government, and in a personal capacity too, that all necessary precautions would be adopted so that the reactor would not enable Iraq to acquire nuclear weapons.

Since this was a research reactor, the minister went on, the principal unease related to the grade of the fuel. But Iraq had no stockpiles of nuclear fuel which were not under French supervision; future deliveries would be in tightly restricted amounts, to serve exclusively for operating the reactor, and in rods unusable for military purposes. Furthermore, French technicians alone would operate and maintain the reactor, so that it could not possibly be converted to any untoward purpose.

It sounded reassuring, but a closer study of Guiringaud's statement revealed a grave omission: at most, he undertook to prevent rods of enriched uranium from being stolen for construction of a uranium bomb. Iraq's other and more probable option, manufacture of a plutonium bomb, was left open.

Israel's hopes now rested exclusively upon Guiringaud's final words, already cited, regarding Caramel-type fuel. But it was a dim hope. There was no certainty that the French scientists could complete their tests on the fuel in time. While talks and contacts proceeded, work on the reactor was also going forward. Israel predicted—correctly, as it turned out—that when construction was completed, the Iraqis would demand delivery of the high-grade uranium specified in the agreement.

At best, Gazit concluded, Caramel was not so much a candy as pie in the sky.

While work at al-Tuweitha advanced, Baghdad continued to make warlike noises. "Iraq doesn't accept the existence of a Zionist state in Palestine," declared Iraq's Ambassador to India Jihad Karem on October 24. "The only solution is war," he added.

Four days later, as Baghdad prepared to host the ninth Arab summit, where the refusalist states opposed to peace or negotiations with Israel would proclaim the "Front of Firm Resolve," or Refusal Front, the Iraqi Ba'ath organ al-Jumhuriya wrote: "The existence of the artificial Zionist entity symbolizes denial of the Arabs' historic right of survival, and offends their dignity. . . . We must combat Zionism with the oil weapon, with our armies and in any manner possible. Arab Jerusalem awaits the Saladin who will redeem it from the defilement with which the Zionists have stained its sanctity." The message was plain; Saladin, it will be recalled, was the great Moslem hero who humbled the Crusader kingdom in the Holy Land when he triumphed in the 1187 battle of Karnei Hittin. Even so, Saddam Hussain showed no inclination toward genuinely emulating Saladin, whose noted traits included chivalry and generosity toward his adversaries. Nor did he intend to defeat Israel on the field of battle, as Saladin did to the Crusaders. In all probability, what the Iraqi leader had in mind for the problem he faced was a "final solution" in the form of a Topolov bomber bearing a nuclear bomb.

After the November 2 Arab summit, whose participants agreed to sever their ties with Egypt should that country make peace with Israel, Iraqi President Bakr hastened to update his French counterpart Giscard d'Estaing; according to FBIS, Bakr's report also embraced the summit's secret decisions.

Giscard's reply, dated December 18, displayed understanding toward the Refusal Front states. Referring to Bakr's revelations, Giscard commended this as striking proof of the "relations of confidence" between the two countries, and their joint wish "to exchange information on important questions of mutual interest."

While some Iraqi experts pursued their nuclear studies in France, a further 150 scientists, engineers and technicians commenced similar advanced courses in Italy in 1979. Their training was, of course, linked with the "July 30" project: production and reprocessing of nuclear fuel, metallurgy of materials for nuclear structures, and advanced metalworking technology—all skills designed to teach them to operate the hot cells Iraq was buying from Italy. In their eagerness for Iraqi oil, the Italians were willing to expand bilateral nuclear cooperation, with proposals foreseeing construction of an Iraqi-Italian plant for production of heavy water, as a byproduct of fertilizer manufacture.

Baghdad had learned that doing business with Western companies was easier than dealing with the Soviet Union, since greed for profit was inducing the Western entrepreneurs to shut their eyes to Iraq's underhand designs. Little wonder that Iraq felt free to put out feelers to Belgatom, a consortium of three Belgian companies with twenty-five years' experience in nuclear engineering, offering it a contract for refurbishing the small Soviet reactor by installation of radiation systems and construction of a store for radioactive waste. The Iraqis also requested that the Belgians act as their consultants with regard to isotope separation. Any person of intelligence had to understand the implications of such a request. The Belgians were further commissioned to prepare a preliminary survey for construction of a nuclear-power station. In all probability, this was a smokescreen: with some of the world's richest oilfields, Iraq had no need of such a station. But the Belgians could seize on the request to placate their consciences.

Iraq also wooed Brazil, with which talks were held on nuclear cooperation. At first sight, such cooperation had little to offer Brazil—until one recalled that, possessing no oil reserves of its own, that country had run up the world's largest foreign debt. Nor was it difficult to discover that Brazil had reached an advanced stage in its negotiations with West Germany for purchase of uranium-enrichment techniques.

All this time, the Iraqis made incessant efforts to stockpile uranium in amounts far exceeding their research requirements, and regardless of their guaranteed supplies of nuclear fuel for their reactors. Iraqi purchasing commissions scoured the markets of West Germany, France, Sweden and Italy; in their quest for the metal, Iraqi agents were willing to go anywhere—the black market included: they recruited the services of arms dealers and other dubious elements, and even tried to lay hands on a quantity of weapons-grade uranium belonging to one of the superpowers.

Iraq's endeavors were, of course, no secret from Israel. Military Intelligence Director Gazit was therefore astounded when senior representatives of a friendly power who had earlier displayed great interest in the Iraqi reactor revealed that they had been instructed "to play it down." Gazit naturally refused to go along: "We told them everything we knew," he recalled.

An intriguing meeting was held in Paris on January 11, when President Giscard hosted Iraqi Vice-President Taha Muhi-a-Din Maarouf. On his return to Baghdad, FBIS cited Maarouf as declaring that there was "a renewed determination to diversify ways and means to strengthen relations between the two countries. These relations are considered ideal in international dealing because they are based on mutual respect, joint understanding and positive and constructive cooperation in the interest of the two countries and peoples." The Iraqi leader added, "The talks also showed appreciation [by France] for the efforts exerted by Iraq to unify Arab ranks within the framework of the [Baghdad] ninth Arab summit conference."

Maarouf did not mention his failure to get a denunciation of Israel included in his joint statement with Giscard. The Iraqi leader probably regarded this as a minor setback in comparison with the practical results of his talks. For their part, the French hastened to seize on Giscard's "defiance" to ingratiate themselves with Israel.

Late in January, coming close on the heels of the Iraqi Foreign Minister, Moshe Dayan arrived in France for an official visit—the first by an Israeli minister since 1975. The French leaders welcomed Dayan, honoring him with effusive personal compliments. "You are a courageous man," President

Giscard told him, "and there are very few courageous men in the world today." Fine words not, however, backed up by any substance acceptable to Israel. On the contrary: flying in the face of the facts, Dayan's hosts tried to convince him that the Arabs were progressively relinquishing their dreams of annihilating Israel. According to Giscard, the idea of destroying Israel, or obliterating its Jewish character, had been given up by both Saddam Hussain and Syria's Hafez al-Assad, if indeed they had ever espoused it.

At his meeting with Premier Raymond Barre, Dayan raised the issue of the Iraqi reactor. Barre withheld any direct answer, contenting himself with the remark that he was familiar with Iraq, having visited that country on several occasions; he cited Vice-President Maarouf, who claimed that his country was stockpiling arms solely out of fear of the Soviet Union. Barre boasted of the absence of anti-Israeli declarations in his joint statement with Maarouf. Dayan naturally found no comfort in that, nor in the cases of fine wine presented by his hosts. His mood was sour: he knew that while he was placated with wine and reassurances the Iraqis were getting something more substantial—a nuclear reactor and the accompanying knowhow.

Two weeks after Dayan left Paris, Franco-Iraqi relations were expanded by a further tier. February 20, 1979, saw the signing of minutes for further economic and technical cooperation, following guidelines agreed between Vice-President Maarouf and President Giscard. Iraqi Planning Minister Adnan Hussain explained, "The signing of the joint minutes will give new momentum to . . . fruitful cooperation."

"Relations between Iraq and France have been given a new impetus . . . in a manner which will serve the joint interests of the two peoples," agreed French Foreign Trade Minister Jean-François Deniau.

That same month, General Shlomo Gazit concluded his term as director of Israeli Military Intelligence. Recalling his period in that post, he noted, "The Iraqi reactor was among the top priorities . . . It was evident that the Iraqis did not require the reactor out of a passion for research; they needed it to develop nuclear arms. This conclusion rested upon reliable and authoritative information, and upon analysis by professionals well versed in the subject. We pursued the matter relentlessly, holding very many meetings with friendly foreign agencies to warn them of developments at al-Tuweitha."

Gazit was succeeded by General Yehoshua Saguy. The Jerusalem-born Saguy had occupied various Military Intelligence posts, serving as intelligence officer under Ariel Sharon during the 1973 Yom Kippur War. The changes brought about by the Agranat Commission's scathing report on the shortcomings of that war led to Saguy's appointment as deputy director for research at Military Intelligence, where he became thoroughly versed in the problem of the reactor. "When I got the job," he related, "it was considered highly probable that Iraq had taken the nuclear path."

At the plant at La Seyne-sur-Mer, near the port of Toulon, work on the reactor proceeded at full speed. The installation was in the final stages of completion. Within a few days it was to be shipped off to Iraq by sea.

At dawn on April 6, 1979, a muffled explosion sounded from the plant. Police and security agents who hastened to the scene discovered that the reactor core had been shattered by explosive charges.

Various French sources pointed accusing fingers at the Israeli Mossad. But the French press came up with its own version, hinting that the Paris government may have benefited from the explosion, which allowed it a breathing space to complete tests on the new Caramel fuel; the event could even offer an opportunity for reneging on the entire deal.

Evidently the early-April shipment date scheduled for the reactor was off. The enraged Iraqis urged France to speed up repairs. Iraqi Defense Minister Adnan Hiralla soon arrived in Paris for meetings with Premier Barre and Defense Minister Yvon Bourgés, pressing them to deliver the reactor at the earliest date possible.

The French had good tidings for their guest: the explosion had inflicted damage assessed at hundreds of millions of francs, but urgent talks with the manufacturers had elicited promises that the necessary repairs would be completed within a few months; that pledge was to be redeemed by October of that year. Moreover, Barre, eager to placate the Iraqis, reportedly directed that the reactor be covered henceforth by France's seven-year guarantee.

By the spring of 1979, it was becoming increasingly clear to Israel that military action against the reactor was unavoidable, and Prime Minister Begin made a statement to that effect to a group of senior ministers and military leaders.

Foreign Minister Dayan advocated diplomatic efforts in West Germany, which was scheduled to provide various components for the Iraqi nuclear complex, whether by way of Brazil or through other channels. But Dayan's thinking transcended the immediate operational problems posed by the Iraqi reactor. Convinced that Israel's neighbors were in the process of nuclearization, Dayan, after prolonged reflection on the subject, began to contemplate an alternative nuclear strategy to replace the traditional proclamation that Israel would not be the first state to introduce nuclear weapons into the Middle East. In conversations with his friend Professor Shlomo Aharonson of the Hebrew University's political-science department, Dayan expressed the fear that Israel could not long pursue the conventional arms race. The added sophistication of new weapons systems was making them increasingly costly. The highest-priced plane used by Israel in 1967, the French Mirage 3, was purchased at a unit cost of $2.2 million; the Air Force having grown to some six hundred aircraft, its first-line plane was now the F-15, with a price tag of $28 million. Similarly dramatic rises were recorded in the prices of tanks, cannon, communications systems, medical equipment and so on. How long could Israel bear such a burden? Dayan demanded. He answered his own question by proposing a new policy, one of whose elements would be overt and decisive nuclear deterrence, Israel in any case being powerless to prevent the region from going nuclear.

But in the meantime the immediate threat from Baghdad had to be met. At the Prime Minister's behest, Dayan now summoned General Aharon Yariv and requested him to form a committee to consider all the problems arising from nuclear development, in conjunction with the current issue. Yariv was a good choice. Commencing his military career as an officer with the British Army in World War Two, he had fought in the 1948 War of Independence and gone on to rise to the peak of Israel's military hierarchy, distinguishing himself as an original thinker and a superb analyst. Following his release from the Army, Yariv was elected to the Knesset and served in the Cabinets of Golda Meir and Yitzhak Rabin; but after one term he exchanged politics for the academic sphere, where he headed Tel Aviv University's Center for Strategic Studies.

Iraq and France continued to cultivate bilateral relations with great gusto. On July 7, 1979, a high-level French delegation headed by Raymond Barre arrived in Baghdad for an intensive three-day visit. The delegation had full authority from President Giscard to tie up all the loose ends.

The joint declaration issued at the end of the visit caused even France's friends to raise eyebrows in surprise at implicit French support for Refusal Front attacks on the Begin-Sadat accords recently concluded at Camp David. This endorsement was reflected in the joint statement, with terms such as "the dangers to the Palestinian people's rights and to peace itself" from the Camp David Accords, and "the efforts being exerted by Iraq and the other Arab countries to eliminate such dangers."

The statement went on to note the satisfaction expressed by Barre and Hussain over the success of the current visit. Iraq consented to increase its oil deliveries to France, thereby providing one quarter of French energy needs at a price 7 percent below the official OPEC figure. As it transpired later, this step had been approved on May 17 by Iraq's RCC, in response to a French request for a 50 percent boost in oil supplies. Iraq's sales to France would grow from $10 billion to $16 billion, and further increases were quite feasible.

Ambitious development plans were making Iraq into a most tempting proposition for French industrialists, building contractors, exporters and other businessmen, all keenly aware that the Iraqi exchequer commanded enormous reserves which were swelling rapidly as oil prices soared. Overtaking Britain, the United States and Italy, France soon gained third place— after Japan and West Germany— in the list of Iraq's Western suppliers. Interviewed early in July 1979 by the renowned French Jewish journalist Eric Rouleau, Iraq's Propaganda Minister Saad Kassem Hamudi adopted a candid tone: "We shall grant France a measure of priority in allotting our development contracts. We appreciate France's attitude toward the Arab–Israeli conflict . . ." He detailed a list of matters, of importance to the Arabs in general and Iraq in particular, which enjoyed French support. Iraq also appreciated France's "understanding" for the concerns which the Israeli-Egyptian peace treaty had aroused among the countries allied in the "Front of Firm Resolve." The Iraqi minister recalled that this "understanding" had been expressed in President Giscard's forementioned December 18 letter.

Barre made one last feeble effort to talk the Iraqis into accepting Caramel in place of military-grade uranium, pointing out that preliminary tests showed the new fuel suitable for use in the research reactor, and mentioning that it was far cheaper than the higher-grade uranium.

Predictably, the Iraqi reply was a flat No. The Iraqis made it plain that they would tolerate no delay in delivery of the reactor and the fuel as provided by the agreement. Saddam Hussein went so far as to warn Barre that unless Iraqi demands were met, Baghdad would not hesitate to turn to other sources.

"Iraq never rejected the idea of using Caramel," Barre later explained Baghdad's position. "The Iraqi authorities were willing to consider any new proposal, beyond the terms of the original contract which provided for two years' deliveries of 93 percent uranium—as long as the substitute fuel achieved a performance which met the terms specified in the agreement."

But Barre's legalistic wording was no more than a smokescreen. The agreement specified that the fuel delivered should be "tested." But the earliest tests on Caramel were scheduled for early 1980—long after the date laid down in the agreement. Iraq could therefore fall back on purely formal arguments, as well as keep the French in line by dangling before their eyes billion-dollar contracts, principally for arms.

On his return to Paris, Barre ordered the repairs on the reactor speeded up. Iraq had triumphed. On October 19, French Foreign Minister Jean François-Poncet told Israeli Ambassador Gazit that the promised enriched uranium would soon be delivered to Iraq, though France would make sure that the fuel was used exclusively at the reactor.

In the meantime, the Iraqis persisted in vigorous diplomatic efforts to camouflage their nuclear intentions. These efforts achieved a new peak of cynicism when Iraq's UN delegation submitted a draft resolution to the General Assembly accusing Israel of developing nuclear weapons and of being "a motivating factor" in the nuclearization of the Mideast; the resolution called for a team of experts to investigate "Israel's nuclear armament." Rammed through by the automatic majority of the Arabs and their supporters, this resolution, like others of its kind, was of no practical significance.

The Saddam Hussain regime operated in a manner which, in spite of its apparent irrationality, was nevertheless guided by its own inner rationale. The few Iraqis with any genuine nuclear expertise found themselves under lock and key.

The first to be detained was Dr. Hussain Shahristani, scientific adviser to the President of Iraq and research director at the country's Atomic Energy Authority (AEA). On September 18, 1979, agents of the Fifth Branch of the Internal Security Police entered the AEA offices, declaring their intention of arresting Dr. Shahristani. The authority's president refused to hand him over, demanding written authorization from President Hussain. When the agents returned that evening with the appropriate authorization, they found the offices locked, but they arrested Shahristani in the street on his way home.

An Amnesty International report alleges that Shahristani was brutally tortured while in detention. To this day, the charges against him remain unclear, though he was apparently suspected of links with the Shi'ite Imam of Iraq, Bakr a-Sadr, a bitter foe of the Hussain regime. Shahristani, who studied nuclear physics at Moscow's Lumumba University, at London's Imperial College and at Montreal University, came from an ancient and noble Shi'ite family. But his connections were of no help to him, no more than the fact that only three years previously he had received an award from the Iraqi President for his contribution to the country's scientific development. He was sentenced to death for "treason and plotting against the regime." Scientists the world over made efforts to save his life, but their appeals made no impact on the "Butcher of Baghdad." In May 1981, Shahristani was executed.

In February 1980, Dr. Ja'afer Dhaieh Ja'afer, head of the AEA nuclear-physics department and one of the men involved in scientific coordination with France, was likewise imprisoned when he had the temerity to protest against the arrest of Shahristani. Like the latter, Dr. Ja'afer was a Shi'ite, and as such both men were detested and mistrusted by Hussain. Having made their contribution, they could be removed, to prevent any disruption to the nuclear designs of their President. The closer Hussain came to realizing his dream of an Iraqi nuclear bomb, the greater his apparent fear of being foiled by "hostile elements."

The military significance Hussain attached to his "research project" is also indicated by the fact that Iraqi nuclear experts who were sent on advanced-study courses in Italy and France were under the constant supervision of Iraqi political commissars, handpicked by Hussain. The "supervisors" came to Europe posing as engineers, but pursued no studies. Their presence was, of course, apparent to the Italian and French authorities, who nevertheless preferred to turn a blind eye. Nothing is more detrimental to official sight that the steady stream of Iraqi oil flowing westward.

Late in September 1979, Brazilian Trade and Industry Minister João Camilo Penna arrived in Baghdad. But Iraqi attention focused on his companion, Paulo Nogueira Batista, one of the heads of Brazil's Atomic Energy Commission. On October 1 the visiting minister signed a "memorandum for extensive cooperation in the nuclear sphere." In spite of its apparently innocuous form, a glancing perusal of the document raises embarrassing questions. Article 3, for example, affirms that both sides "declare their support for the principle of the nonproliferation of nuclear weapons," but almost in the same breath the parties "stress their right to develop nuclear energy and apply it toward peaceful purposes." While oil-deficient Brazil had good cause to develop nuclear energy, what grounds were there for allotting resources to a similar pursuit in Iraq, with its abundance of oil? Moreover, had the Iraqis genuinely intended to implement the memorandum in word and spirit, they, as suppliers of 37 percent of Brazil's oil imports, would have been the first to suffer.

Subsection C of the memorandum's Article 4 affirms that bilateral cooperation would include "the supply of natural uranium and slightly enriched uranium (if possible, in the form of fuel) for use in nuclear reactors." At the time Iraq had long-term contracts with France and the Soviet Union for the suply of uranium to its reactors. Why did Baghdad need additional nuclear fuel? The most probable answer to that riddle is that the Iraqis planned to divert some of the enriched uranium intended for Osirak to the production of plutonium by means of the Italian hot cells. Already aware that the reactor could work on relatively low-grade fuel, like Caramel for example, the Iraqis hoped to use Brazilian nonmilitary uranium to deceive IAEA inspectors when the latter came to oversee how French weapons-grade uranium was being used.

A few months later, persistent rumors circulating in Brazil insisted that the government had undertaken to supply Iraq with uranium enriched to a grade of 20 percent. Brazil's Atomic Energy Commission responded with spluttering indignation. Its chairman, Hervasio de Carvalho, dismissed the reports as "absurd," warning that they were "liable to harm Brazil's reputation in the world." He claimed that Brazil was as yet unable to produce enriched uranium, and that even when production commenced as planned "it would still be uranium enriched to a grade of 20 percent." However, the prominent *O Estado de São Paulo* insisted on the veracity of its information whereby Brazil had undertaken to resell to Iraq enriched uranium purchased in the United States. Incidentally, Carvalho offered no response to the most serious question raised: Why did Iraq need any additional uranium—even of the low-grade 3.3 percent variety—when it already held contracts for the supply of nuclear fuel to its reactors?

But the loudest outcry arose from rumors that the Brazil-Iraq agreement contained a secret codicil whereby Brazil undertook, on completing its projected plant for the reprocessing of radioactive materials, to provide Iraq with plutonium for "scientific experiments." If the agreement did include such a provision, its ominous portent must have been obvious to the Brazilians. But equally obvious was the fact that, as the source of nearly 40 percent of Brazil's oil imports, Iraq had almost unlimited leverage to exert on the Brazilian government—as illustrated when Iraq's ambassador to Brazil, Ziad Haidar, permitted himself to sound off with the rhetorical question "If our enemy Israel is close to building an atomic bomb, or already has one, what prevents us from developing the same capacity?"

The ambassador may have done no more than voice what he read in communications from Baghdad, because shortly after, on October 25, 1979, Saddam Hussain himself spoke out in similar terms. "The struggle against Israel," he declared in an interview, "will be arduous and prolonged. In its course, it is even feasible that Israel will attempt to use an atomic bomb against the Arabs. Consequently, it is incumbent upon the Arabs to prepare all the means necessary for victory." Those "means" were sited at al-Tuweitha, where rapid progress was being made on the infrastructure for victory over Israel.

12 "The Filth of Zionism"

The generally accepted consensus among Israeli experts at the end of 1979 ran as follows:

Within a few months—March 1980 at latest—France would dispatch the first shipment of 93-percent-grade uranium, comprising 12 to 12.5 kilograms out of an overall total of 70 kilograms promised.

On delivery of the fuel, the small Tammuz-2 (Isis) reactor would go into immediate operation, its Iraqi staff receiving French guidance in operating the various systems.

Within three to four months—July 1980 approximately—the larger Tammuz-1 reactor would be ready for activation.

Between May and December 1980, the second phase of the Italian "July 30" project would reach completion, giving Iraq the facilities for extracting plutonium from the spent fuel rods.

No one knew with any certainty when Iraq would receive the rest of the enriched uranium from France. One view held that, on activation of Tammuz 1, France would immediately deliver the outstanding remnant, sufficient to allow the reactor to work at full output for two years. The other, more "optimistic" school believed that deliveries would be phased, with each load of fuel arriving in Iraq shortly before the previous shipment was used up.

However, it was unanimously agreed that by late 1982 the Iraqis would be able to congratulate themselves on completing their nuclear program—just as long as they could acquire 8 kilograms of plutonium each year, and everything indicated that they would have little difficulty in doing so. One possibility open to them would be bribery or intimidation of some of the French experts at al-Tuweitha. A mere handful of collaborators would suffice to enable the Iraqis to divert spent fuel rods to the Italian hot cells for separation of their plutonium.

Acquisition of an adequate amount of plutonium (10 kilograms or more) would permit Iraq to detonate a nuclear device by 1985. Such a device would not be an atomic bomb in the conventional sense of the term: it would be a kind of "demonstration device" of relatively low explosive power, and unsuitable for delivery at a specific target. However, the detonation would undoubtedly elevate Iraq to the status of a nuclear power, with only a short distance to traverse before acquiring the necessary knowhow for the manufacture of genuine bombs.

It emerged subsequently that this problem, construction of the rudimentary nuclear device, was indeed the bottleneck in Iraq's nuclear program. Even when the plutonium they so desperately desired appeared to be within their grasp, the program's directors did not possess so much as elementary sketches of the device they hoped to construct. They appear to have hoped that the problem would be resolved with the return home of the scientists and engineers currently training at nuclear centers the world over. The Iraqis may also have pinned their hopes on the covert cooperation of Pakistan, which had already made great strides toward joining the atomic club.

Even before completing their nuclear program, there was one headache the Iraqis were spared: the means of delivering nuclear bombs. Iraqi airbases housed Soviet-made Topolov-16 and -22 medium-range bombers, as well as MIG-23 combat bombers, all capable of bearing nuclear weapons. Iraq also possessed Soviet "Scud" medium-range surface-to-surface missiles. Some Soviet ground units are equipped with similar missiles armed with conventional or tactical nuclear warheads; but they can also bear any type of nuclear bomb.

The information collated, and the assessments built upon it, now left no further room for doubt: by the mideighties, Iraq would achieve a genuine nuclear option. Consequently, Prime Minister Begin instructed Commander in Chief Raphael Eytan to initiate planning of a military strike at the reactor, and to present possible modes of action to the Cabinet.

Eytan promptly directed Aryeh Levhar,* a colonel at the General Staff's operations section, to prepare the plans. Eytan also summoned Air Force Commander General David Ivry, to brief him on the Prime Minister's directive and the projected attack on the Iraqi reactor. Ivry issued instructions to Colonel Dan Oren,* head of Air Force Command's operations section, to examine all technical aspects of the operation.

The complexities of the operation had been entrusted to two of Israel's foremost military commanders—Eytan and Ivry.

*Fictitious name.

"Rafful" Eytan—a farmer from the *moshav* (agricultural cooperative) of Tel Adashim, and an amateur carpenter—had taken part in every war fought by Israel, commencing with the 1948 War of Independence, when he was wounded in the battle for Jerusalem. Eytan spent much of his service with the paratroops, commanding a battalion in the 1956 Sinai campaign and a brigade in the 1967 Six-Day War. In the 1973 Yom Kippur War he commanded one of the three divisions which fought on the Golan Heights, where they barely managed to halt the oncoming Syrians before they could reach Galilee and the Jordan Valley. After the war Eytan became head of Northern Command and, in 1977, head of the General Staff's operations section.

In 1978, when Mordechai Gur completed his term as commander in chief, Defense Minister Weizman was called upon to pick a successor. After lengthy consideration, he opted for Eytan, a man he regarded as "a fighting machine" of the first order and a superb combat officer who had achieved distinction in every post he was called upon to fill. "I was always fascinated by his personality," Weizman recalled. When Weizman told him of his selection, Eytan responded in characteristically robust fashion: "Okay. You've decided? You have decided! Depend on me. You won't regret it."

Regret it Weizman probably did. It was not long before Eytan, departing from his long-standing image of heavy-tongued reticence, began to deliver himself of various utterances which infuriated politicians and journalists. In addition, his professional performance also came in for criticism. But even his severest critics concede Eytan's mastery of commando tactics, his audacious planning, and his ability to "read the map" of battle even as combat is in progress. Faithful to the paratroopers' slogan "After me!," Eytan always went into battle at the head of his troops, with whom he enjoyed enormous popularity.

Air Force Commander David Ivry had likewise achieved his senior appointment after a covert though tough contest against another officer. Here too, Weizman went through considerable soul-searching before picking Ivry, a tall flier who had risen through the ranks from pilot, by way of flight commander, wing commander and senior staff officer. He was invariably modest and retiring, but Ivry's friend and colleagues knew that his tranquil exterior concealed a mind both cautious and original.

In November 1979, the General Staff began examining the various proposals for destruction of the reactor. It goes without saying that Ivry was careful to keep to a minimum the number of those privy to the secret. Aside from Colonels Levhar and Oren and a number of their closest aides, the officers engaged in the survey were told nothing of its purpose. The women clerks who typed the relevant letters and cables employed code names whose meaning they did not know. Officers were instructed to provide technical solutions for specific problems without being acquainted with the overall objective. Test flights and maneuvers were conducted without their purpose being revealed to the pilots.

The various possibilities considered were, without exception, astonishingly daring. At this phase, late December 1979, the concept called for a mixed force of Skyhawk assault planes and Phantom combat bombers, U.S.-built aircraft which had withstood the harsh tests of the late-sixties "war of attrition" and the Yom Kippur War. However, a further aspect had to be considered: the long flight to Iraq and back dictated aerial refueling.

In issuing a directive for planning of long-range missions and examination of their execution, Ivry sketched out a "mission profile" conforming in every respect to the projected raid on the reactor. The specifications of the various exercises sought solutions for problems such as refueling, bomb-load, the illumination required for the actual bombing, and so on. Phantoms and Skyhawks commenced training for long-distance flights; the exercises produced good results.

In spite of his chummy backslapping relationship with Ivry, Defense Minister Ezer Weizman had not the least intention of ordering the attack— or at least not in the foreseeable future. One of the first to reach this conclusion was Professor Yuval Ne'eman. On January 2, 1980, Yisrael Na'eh,* an adviser to Weizman and his go-between with Ne'eman, reflected the minister's own unfavorable view when he told the professor, "Bombing the reactor would harm [the] peace [treaty] between Israel and Egypt."

Ne'eman meanwhile maintained ongoing contacts with colleagues employed in the nuclear field in other countries, and the often depressing information he received spurred him into redoubling his calls for an immediate strike at the Iraqi reactor.

Knowing nothing of Israel's intentions, the Iraqis pressed ahead with their own plans. They were not particularly upset when the U.S. State Department issued a report which named their country as one of the four most prominent in their support of international terrorism. Iraq was accused of vying with Libya in placing its diplomatic missions and services in various countries at the disposal of terrorist groups.

The Iraqis now instigated talks with Italy for the purchase of a high-output nuclear-power station. It is significant that, in addition to electric power, the reactor's products included plutonium. Its integration into the "July 30" project's hot cells would have made Iraq into a plutonium producer of the first order.

Iraq wove a further strand into its worldwide nuclear net on January 25,

*Fictitious name.

1980, when the memorandum of cooperation concluded with Brazil on October 1, 1979, was elevated to a bilateral treaty. It will be recalled that the agreement's main provisions call for Brazil to provide nuclear aid in return for Iraqi oil.

Five days previously, on January 20, São Paulo Governor Paulo Maluf (the name reveals his Arab origins) had arrived in Baghdad on an official visit and had been accorded a regal welcome. In an interview to Brazilian journalists accompanying Maluf, Iraqi Deputy Prime Minister Tarik Aziz showered Brazil with fulsome praise for its pro-Arab policy. Brazil's support for the 1974 UN resolution which denounced Zionism as a racist movement "opened the doors of the Arab countries to Brazil, and it is considered a milestone in Brazilian relations with those countries," he declared. Brazil's support for the resolution had evoked tempestuous domestic protests, but it pleased the country's large Arab community, which had exerted enormous pressure to that end.

Aziz referred openly to the bilateral agreement for nuclear cooperation soon to come into effect; predictably, he declared that the agreement was "in the context of the use of nuclear energy for exclusively peaceful ends." When the journalists questioned him on technical aspects of the agreement, Aziz declined to reply. In response to a specific query about the agreement's provision for the supply of Brazilian enriched uranium, Aziz explained coyly that the matter was not in his purview. By contrast, he willingly elaborated on those sections providing for Iraqi oil deliveries to Brazil. He stressed that Iraqi policy was largely guided by "the degree of a country's friendship." The hint was plain, but Aziz pressed the point: "According to our President's guidelines, Brazil is considered to be a friendly country."

Indeed, statistics speak for themselves. Brazil was importing Iraqi oil at a rate of 400,000 barrels a day, and in 1978, overall Iraqi exports to Brazil totaled $1.022 billion, while Iraq bought no more than $84 million worth of Brazilian goods.

In fact, the Iraqis were looking beyond Brazil, to West Germany—to be precise, to the 1975 Brazilian–German agreement on nuclear cooperation. It should be recalled that West Germany is in a particularly delicate position with regard to its nuclear development. No one doubts the ability of the Federal Republic to construct nuclear bombs, but it is commonplace that any German attempt to cultivate a nuclear capacity would be regarded by the Soviets as a *casus belli* and would be treated accordingly. Little wonder then that West Germany's entry into the nuclear field has prudently sidestepped its military aspects.

However, in nuclear matters the dividing line between civilian and military spheres is extremely hazy. The knowhow applied at atomic-power stations can also serve reactors designed for plutonium production. Enriched uranium intended as fuel for generating energy can be used for production of plutonium, or directly in bombs. West German knowhow, if transferred to other hands, could serve military purposes.

Diplomatic constraints bearing upon the Federal Republic obviously do not affect Brazil, which can therefore make use of West German nuclear expertise. Small wonder, then, that the Iraqis, eager for access to German uranium-enrichment techniques, forged ties with Brazil as a substitute for the regrettably unavailable direct links with Bonn.

By this time, the African state of Niger, possessing some of the world's richest uranium deposits, had consented to sell large amounts of natural uranium to Iraq. All that the Iraqis now needed to do was acquire the complex technology of uranium enrichment—i.e., purchase it from West Germany by way of a third party: Brazil. At the time of its agreement with Iraq, Brazil had yet to completely master the enrichment technique, but experts predicted that this omission would be corrected within a few years.

Early in 1980, directives were issued in Israel to extend groundwork for the raid on the reactor. A consultation attended by representatives of the various bodies linked to the operation concluded that technical preparations must be complemented by a wide range of information, to come from the Mossad, Military Intelligence and the Air Force's own intelligence section, whether independently or in coordination. At the same time, work went on in mustering all available information about the reactor's internal construction, its components and similar details.

The overall picture was as yet incomplete, but Air Force Commander Ivry was now in a position to brief the Commander in Chief and the Defense Minister on the operation. Ivry's presentation was imposing, but everyone knew, as he did, that his proposals were little more than ideas, falling far short of operational plans.

While keeping a close watch on progress at al-Tuweitha, Saddam Hussain missed no opportunity for an unequivocal proclamation of his intentions with regard to Israel. In a broadcast on Army Day, January 6, 1980, he told his countrymen, "Our Army is preparing itself, by earnest training, by scientific development and by its advanced weapons, for fulfillment of its historic national duties . . . this is the army of the Arab nation, whose duty it is to ward off dangers threatening the Arab nation . . ." Late in January Hussain added, "Iraq aspires to harness the mighty forces of the Arabs to changing the balance of power in the region."

The ultimate aim of those aspirations was sketched out in a January 31 press interview by Iraqi Foreign Minister Dr. Sa'adun Hammadi: "Iraq will not consent to the Zionist presence, whether as a movement or a state. The

Arab nation cannot consent to the theft of a part of its body. The land of Palestine is Arab and we cannot surrender it. . . . The struggle against Zionism is not open to compromise. It comprises stages, with the operation of the time factor."

On February 7, Saddam Hussain indicated how the time factor could be overcome. In an interview to *al-Watan al-Arabi*, he said, "Any state which wants to use the atom for military purposes should attain a special scientific and technological level in all fields, not only in the nuclear field." Hussain is consistent: it was an almost precise word-for-word repetition of a statement he had made ten years earlier, in January 1970, in an interview to *al-Mustakbal*.

A less nebulous opinion on the matter appeared in the February 1980 issue of the Swiss *International Defense Review*, where it was noted that the Iraqi reactor employed highly enriched uranium which could "be used directly for manufacture of nuclear arms."

Under Ivry's systematic direction, the Air Force continued to polish up its plans for the reactor attack. By February, the Air Force commander was in a position to put on a far more advanced "display" for the edification of the Defense Minister and the Commander in Chief. With the termination of the "display," Weizman directed that work on other alternatives still go ahead, but expressed the personal view that an attack by combat planes was the most practical option. While the other alternatives were feasible, the entire defense establishment quickly joined Weizman in judging an air strike to be preferable.

It was now the Air Force's show, and Ivry proceeded to summon Colonel Yitzhal Melrom,* the commander of the airbase which was to receive the F-16s shortly expected from the United States. Ivry put it succinctly: "There's a high probability that, on arrival of the F-16s, they'll be chosen for the operation, conditional upon this gaining top priority in the training schedule."

Anyone in need of a further Iraqi declaration of intent soon got it. "The Zionist entity," Saddam Hussain told the UN General Assembly on February 27, "is not considered a state, but a misformed entity which holds Arab territories."

In the meantime, Aharon Yariv's team of experts had completed its report about the potential consequences of attacking the reactor. Submitted to Begin on March 2, 1980, the report cautioned:

*Fictitious name.

1. Bombing the reactor would alienate world public opinion, mainly because of the danger of radioactive contamination arising from the attack.

2. Israel would be accused of disrupting the Mideast peace process, and, moreover, of violating the broad global consensus against attacking nuclear reactors, particularly when they are active. The international community was liable to apply severe sanctions against Israel.

3. The attack was liable to unify the Arab and Moslem worlds against Israel, to the point of a joint declaration of war, with Soviet backing.

4. U.S. aid was liable to be reduced in response to the raid, which might also give a boost to American cooperation with the Arab states.

Even though Begin read the report intently, it nevertheless failed to convince him that the dangers arising from an attack on the reactor outweighed the threat posed by its activation. He was sure he could overcome all the other difficulties—diplomatic in the main—which the operation would engender; but the report reinforced his view that the reactor must not be attacked after becoming "hot," its activation to be forestalled by preemptive action. He ordered the intelligence services to provide him with precise and reliable information about the date it would go into operation.

Media revelations, domestic and foreign, forced the French government to admit that it did intend to supply Iraq with enriched uranium. On March 4, 1980, a statement by France's Atomic Energy Commission declared: "France has decided to supply Iraq with an Osiris-type nuclear research reactor, and we are therefore bound to supply the fuel for that reactor."

In spite of never signing the NPT, France had reiterated its opposition to dissemination of nuclear weapons outside the existing global nuclear club. Referring to nuclear cooperation with Iraq, President Giscard declared that France would act as though it were a party to the NPT—in other words, ensure that the nuclear materials, technology and knowhow supplied to Iraq would not enable that country to construct nuclear weapons. The promise was, of course, hollow: delivery of Tammuz 1, with the fuel for its operation, was in itself a step toward an Iraqi military nuclear potential.

The dangers inherent in the Iraqi reactor raised a growing clamor. Professor Frank Barnaby, head of Stockholm's SIPRI—which is renowned for its leftist leanings and therefore cannot be suspected of any pro-Israeli sentiments—declared outright that enriched uranium of the grade destined for Osirak would grant Baghdad a nuclear option.

A similar view was expressed by the prestigious French *Défence et diplomatie*, whose March 10, 1980, issue stated: "Since manufacture of a Hiroshima-size nuclear bomb requires a total of 12 kilograms of enriched uranium, supplying a 70-megawatt reactor to Iraq raises in all its gravity the possibility of diversion of the fuel to military purposes."

In Israel, Professor Yuval Ne'eman was more specific in his warnings: "This fuel contains fissionable material from which nuclear bombs can be produced in a relatively brief time. Furthermore, the knowhow that the French intend to supply to Iraq will also give them the alternative possibility of manufacturing an atomic explosive no less dangerous: plutonium."

France was not Israel's sole headache: Italy would also play a most significant role in Iraq's nuclear program. Prodded by a barrage of Israeli reminders, the United States made an indirect attempt to induce the Italians to pull out of the project. Information leaked to the *New York Times* and the *Washington Post* by U.S. intelligence agencies recorded that Italy was selling advanced nuclear equipment to Iraq, as well as training Iraqi engineers and technicians at its nuclear centers. The Carter Administration was particularly concerned—so the two papers reported—over Italy's sale of the hot cells. The leak was, of course, aimed at embarrassing Italy and prompting its government to second thoughts. But the Italians were in no mood to reconsider.

On March 20, 1980, a London newspaper reported: "Next year, Iraq will be capable of manufacturing a nuclear bomb—with the assistance of France and Italy. France provides the enriched uranium, Italy: the knowhow and technology." Two days earlier, the *New York Times*, citing "Administration officials", noted that "the Italian facility was big enough to permit Baghdad to obtain enough plutonium to produce a nuclear weapon in about a year's time."

Iraq was not slow to respond. That same day, an official spokesman bitterly attacked the American "campaign against Iraqi–French and Iraqi–Italian technological cooperation in the field of nuclear energy." The spokesman affirmed that the campaign "demonstrates once again the United States's hostility toward the Arab nation and Iraq in particular." He added that the Administration was pursuing this campaign "so as to solicit Zionist votes at the expense of the independence and freedom of action of nations.... The United States is trying to impose a technological embargo on Iraq and the Arab nation in order to keep them backward and dependent upon others." With typical self-righteousness, the spokesman recalled that Iraq was a party to the NPT "and strongly opposes the introduction of nuclear weapons in the area."

In another statement, the Iraqi Foreign Ministry affirmed: "Removal of Zionism from Palestine is a precondition for the constitution of a nonracist international community."

There was a growing shrillness about the tone adopted by official Iraq. "We want the whole of Palestine," declared Deputy Prime Minister Tarik Aziz on March 24. "We recognize neither the 1967 borders nor the 1948 partition borders." In an address to Iraq's National People's Conference on March 27, Saddam Hussain warned against "recognition of the monstrous Zionist entity."

The Iraqis did not rest content with mere words. Nor were they satisfied with the nuclear agreements already concluded. They sought additional sources of nuclear knowhow, technology and material.

On March 28, 1980, the British *Financial Times* disclosed that Portugal was negotiating a raw-uranium deal with Iraq. The report was soon confirmed by *New Scientist*: the periodical wrote that Iraq had stepped up its oil deliveries to Portugal, in return for which that oil-deficient country would sell Iraq 120 tons of uranium oxide. The periodical added that negotiations were marked by pressure from Iraq, which supplies 45 percent of Portugal's oil consumption.

On September 26, *Energy Daily* cited American intelligence sources as expressing concern over Iraq's purchase, from Portugal and other countries, of hundreds of tons of raw uranium destined for "manufacture of nuclear weapons."

One year later, on February 11, 1981, a Portuguese newspaper reported that its government had sold to Iraq raw uranium to the value of $12 million during the first half of 1980. In return, Iraq had boosted its oil shipments to Portugal by 40 percent—from 2.5 to 3.5 million tons.

On March 28, a delegation headed by Professor Umberto Colombo, chairman of Italy's Atomic Energy Commission, arrived in Baghdad for talks with their Iraqi counterparts "about the development of bilateral cooperation in exploiting atomic energy for peaceful purposes." That statement was backed by some salient facts: over the preceding three years, Iraq's crude-oil exports to Italy had grown from 15 million to 22 million tons, and the overall trade balance between the two countries now inclined in Iraq's favor by a four-to-one ratio.

The Italian delegation was preceded by one day by the Commander in Chief of India's armed forces, General S. P. Malhutra. The topics of his talks with the Iraqis were not made public, but his hosts may have seized on the opportunity to find out whether India, the latest adherent to the atomic club, would be helpful in procuring admittance for Iraq.

On April 6, 1980, Kibbutz Misgav Am in Israel's Upper Galilee was attacked by terrorists; responsibility for the criminal onslaught was taken by the Arab Liberation Front, a terrorist organization controlled and massively supported by Iraq.

Agriculture Minister Ariel Sharon hastened to alert Begin: this was a suitable opportunity for the attack on the Iraqi reactor. A similar proposal came from several of the Air Force officers engaged in planning the operation. Cabinet secretary Aryeh Naor, likewise convinced that this was an opportune moment to act, sent a note to that effect to Ezer Weizman. The Defense Minister's reply was mockingly ironical. Weizman's reservations were shared by Begin, who directed that planning and preparations should continue.

On April 13, the Air Force conducted a trial which included aerial refueling of Phantoms by Hercules transport planes, and a bombing raid at twilight (five-thirty) employing various types of bomb. None of the pilots knew the purpose of the test.

After thorough study, the Air Force commander was now in a position to notify the Commander in Chief: "The feasibility of attacking the reactor by combat planes has been tested and found applicable. The Air Force is now ready for for-real execution at relatively short notice."

Nevertheless, trials proceeded, employing mixed formations of Phantoms and Skyhawks.

A draft mission order surfaced at Air Force headquarters; handwritten, it bore neither date nor authorization. Like similar orders relating to any Air Force operation, it comprised the following headings: forces participating, method, attack, armaments, control, flight routes out and back, communications, protection, interception. Each item constituted an independent entity requiring considerable thought and effort on the part of the relevant experts.

The Air Force also prepared for the contingency that, in consequence of the reactor attack, there would be an attempt to strike at select targets within Israel.

Each passing day brought additional improvements to the plan. In part or whole, it was exhibited before select military forums; every comment was taken into account.

Saddam Hussain continued to whip up his soldiers. In an address on April 25, 1980, the Iraqi President urged his men "to prepare for the liberation of Palestine from the filth of Zionism."

On April 29, Iraqi Oil Minister Tayih Abed al-Karim, speaking in Paris, where he had gone to preside over the Franco-Iraqi joint commission for technical and economic cooperation, offered a declaration to warm French hearts: "France will not have to go short as far as oil supplies are concerned."

Very few of France's citizens were aware of the enormous price—political, economic and, above all, moral—their country was being called upon to pay for that proclamation.

13 "Time is fast running out."

"A military option is now vital": that conclusion was reached during the first half of 1980 by an Israeli decision-maker previously convinced that the problem of the Iraqi reactor could be resolved by other means. He conveyed his assessment to Defense Minister Ezer Weizman.

In May, Weizman, flanked by Commander in Chief Eytan, reviewed the issue before Israel's political leadership. The gist of Weizman's remarks was: I am not certain that I'm in favor, but the armed forces must be prepared for any eventuality.

David Ivry understood Weizman's words to denote that planning was to go ahead even though the attack might not materialize.

Another voice as ever called for action. Agriculture Minister Ariel Sharon declared, "It is vital to execute, by any means feasible, a military operation to ensure destruction of the reactor, which constitutes a threat to Israel's survival."

Other participants dissented, whereupon Sharon flung back, "Gentlemen, I'm afraid you don't completely comprehend the matter."

Deputy Prime Minister Simha Ehrlich, who almost invariably disagreed with Sharon's hawkish views, again backed him, as he had at the preliminary discussion. "It is rare for me to support the Agriculture Minister's proposals with all my heart," he stressed, adding further weight to his endorsement of Sharon's position.

The Prime Minister's other deputy, Yigael Yadin, opposed military action; he remained convinced that there were still numerous other options open before resort to force, which, he feared, would have detrimental diplomatic consequences for Israel.

The dean of ministers, the veteran Dr. Burg, inclined toward Yadin's view, but urged that military preparations be maintained. Burg proposed that the final decision be delegated to a select team of ministers—thereby in effect denying Begin the authority to order the strike at a time he found suitable and binding him to convene the team at least once more.

In response to Burg's demand, Begin promised that the participants would be convened for further thorough deliberations before any military action. The Prime Minister affirmed that planning of the operation would proceed, as would collection of updated information on the reactor and related matters. "All those involved in the matter are well versed in their duties," Begin concluded.

Israel's preparations were overshadowed by the humiliating setback endured by the United States when a helicopter-borne force failed to seize the U.S. Embassy in Teheran and free the fifty-two American hostages imprisoned there by Ayatollah Ruhollah Khomeini's revolutionary guards. The Israeli General Staff endeavored to glean details of that operation, so as to learn the lessons for its own planned attack on Iran's neighbor. The failure of the American rescue operation probably convinced the Israeli planners that the only way of destroying the reactor was by aerial attack.

"Until the abortive U.S. operation," General Ivry related, "we didn't feel bad, professionally speaking. When the unexpected occurred, I thought, Who can guarantee that we don't have a technical hitch? The U.S. operation having deteriorated into catastrophe because of unforeseen events, doubts began to emerge among us too. Of course, our preliminary planning was good, but we were troubled by uncertainty."

On May 28, 1980, after prolonged differences with Begin, Weizman resigned; the Defense portfolio was taken over by the Prime Minister.

Later, following the attack on the reactor, Weizman stated, "I would not have approved the operation, because I feared that it would have an adverse effect on our relations with Egypt, the first Arab state which had made peace with us." As long as he was defense minister, Weizman consequently endeavored to delay a final decision on the matter. But "Begin could talk the Cabinet into any decision he wanted," Weizman recalled, "and he wanted to bomb [the reactor]."

On this issue, Weizman was in total disagreement with his own appointee. Referring to the Commander in Chief, the Defense Minister once remarked to a friend, "Rafful's bug is knocking down that reactor."

Weizman's resignation removed an obstacle which had hitherto blocked a decision—a decision which was, in the view of Yuval Ne'eman, unavoidable. Mordechai Zippori, Weizman's deputy, who stayed on in that capacity under Begin, was equally convinced that "now they'll bomb the reactor." But his mind was uneasy about it.

· · ·

It was business as usual on the Paris–Baghdad air route, with ministers and senior officials hastening back and forth as the two countries continued to trade oil and arms.

In May 1980, Iraq's RCC promulgated a special law for "protection against ionic radiation." At first sight, it was a simple administrative decree of a technical nature designed to protect citizens from radioactive contamination. In fact, however, publication of the decree testified that Iraq was now launched into the nuclear epoch. Baghdad may have regarded it as an "educational" decree to remind Iraqis that their country was rapidly hatching out into a fully fledged nuclear power.

The promised deliveries of French uranium had yet to reach Iraq, but information from varied sources indicated that the first shipment would soon be sent off. By 1985 Iraq would receive some 70 kilograms of weapons-grade uranium, sufficient to manufacture a number of Hiroshima-type bombs.

On June 6, Dr. Yahya al-Meshad, a member of Iraq's Atomic Energy Commission, arrived in Paris. An Egyptian citizen, al-Meshad was a metallurgical expert who had studied nuclear engineering in the United States and the Soviet Union, going on to specialize in control and operation of nuclear reactors. After serving as dean of the nuclear-engineering faculty at the University of Alexandria, he took up a senior position in Iraq's nuclear program.

It was al-Meshad's second journey to France, and, as before, his visit was linked with the Tammuz reactors. Cairo's *al-Ahram* claimed that "on his first trip, Meshad made arrangements for receipt of the equipment and instruments for Tammuz 2, and his second trip was for the purpose of completing discussions and talks with regard to the atomic fuel which is the basis for the production of the atomic bomb."

From Paris, Meshad headed southwest, to the noted nuclear center of Fontenay-aux-Roses, where he spent several days examining materials which France had undertaken to deliver to Iraq. Having completed his task, he traveled back to Paris, where he checked in at the renowned Méridien Hotel for a brief vacation before his return to Iraq.

On Saturday, June 14, a room attendant found the scientist lying lifeless on the floor of his room. The body bore numerous wounds, including a deep gash in the face. The murder had evidently not been committed with robbery in mind: Meshad's money had not been taken, nor had various documents including some of a technical nature.

The hotel management summoned the police. Guesses as to motives for the slaying were varied, even extending to the theory that it had homosexual undertones. The Méridien, which hosts many foreign businessmen, is also frequented by numerous prostitutes, including the male variety. The police investigation elicited that Meshad had been seen with a certain prostitute by the name of Marie-Claude Magalle. Under interrogation, Magalle admitted that she had tried to solicit Meshad, but said he proved indifferent to her advances. Refusing to give up, she remained in the corridor near his door, in the hope that he would change his mind. She related that Meshad then entered his room, from which voices were heard. She stressed that the tone was not loud or quarrelsome.

Magalle was freed. A few days later, when the police sought to interrogate her further, it transpired that she had been killed in a hit-and-run accident. Was her death mere coincidence, or did Meshad's killers fear that she might offer unwelcome revelations?

The British *New Scientist* suggested that Meshad had been killed by the Iraqis themselves, because of his alleged links with Dr. Shahristani, the Iraqi physicist who, as has been related, was imprisoned and subsequently executed. Others recalled that Meshad was involved in Iraq's bid to buy the Iranian government's 10 percent holding in Eurodif, Europe's largest plant for uranium enrichment and refinement. Iran purchased its share under the Shah, but after Khomeini's rise to power the Iranians let it be known that they wanted out, though France had meanwhile frozen their stock. Some theories tied Meshad's death to this matter. Another hypothesis argued that Meshad's interests included a covert link with Soviet curiosity about the French reactor under construction at al-Tuweitha, and that it was this involvement which led to his killing.

It goes without saying that numerous theories posited Israeli complicity in the slaying. Advocates of this view pointed out that, as an eminent scientist and the lynchpin of Saddam Hassain's nuclear program, Meshad was a natural target for Mossad agents.

Be all that as it may, work at the reactor was not held up for a single moment, and the same held true for top-level contacts between France and Iraq.

In June, Iraqi Foreign Minister Dr. Sa'adun Hammadi spent four days in France, meeting with President Giscard, Premier Barre and Foreign Minister François-Poncet. On returning to Baghdad on June 13, 1980, Hammadi cited his French hosts as stressing that bilateral nuclear cooperation rested upon "firm foundations. Certain circles' intrigues and acts of sabotage will not affect this cooperation."

* * *

The French proved true to their word. In mid-June 1980, only three months behind schedule, Iraq received the first 12-kilogram shipment of enriched uranium. The metal was stored at the small Tammuz-2 reactor, which was primed to go into operation.

The uranium was dispatched on instructions emanating from France's top-level political leadership: President Giscard and Premier Barre. Since the uranium came from France's weapons stockpile, execution of the order was delegated to the senior military echelons.

A second shipment, likewise comprising 12 kilograms, was due just a few days before Tammuz went into operation. But the Iraqis now demanded immediate delivery of the entire outstanding amount of 58 kilograms. With that they did not promise to return the spent fuel to France.

Why were the Iraqis so insistent about receiving the rest of the fuel at a time when the reactor was as yet inactive? That is a riddle. The only conceivable answer is that they sought the option of doing without the reactor, and the attendant French aid, while simultaneously leaving themselves large amounts of weapons-grade uranium which would permit construction of a number of Hiroshima-type bombs.

That precisely was the view of one of America's leading authorities on nuclear armament and proliferation, Professor Albert Wohlstetter. Wohlstetter, a fellow at the Rand Institute, served on numerous committees overseeing U.S. military nuclear policy and also officiated as senior adviser to the National Security Council. His essay, published in W. Scott Thompson's *National Security in the Eighties: From Weakness to Strength*, is regarded as a highly original work. Professor Wohlstetter affirmed that "the highly enriched uranium which the French announced they will sell and deliver to Iraq for the purposes of nuclear 'research' [had] only the remotest application in the civilian economy of Iraq, but such concentrated fissile material is the most important and hardest to produce component of nuclear weapons and can be quickly incorporated in a weapon assembly. Highly enriched uranium makes feasible weapons of the simplest design—the gun as distinct from the implosion-type essential for plutonium."

It goes without saying that these details were familiar to Saddam Hussain. An analysis of successive Iraqi demands directed at France indicates that someone in Baghdad with a mastery of all the technical data worked throughout toward one single aim: endowing Iraq with a military nuclear option at the earliest date possible.

On June 25, Hussain delivered a festive address to his troops. "The Iraqi Army," declared the President, who, in spite of never having served in it, now flaunted the resplendent uniform of a field marshal, "has not hitherto engaged in concrete manner in the battle for Palestine. All that the Iraqi

Army has contributed so far is only the beginning of what it is destined to do."

Two days later, in what could have been an elaboration on his President's words, parliament Speaker Naim Haddad told an *International Herald Tribune* interviewer, "The Arabs must get an atom bomb. The Arab countries should possess whatever is necessary to defend themselves."

These declarations were delivered at a time when the first shipment of enriched uranium was already in storage at Tammuz 2. The jubilation at Hussain's presidential palace was great. In no way disturbed by the fact that IAEA inspectors dutifully noted and confirmed delivery of 12 kilograms of uranium, the Iraqi President knew perfectly well that the agency's supervision would constitute no obstacle toward achieving his goal. Having come into possession of an appreciable amount of weapons-grade uranium, Iraq now qualified as a potential member of the world's most exclusive circle: the nuclear club. The only thing needed was Hussain's directive for an effort to get Tammuz 1 active by the end of 1980.

American officials who went to Israel in May for a routine exchange of information about the Iraqi reactor endorsed the views of their Israeli colleagues regarding Baghdad's intention of manufacturing nuclear bombs at the earliest date possible. At this phase, Israel's assessment of Iraq's designs did not greatly diverge from the views held by other countries that were following developments at al-Tuweitha. But there were differences as to the projected date.

"Under certain circumstances," said Theodore Taylor, an engineer employed in bomb design for U.S. nuclear-arms programs, "at least one nuclear bomb could be made out of that amount, 12 kilograms of uranium, which comprises one full fueling of the facility." Taylor, who had worked at the Los Alamos laboratories and at General Dynamics, as well as holding a Princeton lectureship in nuclear engineering, indicated that, with delivery of the first shipment of enriched uranium, the Iraqis were free to confiscate the metal and swiftly divert it to construction of one Hiroshima-type bomb. No one disputed the validity of his assertion, though Israel and the United States agreed that the Iraqis would opt for the plutonium course, which, while more time consuming, required a smaller amount of fissionable material for each bomb. If the Iraqis pursued the plutonium course, their first bomb could be completed by 1983.

In June 1980, two Brazilian nuclear scientists arrived in Iraq, where there could have been little pleasure over the tidings they bore: Brazil was still several years away from production of the enriched uranium the Iraqis so desperately craved. The Iraqis suffered a further disappointment on learning that the Brazilian engineers and technicians who were to have assisted them had only now left for West Germany for advanced training in uranium-enrichment techniques. A considerable time would elapse before they were capable of training others.

However, the same month brought two additional visits to Iraq, with somewhat more gratifying results. On June 17, Niger's Foreign Minister Daouda Daillo arrived in Baghdad, where he engaged in intensive talks with Iraqi officials headed by Hassan Ali, trade minister and RCC member. According to the official statement, the talks explored ways "to promote economic and technical cooperation between the two friendly countries, Iraq's contribution to the implementation of the five-year development in Niger, and Iraqi aid to assist Niger in overcoming the difficulties it is facing in the wake of the 1974 drought."

The only point omitted from these flowery phrases was the fact that Niger has the good fortune to own some of the world's largest deposits of uranium ore.

Five days later, on June 22, Italy's Industrial Cooperation Minister Gianni de Michelis reached Baghdad, where he was received by Oil Minister Tayih Abed al-Karim and held intensive talks with other officials. The topic was depicted under the vague heading of "relations of industrial and economic cooperation between the two friendly states." Here too, a hidden hand erased any reference to nuclear cooperation.

The same month, European Common Market prime ministers issued their Venice declaration recognizing "the legitimate rights of the Palestinian people." The EEC declaration evoked indignation and concern in Israel and was universally regarded as a marked shift toward the Arab viewpoint on the part of Western Europe. However, even that failed to satisfy the Iraqi leaders, who denounced the statement and declared that they would accept no solution short of "wiping the Zionist entity off the map."

Still perceiving only one way of resolving the "Zionist problem," Baghdad now took a further significant step toward that "final solution." On June 20, the small Tammuz-2 reactor became operational.

The first of the new U.S. F-16s reached Israel on July 2, with the rest of the first delivery due to follow within one month. Air Force Commander Ivry promptly summoned the two officers designated to take command of the new planes, Colonels Aryeh Ran* and Eliezer Malachi,* and, without specifying the target, instructed them "to develop preparedness for aerial defense and attacks in depth."

The pilots practiced long flights culminating in simulated attacks. After

*Fictitious name.

several such exercises, Ivry concluded that the planes would be able to fulfill their assigned roles in the attack on the reactor. He reported to the Commander in Chief, "We are in the stages of testing the fitness of the plan to accomplish the attack."

With the arrival in Washington of its new ambassador, Ephraim Evron, Israel maintained its diplomatic pressure on the United States. The new post fitted Evron to perfection. He was widely experienced, having served as chief aide to the Defense Minister and as director general of the Foreign Ministry, with a diplomatic record as ambassador to Sweden and to Canada and as minister in Washington.

On July 16, Evron met with the new Secretary of State, Edmund S. Muskie. Instructions had been sent from Jerusalem requesting Evron to raise the issue of the Iraqi reactor, but the cable arrived after his return from the State Department. Evron therefore had to settle for a telephone conversation with Assistant Secretary of State Harold H. Saunders, requesting him to acquaint Muskie with all the information regarding France's involvement in the Iraqi nuclear project.

Saunders, a career diplomat boasting a long-time acquaintance with the Mideast, told Evron that the United States took a grave view of Iraq's nuclear endeavors. America had already taken action in Rome, he said, promising to see "what can be done in France"; the United States was even prepared to approach the Soviet Union with the aim of bringing Russian influence to bear upon Iraq.

What precise form did the American approach to France take? That is a matter of disagreement: some hold that it never went beyond a mere expression of views, while others insist that diplomatic intervention was direct and unabashed. However, America was powerless against France's independent demarches. By the time Washington made its approach, the French could metaphorically finger their noses: their first shipment of enriched uranium had already reached Iraq.

In the meantime, the media published a startling declaration by President Carter: the United States would not attempt to impose its views upon states with a nuclear capability—such as France—with regard to the Mideast. If that was indeed what Carter said, he thereby gave France a free hand to go ahead with full implementation of its agreement with Iraq.

French spokesmen rejected American criticism—official or semiofficial —of their country's policy. They found a measure of support for their position in a row which erupted in Congress over Carter's decision to send 38 kilograms of enriched uranium to India, in accordance with an agreement between the two countries. Numerous congressmen called for abrogation of the agreement, but Administration spokesmen warned that such a course was "liable to jeopardize U.S. relations with India, and facilitate Soviet moves in Southeast Asia."

The controversy was exploited to the full by the French. "Enriched-uranium deliveries are a routine matter," they argued, pointing to the American uranium shipped to India after that country had demonstrated its nuclear capability. The French counteroffensive also referred to Iraq's assurances—to France and to the IAEA—that all its nuclear facilities would be employed exclusively for peaceful purposes and would come under international supervision. The French recalled the presence of four hundred of their engineers and technicians at al-Tuweitha as a further guarantee that the reactor's uranium would not be employed for military purposes.

The French spokesmen conveniently overlooked a recent meeting in London where representatives of eight states commanding advanced nuclear technology considered supervisory methods that would be more effective than those hitherto applied by the IAEA. France initially agreed to attend the meeting, but pulled out under Iraqi threats to call off all the arms deals concluded between the two countries.

Israeli leaders made no secret of their indignation over France's conduct. On July 13, Transport Minister Haim Landau declared, "We are conscious of the threat posed by Iraqi efforts to construct a nuclear reactor. Israel will not be able to tolerate such a situation, and will do its best to prevent it, by better means or worse." The following day, Landau and two other Knesset members boycotted the traditional Bastille Day reception at the French Embassy in Tel Aviv. "There are times when I imagine that we are living in the period of the Vichy regime," Landau said in defense of his action. "France is taking upon itself a very heavy responsibility." Landau was a long-standing friend of Menahem Begin, having served under him in the forties as chief of staff of the Etzel underground. During Begin's first year in office, Landau served in the Prime Minister's office as minister without portfolio, in which capacity he attended Begin's regular meetings with the heads of the intelligence services. It is therefore probable that Landau's step was no mere private protest.

Deputy Prime Minister Yigael Yadin, who disagreed with Begin over policy with regard to the Iraqi reactor, was nevertheless unsparing in his criticism of France. On July 15 he declared publicly that, Israeli concern having been conveyed to France, "further steps" would be taken. He did not elaborate.

That same day, another warning came from the director general of the Prime Minister's office, Matti Shmuelevitz, whose duties gave him access to confidential material. In an interview to the German *Die Welt*, Shmuelevitz—once sentenced to death by the British mandatory authorities for his membership in the Lehy underground—stated, "Israel cannot afford to sit idle and wait till an Iraqi bomb drops on our heads."

It should be noted that France did not speak with a single voice. That country's contribution to the nuclear programs of other states evoked horror among many of its citizens; one of these was National Assembly Deputy Paul Quilès, who addressed a written question to the Foreign Minister pointing to the contradiction between the government's professed opposition to nuclear proliferation and what he defined as "the pursuit of contracts for supply of nuclear equipment which can lead directly to the fabrication of nuclear explosives for military purposes, to Pakistan and Iraq." Quilès demanded to know why Iraq had been given uranium enriched to a grade of over 90 percent for a research reactor, even though it—like others of its type in France—could be fueled by low-grade uranium.

It was three months before the minister deigned to provide an answer, which was phrased in terms drearily familiar. "Most of the world's research reactors—seventy-five reactors have been exported to some thirty countries —are fueled by highly enriched uranium," he stated in response to the final section of the question, going on to argue:

> Therefore there is nothing new in the supply of this fuel to Iraq. France is nevertheless making efforts to promote the use of less enriched uranium and make it into the normal material for research reactors. Tests are now being conducted in France, with very promising results, so as to establish the quality of this type of fuel.
>
> With regard to the delivery of highly enriched fuel to Iraq, in an agreement signed by the two countries in 1976 all necessary safeguards are guaranteed: Iraq, having adhered to the treaty for nonproliferation of nuclear weapons, has, unlike other countries, submitted all its nuclear activity to the inspection of the IAEA. Furthermore, Iraq has undertaken (by the terms of the Franco–Iraqi agreement of January 18, 1975) to subject to such inspection the materials, equipment and facilities received in the framework of cooperation between the two states. Finally, modalities of delivery of the fuel correspond solely to requirements of the research reactor supplied, have been programmed accordingly, and are encompassed by all necessary precautions.

Having himself received similar answers from French officials, Professor Yuval Ne'eman naturally found little difficulty in refuting them outright. However, Ne'eman's discreet talks with U.S. representatives in Israel failed to spur the Administration into adopting more drastic steps. In desperation, Ne'eman approached Israel's mass circulation *Yediot Aharonot* and asked to be interviewed on one sole topic: the threat to Israel posed by the Iraqi reactor.

In the interview, published on July 18, 1980, Ne'eman declared, "The reactor purchased by Iraq can have only a military purpose. Iraq has no nuclear research, and the Osiris-type reactor is too small for generating electricity. Consequently, its only significance can be military.

"The Iraqis will have two possibilities," Ne'eman went on. One was production of a Hiroshima-type bomb employing the enriched uranium itself. "This is not simple, but neither is it overly complex. Iraq has sufficient enriched uranium for seven or eight such bombs.

"The second possibility is more complex and requires a longer time, but it will allow the Iraqis to construct more bombs." The enriched uranium could be utilized to produce plutonium, which the Iraqis could then extract with the equipment bought from Italy. "In my opinion, Osiris can produce three or four plutonium bombs per year."

Ne'eman's final conclusion was unambiguous: If the Iraqis chose to construct enriched-uranium bombs, with technical aid from another country (Pakistan, perhaps) they would have their first atomic bomb within six months to a year of receiving the uranium.

One of the few men to foresee what lay in store was Winston Churchill, grandson of Britain's wartime leader, who had emulated his famous forebear by first becoming a journalist and later entering Parliament. A frequent visitor to Israel who had written a fascinating book on the Six-Day War, Churchill did not rest content with criticizing France for abandoning moral principle in its dealings with Iraq. He was one of the earliest observers to grasp that Israel could not stand by idly. "Time is fast running out," Churchill warned on July 11. "Few who know Israel well can imagine that she can permit a situation to come about in which Iraq—which is in a self-proclaimed state of belligerence with Israel—has a nuclear weapon sitting in one corner of a hangar with a Soviet-supplied TU 22 Blinder strike bomber."

If these truths were self-evident to Churchill, they were doubly so to a man of the caliber of former Foreign Minister Moshe Dayan. On July 13 he declared, "The nuclear option will not be restricted exclusively to the Arabs." Israel had always declared that it would not be the first state to introduce nuclear weapons into the Mideast. However, Dayan added, Israel had never declared that it would not use such weapons "or that we would be too late in employing them."

French spokesmen continued to varnish the facts. When an Israeli television reporter asked French Ambassador Marc Bonnefous why his country was helping Iraq in such a sensitive sphere, the diplomat gave the stock answer: The uranium was under "effective French and international supervision . . ."

On July 15, 1980, just 191 years and a day after the banner of freedom was hoisted over the Bastille, Ma'ariv's Shmuel Shnitzer delivered a vitriolic response: "I am ashamed of present-day France—a France which, with the cynicism of conscienceless merchants of death, gives an Arab state the tools and means for the manufacture of the most lethal weapon of mass destruction hitherto designed by the human brain."

14 "The Administration is concerned . . ."

During the first week of July 1980, Menahem Begin suffered a minor heart attack. Hospitalized at Jerusalem's Haddassah Hospital, he was still able to work from his sickbed and receive current reports. One of the documents submitted for his perusal dealt with the rapid progress of work at al-Tuweitha; having studied it carefully, he turned to his personal aide Yehiel Kadishai and said, "When I get out of hospital, be good enough to summon Ambassador Lewis to see me urgently."

On his departure from the hospital on July 14, Begin found dozens of journalists awaiting him outside. One of them wanted to know what Israel intended to do about the Iraqi reactor, then very much in the news with frequent reports about its rapid construction and its military potential.

"That is a very grave development," Begin replied tersely.

July 16 was an eventful day for Iraq's nuclear program.

In Baghdad, Trade Minister and RCC member Hassan Ali met with Brazil's Minister of Industry and Trade João Camilo Penna, who had arrived at the head of an economic delegation. In all probability, the meeting hinged upon bilateral nuclear cooperation in return for enlarged deliveries to Brazil of Iraqi oil on preferential credit terms.

In Paris, Premier Raymond Barre publicly congratulated Saddam Hussain on the first anniversary of his assumption of the presidency. In France and elsewhere there was astonishment at Barre's fulsome praise for the Iraqi tyrant. "Saddam Hussain," Barre affirmed, "is the statesman who can assume the burdens and responsibilities of the hour." Barre highly commended Hussain's leadership of "brave and independent Iraq."

In Jerusalem, the Knesset's Foreign Affairs and Defense Committee, convened on the initiative of former Prime Minister Yitzhak Rabin, listened with great concern as a senior Military Intelligence officer warned that if Osirak went into operation on schedule, within the year, and if high-grade nuclear fuel continued to reach Iraq, it would take that country no more than a few years to attain the military nuclear capability it sought to promote its strategic aims in the Arab–Israeli conflict and to buttress its position in the Persian Gulf. By the mideighties, the officer added, the Iraqis would be able to construct several nuclear bombs.

The committee's chairman, aeronautical-engineering professor Moshe Arens, warned that Iraq's possession of nuclear weapons was liable to spark off a global conflagration. Consequently, heavy pressure should be exerted upon the Western countries to induce them to prevent the nuclearization of Iraq.

Other committee members called for urgent action against France, which was giving nuclear aid to Iraq in defiance of its express international obligations. They also called for a propaganda campaign to alert public opinion in the world at large and in France in particular.

On July 17, Begin received U.S. Ambassador Sam Lewis. A career diplomat who specialized in European and Latin-American affairs, Lewis had served as assistant secretary of state for international organizations before taking up his post in Israel. He arrived shortly before Begin's 1977 election victory and soon befriended the new Prime Minister. The ambassador became a regular visitor to the Prime Minister's office, often serving as the principal channel for conveying Israel's views to Washington, and playing an active role throughout the peace talks with Egypt.

Commencing the conversation, Begin declared that there was something "bearing upon" Israel's security and requested that his words be transmitted directly to the White House. The nuclear weapons liable to be constructed in Iraq were "causing us sleepless nights," he said, repeating the assessment of Israeli and foreign experts that French deliveries of 70 kilograms of enriched uranium would leave the Iraqis a short path to traverse toward construction of three Hisoshima-type bombs.

Recalling the previous month's visit of U.S. experts who shared the Israeli view that Iraq was bent on early construction of nuclear bombs, Begin reminded Lewis that Iraq possessed Soviet-built Topolev bombers capable of carrying the bombs to Tel Aviv. The President should take into consideration that the Iraqi tyrant was "the bloodiest of them all." Begin related an episode he had heard about from Hosni Mubarak, then Egypt's vice-president. On one of his visits to Iraq, Mubarak went to see Hussain at the latter's Baghdad office. In the course of their conversation, Hussain unexpectedly pulled out his pistol and laid it on the desk. Startled by this unusual act, Mubarak could not refrain from asking his host what the pistol had to do with their conversation, and the Iraqi President replied, "That's the way we live." Begin pointed out that on his path to power the "Butcher

of Baghdad" had killed dozens of his friends and colleagues. The Prime
Minister also recalled the Jews hanged in Baghdad in 1969 on Hussain's
instructions.

Iraqi troops had taken part in every war between Israel and its neighbors.
Iraq did not even adhere to the 1949 armistice agreements signed by all the
other Arab states. Next to Qaddafi's, Hussain's regime was "the most irresponsible" and would use its nuclear weapons to destroy Israel's civilian
population. Stressing "the grotesqueness of French behavior toward the
Americans," Begin nevertheless considered the issue serious enough "to ask
the President to ask the French to refrain" from sending more enriched
uranium to Iraq.

"I repeat," Begin said, "it is a crucial issue for us. There is justified
nervousness here." It was not a matter of "another squadron of planes"; it
was an atomic bomb!

Lewis displayed full understanding for the Prime Minister's anxiety,
which he linked with concern over developments in Pakistan and "their
evidence of cooperation" with Iraq.

Begin pointed out that Iraq, unlike Pakistan, already possessed a "delivery vehicle" in the form of the Topolov bombers. It was not a matter of four
or five years; Israeli experts spoke of two years as a possibility. Even if the
Iraqis took the longer course, they could have their first primitive plutonium
device by 1983.

Lewis quoted American assessments whereby Iraq's "most likely course"
would be to develop "a full fuel cycle" to produce plutonium. It was merely
a question of time, and "the three-to-five-years estimate is itself dismaying
enough." Lewis repeated the contention of the French that their uranium
shipment had been "checked in by IAEA inspectors," and that if it should be
diverted to make weapons, "then, under the safeguard agreement, it would
be immediately noted." He admitted that this was "a small reassurance."

Begin: "It is not foolproof."

Lewis conceded that there were ways of concealment. But he urged
Begin to put his trust in President Carter. "No President has been so concerned and so active in trying to stop the spread of nuclear weapons. I am
certain, if he can find a way to stop the French, he will do so."

Returning to his embassy in Tel Aviv, Lewis hastened to send a report on
his conversation with Begin to the President and the Secretary of State.

In 1980, following disagreements with Begin, Moshe Dayan resigned
from the Cabinet, to be succeeded as foreign minister by Yitzhak Shamir.
Shamir, in his sixties, had entered politics following decades of clandestine
activity, first as commander of the hard-line anti-British Lehy underground,
and then, after Israel's independence, as an employee of the Mossad, where

he soon achieved prominence. Shortly after terminating his work for the secret agency, Shamir accepted Begin's invitation to join his Herut movement, the mainstay of the Likkud confederation; here too he advanced to senior positions. When Begin became prime minister in 1977, he offered Shamir the post of Knesset speaker, arguing that "it should be recorded in history that a Lehy commander officiated" in that role.

As a new foreign minister, Shamir now departed from conventional diplomatic usage by sending a handwritten letter to his Italian colleague Emilio Colombo, whose acquaintance he had made during his term as Knesset speaker, when Colombo presided over the European parliament. Shamir's letter, dated July 20, 1980, was written in French, a language he had mastered as a political exile in France after escaping from a British detention camp in Africa. Shamir drew attention to the "growing and unprecedented threat" posed by Iraqi efforts to attain a military nuclear capability, which constituted a threat to peace "whether in this region or to the world at large." He wrote of the Italian-supplied installations for plutonium extraction, and of current talks for sale to Iraq of an Italian natural-uranium reactor capable of producing fissionable material. Urging Italy to give no help to Iraq's efforts, which threatened Israel's existence, Shamir concluded: "it is of the gravest when nuclear capability is endowed to a regime which achieved power by force, and which is constantly sustained by its fierce antagonism toward the Israeli people."

Shamir could only hope that Colombo (Italian for "dove") would not be overly soft and yielding in dealing with the topic of his communication.

The day that letter was composed, Iraqi parliament Speaker Naim Haddad delivered an impassioned address to "representatives of the Palestinian revolution" who adhered to various terrorist groups under Iraqi patronage. "Iraq is placing all its resources at the disposal of the national revolution," he declared. "We are preparing our Army to defend the Arab nation and the Palestinian cause, on a sophisticated scientific basis and on the basis of our principles, which bind us to take part in liberating every inch of the Arab homeland."

On July 18, reports emanating from a "senior official" in Paris disclosed that the small Tammuz-2 reactor, having received its first load of uranium, was now active. Two days later, July 20, witnessed the first public mention of a possible Israeli air strike at al-Tuweitha. That day's *Boston Globe* cited "observers discussing a worst case scenario" to predict that "Israel could launch a pre-emptive strike to put the reactors out of commission." The article also referred to the nightmarish vision of a senior Administration official: three of the world's craziest and least stable regimes, Iraq, Syria and Libya, were liable to acquire nuclear arms. "Maybe they'll drop one on us," the official was quoted as speculating, "but more likely they'll drop them on each other first." From Israel's viewpoint, that was a highly optimistic prediction, but no Mideastern state could have found much reassurance therein.

On July 21, the biweekly *Nuclear Fuel* published a secret intelligence report alleging that Iraq was using extortion against Brazil to gain nuclear knowhow purchased from West Germany. The nuclear-cooperation agreement signed by Iraq and Brazil one year previously was "a direct outcome of Brazil's oil deficiency." The journal added that Iraq also received nuclear knowhow from Pakistan.

The Iraqis sent up a smokescreen. Saddam Hussain, whose utterances for domestic consumption showed no inhibitions about proclaiming his intention of developing nuclear weapons, hotly denied any such plans when questioned by foreigners. At a press conference on July 21, Hussain expressly denied that his country sought to construct nuclear arms. In its report the following day, the London *Times*, recalling Hussain's frequent references to the Arabs' ability to acquire nuclear weapons, quoted him as saying, "Whoever wants to be our enemy can expect that enemy to be totally different in the very near future." That prophecy proved to be literally true: only a few months elapsed before it turned out that Iraq's military efforts were directed not westward, against Israel, but eastward, against Iran.

American endeavors to block France's nuclear aid to Iraq failed to bear fruit, to Israel's bitter disappointment. On July 22, Ambassador Evron told Assistant Secretary of State Harold Saunders that France, aware of America's own eagerness to improve relations with Baghdad, was indifferent to U.S. pressure. Although expressing himself with diplomatic reserve, Evron made his meaning plain: Israel suspected Washington of insufficient concern about developments in Iraq.

Saunders denied the implied charge. For the past five years, he claimed, the United States had, even before being approached by Israel, been following Iraq's nuclear program. He reiterated that the U.S. took a grave view of nuclear proliferation.

On July 23, an official report published in Baghdad defined mastery of nuclear technology as "a form of scientific progress required to achieve a high level of overall development." Nuclear technology was now vital for advances in a variety of scientific and industrial spheres, including medicine, generating electric power, farming, geology, physics, chemistry and so on. The true aim of Iraq's nuclear program, weapons production, was only hinted at in roundabout terms: overall development required an increasing application of nuclear progress so as to provide a broad basis for development "and to achieve national security for the Arab people. In this sphere, Iraq plays a pioneering role."

On July 21–22, Israeli experts convened to draw up an assessment of the situation at al-Tuweitha. "The reactor," they concluded, "is capable, by irradiating natural uranium, of producing plutonium that can be extracted by means of installations which Iraq is buying in Italy. This combination permits Iraq to advance toward attainment of the nuclear option." They foresaw that French deliveries of enriched uranium would enable Iraq—by resort to the technological facilities it was receiving—to construct three or four atom bombs without particular difficulty. Should Iraq decide to produce plutonium bombs, one bomb could be constructed each year with the plutonium produced by the reactor and refined by the hot cells. However, certain technical modifications would enable the reactor to produce a greater amount of plutonium, allowing Iraq to build up a nuclear arsenal within a few years.

(A similar assessment was reached by Lewis A. Dunn, a nuclear-proliferation expert at the Hudson Institute, in a working paper composed in June 1981, after Israel bombed the reactor: "Since the mid-1970's, Iraq had been purchasing nuclear material and facilities that, once completed, could have been illegally used to produce enough plutonium for about one Hiroshima-type bomb per year." Recently appointed assistant director at Washington's Arms Control and Disarmament Agency, Dunn argued that any Iraqi attempt to divert the reactor to military use would have come to light. But he believed the Iraqis willing to run the risk of international sanctions, as long as they could achieve their aim.)

The Israeli experts warned that nuclear cooperation between Iraq and Pakistan was quite feasible, and possibly already in effect, greatly shortening Iraq's path to a military nuclear capability. One of the leading experts pointed out that it was not possible to rely upon supervision, and certainly not on Iraq's pledges to refrain from employing for military purposes the nuclear technology it acquired. It was Iraq's intention, in spite of being a party to the NPT, and in spite of supervision by France and the IAEA, to use the reactor for military ends. Being a hard-line radical state, Iraq was quite capable of disowning all its international obligations. Furthermore, Article 10 of the nonproliferation treaty allowed Iraq, like any other signatory, to cancel those obligations unilaterally, at three months' notice.

The morning of July 24, 1980, just one week after their previous meeting, Ambassador Lewis paid a return visit to Begin to deliver "an interim report." He assured the Prime Minister that the report on their previous meeting "was carefully read by the President and the Secretary of State," who were preparing "a serious and complete response." Lewis added that the United States had been "watching the Franco–Iraqi cooperation very closely . . . and speaking to the French about this."

The Iraqis were acutely conscious of U.S. efforts to dissuade France and Italy from persisting in their nuclear aid. On July 24, the day Begin received Lewis, Iraqi Oil Minister Karim received the Arab ambassadors accredited in Baghdad. "Attacks and threats," the minister declared, "will not deter Iraq from maintaining its firm resolve in continuing to implement its industrial, scientific and technological initiative in the service of the Arab nation. The Zionists are . . . behind the attacks and threats, which are aimed at preventing scientific progress in the Arab states."

In Washington the following day, Ambassador Evron met with Dr. Thomas Pickering, Assistant Secretary of State for Scientific Affairs (and later U.S. ambassador to Israel). Pickering's office had accumulated data on nuclear activity the world over, and the Iraqi program was one of his principal spheres of interest.

"The Administration is concerned about Iraq's efforts," Pickering declared. "We've been watching them for a number of years." The United States knew that Iraq had no hope of accomplishing its nuclear plans without outside assistance. Pickering reported that the 12 kilograms of French uranium, having undergone irradiation at Tammuz 2, had been transferred to Tammuz 1—which, he claimed, would make it difficult for the Iraqis "to misuse this amount."

Furthermore, he added, France had undertaken to deliver no more than the bare minimum of uranium required for the operation of the reactor. The French also claimed to have taken all necessary measures to oversee Iraqi activity at the reactor, the presence of French personnel presenting "a certain obstacle" to diversion of the fissionable material to undesirable ends. Pickering assured Evron that, in addition to being aware of U.S. concern, the French shared it. The Administration hoped to reach an understanding with them about the spent fuel, proposing that it be sent to laboratories either in France or in the United States, just as long as it did not remain in Iraq.

Italy's activities were also a source of anxiety to the Administration, Pickering went on. Italian leaders "of the very highest rank" had informed Washington that they were keeping watch on developments in Iraq, in accordance with the provisions of the NPT to which Italy is a party. The Administration told the Italians that their answer was inadequate, and there would therefore be further contacts between the two governments.

The United States, Pickering concluded, would not relax its pressure on France and Italy and would also approach other governments linked with Iraq's nuclear program.

Evron and his aides listened intently to everything Pickering had to say, but were not reassured. Israel, Evron declared, was still highly disturbed by Iraq's possession of nuclear fuel, and by the technological potential represented by the Osirak reactor and the hot cells. Iraqi statements, in conjunction with the evasive replies of France and Italy, further heightened Israel's concern.

Endeavoring to play down the gravity of the situation, Pickering, admitting the disparity between Italy's explanations about its aid to Iraq and the information Washington had received, promised that the matter would be investigated.

Evron still suspected the Americans of insufficient alertness. "Are you aware of the declarations of Iraqi leaders about use of a nuclear bomb against Israel?" Pickering confessed his ignorance, whereupon Evron read out a selection of declarations by Saddam Hussein and Naim Haddad.

Sensing that Evron suspected him of underestimating the matter, Pickering tried to correct that impression. "Iraq is spending a fortune on nuclear research and development. The United States is in no doubt as to Iraqi intentions, even without knowing what Saddam Hussein said. The Administration understands perfectly the catastrophic results which can arise from Iraq's actions."

Two days later Pickering would have been able to read the declaration of Iraq's ambassador to Kuwait, Abdel Jabar Amer Aini al-Dori, who quoted his President: "We shall acquire the atom, and Israel will be unable to disrupt our actions. The might of Iraq is the might of the Arabs, and the might of the Arabs is the might of Iraq."

Iraq's Foreign Ministry and intelligence services paid close attention to Western media revelations about their country's nuclear program, some of which evidently emanated from covert American sources. The Iraqis also received updated reports from Paris about American pressure to halt, or at least delay, French nuclear aid to Iraq. Among other reasons for keeping Iraq informed, the French probably sought to enhance the value of their aid in Iraqi eyes.

On July 25, Iraq's ambassador to Paris, Nuri Ismail al-Ways, sounded the alarm about Israeli military action against Iraq: "The Zionist enemy is planning military aggression against Iraq. It should be stressed that the enemy possesses U.S.-built aircraft capable of attacking Iraqi territory. The Zionist entity is preparing to launch an air strike at the Iraqi nuclear reactor, in an effort to sabotage Iraq's scientific and technological development, and to prevent the Arab nation's progress in that sphere." His statement ended by reiterating firmly, "The Iraqi nuclear program is designed solely for peaceful purposes."

• • •

On July 28, Israeli Foreign Minister Yitzhak Shamir met with the French chargé d'affaires, Jean-Pierre Chauvet. Flanked by two aides, Shamir began by expressing Israel's concern over Franco–Iraqi nuclear cooperation. Israel was in no doubt that Iraq—in spite of being a party to the NPT, in spite of IAEA supervision, in spite of Baghdad's undertakings to France—intended to use the reactor for military purposes. Shamir pointed to a number of facts which made such a conclusion unavoidable: Iraq's insistence on 93-percent-grade uranium, which could only denote that the fuel was to be used for plutonium production, or directly as a nuclear explosive; Iraqi declarations of intent about acquiring nuclear weapons; Iraq's nuclear cooperation with Pakistan; Iraq's refusal to countenance Israel's existence, even on terms that other Arab states were prepared to consider.

Shamir went on to a topic even less pleasing to French ears: France's undertakings to Israel, conveyed to Israeli foreign ministers and diplomats by their French counterparts during the years 1977–79. Shamir recalled France's promise that the uranium supplied to Iraq would be of a low grade. France had also pledged that the amount of uranium in Iraq's possession at any time would be the bare minimum required to operate the reactor, that Iraq would not stockpile fuel beyond the control of French experts, that immediately on delivery of the fuel rods they would be irradiated so as to preclude any other use, and that when spent they would be returned to France. There was considerable uncertainty about these pledges, which Shamir, urging their fulfillment, now proceeded to list in detail:

1. France would henceforth supply Iraq solely with low-grade uranium unsuitable for military purposes.

2. France would take the strictest measures to ensure that the fuel was not diverted to such purposes.

3. France would be on the alert to prevent any technical modification that could make the reactor capable of producing plutonium in larger amounts.

4. France would not permit Iraqi engineers and technicians to receive advanced training in "sensitive" subjects—i.e., in fields likely to aid Iraq in acquiring a military nuclear option.

"Monsieur le Chargé d'Affaires," Shamir concluded, "Israel holds France exclusively responsible for the results liable to arise from operation of the reactor and misuse of the nuclear fuel."

Having listened attentively to Shamir's charges, Chauvet replied, "My task is to be the defending attorney for my country, just as you have been the prosecutor for yours." He pointed out that France had supplied research reactors to Zaire and several South American countries. Such reactors do not, in themselves, constitute any immediate danger. The French government did not believe Iraq to possess scientists or technicians of a standard capable of constructing nuclear arms. France trained scientific and technical staff in the operation of research reactors, never in the manufacture of nuclear bombs. The moment the French personnel employed at al-Tuweitha detected Iraqi attempts to misuse the reactor, "we shall pull our cards out of the game." Chauvet proclaimed his understanding of Israel's long-term worries: no one could guarantee that Iraq would not ultimately acquire a nuclear bomb. But for that purpose, it would long require the services of mercenary scientists. France would offer no aid to that end.

Chauvet tried to put himself in Hussain's shoes. Acquisition of nuclear arms would be lunacy on the part of Iraq, he argued. After all, Israel's Jewish and Arab populations are intermingled, and anyone dropping a nuclear bomb on Israel ran the risk of annihilating many thousands of Arabs.

Shamir voiced his skepticism on that last point. Saddam Hussain had shown no mercy toward Iraqis or Iranians or Kurds—why should he spare the lives of Israeli Arabs? Shamir expressed his dissatisfaction with the other replies offered by Chauvet. "You claim that France trains Iraqi scientists," he argued. "If that is for research purposes, Iraq evidently does not require a reactor as large and advanced as Osirak; it possesses a Soviet reactor quite adequate for scientific experimentation."

Chauvet claimed that Iraq was interested in constructing a network of electric-power reactors and had a detailed plan to that end. Iraq did possess large oil reserves, but in view of their depletion, and rising oil prices, power reactors were a profitable investment. The governments of France and Italy had a clear interest in so lucrative a project. With that, the Frenchman conceded, "I won't say the Iraqis don't have hidden ambitions."

Following upon this meeting, Israel promptly published a detailed statement about its main points, with the aim of exerting additional pressure upon France. The statement concluded with the warning that nuclear aid to Iraq was liable to "reignite the flames of conflict in the region" and foil peace efforts. Shamir had "reiterated Israel's request that France do everything to prevent Iraq from attaining a military nuclear capability."

Chauvet left Shamir's office with a detailed list of Israel's complaints, which he hastened to forward, with a report of his conversation, to the Quai d'Orsay. The report prompted the French President to meet with his Foreign Minister, followed by an official statement hotly denying the truth of France's nuclear cooperation with Iraq. Transmitted without delay to Shamir, the statement read:

"The French government is astonished by the fantastic statements and accusations recently propagated on the subject of its nuclear cooperation with Iraq, in spite of the precise information furnished by the competent

French authorities and agencies." The statement, like that proffered by Chauvet, was open in its advocacy of Iraq's right to nuclear development. After defending France's nuclear aid, the statement concluded by affirming that France's cooperation with Iraq was directed toward "perfectly legitimate objectives" and was encompassed by "all guarantees."

The statement was a masterpiece of coy hypocrisy, and its release further heightened Israeli anxieties. Had the French government undertaken to review its cooperation with Iraq, it would hardly have reassured Israel, but it would at least have demonstrated French sensitivity to Israel's complaints. But the latter were effectively dismissed by the French statement in total disregard—probably deliberate—of the grave charges put forward by Israel and the United States.

On July 30, 1980, Yitzhak Shamir, replying to a motion to the agenda submitted by Communist leader Meir Vilner, announced that every year since 1974 Israel had regularly proposed that the Mideast be proclaimed a nuclear-free zone. Israel was prepared to enter into direct negotiations on this matter with all the Arab states, or with any one of them, at any time, anywhere, and with no preconditions. To date, the minister added, the Arab states had rejected these proposals.

One day later, the Iraqi delegation to the United States distributed a document entitled "Zionist Threats to Iraq's Program of Nuclear Development for Peaceful Purposes." It stated: "The Zionist entity . . . is perhaps preparing to launch an air attack on the Iraqi nuclear reactors in an attempt to obstruct the scientific and technological development in Iraq. . . . The Zionist entity, which is threatening Iraq, has possessed nuclear weapons for years and has refused to abide by the treaty for the nonproliferation of nuclear weapons."

Two days later, Foreign Trade Minister Jean-François Deniau visited Baghdad as head of the French delegation to the Franco–Iraqi joint committee. On his return home Deniau declared, "France regards the tempest around the supply of the nuclear reactor to Iraq as terminated."

If Israel needed any further vindication of its anxieties, that was provided on August 5 by an impartial authority. The son of Nobel laureate Jean Perrin and himself one of France's leading nuclear physicists, François Perrin had played a crucial role in building up France's independent nuclear Force de Frappé. Perrin told a *France-Soir* interviewer that Osirak could serve for plutonium production in spite of not having been designed for that purpose. Perrin proved his point by citing India, which had followed precisely that course. For Iraq, "this is a question of prestige." Atomic weapons are the most powerful means of international blackmail. Anyone possessing such weapons could threaten to employ them if his demands were not met promptly. From Israel's viewpoint, Perrin said, Iraq's possession of nuclear arms implied direct blackmail.

On August 4, French National Assembly Deputy Didier Bariani addressed a question to the Foreign Minister querying Iraq's willingness to fulfill its obligations, which were in any case "precarious" because whenever the Iraqis decided to disregard them Baghdad would retain sufficient enriched uranium for construction of a nuclear bomb.

Predictably, Foreign Minister François-Poncet defended his government's policy, attempting to reassure Israel by pointing out that research reactors the world over use similar uranium. He added that Iraq was perfectly entitled to employ nuclear energy for peaceful purposes. France scrupulously observed all the rules of international nuclear commerce, he said.

That same month, the menacing conglomerate comprising the French reactor and the Italian hot cells was mentioned in Congress. One year earlier, on the initiative of Congresswoman Millicent Fenwick, the House of Representatives had branded Iraq "a supporter of international terrorism" whereupon any American export exceeding $7 million required prior approval by the foreign relations committees of both houses of Congress.

Shortly after adoption of that measure, Italy sought to buy eight General Electric gas turbine engines to install in frigates being constructed for the Iraqi fleet in Italian shipyards. In January 1980, the Carter Administration approved the sale without first notifying the congressional committees, and a storm erupted in Congress. In June 1980, members of the foreign-relations and banking committees of both houses sent a sharply worded letter to President Carter, voicing their objections to the sale. The letter mentioned that on April 7 a PLO group backed by Iraq had attacked the children's nursery of Kibbutz Misgav Am in Upper Galilee, resulting in the deaths of three civilians and injuries to sixteen. The Administration's consent to sale of the engines "clearly violates a provision of law . . . Iraq has long been considered as one of the prime supporters of terrorist activity."

Senator Richard Stone of Florida, a member of the Foreign Relations Committee, urged the Senate to direct the President to withdraw the permit issued to General Electric. None of the senators objected. Behind-the-scenes contacts between Stone and Congressman Jonathan Bingham of New York, a veteran member of the House Foreign Relations Committee and a vigorous opponent of the Arab boycott against Israel, brought up a further idea: Congress would meet the Administration halfway with regard to the engine sale, on condition that Italy call off its nuclear aid to Iraq.

"I said to Senator Stone," Bingham recalled, "that I felt the danger to Israel from Iraq's acquisition of a nuclear-weapons capability was infinitely greater than the threat posed by the acquisition of . . . frigate engines, and that therefore the most important thing was for the United States to try to persuade Italy to cease or drastically limit its cooperation with Iraq in the nuclear field."

In the first week of August, the Italian government gave the Carter Administration an undertaking (in writing, according to one source, verbal according to another) to discharge all obligations arising from its signature of the NPT.

The Administration attempted to convince Bingham that the Italian response was "better than expected," and various reports claim that he agreed; but Bingham himself later denied buying the Administration's story. "The Italian pledge was never very specific and was not really satisfactory. Such as it was, it was made at the highest level of the Italian government, and was not effectively relayed to the technicians and others working on the export of a hot cell and other nuclear cooperation with Iraq."

Richard Stone added, "I was not satisfied that the Italians would follow through on their oral assurances of tight supervision of Iraq's nuclear program. This was the major concern. The nuclear materials which the Italians were giving to the Iraqis were extremely important, and I did not feel comfortable with the degree of their supervision promised by the Italians."

The engines were ultimately sold to Italy and duly installed in the Iraqi frigates. But just as Bingham and Stone had feared, Italy continued to supply Iraq with nuclear equipment and technology, sheltering behind the pretext of "international supervision." What clinched the matter as far as the Italians were concerned was a gigantic arms deal, principally for naval equipment, for which Italy would be paid in Iraqi oil.

At the same time, Iraq made preparations for ridding itself of international encumbrances and restrictions. On August 17, 1980, RCC secretary Tark Hamed issued a dramatic appeal to Arab nuclear experts to take up residence in his country and take part in Iraq's nuclear program.

Two days later, in an address at a Baghdad housing project, Saddam Hussain threatened Israel in terms not heard for a long time. He referred to the recent decision by Iraq and Saudi Arabia to boycott any country which transferred its embassy from Tel Aviv to Jerusalem—from which one might deduce that the Arab–Israeli conflict hinged solely upon Jerusalem, and that the Arabs were willing to recognize Tel Aviv as Israel's capital. Hussain expressly denied this interpretation, adding that the best thing would be to "destroy Tel Aviv with bombs. But we have to use the weapons available until it is actually possible to respond to the enemy with bombs." He reiterated his pledge that "when the time comes for Iraq to vent its anger on the Zionist entity, it will do so."

The U.S. State Department sharply denounced these statements, but Hussain ignored the rebuke. On August 25, in his closing address to the national convention of the Union of Iraqi Workers' Organizations, he reiterated his pledge: "The Arab nation will without doubt defeat the Zionist enemy, after eliminating the divisive factors and achieving scientific and technological parity with the Zionist enemy."

15 "You'd better believe it!"

During the second half of August 1980, authoritative confirmation of Iraq's pursuit of a military nuclear option was laid before the Senate Foreign Relations Committee when the chairman of its Mideastern subcommittee, Richard Stone, convened it for a confidential hearing attended by scientists from California's Livermore Laboratories, among the most outstanding nuclear research centers in the West. At the scientists' request, no record was kept of their presentations. But they are known to have expressed their conviction that, under the guise of "legitimate" objectives, Iraq was making unabashed efforts to achieve a military nuclear capability. By the mideighties Iraq would be capable of mounting a test detonation of a nuclear device similar to the one set off by India in 1974. As for operational military applications, these might be delayed by a few years, due to the technical difficulties involved in constructing a bomb. Attainment of the aim Iraq had set itself depended solely upon the resources it channeled to that end. The United States could do nothing to thwart Iraqi ambitions, whose perilous consequences could be avoided only by diplomatic efforts to steer Baghdad toward moderation and "a more responsible attitude."

The mere notion would have brought a smile to the lips of Saddam Hussain.

The new Israeli ambassador to France was Dr. Meir Rosenne, a former Foreign Ministry legal adviser and an expert negotiator (he took part in the "Kilometer 101" talks with Egypt after the 1973 Yom Kippur War and helped formulate the Camp David Accords). Shortly after his arrival in Paris, Rosenne approached the French government, repeating his predecessor's appeals to halt or limit nuclear aid to Iraq. All he got were evasive answers, and advice such as "You should show more concern over developments in Pakistan." He was told that uranium purchased from Niger by Libya had been transferred to Pakistan.

• • •

Work on the Iraqi reactor advanced at a rapid tempo. So did preparations for Israel's aerial strike.

On August 23, the Israeli Air Force held a preliminary model test attack, with the planes staying in the air for a lengthy time.

On August 28 *New Scientist* reported: "Iraq is on the brink of acquiring the expertise and the technology it needs to join the nuclear club." Citing "a reliable source in Iraq's nuclear community," the journal claimed that Iraq now has "enough enriched uranium to meet its needs." Predictably, the Iraqi source denied that his country wished "to build or to stockpile atomic bombs," saying that it merely sought to possess "the technology and expertise to make this possible."

The reply from Italian Foreign Minister Emilio Colombo to his Israeli colleague's July 20 letter reached Shamir on September 4. The lengthy time lapse in itself indicates that Italy did not share Israel's grave view of developments in Iraq. If Shamir hoped that his impassioned personal appeal would spur Rome into a turnabout, he was in for a disappointment. Colombo persisted in the tone now drearily familiar: part denials, equivocation and a legalistic smokescreen.

Colombo recalled that his country's Atomic Energy Commission had concluded a framework agreement with its Iraqi counterpart for scientific and technological cooperation. In the wake of the 1975 agreement, Iraq contracted with an Italian company for the supply of five laboratories, of which only one, for nuclear radiochemistry, had been delivered. (The letter failed to mention that, of the five, this was the most important, being designed for the extraction of plutonium from the spent fuel rods.)

"The Italian government," Colombo went on, "is vigorously opposed to dissemination of military nuclear technology. Italy's decision in favor of nuclear cooperation with Iraq rested in part on that country being among the few Mideastern states which had signed and ratified the NPT." (This was an open jibe at Israel, which refused to sign the Non-Proliferation Treaty as long as its own existence was not recognized by its Arab neighbors; even so, Israel had repeatedly proclaimed its willingness to declare the Mideast a nuclear-free zone.)

"We have thoroughly examined the Israeli concerns brought to our attention," Colombo went on. "It transpired that the technical traits of the Italian laboratory delivered to Iraq fall short of the equipment supplied by France and the Soviet Union, as testified by the fact that the Italian facility was not subject to IAEA supervision, and there had never been any comment thereupon."

(This was a typical piece of diplomatic doubletalk. It goes without saying that, on its own, a nuclear reactor poses a greater threat than an unsupplemented radiochemical laboratory—but the combination of the two is a double menace. As for the IAEA's nonsupervision of the Italian laboratories, that could be attributed to the clumsy bureaucratic procedures prevalent in the agency, whose experts' tardiness in grasping the dangers inherent in the reactor hot-cell complex delayed the listing of the Italian laboratories among the facilities requiring supervision.)

Replying to Shamir's query about Italy's intention of selling to Iraq a high-output reactor operating on natural uranium and heavy water, Colombo stated that a preliminary survey by the Iraqi government had indeed led it to the conclusion that it required such a reactor for its long-term energy program, but, he said, it should not be deduced therefrom that Italy intended to supply Iraq with such a reactor in the near future.

The letter concluded with the conventional diplomatic formula: "I hope the information I have provided will assuage your concerns, of which you can be sure the Italian government is aware."

It goes without saying that the letter failed to assuage Shamir's concerns. The Israelis merely noted that the Italians had taken a leaf out of the French book with regard to prevarication.

Not resting content with official diplomatic channels, Israel conveyed updated information and assessments to Italy's security agencies. But the response was cautious and conditional: If there were indications that Italy had misjudged the significance of its aid to Iraq, or concerning Iraqi intentions in relation to that aid, it would be necessary to suspend nuclear links with Iraq.

Israeli efforts to curtail French aid to Iraq's nuclear program included a bid to recruit the services of West German Chancellor Helmut Schmidt. Schmidt was in continual contact with Giscard on a variety of bilateral and international issues, and the two leaders were known to be on excellent personal terms; if the Chancellor intervened on Israel's behalf, the French President could hardly ignore his appeal. In approaching Schmidt—a former Wehrmacht officer though never a Nazi Party member—it was probably assumed that he would display sensitivity on a matter which jeopardized the survival of the Jewish state.

Israel's ambassador to Bonn, Yohanan Meroz, accordingly met with the head of Schmidt's office; submitting detailed and well-documented information on France's nuclear aid to Iraq, he requested Schmidt's intervention with the French President. The official conveyed the material, and the accompanying request, to the Chancellor.

On September 4, Meroz was summoned to meet with the Chancellor, who, while employing diplomatic terms, proceeded to make it plain that there was nothing doing. Schmidt claimed that he had put out cautious feelers in Paris but had decided against active intervention. I understand Israel's concern, said the Chancellor, but the Franco–Iraqi agreement is signed and sealed; any attempt at intervention now is liable to damage West Germany's relations with France, as well as harm current efforts toward a rapprochement between the United States and Iraq.

Schmidt repeated the French claim to have subjected the reactor to all the precautions necessary and feasible. Paris was convinced it had total control and supervision of the reactor—"to the extent that agreements and undertakings have any value," Schmidt added prudently. The Chancellor did not disregard the danger of the Mideast becoming a nuclear arsenal—a horrifying thought, he said; nevertheless, he advised Israel to rest content with France's pledges.

After attempting to point out the basic error in the Chancellor's deductions, Meroz realized that it was hopeless. "France's promises must suffice," Schmidt insisted. "I do not see what can be done now."

"At least be good enough to appeal to France to tighten up its supervision of the reactor," the ambassador requested.

"I'll think about it," the Chancellor replied. "I do not promise."

Israel's campaign against the Iraqi nuclear program had hitherto been conducted behind closed doors. But the international media were given various signals of Israel's resolve to deny Iraq a military nuclear option.

On September 14, 1980, Deputy Defense Minister Mordechai Zippori issued one such warning by means of an American newspaper: "If it is impossible to halt the Iraqi program by diplomatic means, Israel will have to reconsider its options." The message was plain: if diplomacy failed, Israel would resort to other means.

Zippori's warning coincided with an interview to the Kuwaiti *al-Kabass* by Dr. Ibrahim Hamouda, chairman of Egypt's Atomic Energy Commission: "If Iraq succeeds in realizing its plans, by 1985 it may be capable of detonating a nuclear device." His prediction was an ironical comment on the denials and evasions emanating from France and Italy.

In September 1980, Foreign Minister Shamir arrived in the United States to attend the UN General Assembly. But most of his visit was devoted to diplomatic efforts to counter Iraq's nuclear project.

On September 18 he held a meeting with Secretary of State Edmund Muskie. Shamir was accompanied by Ambassador Ephraim Evron, Washington Minister Yaakov Nehushtan and aides. Muskie was likewise backed by a large team of advisers.

Shamir voiced Israel's dismay over Iraq's nuclear program and the aid it drew from France and Italy. I do not know, said Shamir, whether the United States is capable of influencing France and Italy, but there is a clear need for action. Israel regards developments in Iraq as a threat to its very existence.

Muskie replied that the United States, being equally concerned, had voiced its anxieties to the governments of France and Italy. But the Europeans claimed that their nuclear ties with Iraq were restricted to delivery of research facilities and the fuel required for their operation, and that under no circumstances would they assist Iraq in achieving a weapons capability. On this matter, Muskie admitted outright that, in spite of being the leader of the West, the world's greatest superpower did not wield unlimited power. We are unable to judge, he said, whether the promises of France and Italy are genuine.

Undersecretary of State for Political Affairs David D. Newsom conceded that there was a problem concerning European deliveries of nuclear materials to certain countries whose motives were questionable. The current Administration had put nonproliferation high on its list of priorities.

The Americans reported on their talks with various European countries about nuclear-fuel sales to Pakistan and Iraq. The Europeans insisted that adequate precautions had been taken to prevent the reactors being put to military use, but the Americans did not quite go along with these claims. Washington questioned the efficacy of the safeguards imposed by the Europeans and made no secret thereof, Muskie's aide concluded.

Muskie confessed his own concern about the facilities the Italians were constructing in Iraq, and about Italy's capitulation to oil extortionism. He also admitted that international bodies experience difficulty in effective supervision of nuclear activity, because nuclear materials are available from a variety of sources, not all subject to control.

The Secretary of State promised that the United States would persist in its diplomatic efforts to convince France and Italy to halt, or at least cut back, their nuclear aid to Iraq. But he was careful to avoid fostering any illusions. "I assume," he said, "that we shall receive further promises; to what extent those promises can be considered adequate and satisfactory I do not know."

The meeting ended with an undertaking from Shamir that Israel would keep the United States up to date on all developments.

"In the free and easy atmosphere of a banquet," adviser Eytan Bentzur would recall later, "careful attention to the words of our hosts revealed their uncertainty as to the influence the United States could exercise on France in a matter so painful and perilous. In my heart, I doubted whether the current Administration, whose term of office was ending, would act with the vigor appropriate to and dictated by this matter."

The following day, September 19, Shamir met with Defense Secretary

Harold Brown and pointed out that Iraq's nuclear program ought to be a source of anxiety to the United States no less than to Israel. Brown, himself a nuclear scientist by training, did not argue the point. He promised that the United States would persist in its pressure on its European allies. The Administration would point out to them, he said, the dangers involved in Iraq's advance toward a weapons capability, even if that advance was at an apparent snail's pace.

But Brown likewise refrained from holding out false hopes. He admitted that America had no direct influence on Iraq, which received no U.S. economic aid and bought its arms in the Soviet Union or Western Europe. The only course open to the United States was that of diplomatic efforts in the European countries.

Shamir now began to prepare for his crucial meeting with another prospective participant at the UN General Assembly: French Foreign Minister Jean François-Poncet.

That personage had meanwhile engaged in a tempestuous exchange of letters with the chairman of the Israel-France Friendship Association, French war hero General Georges Laconte.

On August 11, Laconte wrote to François-Poncet posing pointed questions about France's nuclear aid to Iraq. He demanded to know why Iraq had been so outright in its rejection of France's offer to replace the 93-percent-grade uranium with the lower-grade Caramel, in view of the fact that the latter fuel was adequate for quite advanced scientific experiments and, moreover, cheaper.

It was September 16 before Laconte received the minister's reply. Referring to Caramel, François-Poncet argued that the fuel had yet to reach commercial production, and it was therefore out of the question to make binding promises about its delivery. Formally, that was correct, but the minister, like Laconte, knew that the argument ran well wide of the truth.

François-Poncet went on to promise that the guarantees provided to France would "make it possible without delay to detect any attempt to divert the material supplied to Iraq to military purposes" and would "in practice forestall any such attempt." Iraq's international commitments precluded its acquisition of nuclear arms and subjected all nuclear equipment and materials on its soil to supervision, he claimed. Elaborating on that supervision, the Foreign Minister listed the stock books which would register the incoming nuclear material, the automatic cameras to record everything going on at the reactor core, the lead seals on the fuel rods, the periodic visits of IAEA inspectors. All these safeguards would facilitate early detection of any suspicious use of the material, argued François-Poncet. There were, he claimed, no grounds for questioning the efficacy of such supervision, currently in force in respect of forty-seven countries. To date, no nuclear material in any state under IAEA supervision had been diverted for use in a nuclear explosion.

The minister also listed the safeguards and controls provided for by the Franco–Iraqi agreement of November 18, 1975. It was not credible that such a network of guarantees could fail to achieve its purpose, he wrote. Violation of these agreements, or their abrogation, would provide a clear signal to raise the alarm about the evil designs of those concerned, and the necessary conclusions would be drawn without delay or hesitation.

The letter was literally correct in every respect, but it overlooked Israel's most serious charge: unlike other countries, Iraq had demonstrated, by word and deed, that its ultimate aim was a military nuclear option. Consequently, as he read the Foreign Minister's reassurances, Laconte could only sigh and murmur a skeptical "You'd better believe it!"

16 "No Grounds for Concern"

On September 17, 1980, the Persian Gulf region erupted into war. Only a few years after signing his agreement with the Shah concerning joint use of the Shatt-al-Arab waterway, Saddam Hussain proclaimed its unilateral abrogation. Large forces of Iraqi armor, with massive air support, lunged into southern Iran, threatening that country's oil ports and coincidentally violating every international convention on the conduct of war.

The confrontation was between two leaders who recognized few inhibitions. Ayatollah Ruhollah Khomeini, Iran's glowering religious tyrant, was pitted against Saddam Hussain, who dreamed of Iraq's imperial hegemony over the Persian Gulf and the entire Middle East.

The direct pretext for the outbreak of hostilities was a years-long dispute over various stretches of territory on the border between the two countries, principally along the Shatt-al-Arab and in western Iran's Khuzistan. But the underlying reason arose from a thousand years of Arab–Persian hostility exacerbated by a violent religious dispute. Over half of Iraq's population belong—like the Iranians—to the Shi'ite sect of Islam; but military and political power in Iraq is the exclusive preserve of their Sunni Moslem rivals. In Khomeini's eyes, the Sunnis represented a heresy no less repugnant than Judaism or Christianity, while Saddam Hussain and his cronies were usurpers repressing the Shi'ite faithful.

Like most military observers the world over, Saddam Hussain was convinced that Iran's military might had been eroded by Khomeini's religious revolution. Many of Iran's senior officers had indeed been sentenced to death by revolutionary tribunals, while others fled or went into retirement; as a result, professional standards in the country's armed forces had plummeted. Ruptured relations with the West gave rise to a shortage of spare parts for planes and tanks, as well as grave maintenance problems. In view of Iran's predicament, Saddam Hussain found this an opportune moment to fling his troops across the border.

To all those who had eyes to see, Hussain's aggression demonstrated the worth he attached to his own undertakings, as well as highlighting his political and military objectives. But the French government kept its eyes firmly shut and adhered stubbornly to its own agreements with Iraq.

Two days after the outbreak of fighting, Foreign Minister François-Poncet held a press conference in New York, where he was attending the UN General Assembly. In reply to a question, the minister said that his country's nuclear cooperation with Iraq would proceed normally, since it "pursued purely peaceful purposes."

The same day, the French official gazette published the minister's reply to a question submitted by Senator François Palméro of the Gaullist party, about French deliveries of weapons-grade uranium to Iraq. The reply— again belated—argued in substance that supplying highly enriched uranium was "not an exceptional act." The uranium delivery corresponded "exclusively to the needs of the research reactor supplied" to Iraq, was "programmed accordingly" and was "encompassed by all necessary safeguards."

In publishing question and answer, the French press did not neglect to note that the uranium supplied to Iraq was "usable for military purposes."

Iraq's invasion of Iran could have been expected to strengthen Shamir's hand when he met France's François-Poncet in New York. Now that Hussain had disowned a formal agreement with Iran and subjected that country to an unprovoked onslaught, it would be pertinent to demand what guarantees France had that the Iraqi tyrant would live up to his nuclear commitments. Shamir had learned on good authority of the French government's secret decision—adopted after the outbreak of the Gulf War—to evacuate its scientists and technicians from al-Tuweitha, thereby leaving the reactor without supervision.

Yet in spite of all this, the September 26 meeting did not live up to Shamir's expectations. It turned out to be nothing more than a rerun of previous exchanges on the same topic and, like its predecessors, a grievous disappointment to Israel.

Shamir commenced by pointing out that Iraq, not having signed the 1949 armistice, still regarded itself as being at war with Israel. Saddam Hussain aspired to inherit the mantle of Gamal Abdel Nasser as the acknowledged leader of the Arab world, and his ambitions were an unfailing source of strife. Iraq is rich enough to purchase anything money can buy. In recent years, the Iraqis had channeled enormous sums to acquisition of nuclear equipment, materials and knowhow. The enriched uranium in Iraq's possession provided an almost immediate option for construction of a bomb; even if Baghdad chose the longer and surer "plutonium course," it could possess its first nuclear weapon by 1985. The matter was made even more complicated by the war with Iran and the consequent withdrawal of Western scientific and technical staff, demolishing France's claim to exercise strict control over the reactor and its equipment.

François-Poncet prefaced his reply with the traditional "I comprehend your concern," to which he appended the equally traditional "but in my opinion it is groundless." His country supplied Iraq with nuclear knowhow, material and equipment "exclusively for research purposes." Osirak, "like research reactors the world over," employed highly enriched uranium, but enormous amounts of that fuel—far more than Iraq possessed—were required for construction of a bomb. The fuel rods underwent irradiation, which made them unsuitable for such a purpose (the minister neglected to mention that to anyone in possession of a hot cell the rods were an excellent source of plutonium). All in all, France could not disown its obligations toward Iraq. As evidence of his government's sensitivity and balanced judgment, François-Poncet recalled its negotiations with Pakistan over delivery of nuclear equipment and technology. "The moment we got confirmation of our suspicions that the Pakistanis intended to manufacture a nuclear bomb, we called the deal off." The minister conveniently overlooked Pakistan's lack of the oil weapon brandished so effectively by Saddam Hussain.

Contacts with Baghdad had not kindled French suspicions. "Iraq has no intention of constructing nuclear weapons—not now, at least." François-Poncet conceded that no one could offer assurances about the distant future, but Israel's proposal, effectively denying nuclear knowhow and technology to Iraq, was "unacceptable to France." Israel's concerns were understandable, but France could not undertake to act in accordance with them, particularly as they were unfounded, the minister claimed. "I have personally examined the file," he said, "and found no grounds for anxiety."

In spite of the evident determination behind his colleague's courteous tone, Shamir did not give up easily. If it were only a matter of Iraq's nuclear cooperation with France, he said, Israel might content itself with such explanations. But the matter was far more complex. Alongside its purchases in France, Iraq had ordered radiochemical laboratories in Italy and was conducting secret contacts for similar deals in Brazil. In combination, these transactions posed a grave threat to Israel.

Such a formulation ought to have been a clear signal to the French Foreign Minister that Israel did not intend to sit idle. International law recognizes the right of a state so threatened to take the necessary steps, including resort to arms, to defend itself. Shamir could safely assume that François-Poncet, as the latest in a long family line of French diplomats, would get the message.

Abandoning chilly courtesy, the French minister now went over to the attack. First, if Iraq had nuclear links with other states, why was Israel directing its fire exclusively at the Franco–Iraqi deal? Second, Iraq had signed the NPT, "unlike certain other states." It would be hard to imagine Iraq violating the Non-Proliferation treaty, he argued, pointing out that Israel, a nonsignatory, had a nuclear program of its own.

Shamir denied that Iraq's adherence to the NPT offered any guarantee. Israel, he said, was familiar with Saddam Hussain's declarations about acquiring nuclear arms and about resolving the Zionist problem. Shamir seized the opportunity to recall that Prime Minister Raymond Barre had given directives to bypass a specific decision of the National Assembly forbidding French companies to capitulate to the Arab boycott against Israel.

"That is an internal French matter," François-Poncet muttered tersely.

The meeting with the French Foreign Minister having proved fruitless, Shamir could claim no greater success in his subsequent encounter with his Italian colleague, Emilio Colombo.

Developments in Iraq, Shamir told the Italian minister, called for an urgent reassessment of Iraq's intentions with regard to development of nuclear facilities. But Colombo obstinately refused to budge from the terms of his September 4 letter.

Despondent and uneasy, Shamir reported to Begin on his conversations, which testified that the moral principles to which European politicians paid such eloquent lip service were heavily outweighed by their greed for Iraqi oil and lucrative contracts for nuclear equipment. Like several of his Cabinet colleagues, Shamir sensed that European cynicism left Israel with no choice other than the one it had repeatedly adopted in the past: to take its fate into its own hands.

On September 20, Israel television screened an interview with Major General Eytan. The Commander in Chief spoke principally about the implications for Israel of the Iraq–Iran war. Referring to the Iraqi reactor, he said: "At present, we are following developments."

A leak from French sources now confirmed what Israel already knew: the French government had withdrawn most of its scientific and technical staff from al-Tuweitha, leaving behind a few volunteers who, for handsome remuneration, had consented to stay on and prevent radioactive contamination in the event of the reactor being bombed. The same sources also reported that the French technicians had halted tests on the first delivery of enriched uranium. On September 22, the fuel rods were housed for safekeeping in Transit Channel 2 within the reactor structure. Prior to being stored, the rods were irradiated sufficiently to render them unfit for use in a uranium bomb, though that, of course, did not preclude their use for plutonium production when the Italian hot cells went into operation.

On September 25, Iraqi Deputy Prime Minister Tarik Aziz came to Paris on an urgent mission for Saddam Hussain. Aziz's report to the French leaders about the outbreak of hostilities with Iran also touched upon the dangers now facing the reactor. Al-Tuweitha was too far from the border to suffer Iranian artillery bombardment, but Iran's Air Force was quite capable of attempting to bomb the site.

Indeed, on September 27—just as Israeli Military Intelligence Director Saguy, in conversation with an Israeli journalist, was expressing his surprise at Iran's failure to attack al-Tuweitha—Iranian warplanes circled the reactor and fired missiles at it. The Iranians launched a further strike at the reactor on September 30, and there were even reports of a third raid. But the Iranian pilots were unsuccessful. There was some damage to pumps and pipes in the cooling tower designed for storage of radioactive waste, and to the structure for treatment of the waste; but the more sensitive equipment remained intact, as did the cores of both reactors. All the damage inflicted—to a value of no more than a few million dollars—was superficial and would scarcely delay completion of the project.

Suspicions were voiced in Iraq—and in France—that the attacking planes came, not from Iran, but from Israel. Iraqi Defense Minister Ednan Hirallal Talpeh openly accused Israel of having a hand in the raid—a view secretly shared by the French Premier and several of his chief aides. Similar hypotheses were aired in the media. In a comprehensive article on the Iran–Iraq war published in the London-based Arabic paper a Shark al-Aussat, Fawzi al-Asmar alleged Israeli involvement in the raid. The charge surfaced again on October 16 when the BBC's Outlook magazine featured an interview with Paul Webster, Paris correspondent for the Manchester Guardian, who cited "evidence . . . coming from the French intelligence services" to back up his claim that the September 30 rocket attack was carried out by two U.S.-built Phantoms which, though "unidentified," came from the Israeli Air Force. Webster backed up his claim by circumstantial evidence: the reactor had been "a point of tension between France and Israel now for four or five years," he pointed out. Fearing that Tammuz would "one day be used to help Iraq develop nuclear weapons," Israel was determined to destroy it before it came into operation. Webster recalled the sabotage of the reactor core eighteen months previously, attributing it to "Israeli agents." He also referred to the murder of the Iraqi nuclear project's director, Meshad, "and again a shadow of the Israelis does seem behind it."

As was to be expected, Israel emphatically denied all these charges. Several months later, when Israel set out in earnest to destroy the reactor, the results far exceeded those achieved by the Iranian raids—clear testimony that the earlier accusations had been unfounded.

In a press interview, Military Intelligence Director Saguy claimed that

Iraqi plans for early activation of the reactor had been postponed due to the Gulf War. Recalling Israel's assessment of the timetable for the nuclear project, Saguy predicted that Iraq could be in possession of nuclear weapons by the mideighties. He defined the reactor as "a prime Iraqi strategic objective," adding, "Nuclear weapons in the hands of an intransigent and bloodthirsty ruler like Saddam Hussain constitute a threat to all the states in the region, including Iran, Saudi Arabia and Kuwait." Saguy's words may have been designed to spur Iran on to greater efforts toward destroying the reactor. But it soon became evident that Israel could not pin its hopes on others.

Unrelated to the Iranian air attacks, Washington columnist Jack Anderson reported on a special Pentagon investigation which foresaw an Israeli preemptive strike aimed at the utter destruction of the Iraqi reactor. Defense Department intelligence (which is distinct from the Central Intelligence Agency) was convinced that Iraq would be the first Arab state to build up a nuclear arsenal, and that it could have a number of nuclear warheads ready for deployment as early as 1981!

Anderson's revelations caused less concern in Baghdad than did the war with Iran, which was not unfolding as foreseen. The Iraqi Army was advancing, leaving a wake of blood and devastation, but the Iranian forces were a long way from surrender. Iran's deficiencies in equipment, ammunition and arms, and the faulty maintainance of its military machine, were more than compensated for by the fanatic zeal of Khomeini's revolutionary guards.

Iran's raids on the reactor were a source of profound anxiety to Iraq. Its costliest and most prestigious project, the mainstay of Saddam Hussain's dream of becoming a new all-Arab caliph, was in danger of destruction. The Iranians therefore took various steps to dissuade Iran from persisting in its attacks on al-Tuweitha. On September 27, Deputy Prime Minister Tarik Aziz went out of his way to tell a Jordanian interviewer that Iraq's principal war effort was directed, not at Iran, but "against the Zionist foe." On October 4, an editorial in the official Baghdadi al-Jumhuriya declared: "The nuclear reactor cannot be a threat to Iran because Iraq looks upon the Iranian people as brethren. . . . The Zionist entity is the one that fears the Iraqi nuclear reactor . . . [which] constitutes a grave danger for 'Israel.'" The same day, another Iraqi paper, ath-Thawra, wrote: "The Iranian people should not fear the Iraqi nuclear reactor, which is not intended to be used against Iran, but against the Zionist enemy."

Ath-Thawra, echoed by Iraq's official news agency, openly implied that Israel had abetted Iran's attack on the reactor. This falsehood was, of course, aimed at embarrassing the Iranians by depicting them as undermining Iraq's military preparations against Israel.

• • •

That same day, Foreign Minister Shamir met with the French President. Giscard d'Estaing proffered a specific pledge: "The moment we sense that Iraq is turning to production of nuclear weapons, we shall prevent it." But he rejected a direct Israeli request for an immediate halt on transfer of material or knowhow liable to carry Iraq beyond the point of no return in its nuclear-weapons program.

In the meantime, French newspapers, citing returning French technicians, reported on modifications already effected in the design of the small Tammuz 2 to adapt it to plutonium production. There was a further outcry in France when it emerged that the 12 kilograms of enriched uranium withdrawn from the reactor core at the outbreak of hostilities, and as yet unirradiated, had been entrusted to the Iraqis, in flagrant violation of express promises that the fuel rods would be under constant French supervision. National Assembly Deputy Paul Quilès, who had already submitted parliamentary questions about France's nuclear cooperation with Iraq, now demanded to know how supervision of the enriched uranium left in Iraq was being exercised when almost all the French technicians had quit that country.

The reply Quilès received was innocent—or coy: Foreign Minister François-Poncet explained that international supervision of the reactor "continues to be exercised by the inspections and verifications with which the IAEA is entrusted." Departing from the traditional French answer which invariably pointed to the presence of French technicians as a further safeguard, the minister claimed on this occasion that "control of peaceful use does not require resort to French technicians."

In the meantime, in apparent consequence of the talks with the Iraqi Deputy Prime Minister, France began to work out a new timetable for activation of the reactor. As already noted, the Iranian raids had inflicted nothing more than superficial damage; repairs, French experts believed, could easily be completed by November 1981. Furthermore, there having been no damage to the sensitive portions—above all, to the core itself—Iraqi contractors were capable of effecting the repairs unaided.

17 "The Choice of Two Evils"

"The problem is complex, and a word to the wise is sufficient..." So wrote Prime Minister Begin in a note to Knesset Foreign Affairs and Defense Committee member Yosef Rom when the latter expressed his conviction that the newly erupted Gulf War offered a good opportunity for destroying the reactor. At a committee meeting held shortly after the eruption of the Iraq–Iran war, Rom, reluctant to raise the matter overtly, conveyed his opinion in a note to Begin. The Iraqi reactor would continue to function, wrote Rom, coincidentally with, and in spite of, the war.

Aeronautics Professor Rom, an Israel Prize laureate, had unwittingly expressed Begin's own view. The time had come, the Prime Minister decided in the second half of October 1980, to reach decisions. With regard to Iraq's course toward a nuclear-weapons option, Begin entertained no further illusions about blocking action by international authorities. Activation of the reactor was merely a matter of time, whether two years or a few months.

The General Staff had decided in principle that, if directed to destroy the reactor, it would delegate the task to the Air Force. Planning the operation now became the principal occupation of the Air Force's new head of operations, Colonel Ahiam Tzur.*

On October 14, Begin summoned a group of ministers to consider the issue. In addition to participants in earlier discussions—Yadin, Ehrlich, Sharon, Hurwitz, Burg and Zippori—the group was now joined by Justice Minister Moshe Nissim, Education Minister Zvulun Hammer, Health Minister Eliezer Shostak and Foreign Minister Yitzhak Shamir. Also attending

*Fictitious name.

were the Commander in Chief, the Air Force commander, heads of the Mossad and Military Intelligence, and others.

It was Begin's regular habit in such deliberations to listen to other opinions before voicing his own views. But on this occasion he departed from his usual custom by initiating the discussion, with the declaration "We have the choice of two evils."

The first "evil" was an attack on the reactor, with the risk of adverse reactions. Iraq was at war with Iran, hopes of a rapid victory had failed to materialize, and its military situation was deteriorating; but an Israeli attack on the reactor could induce Iraq to direct its military might against Israel, an end for which Baghdad might even make its peace with Syria.

Consideration should also be given to the Egyptian position. Egypt was awaiting April 26, 1982, the date of Israel's final withdrawal from Sinai under the peace treaty between the two countries. An Israeli attack on the Iraqi reactor could in no way be interpreted as a violation of that treaty, and Cairo was aware that in the event of an Egyptian violation Israel would respond accordingly; nevertheless, Sadat's reaction to a strike at the reactor was impossible to predict. The operation was, therefore, risky.

The second "evil": to refrain from action; in other words, to sit by idly and do nothing to prevent Iraq's continued efforts toward manufacture of nuclear weapons.

After thorough consideration, Begin declared, "I have come to the conclusion that we must choose the first of the two evils. Why? First, because now is an opportune moment. The Gulf War has weakened Iraq and has also put a halt to work at the reactor, which is still 'cold.' That means it is feasible to bomb it without the risk of radioactive contamination of its vicinity. Who knows if such an opportune moment will recur? It must be clear that if Israel does not prevent it, Iraq will manufacture nuclear weapons. Everything points to that. Saddam Hussain is a vicious and bloodthirsty tyrant. Why does he need a nuclear reactor, and nuclear weapons?" Begin left his rhetorical question unanswered, but its thrust was unassailably clear.

"Somewhere in the vicinity of Baghdad," the Prime Minister concluded, "weapons of mass destruction are being prepared for use against us. Are we at liberty to sit by with folded arms in view of that terrible danger? It is our duty to our people to take the risk—and act."

Agriculture Minister Ariel Sharon wasted no time in concurring with the Prime Minister's view. The Gulf War provided an opportunity to act against Iraq's attempt to construct nuclear weapons, which should be seen as a *casus belli*. "We will come to no harm if we destroy the reactor," Sharon reassured his colleagues. "When Iran attacked the reactor and Iraq accused us, the world was not shocked. Nor is there any point in dissembling. The main thing is to act, thus forewarning any Arab state against embarking upon a similar adventure."

The opposing view was voiced by Deputy Prime Minister Yigael Yadin, who counseled against haste in reaching a decision. "Israel's present situation is very good: the Arab states are fragmented and divided, and the Gulf War is the best evidence thereof. The Israeli–Egyptian peace treaty has exacerbated conflicts within the Arab world. It is vital to maintain a policy which guarantees peace to Israel, and not take drastic action which will unite the entire Arab world against us. It cannot long be concealed that it was Israel which destroyed the reactor, and that will lead the Arab states to a general reconciliation and to unification against 'the Zionist menace.' Furthermore," Yadin pointed out, "there is no historical precedent for the destruction of a reactor. How will the superpowers react? What will the Americans say? What will Israel do if the bombing should prompt the Soviet Union to step up its active aid to the Arab states? The risk is not worth taking: the reactor is not in operation at present. By the time it is activated —no one knows when that will be—diplomatic pressure can be renewed on Iraq and its Western nuclear partners." Yadin urged Begin to submit the issue to the full Cabinet.

Begin hastened to respond: "If this group of ministers supports that proposal, I'll convene the full Cabinet."

Begin's other deputy, Simha Ehrlich, supported the Prime Minister's view. "There are risks," conceded the ever prudent Ehrlich, "but standing by idly involves greater risks. We have no response other than seizing on this present opportunity to bomb the reactor. I do not believe in a Mideastern 'balance of terror' similar to that prevailing between the two global blocs. Matters are different here: if the Iraqis get nuclear weapons, they are quite capable of using them."

The veteran Dr. Burg supported Yadin's position. "The risks," he argued, "outweigh the prospects. Bombing the reactor will not foil Arab efforts to acquire nuclear arms. At most, it will obstruct the process without halting it. On the contrary: the proposed operation will unify the Arab world against Israel, overcoming its present polarization." Burg too inclined to the view that the final decision should be left to the full Cabinet.

Disagreements were not confined to the ministers; there was an equal lack of unanimity among the experts Begin had insisted on inviting. Opposition to the proposed attack came from Mossad chief Hoffy, from Military Intelligence Director Saguy, from the head of the Defense Ministry's national-security unit, General Avraham Tamir, and from other officers.

Their deputies held the opposite view. Assistant Military Intelligence chief Brigadier Aviezer Ya'ari affirmed unreservedly that the bomb being prepared in Iraq was directed against Israel, not Iran. Hoffy's deputy at the Mossad argued that striking at Iraq would be a lesson to others.

Veteran General Avraham Tamir had taken a share in formulating Israel's military doctrine back in the fifties; he has authored numerous works on military theory, strategic planning, and assessment of diplomatic contacts. Tamir rested his opposition to the projected raid on these arguments: the reactor attack would precipitate nuclear development the world over, the Mideast included; delaying construction of Osirak by a few years would not prevent its completion in the future; as to radioactivity, the problem was not merely whether or not the reactor was "hot"; from the moment a reactor goes into operation and starts producing plutonium, three years must elapse before production of a nuclear bomb.

General Saguy expressed his foreboding that the reactor bombing would induce Iran and Iraq to bury the hatchet and direct their resources against Israel. Was it not preferable that they continue to slaughter one another for a further year or two?

The Commander in Chief had come well prepared. Major General Eytan's predictions were somber: "A nuclear balance implies accepting that Israel will not continue to exist. The Arabs are more capable than we of paying a heavy price, and it will therefore be impossible to deter them. The threat of a second-strike response—after we have taken an atomic bomb—implies a Samsonlike 'Let me die with the Philistines.'"

Begin exhibited respect for every viewpoint, whether favorable or not. But he was disturbed by the stubborn opposition of Yadin, whose declaration that he would not bear collective responsibility for a decision to attack the reactor foreshadowed a Cabinet crisis if it went through.

In the ensuing vote, the raid was endorsed by Begin, Shamir, Sharon, Ehrlich and Hurwitz. Yadin, Burg, Hammer and Shostak voted against it, demanding that a final decision be left to the full Cabinet.

Begin announced that he would convene the full Cabinet for comprehensive deliberations; subsequently, he would brief leaders of the Labor opposition.

Though convinced that military action against the reactor was now unavoidable, Begin nevertheless ordered further discreet diplomatic contacts with France. Israel continued to sound the alarm, while France continued to make reassuring noises. French officials reiterated their drearily familiar refrain: the uranium supplied to Iraq underwent irradiation which rendered it unfit for use as an explosive; the reactor was under the direct control of French experts, and subject to inspection by the IAEA. Further, the French dropped dark hints about the secrets of their agreement with Iraq. "If only you knew [its provisions], your anxieties would decrease or be banished altogether."

This bizarre contention could prompt the Israelis to nothing more than wry smiles: if matters were so rosy, why was the French government so obstinate in rejecting demands by politicians and journalists, French and foreign alike, for detailed publication of the agreement with Iraq?

French officials also attempted to channel Israeli anxieties toward more distant dangers, pointing out that Israel should be uneasy over France's help in training a new generation of Iraqi nuclear scientists and technicians. It goes without saying that this was a further source of Israeli concern, but it could not overshadow the immediate menace.

At this time, Ambassador Ephraim Evron in Washington received a detailed memorandum from Hanan Baron, deputy director-general of the Foreign Ministry, listing Iraq's nuclear efforts and their military significance. "Iraq now has 24–30 kilograms (!) of enriched military-grade uranium, which can serve for construction of a primitive nuclear weapon," the document warned, adding:

· Cooperation with Pakistan might offer Iraq a shortcut to a military nuclear option.
· Iraq could disown its commitments under the NPT, withdrawing its signature at three months' prior notice.
· Iraq was active in the international arena, striving to fend off outside pressures by seeking recognition that its nuclear program was for exclusively peaceful purposes.
· Iraq was making continual efforts to elicit a UN decision for a team of experts to inquire into "Israel's nuclear armament." Israel could be expected to reject such an inquiry, thereby granting the Iraqis an alibi for their own nuclear program.
· Iraq's professed interest in generating electricity from nuclear reactors should be rejected out of hand. First, Osiris was not designed for that purpose, nor could it serve as a training laboratory for familiarization with power reactors. Second, as one of the world's richest oil states, Iraq had not the least grounds for channeling such enormous resources to generating electricity by means of nuclear power.

On October 28, Begin summoned the Cabinet to his Jerusalem office for an extraordinary Tuesday meeting (regular Cabinet sessions are held on Sunday). One by one, the ministers took their seats in the heavily curtained conference chamber. The windows face south upon a magnificent vista: the Judaean hills, the Hebrew University, and Jerusalem's carefully tended residential neighborhoods. Within the chamber, the table bore the traditional refreshments: cheese sandwiches, olives, vegetables and fruit, coffee and tea.

The atmosphere was sober. The ministers knew that they had been summoned to weigh an issue of crucial importance for the future of their country.

Initiating the meeting, the Prime Minister said, "Gentlemen, today we are about to engage in a matter of life and death. I shall lay before you a topic of the highest confidentiality, and I adjure you to say not a word to anyone, whether in your homes or in your offices. This matter is among those known only to those required to know. I have no choice but to rely upon not one word leaking out of this closed room."

Those ministers who had attended earlier consultations concerning the reactor knew what Begin was referring to; the others listened intently.

Begin resumed: "A group of ministers has long been monitoring reports on the construction of the nuclear reactor in Iraq. Two weeks ago, I submitted a certain proposal to that group, most of whose members supported it. Before detailing the proposal, I shall call upon the experts to explain the matter to you."

In succession, the Commander in Chief, the director of Military Intelligence and the head of the Mossad now delivered concise reports on the Iraqi project—its construction, its military potential, the previous month's Iranian raid which had temporarily halted work at the site, and other developments.

Begin now resumed his presentation. "I want to put it in brief: a great clock is hanging over our heads, and it is ticking. Somewhere on the banks of the Tigris and the Euphrates, there are men plotting to annihilate us, and they are preparing the means for implementing their criminal design. Every passing day brings them closer to their goal.

"We must ask ourselves the significance of nuclear weapons being constructed by a state like Iraq. The significance is: a threat to the life of every man, woman and child in Israel. In another five years, or maybe just three years, the Iraqis will have two or three atomic bombs, each of the power of the bomb dropped on Hiroshima. Saddam Hussain is a bloodthirsty tyrant who seized power by killing his best friends with his own hands. He will not hesitate to employ weapons of mass destruction against us. We must take that as our point of departure. It is our duty toward the nation which elected us to conduct its affairs.

"Employment of such weapons against concentrations of our civilian population will entail bloodshed the like of which there has not been since 'those days' in the forties. In the face of such a danger, are we at liberty to sit with arms folded? Will we discharge our duty by acting in such a manner?

"If nuclear weapons fall into Iraqi hands, one of two things can happen: we shall be obliged to either surrender to their demands or run the risk of mass annihilation. Atrocious! We must ask ourselves: is there no way of preventing it? Since the day I learned of Iraq's intentions, the matter has given me no rest. We have done much to delay those preparations. But a nation does not live on borrowed time. The hour has come to reach a decision. To prevent the reconstruction of the reactor and its activation, there is no course other than military action, and that is the proposal I submitted recently to the group of ministers which has followed the matter. Military action naturally entails great risks, above all to those carrying out the operation. We shall do everything to reduce those risks to a minimum. In addition, there are political risks. It is necessary to take a calculated risk, and to realize that the risk of inaction exceeds the risk involved in acting. If the operation is followed by a diplomatic onslaught against us, we shall withstand it. Even if the enemy attempts a military response, it will be immeasurably less severe than the terrible danger in store for Israel should nuclear weapons fall into the enemy's hands. If we do not act now, we shall not be able to excise this terrible danger to ourselves and our children."

Begin made no explicit reference to a similar dilemma which had been posed seven years previously, when Egyptian and Syrian forces deployed for the assault which was to spark off the 1973 Yom Kippur War. A few hours before the impending attack, Golda Meir's Cabinet faced a painful choice: either to order a preemptive aerial strike, thereby incurring the risk of saddling Israel with the blame for unprovoked instigation of hostilities, or to withhold such action, so as to face the world with a clear conscience. As Begin's ministers now recalled, Golda Meir and her colleagues decided against a preemptive strike. While achieving undeniable political advantages, that decision certainly had a detrimental effect on the course of the war, particularly in the early days of the fighting, and probably took its toll of Israeli soldiers' lives.

With the historical analogy left unstated but nevertheless hovering in the shadows, Begin now urged the Cabinet to adopt a decision in principle, as recommended by a majority of the ministerial team, in favor of destroying the reactor. The details would be worked out by the same group of ministers, which reflected all the political hues represented in the ruling coalition.

In the ensuing discussion, the ministers touched upon every relevant aspect. Although the Prime Minister had flung the full weight of his authority behind the attack, he did not present it in a one-sided light. He now gave his colleagues free rein to express the full range of pros and cons. Every conceivable facet was illuminated: For or against the strike. When to launch it. Now, when the United States was embroiled in an election campaign? In the interim period between one American administration and the next? How would the United States react? Would the Russians rest content with verbal condemnation, or would they actively support Arab designs against Israel? Would the Arabs launch an all-out war? What would Egypt do? Would the Iraqis take it lying down, or would they respond by dispatching their Soviet-built long-range missiles toward Israel? Would another Arab state closer to Israel's borders volunteer to do so in place of Iraq? Would the enemy respond by attacking vital objectives in Israel?

Deputy Defense Minister Mordechai Zippori, one of the opponents of the proposed raid, espoused the proposal of Mossad chief Hoffy, who advocated preparation of a plan of action, meanwhile adopting a wait-and-see stance. The departure of the French experts had convinced Begin that now was the opportune moment (with foresight, he predicted that the Iraqis would not freeze construction of the reactor, and he called for early action so as to avoid casualties among the French technicians); but Zippori, departing from the identical premise, reached the diametrically opposite conclusion. Furthermore, he argued that destruction of the reactor would not stop the Arabs from "going nuclear." He rejected the view of the Commander in Chief, who warned of the extinction of Israel. "On the contrary: our overweening ambition is liable to induce the Arabs to manufacture bombs at remote sites."

Simha Ehrlich stuck to his guns: "The reactor is a danger to our existence. We are dutybound to destroy it."

Yadin dug in his heels with equal firmness: "Even experts such as the director of Military Intelligence and the head of the Mossad are opposed to the attack."

Military Intelligence Director Saguy was indeed most outspoken in his opposition, which he detailed in a document submitted to the Prime Minister, the Foreign Minister and the Commander in Chief. Saguy denied that nuclear weapons in the hands of an Arab state implied the end for Israel. Even if the reactor were destroyed, production of nuclear weapons would be resumed, either by Iraq or by some other Arab state. Furthermore, Saguy argued, Israel could survive even if confronted with a nuclear threat; the Arabs would have to learn that any weapons they got their hands on could almost certainly be acquired by Israel. Saguy also cited a professional opinion which denied that Iraq could manufacture nuclear weapons before the early nineties. Saguy made no secret of his apprehension about the response of the Americans, and that of the Arabs. The Prime Minister wished to bomb the reactor before it became hot, to preclude massive loss of life through radiation; but the Arabs were not guided by such considerations. Saguy was convinced that there were other ways of blocking Iraq's nuclear development.

Shamir sided with Begin, denying that the diplomatic risks involved were overly great.

Dr. Burg opposed the operation.

While experts and ministers presented their views, Moshe Nissim scribbled rapidly on some of the tiny memo pads scattered over the table. Being one of the select group of Cabinet members who had already considered the matter, the Justice Minister was more thoroughly versed than many of his colleagues; consequently, he took it upon himself to reply to the opponents. At forty-five still relatively young for a minister, Nissim had embarked upon his political career at the age of twenty-three, when he was elected to the Fourth Knesset on the slate of the General Zionists (now the Liberal component of the Likud confederation). Since then he had gradually clambered up the rungs of the political ladder, forging close personal ties with Begin. Being well acquainted with the views of the Prime Minister, he now attempted to serve as his spokesman.

Nissim saw no grounds for the anxieties voiced by the more hesitant ministers. The Soviet Union would do nothing out of the ordinary. The United States would condemn Israel, but would not loosen its ties with Jerusalem. France would go no further than vent its indignation. The Arabs would not unite to go to war. Egypt, waiting to regain the final portion of Sinai, would rest content with verbal condemnation.

Iraq was already an oil power, Nissim recalled. France and Italy were already ensnared in Baghdad's web. Iraq was now on a course which would make it into a nuclear state. Its reactors already housed some of the enriched uranium, and the remnant would be delivered in the near future. If the raid were postponed, Israel was liable to miss the bus: bombing a hot reactor could cause radioactive contamination, entailing the risk of adverse reactions. The projected attack could only benefit from Iraq's war with Iran, without which Baghdad was liable to attain its sought-after status of leader of the Arab world, with both the United States and the Soviet Union paying court.

When Nissim concluded his address, he received a note from Cabinet secretary Aryeh Naor: "However symbolical, you were 'a bomb.'" The colloquially phrased compliment from Begin favorite Naor may be assumed to have reflected the Prime Minister's own view of Nissim's performance.

After Begin wound up the deliberations, a vote was called. The Prime Minister's proposal won ten votes: Begin, Ehrlich, Sharon, Shamir, Landau,

Hurwitz, Nissim, Housing Minister David Levi, Minister of Religions Abu Hatzeira, and Energy and Infrastructure Minister Yitzak Moda'i. The last-named three ministers displayed some hesitancy during the discussion, but ultimately came around to Begin's view.

Six ministers voted against the proposal: Yadin, Burg, Labor and Welfare Minister Yisrael Katz, Commerce and Industry Minister Gideon Patt, Hammer and Shostak. The last two did not attend the meeting, but made known their views.

Held on a day when the ministers rarely convene, the extraordinary Cabinet meeting naturally aroused the curiosity of media representatives, who inquired about its agenda. Naor resorted to a white lie: the Cabinet secretary told journalists that two ministers were at loggerheads over the government's position in relation to a private member's bill that was pending in the Knesset; the Cabinet had been convened to reach a decision on the matter. At the same time, Naor added, the Cabinet had taken the opportunity to hear a defense review whose substance was classified material that could not be reported. (The following day Naor approached the chief military censor to inquire what the journalists had sought to publish about the special Cabinet meeting. The reply: Nothing.)

When the Cabinet dispersed, Yadin requested a brief meeting with the Prime Minister. This is how Yadin later described their exchange:

"On this matter," I told him, "I am not prepared to accept responsibility. I have never used resignation as a threat, but I shall leave the Cabinet if it decides to bomb the reactor. I don't want you to 'trap' me in the government when the operation is carried out. I want to leave the government in such a way that no harm is caused, either to the operation or to me. I don't want to resign a day or two before the operation, because there would be an immediate linking between the resignation and the attack. On the other hand, I don't want you to place me in a situation where I hear that the operation has gone through and then have to resign."

Begin: "That is out of the question. If you leave, the matter will come to light. I am not prepared to accept such an arrangement. I shall postpone the operation. Meantime, you will be convinced that I am right."

Yadin: "We shall have to find some agreed formula. Maybe we'll link it to the issue of the settlements in the occupied territories to which we [Yadin's party, the DMC] are opposed. I shall quit the Cabinet in connection with the alleged disagreement over the settlements. That will certainly arouse no suspicion."

Begin: "I can't accept such an arrangement. After all, it is not the truth."

Yadin: "So what do you propose?"

Begin: "I assure you you won't be 'trapped' in the Cabinet when the operation is carried out."

Yadin: "I repeat, I don't want to hear of it a day or two ahead, but in sufficient time."

Begin: "All right."

On October 29, Commander in Chief Eytan notified Air Force Commander Ivry that the Cabinet had decided to attack the reactor "at an early date," sometime or other after the November elections in the United States. Eytan ordered preparations speeded up, so that the attack could go ahead anytime after the date specified. Ivry summoned his head of operations and issued the appropriate instructions.

From this point onward, a heavy burden fell upon the various intelligence agencies. They were instructed to provide the planners with comprehensive and updated information on antiaircraft deployment at the reactor site and along the entire flight route, the hours appropriate to the strike, weather conditions, and similar details. The intelligence had to be supplied on a daily basis, since the action could be ordered at any moment.

Early in November 1980, four F-16s set out on a test flight in preparation for the attack. One of the fliers was Major Ehud Ben Amitai, scion of a military family. The major had been picked to take part in the reactor strike, but he did not live to see it: he was killed during another aerial exercise.

At a General Staff meeting on November 10, Ivry presented the Air Force's plan for the reactor attack. Ivry himself was not entirely convinced that aerial bombing alone was the best available option, but he now assumed that this would be the sole plan, with no alternative proposed.

Having presented his plan to the General Staff, Ivry went on to submit it to the political echelons. For the moment, however, the plan could not be executed, with only five F-16s in Israel's possession. The Air Force was awaiting delivery of additional aircraft to complete the complement of two full squadrons.

The operational plan having been submitted to the military and political echelons, the Commander in Chief issued basic guidelines to all those privy to the secret:

The object of the operation: to hit the installation and put it out of commission for as long as possible.

It will be impossible to conceal our identity in the operation.

Preparations shall be made for the contingency of reactions and operations against us after the attack is carried out.

* * *

The war with Iran still kept work at al-Tuweitha at a standstill, but Iraq did not halt its diplomatic efforts. Iraqi emissaries continually toured Europe, particularly France and Italy, to ensure that the nuclear project would suffer no harm beyond postponement.

On October 26, 1980, RCC member Abdel Fattah Muhammad Amin, Iraq's minister of local government, arrived in Italy bearing a message from Saddam Hussain. The reply of Italian President Alessandro Pertini reached Baghdad in a special message delivered by Ambassador Valerio Brigante Colonna Angelini to Iraqi Foreign Minister Sa'adun Hammadi.

On October 27, personal emissary Jacques Forisier brought a letter from the French President to his Iraqi counterpart. The meeting between Hussain and the emissary was also attended by Tarik Aziz, the Deputy Prime Minister to whom the President had delegated the diplomatic aspects of the nuclear project; by Foreign Minister Sa'adun Hammadi; and by the French ambassador to Iraq.

Two days earlier, on October 25, French Premier Raymond Barre had delivered a scathing attack on the campaign against Franco–Iraqi nuclear cooperation. Questioned by a journalist while on a visit to Tunis, Barre declared, "The campaign being conducted by certain circles will not make France reconsider its nuclear cooperation with Iraq. Franco–Iraqi relations are extremely good and solid. France is putting forth every possible effort to further strengthen these relations in all fields. France will respond to all of Iraq's requests, as defined by President Hussain."

On November 5, Deputy Prime Minister Tarik Aziz arrived in Paris, where he held a seventy-five-minute meeting with President Giscard. The meeting was also attended by Foreign Minister François-Poncet and Iraqi Ambassador Nuri Ismail al-Ways. The exchange of letters between the two presidents, like the declarations of Premier Barre and the meetings in Baghdad and Paris, reflected French support for Iraq in its war against Iran, and foreshadowed further massive French aid to Baghdad.

In mid-October 1980, two prominent scientists, one American and the other Italian, unmasked the self-righteous posturing of Italian politicians and nuclear scientists who denied that there was anything unusual about the nuclear equipment Italy was selling to Iraq.

At that time, Professor Yuval Ne'eman came to Austin, Texas. A renowned American nuclear physicist, an old friend, urgently summoned Ne'eman to come and see him. When the two men met on October 30, the American scientist told Ne'eman that he had recently spent time in Italy, where he met a colleague, a leading nuclear physicist directly connected with the hot cells being sent to Iraq. "Outwardly," the Italian related, "everyone pretends that everything is okay, that it's all based on what's known as 'nuclear energy for peaceful purposes.' But that's not true. I see the Iraqi scientists and technicians who come to Italy; I know what equipment they purchase, what they study and what they are taught. I am most concerned. If you have connections in the right places, be good enough to convey the following message: 'Here in Italy, disturbing things are afoot.'"

For Yuval Ne'eman, it was further vindication of the alarm he had been sounding for many months.

18 Covering the Traces

On November 7, 1980, Iraq announced that it was halting regular visits by IAEA inspectors at the reactor, the excuse being "an act of God." The "act" was, of course, the war with Iran. The Iraqi step underscored Israel's principal criticism of IAEA control, whose dubious effectiveness was further compounded by another flaw: any state voluntarily placing itself under the agency's supervision incurred no punitive action if it unilaterally abrogated that supervision.

Furthermore, the handful of foreign engineers and technicians remaining at al-Tuweitha were now barred from the nuclear installations. The official pretext was that this was to "protect the foreigners from the danger of an Iranian bombing raid." But the true reason appeared to be Iraq's decision to conceal the fuel rods in a water channel in the reactor structure, on the probable calculation that in the event of their failure to manufacture plutonium bombs, or of the reactor's destruction, the hoard of enriched uranium would constitute a strategic reserve for the production of at least one primitive uranium bomb.

France demanded written Iraqi undertakings that the enriched uranium had been removed from the core of Tammuz 2, but the Iraqis declined to provide them. They also refused to resume negotiations with the IAEA about special supervisory arrangements for the reactor, even though their 1972 agreement with the agency bound them thereto.

French National Assembly Deputy Paul Quilès submitted a further parliamentary question to Foreign Minister Jean François-Poncet, regarding the IAEA's inability to enforce supervision of Iraq's nuclear facilities. The question recalled that Iraq had effectively terminated international supervision of those facilities: what conclusions did the Foreign Minister draw from this disturbing information? What steps did the minister intend to take, in the framework of Franco–Iraqi nuclear cooperation?

This time the reply came without delay. François-Poncet produced his trump: an IAEA statement that the agency had received full details from Iraq concerning the condition of the nuclear fuel rods. Simultaneously, Iraq had also undertaken to permit IAEA inspectors to visit the reactor "as soon as this is made possible by the state of war between Iraq and Iran." The Foreign Minister stated that neither the French government nor the IAEA questioned Iraq's commitment, and that the government did not share the pessimistic views of Deputy Quilès.

Taken at face value, the Iraqi document should have reassured those who entertained doubts about the sincerity of Baghdad's intentions. However, anyone acquainted with the IAEA's supervisory apparatus knew that it is at best a broken reed, and at worst a smokescreen behind which any state so inclined can conceal its true intentions.

As various publications confirm, any state subject to IAEA supervision still retains numerous loopholes for the manufacture of nuclear weapons, principally because the agency is incapable of mounting snap checks. Even if it attempted an unannounced inspection, someone at its headquarters— which is staffed, like all UN agencies, in accordance with national "quotas" —would be sure to tip off the state in question that the inspectors were on their way. Given prior knowledge of an imminent inspection, there is little difficulty in covering the traces by removing or concealing equipment. The IAEA's lack of credibility is further compounded by its manner of picking the inspectors to be sent to a given country. Since the agency is utterly politicized, diplomatic pressure can easily be exerted upon the selection committee so as to ensure the choice of inspectors closely identified with the interests of the state they are to visit.

In time, these misgivings, along with even graver suspicions voiced during the course of the past twenty years, would be confirmed by IAEA chief inspector Roger Richter when he testified at U.S. congressional inquiries. But even earlier, in May 1981, three senior French scientists submitted a report to their government wherein they explained why IAEA supervision could not be counted upon to prevent Iraq's resort to the weapons potential offered by the combination of the Osirak reactor and the Italian hot cells.

The report's authors were prominent members of the National Center for Scientific Research, France's most prestigious research body. Founded forty-five years previously by Léon Blum, France's Jewish premier in the years preceding World War Two, it is in the top league of Western research institutes.

The three men were Georges Amsel, research director at the center and head of the solid-physics department in France's most prestigious college, the Ecole Normale Supérieure; Jean-Pierre Pharabaud, an engineer at the center, a member of the energy committee of the Socialist Party (which was to take power shortly after the report's completion) and chief engineer at the high-energy laboratory of France's top technical college, the Ecole Poly-technique; and Raymond Sène, a senior researcher at the center and head of the laboratory for particle physics at the renowned Collège de France.

Resting upon a highly detailed report which explored every conceivable aspect, the three scientists worded their conclusions in terms of a terrifying simplicity:

· The French reactor, in combination with the Italian laboratories, guaran-teed Iraq "a complementary nuclear capability" (reinforcing its existing capa-bility) within a short time, and no later than the mideighties.
· Notwithstanding the manner in which it was depicted, the Osirak project did not constitute scientific cooperation; rather, it involved transfer of high technology which could neither be defined nor be justified as meeting Iraq's scientific, educational or cultural requirements.
· Iraq would encounter no difficulty in channeling the material, the equip-ment and the knowhow received from France and Italy away from the pur-poses for which they were intended, to manufacture of nuclear bombs.

The trio of scientists foresaw matters in Iraq developing into "a nuclear Sarajevo." It was an ominous term: the Serbian town of Sarajevo gave the signal for World War One when it was the scene of the assassination of Austrian Archduke Franz Ferdinand and his wife.

On November 11, Military Intelligence chief Saguy briefed the Knesset's Foreign Affairs and Defense Committee, reporting that the Iraqi reactor was then at a standstill due to the withdrawal of the French experts. It goes without saying that he gave not the slightest hint of the Cabinet's decision to bomb the reactor.

On November 13, Prime Minister Begin met with President Carter. Carter was now a lame-duck president, having suffered a resounding defeat at the hands of Ronald Reagan. All the same, three months would elapse before Reagan took over, and until then Carter remained the leader of the world's preeminent superpower.

A private talk between the two leaders touched upon the Iran–Iraq war and the Iraqi reactor. They also discussed effective action to prevent nuclear proliferation, and the danger to world peace should nuclear weapons fall into the hands of states like Iraq and Pakistan. Begin urged the United States to step up its endeavors in this sphere. Carter assured his guest that he would discuss the matter with his designated successor when they met the following week.

Did Carter indeed discuss the Iraqi reactor with Reagan? Was the relevant material that had been accumulated by the Carter Administration transmitted to the Reagan team?

In both cases, the answer appears to be negative. There must have been some slipup in the transition from one administration to the next. Carter was to explain the omission by pointing out that Reagan appointed his Secretaries of State and Defense "at the last moment"; consequently, there was no one to receive the information.

Prior to a handing over of power in Washington, the outgoing administration prepares a "transition file" on every important matter still outstanding. According to a most reliable American source, there must have been such a file on the Iraqi reactor. "However," the source added, "for some reason it didn't get the attention it deserved from the Reagan Administration."

The oversight was to strike home with stunning force some months later, when Israeli Air Force planes devastated the reactor, and the United States responded with unexpected fury. The Israelis would then learn, to their consternation, that President Reagan and his senior advisers knew next to nothing about the intensive bilateral contacts in the course of which Israel had made it plain to the United States that it regarded the Iraqi reactor as a genuine threat to its very existence.

On November 30, Foreign Minister Shamir met with his French colleague François-Poncet in Paris. Predictably, Shamir again brought up the subject of the Iraqi reactor. By this time, the French could have been expected to entertain suspicions as to Iraq's true intentions. They did not. François-Poncet's declarations to Shamir were a well-nigh precise rerun of everything said at previous meetings.

A few days later, on December 4, Shamir went to the Élysée Palace for a personal meeting with President Giscard.

Israel was aware of Giscard's opposition to nuclear proliferation, Shamir said. But France was familiar with Saddam Hussain's uncompromising attitude toward Israel, for whose destruction the Iraqi President declared all means to be justified. Consequently, France, like the rest of the world, was bound to take a doubly grave view of what was happening in Iraq.

France was aware of Hussain's views, Giscard replied. The French technicians had been instructed to keep a sharp watch on everything that went on at the reactor site. If there were any sign of Iraq attempting to develop nuclear arms, the technicians would sound the alarm, and France would immediately take every measure called for. To this day, the French technicians had detected nothing suspicious. Eager to illustrate his goodwill toward Israel, Giscard related that when a French company concluded a contract with an Arab state for the sale of a certain class of weapon which he regarded as a threat to Israel's existence, he had ordered the deal canceled. "That is my position and I am sticking to it," the President affirmed.

Shamir was not reassured. His report to Israel was pessimistic in tone. When U.S. Ambassador to Israel Sam Lewis asked whether Shamir had made any headway in his talks with the French leaders, the Israeli Foreign Ministry director-general, David Kimche, replied laconically, "Shamir wasn't too happy with the talks."

By mid-December 1980, Israel and the United States had clarified their respective views on the issue of the Iraqi reactor. Both governments displayed a shared concern, but whereas Israel affirmed outright that Iraq planned to manufacture nuclear weapons, the Americans denied that the evidence was irrefutable, though they believed that Iraq's nuclear program was aimed at creating a future option for weapons production.

Israel complained of the assistance rendered by France and Italy, without which Iraq would have been powerless to promote its nuclear designs. Drawing upon its own sources, the Carter Administration acknowledged the accuracy of Israel's assessments. Washington urged its two European allies to exhibit restraint in transferring sensitive nuclear materials and technology to Iraq. France was pressed to reduce to a minimum the stock of enriched uranium stored in Iraq, and to remove the spent fuel rods, whether or not there were facilities for their reprocessing. The Americans were equally conscious that the Italian installations could enable Iraq to extract small amounts of plutonium from the spent reactor fuel. Italy was also training Iraqi scientists, as well as pursuing joint nuclear research to induce Iraq to purchase an Italian natural-uranium reactor which produced considerable amounts of plutonium. The United States undertook to obstruct Iraqi attempts to acquire nuclear materials and technology. The Americans hoped that the Iran–Iraq war would convince France and Italy to curtail their nuclear aid to Iraq, but Israel held that this assessment was overoptimistic and could not be relied upon.

Washington claimed to be "under no illusions as to the gravity of the danger to be expected from Iraq's possession of nuclear weapons"; however, the Administration held it preferable to pursue diplomatic approaches to France and Italy, rather than countenance direct Israeli pressure upon Iraq which, the Americans feared, could place obstacles before Mideast peace efforts.

19 "That's the whole secret..."

At eight-fifteen in the morning of December 17, 1980, U.S. Ambassador Sam Lewis entered the office of Prime Minister Begin. The two men commenced their conversation on a friendly note.

Begin: "I heard on the radio that with the change of administrations you're to be head of the State Department's Mideastern desk."

Lewis: "I don't know anything about that. There are lots of jobs I don't want, and that's one. I'd rather stay here."

Begin: "That's what we want, too."

Lewis (with a smile): "I have enough business with Jews. I don't want to have to deal with Arabs as well."

The ambassador got down to business. He recalled Begin's past approaches on the issue of the Iraqi reactor. "At your request, I have assembled all the information the United States has on that matter." He opened his briefcase and produced a document. "This is the summary drawn up in Washington. I'll read it to you and you'll see that there is a considerable proximity in the basic assessments of the two governments."

The nineteen-point document is believed to have been drawn up by a specialized Administration agency, whose employees diligently collated information about nuclear activity the world over, including, of course, Iraq and its French and Italian collaborators. Begin listened intently as the ambassador read it out. In conclusion, Lewis extended the paper to the Prime Minister.

Begin could not have been more gratified. Confirming Israel's anxieties, the memorandum also highlighted America's own concerns about developments in Iraq.

"We assume," Lewis said, "that as long as the Persian Gulf War goes on, the French won't send any more uranium to Iraq. In the long run, the United States fears that the Italians will be more of a problem than the French, because the Italian equipment is liable to give the Iraqis the capability to extract plutonium from irradiated natural uranium. Massive Iraqi purchases of hundreds of tons of natural uranium from Niger, Portugal and other countries testify that this option is being taken seriously in Baghdad."

Thanking the ambassador for the U.S. efforts, Begin recalled Saddam Hussain's declaration a fortnight earlier: the war against Iran marked the beginning of the march on Jaffa and Jerusalem. Begin added that the Iraqis would probably seek plutonium from Pakistan, which appeared to have developed a capacity for production of nuclear explosives.

Lewis: "We are exerting pressure on the Italians and the French, but they are dependent on Iraqi oil."

Begin (with bitter irony): "That's the whole secret: Iraqi oil."

Lewis went on to meet with Foreign Minister Shamir, who reported on his recent talks with the French leaders. It was no news to the ambassador, who had been briefed by Shamir's director-general, David Kimche. Lewis told Shamir that, in view of the Iran–Iraq war and the instability prevalent in the Gulf region, France and Italy were now more attentive to U.S. concerns about nuclear proliferation in general and transfer of nuclear knowhow to Iraq in particular.

That assessment soon proved overoptimistic.

Saddam Hussain continued to pursue his designs. His statement to the Iraqi Cabinet, as reported on December 25 by Baghdad radio, spoke for itself: ". . . We recall the deterioration in talk about the Iraqi atomic bomb. Before the [Gulf] war they said, We shall not permit such a bomb to see the light of day. . . . They forgot that no one gave this scientific potential to Iraq on account of her dark eyes; rather, it was acquired through the competence and firm resolve of the Iraqis. Whosoever could bring a laboratory or a reactor can now bring ten. That is the direct price of Zionism."

Late in 1980, Military Intelligence chief Saguy notified Commander in Chief Eytan and Air Force commander Ivry that the Iraqis were taking various defensive precautions around the reactor, encompassing it with a 100-foot-high earth ramp to protect it from observation or from access on the ground; they were also floating balloons, a familiar device to obstruct low-altitude overflights, whether for reconnaissance or for assault.

Major General Eytan had news of his own to impart to Ivry: "The Deputy Prime Minister [Yadin] has withdrawn his objections to the reactor attack."

"Rafful" was to recall, "There was important intelligence data which confirmed our suspicions about the Iraqis' true intentions. I took this evidence to Yadin's home. We discussed the information, and following our talk Yadin withdrew his objections."

For his part, Yadin recalled Begin telling him, "Yigael, Rafful has a report that the French technicians are about to return to the reactor, to activate the system and get it hot." (Among his other objections to the projected raid, Yadin had argued that work at the reactor was at a standstill because nothing could be done without the French technicians who had departed after the Iranian attacks.)

A skeptical Yadin recalled his membership of the Agranat Commission which inquired into Israel's conduct of the 1973 Yom Kippur War, with particular attention to the intelligence shortcomings which allowed Israel to be taken unawares by the Arab onslaught. "Dado (the late Major General David Elazar, who was Israel's commander in chief in 1973) told the commission that prior to the war he had not read intelligence material, the raw data. Now," Yadin told Begin, "I want to read the intelligence material."

On Begin's instructions, Eytan brought the raw data to Yadin. "I was not sure that Rafful's interpretation was the correct one," Yadin related. "Consequently, I decided to consult Military Intelligence chief Saguy and Mossad head Hoffy. They told me it was not certain that Rafful's interpretation was entirely correct, but there was something to that effect in the raw data."

"It should be recalled," Yadin went on "that Begin wanted to hit the reactor without harming the French technicians. He even thought of carrying out the raid at Christmas, when the foreigners were off work and before the reactor went into operation. At that stage," Yadin added, contradicting Rafful's account of his alleged change of heart at this time, "I had yet to give my consent. I thought—after the manner of the well-known Jewish joke—that the lord of the manor would die at the last moment; in other words, that the project in Iraq would not go ahead. In time, it turned out that at the phase in question the report brought to me by Rafful was not quite correct."

But in the meantime the Commander in Chief had given the directive: "Stand by for the raid, commencing January 1, 1981."

True to his promise to the Cabinet, Begin summoned opposition Labor Party leader Shimon Peres. They met on December 30. Subsequently, after the reactor raid, the two leaders would offer conflicting versions of their conversation.

Peres: "I did not understand from Begin that a date had been set for the raid. I thought it was only a matter of reflection or intent, nothing more. Begin did not ask for my comment, and under the circumstances I made none, though my instinctive feeling was against the plan."

Begin: "Peres did not express his consent, but neither did he voice objections."

Peres: "I did not express objections, because I did not wish to be burdensome."

However, in the course of their conversation, Peres did proffer one significant remark which the Prime Minister hastened to bring to the attention of the Commander in Chief—though it transpired that the matter was being attended to.

The first man in whom Peres confided—with the apparent blessing of the Prime Minister—was former Commander in Chief Haim Barlev, at that time Labor's candidate for defense minister. Barlev: "We did not think this was a correct step, from the viewpoint of Israeli security."

Another Labor leader with whom Peres shared the secret was former Prime Minister Yitzak Rabin. Rabin was already updated, since, with Begin's approval, he was in current contact with Aharon Yariv, the head of the special committee named to deal with the problem.

Peres also confided in Yisrael Galili, a man of great military experience who had officiated as a senior minister in successive Labor governments, where he had been the confidant of Prime Ministers Levi Eshkol, Golda Meir and Yitzhak Rabin. For his part, Galili consulted former Military Intelligence Director Shlomo Gazit. Later, Gazit also met with Peres. Gazit was in entire agreement with the assessment which perceived the Iraqi reactor as a menace to Israel's existence. "The government's information is one hundred percent reliable," he told Galili and Peres. But he had his reservations about the notion of destroying the reactor by military action. In his view, it was both necessary and possible to block Iraq's nuclear project by other means.

Yuval Ne'eman espoused an entirely different outlook. Invited to address an international symposium on science and disarmament held in Paris on January 16–17, 1981, Ne'eman stunned his audience—which included French Cabinet members—when he denounced the French government for its nuclear aid to Iraq.

One of Ne'eman's listeners was Pierre Mayer, a French Jew who served as inspector general of finances at the Ministry of the Economy and the Budget. Mayer hastened to send Ne'eman a most sharply worded letter. In his speech, Ne'eman had characterized France as "an irresponsible medium power." Mayer, more of a French nationalist than his Gentile fellow citizens, replied that France's irresponsibility had "found its expression in its attitude toward Israel in a period, happily passed forever, during the Fourth Republic, when France assisted Israel in commencing its nuclear research." Mayer's letter bristled with disparaging terms about Israel ("a pariah state") and its Prime Minister ("a former terrorist").

The French made every effort to convince Israel that its concerns were unfounded. On January 8, Élysée secretary Jacques Wahl told Ambassador Rosenne that twenty French technicians remained at the reactor site, where they effectively denied the Iraqis access to the enriched uranium. (This claim was questionable, since, as will be recalled, the fuel was not under direct French supervision.)

The Iraqis, sensing that this was the moment to persuade the world of the probity of their intentions—without the least harm to their own interests—now took a wily step: they permitted an IAEA delegation to visit the reactor. The delegation arrived on January 22; predictably, it found "everything in order"—hardly surprising, since the reactor was as yet inactive.

In January 1981, Labor Party leader Peres left for Europe for a series of meetings. On January 23 he met with French President Giscard, bringing to his attention the grave view taken in Israel—"without distinction between government and opposition"—of the threat to world peace posed by nuclear development in countries like Libya and Iraq.

Giscard replied, "I am bound to carry out an agreement which I did not sign." In an unabashed evasion of responsibility for the Franco-Iraqi accord concluded during his term of office, Giscard tried to pass the buck to former Premier Jacques Chirac, now one of his bitterest adversaries.

However, Giscard went on, Iraq did not intend to manufacture atomic bombs. "We make sure that the quantities of fuel delivered to Iraq are extremely restricted. Should we find that Iraq is taking steps liable to lead to construction of a bomb, we shall halt implementation of the agreement." The President also offered his counsel: "The best thing for Israel is a military pact with the United States. Thereby, your security will be guaranteed by the world's number-one superpower."

Peres: "Israel does not want to be an American, or a European, protectorate."

Peres also held talks with Jacques Chirac. "Don't believe the fiction that I've sold out to the Arabs," the Premier cautioned Peres. "True, I have numerous friends in the Arab world, but that can only help promote peace. I assure you that if Israel's security is jeopardized, I shall be the first to demand total French support for Israel."

Peres also met with his old friend François Mitterrand, leader of the French Socialist Party and its candidate for President. It was their second encounter in the space of two months: the two men had met in November at the convention of the Socialist International in Spain.

Peres recalled later: "I had two very thorough talks with Mitterrand on the nuclear issue. He told me that [if he became President] he was committed to doing everything to excise the Iraqi reactor of its military potential."

After the reactor bombing, Mitterrand, by now installed in the Élysée Palace, was to claim that he told Peres of his reservations about his country's agreement with Iraq. Mitterrand could not say whether Peres had briefed

Begin on the substance of their conversation, but the President assumed that his views had also been conveyed to Jerusalem by French Jewish bodies.

In retrospect, Peres does not appear to have informed Begin on his talks with Mitterrand, while his report to Jerusalem on the meeting with Giscard was incomplete: for example, it lacked one important detail recalled by his aide, Dr. Yossi Beilin, whereby the French President proposed a joint Franco-Israeli monitoring commission. As far as is known, Paris embassy reports to Jerusalem on Peres' meetings with Mitterrand likewise made no reference to the relevant portions of their conversations. Peres' relations with Begin were frosty, and this is probably why he gave the Prime Minister no verbal reports on his meetings with the French leaders.

Wing commander Yitzhal Melrom, in command of Israel's F-16 squadrons, was notified that the reactor strike date would be fixed as soon as the second squadron of F-16s arrived from the United States. In the meantime, training was to proceed.

Exercises demonstrated that the planes would be capable of accomplishing their mission and returning to base without refueling en route. Air Force experts made various suggestions aimed at maximizing the amount of fuel the planes could carry in their tanks. Finally, a test flight vindicated the view advocated by Colonel Aryeh Ran, the man designated to lead the bombing mission.

Colonel Eliezer Malachi, who was to lead the assault force's second formation, related: "From the start, we were invited to attend discussions about how the operation was to be accomplished. There was talk of 'long-range missions.' When I was appointed to command the F-16 squadron, the Air Force commander requested that I award equal importance to all of the plane's functions, not merely aerial combat. Ivry is notoriously economical with his words. At one stage, we listened to the plan in the company of the Commander in Chief. Afterwards Rafful asked us, 'Do you think it can be done?' We replied, 'Yes.'"

Following the trials, it was decided finally that the operation would be carried out by a certain number of planes. The decision rested upon the assessment that for an effective strike within a highly restricted timespan, without need for a second assault wave, the optimum is a certain number of planes which would guarantee that, even in the event of hitches—mechanical misfunction, faulty armament, human error, one or two planes being hit by antiaircraft fire—the reactor would nevertheless be destroyed.

Early in January 1981, Iraq's security services ferreted out a group of local Shi'ites who planned to assassinate the foreign technicians at al-Tuweitha. On January 13, the *London Daily Mail* reported that the group included about ten suicide attackers who managed to penetrate the nuclear compound's residential quarters before being caught. All were executed.

A further report, dated January 20, related that the Iraqis had discovered two 10-pound bombs in the quarters of the foreign staff at al-Tuweitha. The bombs were dismantled without causing any damage.

If these reports were accurate, the Shi'ite terrorist plans were presumably prepared in Iran, which continued to regard Iraq's nuclear reactor as a threat.

Iraq maintained its pressure on France for additional engineers and technicians to complete repairs at the reactor: Hussain was eager to see his costly toy in operation. The Iraqi government notified France that it no longer feared raids on the reactor. "No one can impose an embargo on the Arab nation with regard to nuclear technology," Saddam Hussain proclaimed in a January 19 press interview.

France skipped to his tune. Early in March, the number of French experts at the reactor rose to eighty, as compared to the twenty who remained there after September's Iranian air raid. The experts examined the repairs and assessed the delay occasioned in the original timetable for the reactor's activation. They predicted that repairs would be completed by November 1981; during the second half of that month, Tammuz 1 would be loaded with uranium and activated.

The proposed schedule did not meet with the approval of the Iraqis, who were unwilling to wait so long to see the reactor hot. Saddam Hussain wanted the reactor operational on July 14, 1981, Iraq's Revolution Day, they explained.

After a prolonged series of tests and consultations, the French worked out an expedited timetable whereby a supreme effort would seek to have the reactor active by July 14, or in the second half of September at latest. August marks France's sacrosanct *vacances*, and almost all the French experts planned to leave then for home. Consequently, even if the reactor did not go into operation on July 14, most of the work had to be completed by early July.

The French kept their word. Dozens of experts labored day after day, overtime included. Everything went according to plan, and some sections were even completed ahead of schedule. After the reactor bombing, the Lebanese weekly *al-Watan al-Arabi*, published in Paris but known for its pro-Iraqi leanings, would write: "The main reactor ('Tammuz 1') was to commence operation on July 1, or at the beginning of September. . . ."

On February 18, French Ambassador Marc Bonnefous hosted Professor Ne'eman for lunch at his Jaffa home. Bonnefous showed his guest documentary information dispatched from Paris in response to Israeli allegations.

The affable ambassador asked Ne'eman for his comments, which were forthcoming unstintingly. But as events unfolded, they demonstrated that Ne'eman's views had failed to convince the French authorities.

On March 15, Begin summoned a meeting in Jerusalem; it wwas attended by the ministerial team, the Commander in Chief, the Air Force commander, the director of Military Intelligence and the senior officers involved in the operation, including the commanders of the F-16 squadrons.

Begin again elaborated on the dangers facing Israel as a result of Iraq's intent to manufacture nuclear weaponry. In conclusion, he requested that the ministers voice their views on two points: Should the reactor be attacked? If so, when?

Several ministers wished initially to get an overall picture of the situation, together with details of the Air Force's operational plan, before expressing their own views. But Begin insisted that they express their opinions first, irrespective of the operational preparations.

As David Ivry recalled the meeting: "To the best of my recollection, the ministers requested that we present the assault plan. I did so in brief. I was asked to gauge the risks. How many planes were we liable to lose? My reply was, 'The risks are the risk of combat.' There was no certainty that they would all return. Our experience in the Yom Kippur War indicated that we lost one percent of the planes sent out on long-range sorties. Even so I refrained from specifying figures."

The reactor attack was supported by all the ministers participating, with the exception of Yadin and two others. As Yadin related later: "Begin told me, 'The situation is deteriorating. Here before you is new information which effectively endorses the data you queried.' I had thought earlier that there was room for doubt, but a new situation had now indeed emerged. However, the intelligence chiefs persisted in their opposition. Begin told me, 'I can no longer wait with the decision to act. The fact is that I have waited a considerable time.'

"I replied, 'I can't confront you all with my ultimatum [of resignation] as I have done hitherto. I agree that if it is necessary to bomb the reactor, now is the time, even though I adhere to my conviction that the risk involved in the bombing is not worth running, particularly as the reactor itself will not be operational [in the military sense] for several years.' Begin said he would submit the matter to the decision of the ministerial forum. I replied, 'I shall vote against the operation, but I shall make it known that I no longer insist on resigning in consequence of the decision.'"

The two men came to an agreement whereby Yadin would give Begin a handwritten letter explaining his October 1980 declaration that a decision in favor of the operation would leave him with no choice other than resignation, and why he now withdrew that threat. The letter would be deposited with the Cabinet secretary, and any minister so inclined could read it. After the operation the letter would, of course, no longer remain classified.

After three hours of deliberations, the ministerial forum approved the proposed strike as exhibited by the planners. The resolution empowered the Prime Minister, in the course of the coming month, to fix the attack date. If necessary, the date would be submitted for approval by the Cabinet or the ministerial team. The Commander in Chief was instructed "in the meantime to make all preparations."

Just like the government, the General Staff was divided over the operation. Military Intelligence Director Saguy continued to voice his reservations. At a session of the General Staff held after the Cabinet meeting, Saguy and other generals expressed apprehension that the bombing might fail to destroy the reactor. On top of falling short of its objective, the raid would then incur needless diplomatic harm.

However, the Air Force commander and his aides were convinced that the reactor would be destroyed. As for losses, they hoped there would be none, or at most not more than a reasonable number.

In view of these replies, Saguy and the other generals withdrew their objections. "Those present supported the plan for an aerial strike, and recommended execution of the operation," concluded the summary of the General Staff meeting.

On March 17, 1981, Democrat Alan Cranston of California dropped a bombshell on the U.S. Senate floor: "I have recently received information that Iraq, though at the present time a party to the Nuclear Non-Proliferation Treaty, is embarked on a full-scale program which appears designed to develop the capability to extract plutonium suitable for weapons purposes."

Cranston conceded that there was no evidence of Baghdad actually engaging in planning a nuclear bomb, "but Iraq is demonstrating graphically the danger that radical oil powers will use the oil weapon to blackmail other nations into imprudent sales of sensitive nuclear technology and cooperation in its use." It was a broad hint pointing to U.S. allies France and Italy.

Pakistan, Cranston went on, was currently on the threshold of a nuclear-weapons capability—and might even have crossed that threshold. Iraq, he added, referring to intelligence sources, was currently at a juncture similar to the one passed through by Pakistan five years previously, but it could be assumed that Baghdad's path to a weapons capability would be shorter and swifter than that of Pakistan, because of Iraq's greater financial resources and the massive aid from France and Italy.

Cranston's declaration drew a swift reply from the State Department, which admitted "concern" over the Iraqi nuclear menace, but disagreed that such an eventuality would arise within one year, foreseeing that several years would elapse before that came about.

Britain and West Germany also probed the matter, concluding that Iraq did indeed intend to exploit the reactor and other facilities for production of a nuclear bomb, though it had no hope of success before 1990 (Israel, it will be recalled, set the date in the mideighties).

The nuclear genie, having long been contained in its flask, appeared to be on the verge of breaking out. Algeria, likewise a wealthy oil state, put out feelers for purchase of a French reactor similar to the Osiris delivered to Iraq. Saudi Arabia and Egypt also began to show an interest in large-scale nuclear projects. There was general unanimity that Pakistan stood close to completion of a nuclear bomb. India, which had already demonstrated its ability to detonate a nuclear device, left no room for uncertainty: if Pakistan developed a nuclear-weapons capability, India would exercise its existing potential to build up an effective nuclear force.

With each passing week, additional French experts were reaching Iraq. The French contingent at al-Tuweitha would soon be back to its size before the outbreak of the Gulf War—three hundred engineers and technicians. According to Israeli assessments, the time lapse from the moment the reactor was loaded with uranium until it became hot would be about four months. It was learned that the French were making vigorous efforts to expedite its activation.

The energy and efficiency displayed by the French experts filled Begin with horror. "For heaven's sake!" he cried to his colleagues. "What are we discussing? Our very existence! Why do we hesitate?" He repeated insistently that Iraq was preparing "a second Holocaust," with the assistance of France and Italy. His renowned sensitivity on the subject of the Holocaust led him to remind the French of World War Two, when their Vichy government abetted the Germans in sending French Jews to the gas chambers.

20 "Are you out of your minds?"

Early in 1981, Alexander M. Haig, Jr., became secretary of state in the Reagan Administration. One of Haig's first foreign trips after taking up his appointment was to Israel, where he arrived in April to hold comprehensive talks with Prime Minister Begin, Foreign Minister Shamir and other Israeli leaders.

As is the custom, Begin and Haig also held a private talk of which no written record was kept. But subsequent remarks by both men indicated that the areas of U.S.–Israel agreement outnumbered the points of disagreement.

Among other topics, Begin brought up the Iraqi reactor. After reporting on progress at the reactor and the threat it posed to Israel, he demanded: In view of Israel's incessant appeals to block Iraq's nuclear program—which, beyond any doubt, was directed toward a weapons cability—what had the United States done?

Haig's reply offered little comfort. He related what Begin already knew: the previous Administration, Carter's, had made efforts to halt Iraq's nuclear program, or at least ensure that it did not endow that country with a weapons capability. Asked on the matter, Carter himself confirmed that he had discussed the proliferation issue with the French President (regarding nuclear programs in Iraq and Argentina) and the West German Chancellor (with regard to Brazil's program). When asked why his Administration had failed to convince its French and Italian allies to refrain from supplying Iraq with nuclear knowhow of a weapons potential, Carter replied ironically, "They—France and Italy—are sovereign states, just like Israel." This confirms what Haig told Begin: "We have intervened with France and Italy—but in vain."

Later, after the reactor attack, when Reagan envoy Robert C. McFarlane came to Israel, Begin told him hotly, "I am willing to swear on the Bible that that is what Haig told me: 'There was intervention—but in vain.'"

By this time, Begin's resolve to bomb the reactor needed no reinforce-
ment. Nevertheless, his conversation with Haig probably stiffened his determination. As he put it: "To sit with arms folded? After the Secretary of State
of the United States said that all efforts were in vain?!"

Did Haig say anything further, beyond admitting the failure of America's
diplomatic efforts? Begin has never made any public reference thereto, and
Haig is equally silent—so far, at least. After his resignation from office,
Haig, though embittered, nevertheless withheld any revelations which could
have embarrassed President Reagan. In his memoirs, Haig mentions the
conversation with Begin solely within the context of the controversy about
the sale of AWACS surveillance aircraft to Saudi Arabia.

But shortly before the death of Simha Ehrlich—Begin's deputy and probably his closest Cabinet confidant—he recalled, "When Haig visited Israel,
Begin received the [additional] impetus to bomb the reactor." Ehrlich may
have been referring to Haig's admission that American efforts to convince
France and Italy had been "in vain."

Late March 1981 witnessed a heightening of Syrian–Israeli tension in
connection with the Lebanese Civil War. Israel's Falangist Maronite allies
attempted to pave a new road to the Christian town of Zahleh, which lies in
an area of northern Lebanon that is predominantly Shi'ite Moslem. Regarding the road as an affront to their control of the area, the Syrians dispatched
helicopter-borne commando units to keep the Falangists from linking up
with Zahleh. On April 1, fierce fighting broke out between the Syrians and
the Maronites. The latter sent two representatives to Jerusalem with an urgent appeal for help addressed to Prime Minister Begin. The emissaries did
not neglect to mention that the Syrians attacking Zahleh were also constructing SAM-6 launch sites and installing electronic-warfare equipment.

On April 8, Begin summoned a group of ministers to consider events in
Lebanon; a further item on the agenda was the Iraqi reactor. Justice Minister
Nissim, who arrived late, was greeted by Begin with an upturned thumb,
the Prime Minister's comment on the previous day's elections in the Hista-
drut labor confederation, where the Likkud confounded pessimistic predictions by gaining a relative success. After a prolonged bout of depression,
Begin was now once more his old self. His government had long been
plagued by what he termed "snags," which he failed to overcome; but he
was now back "in form."

In the course of the consultation, it was suggested that the reactor strike
be set for the following Sunday, April 12. But Nissim, in spite of his enthusiasm for the strike, proposed a later date. The Justice Minister, whose
opinion Begin respected, feared that Israel would be in no position to with-

stand the international repercussions of its intervention on behalf of the Maronites if that coincided with its attack on the Iraqi reactor. The Lebanon issue being urgent, Nissim therefore proposed that it take preference.

"Well done!" Deputy Prime Minister Yadin wrote in a note to Nissim when the latter concluded his words. But they displeased Ariel Sharon, who, having long pressed for the strike to go ahead, took a poor view of any further postponement. Begin and most of the other ministers sided with Nissim, however.

No decision was reached on a new date, that being delegated to a three-man team comprising Prime Minister Begin, Foreign Minister Shamir and Commander in Chief Eytan.

Maronite cries for help now rose to a clamor. The Falangists requested Israel's aid in breaking the Syrian siege of Mount Snin, whose imminent conquest would give the Syrians control of the Christian hill country. The Commander in Chief proposed a sortie against the Syrian helicopters, and Begin gave his approval, perceiving the action as a stark warning to the Syrians, and equally stark proof to the Christians that Israel would not tolerate their destruction. Israel's Air Force acted swiftly, shooting down two Syrian helicopters, with their complement of troops. Syria hastened to respond by moving SAM-6 antiaircraft missiles into Lebanon's Bekaa Valley.

Begin gave notice that Israel would act against the missiles. Tension mounted. The Air Force made preparations to attack the SAM batteries during the afternoon hours of April 30, but one hour ahead of the scheduled time it turned out that weather conditions made it impossible to go ahead with the strike.

The delay was welcomed as a heaven-sent piece of good fortune by some of Israel's military leaders. One of these was the Commander in Chief. Though he favored the attack on the missiles, Major General Eytan feared that its present timing was liable to obstruct the planned reactor raid. "I argued that if we attacked the missiles first, the Middle East would be in such uproar that the operation in Iraq would be forestalled. Aside from that, the missiles were the subject of diplomatic negotiations directed by the U.S. President's special envoy Philip C. Habib. Above all, I regarded the reactor as a far greater threat to Israel than the missiles in Lebanon."

On this point, Rafful disagreed sharply with his Military Intelligence chief. General Saguy advocated priority for the attack on the missiles, which disrupted Israel's early-warning network.

In the meantime, the pilots earmarked for the operation in Iraq engaged in various missions in Lebanon. One of the two fliers who downed the Syrian helicopters would later take part in the attack on al-Tuweitha. His colleagues carried out attacks on terrorist headquarters, artillery batteries and similar targets. Their operational performance progressively improved, as did their mastery of the new F-16s.

General Ivry related: "I purposely pressed for use of the planes in attacks in Lebanon, so as to prepare the pilots for this [the reactor attack]. But all those weeks they didn't know that they were on constant alert [for the operation in Iraq]."

Saddam Hussain was in trouble. His hopes of an easy victory over Iran's Khomeinist regime had been dashed. The fighting was taking a bloody toll of the Iraqi forces. Iran's enormous superiority in land mass and population began to make its impact on the field of battle.

But the Iraqi President pursued his policy of active war on all fronts. In an interview to the Lebanese *al-Hawadet* on April 17, he expounded the basic planks of his ideology: "As for the Iraqi, when we tell him that he is called upon to stand at the head of the liberation of Palestine, he understands what the intention is and what he must do, as this [the liberation of Palestine] is the basis of the Ba'ath Party." Even with his armies deeply embroiled on the Iranian battlefront, Hussain continued to regard "the liberation of Palestine" as his regime's supreme goal.

Senator Alan Cranston would not allow Congress to ignore his warnings about the pursuit of nuclear arms by Pakistan and Iraq. In a speech to the Senate on April 27, he pointed out some implications of Pakistan's nuclear program: "A nuclear-capable Pakistan could be put under extreme pressure from radical Arab states to become embroiled in dangerous Middle East fighting." He urged the Congress and the Administration to lose no time in taking steps against military nuclear projects in the Mideast and Southeast Asia, warning that they might spark a direct confrontation between the superpowers.

But even if Cranston's warnings alerted some of his listeners, the new Congress and Administration were sluggish in their response. It was evident that no concrete action would ensue.

On April 27, a final decision designated the F-16s as the planes to attack the reactor. Almost all the bombs were to be directed at the main objective, Tammuz 1, on the assumption that adjoining targets would also be damaged. According to preliminary estimates, the number of planes chosen for the mission gave odds of 99.88 percent that Tammuz 1 would be hit, and 100 percent certainty of some damage to the structure. The directives specified the number of bombs to be borne by each plane, and there were precise instructions about communications.

By late April the planners possessed detailed information on every subject they had requested. They knew that the Iranian raid of September 1980 had prompted the Iraqis to boost antiaircraft precautions at al-Tuweitha, where the reactor was now encompassed by canvas-covered conelike mounds. The reactor dome had been daubed with camouflage colors to hinder its identification from the air. Antiaircraft defenses included cannon as well as various types of missiles—SAM 6, SAM 2 and improved SAM 3—all controlled by a sophisticated radar system.

A team personally headed by General Ivry drew on intelligence data to prepare instructions on the flight route, formation, assault tactics, etc. It goes without saying that plans included a number of alternative routes to the objective and back—nearly six hundred miles each way. The Air Force continued to conduct a variety of tests, pinpointing obstacles and updating maps and directives.

On May 3, Begin briefed his ministers, giving further reliable information about Iraq's intention of using its reactors for the production of nuclear weapons. In view of current predictions of a Labor victory in the upcoming June elections, he also voiced the fear that a Cabinet headed by Labor Party leader Shimon Peres, and including the latter's dovish colleague Abba Eban, would not summon up the resolve to bomb the reactor.

Replying to critics, the Prime Minister explained why the operation had not been launched the previous January; he recalled that even outright supporters, such as Ministers Ehrlich and Nissim, had argued that it might be viewed as a provocation if carried out so close to the swearing-in of the new U.S. President.

As before, there were disagreements among the ministers and the experts. Military Intelligence Director Saguy argued that destruction of the reactor would set a precedent. There was a rapprochement between Iraq and the United States. "We must not, with our own hands, stir up an eastern front against us. . . . Iraq will not have a nuclear bomb tomorrow morning."

Begin, however, questioned the alleged U.S.–Iraqi rapprochement. The final date had arrived, he said. The reactor was not yet hot, but soon would be. "Suffice it," he said, "if we manage to postpone construction of the Iraqi bomb by just three years; thereby, we save an entire generation."

Commander in Chief Eytan criticized Saguy's remark that there would be no Iraqi bomb "tomorrow morning." "When the reactor is hot," he said, "we shall be unable to act." Waiting would tie Israel's hands. Conscious that an implacable foe was preparing a nuclear bomb, Israel would nevertheless be powerless to act against the reactor for fear of radioactive contamination which could kill tens or perhaps hundreds of thousands in Baghdad and its vicinity.

Deputy Prime Minister Yadin persisted in his opposition, but Begin was supported by Shamir and Sharon, and by Yoram Aridor, the new finance minister, who had joined the team following the resignation of his predecessor, Yigael Hurwitz. After Begin argued against the attack being mounted that same day, Aridor and Shamir came up with a new idea: with the French election campaign nearing its conclusion, would it not be profitable to dispatch an emissary to Mitterrand and attempt to elicit undertakings which, in the event of his election to the presidency, would enable the operation to be shelved?

The Prime Minister rejected the notion. He feared that such a demarche, without changing the situation, would merely delay the necessary Israeli steps. It was not a French reactor, he said, but an Iraqi reactor. The problem was not France, but the existence of the state of Israel. There was therefore no point in waiting for the election of a new French President.

The new date for the reactor attack was fixed for May 10.

On May 5, droves of mourners shuffled along the narrow track leading to the small cemetery of Moshav Tel Adashim. The crowd included the Prime Minister, both his deputies, ministers, opposition leader Shimon Peres, and senior officers. All had come to pay homage to Rafful's flier son, Major Yoram Eytan, who had lost his life the previous day in a training accident. At the time of his death, Major General Eytan had been in a meeting with the Prime Minister.

Among the thousands of mourners mounting the slope, two figures advanced slowly. The lofty Ezer Weizman stooped a little as he poured a torrent of words into the ear of the somewhat shorter Ariel Sharon. Knowing Sharon to be one of the fervent advocates of the reactor attack, Weizman was endeavoring to talk him out of it. But Sharon declined to discuss the matter with the former Defense Minister.

Weizman turned to Interior Minister Dr. Burg. "Are you all out of your minds?" he demanded. "How do you have the temerity to do such a thing?"

"I voted against it," Burg retorted defensively. "However, there is collective responsibility." But Burg, a man of enormous political experience, felt uneasy. How had such a closely guarded secret leaked out? The question gave him no peace.

Deputy Prime Minister Simha Ehrlich felt equally uneasy when Weizman approached him on the same matter. Earlier, Weizman, attempting to contact Ehrlich at home, had urged the latter's wife, Tzilla, "Tell your husband not to be a hero." Now he glared down at the slightly built Ehrlich. "I hear you're a hero," he remarked with bitter scorn. A startled Ehrlich tried to reply, but Weizman got in first. "I've got to talk to you on a matter which I know must not be talked about." Ehrlich, grasping instantly what Weizman was after, elected to hold their conversation elsewhere. The two men arranged to meet at Tel Aviv's Dan Hotel the following afternoon, May 6—the eve of Israel's Independence Day.

"How could you consent to support the reactor bombing?" Weizman demanded.

"How did you find out?" Ehrlich flung back.

"Trust me, I've got my sources," Weizman said, and he proceeded to rattle off a long list of arguments against the proposed attack. His principal objection: it would harm Israel's peace treaty with Egypt—the apple of Weizman's eye.

When Ehrlich remained unconvinced, Weizman urged that the attack be postponed till August. Ehrlich was fully aware of pollsters' predictions that August would find Israel under a Labor government. Such an administration being unlikely to order an attack on the reactor, Weizman's proposed postponement was clearly designed with the aim of altogether foiling an operation of whose urgent necessity Ehrlich was convinced, and whose early implementation he had urged on Begin. The Deputy Prime Minister therefore rejected Weizman's suggestion.

"Fix me a meeting with Begin," Weizman now begged.

But Ehrlich did not wish to get involved in the fractious relationship between the Prime Minister and his former Defense Minister, whose resignation had been marked by resounding criticism of Begin. "If you want a meeting with Begin," Ehrlich retorted, "request it directly."

A few hours previously, while attending the Air Force's commemoration ceremony—the eve of Independence Day is the occasion when Israel remembers its war dead—Weizman had tried to convince the force's commander to veto the operation. General Ivry recalls: "At the service beside the memorial to the Air Force's dead, Weizman put the pressure on me. He used terms like 'Are you all crazy? What are you about to do?' His tirade indicated that he knew a great deal. If my memory doesn't deceive me, Ezer even knew the date of the raid. He wouldn't give up, but I broke off contact. After all, he knew it wasn't me he should be putting under pressure: I didn't make the decisions, I just carried them out."

But Weizman refused to be silenced. Convinced that the reactor attack would entail disastrous consequences, he made feverish attempts to stop the operation. "I had conversations with David Ivry and Simha Ehrlich and Yosef Burg," Weizman related. "I talked with Shimon Peres twice, indirectly," he added, refusing to elaborate on "indirectly." Did he contact Peres by way of some third party? On that point, both men remain tightlipped.

On Friday, May 8, the aerial assault force, supported by maintainance units, flew to the airbase designated as the jump-off for the strike. The pilots conducted a further dummy attack, carried out aerial refueling and completed a general check of all systems. On Saturday, May 9—one day ahead of the date scheduled—the pilots were given detailed directives for the operation.

Unbeknown to the Prime Minister, the Commander in Chief or the Air Force commander, a most determined behind-the-scenes effort was under way in a bid to abort the projected operation. Equally unknown to them, what they regarded as a top secret was shared by all too many individuals not required to be in the know.

Deputy Prime Minister Yigael Yadin recalled: "Saturday, May 9, I was at my summer home in Mikhmoret when the phone rang. On the line was Ezer Weizman. He told me he had learned there were preparations for an attack on the reactor. 'It's madness, it's suicide,' he shouted into the phone. 'I've spoken with Burg and Ehrlich, and I'm telling you too: You are undertaking a great responsibility.' He cursed and reviled the Prime Minister. I told him, 'Ezer, I'm not prepared to discuss this with you over the phone.'

"I don't recall," Yadin went on, "whether it was the same Saturday, May 9, or the Saturday before or after, that Uri Eran* (a reserve brigadier and one of the leading authorities on the matter) came to Mikhmoret to see me. He asked me to persuade Begin to halt the attack. Weizman and Eran appeared to be aware of my opinion on the matter. I told Eran, 'I'm sorry. Whatever I could do or say, I did and said. The die is cast.'"

The assault plan also came to the attention of Shimon Peres. He refuses to divulge his source, but it was probably some establishment personage— whether civilian or military—who was privy to the secret. Be that as it may, that evening Peres decided to act before the strike could go off as scheduled the following day.

In matters of military policy, Peres was in his element, having spent many years at the pinnacle of Israel's defense establishment. He was only twenty-nine when Ben Gurion chose him to serve as director general of the Defense Ministry, a post he filled for many years. In addition to administering the widely ramified ministry, Peres also directed his efforts toward promoting Israel's electronics and aviation industries. With his eyes fixed on the future, he laid Israel's nuclear infrastructure with construction of the reactors at Nahal Shorek and Dimona; when critics, including authorities in the field, dismissed these projects as premature, Peres refused to be deterred.

Peres could therefore claim to be an authority on the matter at hand. Now, convinced that Begin's decision to attack the reactor was misguided, he took a sheet of his personal notepaper and proceeded to formulate his thoughts, setting them out in his cramped handwriting.

*Fictitious name.

PERSONAL—TOP SECRET

PRIME MINISTER,

At the end of December 1980, you summoned me to your office in Jerusalem, and told me of an extremely grave matter. You did not solicit my comment, and I likewise (in spite of my instinctive feeling), under the circumstances then existent, made no comment.

I feel this morning that it is my supreme civic duty to advise you, in all earnestness and out of national considerations, to desist.

I speak from experience. The dates reported by us (and I comprehend the concern of our people) are not the real dates. Material can be replaced with (other) material. What is aimed at prevention could provide a spur. On the other hand, Israel will be like a thorn in the wilderness. And she too has grounds for concern.

I add my voice—and it is not mine alone—to those who tell you not to act, certainly not under the present timing and circumstances.

SHIMON PERES

Seeking to preserve confidentiality, Peres employed imprecise terms, without directly specifying the subject; he assumed, correctly, that Begin would find no difficulty in deciphering his meaning:

· "an extremely grave matter": the decision to attack the reactor.
· "the circumstances": those whereby Peres was notified of the Cabinet decision without his counsel being solicited.
· "this morning": the day of the French presidential elections.
· "to desist": from attacking the reactor.
· "from experience": Peres' share in construction of Israel's own reactors.
· "the dates reported by us": by Israel's intelligence agencies.
· "not the real dates": the dates Begin gave for activation of the reactor were unrealistic; the installation would go into operation at a later time.
· "material can be replaced by (other) material": there was a chance of convincing the French government—particularly if power passed to the Socialists, who were unencumbered by the previous Administration's undertakings—to replace weapons-grade uranium with a nonexplosive fuel (probably Caramel, of which Peres had heard during his talks in France).
· "what is aimed at prevention could provide a spur": instead of halting the nuclear-arms race in the Mideast, the reactor attack was liable to precipitate it.
· "like a thorn in the wilderness": Israel would be isolated in the international arena.
· "and she too has grounds for concern": Israel was liable to suffer reprisal in kind if the Iraqi reactor was destroyed.

· "to those who tell you": ministers, including Deputy Prime Minister Yadin, as well as other experts, civilian and military.
· "the timing": May 10.
· "circumstances": a further reference to the French presidential elections.

Before dispatching his letter to the Prime Minister, Peres held a highly confidential consultation with several party colleagues who knew of the planned reactor bombing: Yitzak Rabin, Haim Barlev, Mordechai Gur, Abba Eban and Simha Dinitz.

Abba Eban recalled: "Peres said that attacking the reactor was liable to alienate Mitterrand, who might be the next French President. If Mitterrand were elected, Peres saw prospects of the material [weapons-grade uranium] being withdrawn from Iraq."

"My colleagues who attended the consultation were familiar with the matter," Peres related. "I consulted them so as to give my letter the official imprint of the Labor Party."

Rabin, who was continually briefed by Aharon Yariv's team of experts, appears to have known more than any of the other Labor leaders, including Peres himself. In general, Rabin shared his party colleagues' view that there was no justification for the attack on the reactor. "The data we possessed," he was to recall, "indicated that the reactor was not an imminent threat. Likewise, the experts' assessment said, 'It is doubtful whether the reactor can be profitable [to Iraq].'"

Haim Barlev, at that time general secretary of the Labor Party and its candidate for defense minister, recalls the exchange of views within the party leadership, and the general consensus that attacking the reactor would be a mistake. It was accordingly agreed that Party Chairman Peres should send an official letter to Begin.

Peres remembers writing the letter at four in the morning. Yisrael Galili was at his home in Kibbutz Na'an when he received a photostat of the letter, with a covering note stating that its original would reach Begin in the morning of May 10; this being about the time Galili himself received it, he would have been unable, even had he so wished, to amend the text or expand upon it.

Peres gave the letter to Simha Dinitz, requesting him to transmit it to his friend Haim Yisraeli, a man of great influence as the Defense Minister's bureau chief ever since the days of Ben-Gurion. Yisraeli, having been requested to make sure Peres' letter reached Begin without delay, sent it by special delivery to the Prime Minister's office in Jerusalem.

As the messenger made his way to the capital, preparations for the raid were in full swing. Execution that very day now seemed a certainty.

• • •

Sunday morning, May 10, all the officers involved with the operation assembled at the Etzion airbase in Sinai. At ten, General Ivry issued his final instructions to the pilots.

Then Commander in Chief Eytan addressed them, stressing the operation's national importance and strategic value. Just six days had elapsed since the death of his son Yoram, but Rafful, bearing himself in the manner of which he alone is capable, gave no sign of his bereavement. Even though he had loved his son dearly, and even though the matter at hand was of the utmost gravity, he laughed and joked with the pilots as they prepared to set off for combat. Asked later about his feelings on being forced to curtail the seven-day *shiva* of mourning, the Commander in Chief replied, "In the Eytan family we don't take these things the way other people do."

At the end of the briefing, the pilots were instructed on how to behave in the event of falling into captivity. Like everyone present, they hoped fervently to be back in Israel that same day without ever having to resort to the counsel they had just received.

That Sunday morning, the Cabinet convened in Jerusalem for its regular weekly meeting. Begin, Shamir and a few other ministers knew that it would be only a few hours before the planes set out on their mission; but the other ministers sensed nothing unusual. The topics on the agenda had been determined beforehand.

No one attached any importance to the buff envelope delivered to Begin; since he was also the acting defense minister, numerous messages and papers reached him at almost every Cabinet meeting.

Delving into the envelope, Begin drew out a sheet of writing paper folded in half, with Shimon Peres' name printed at the head. Having read the contents carefully, he sank into reflection; he then decided to cut the Cabinet meeting short, though not before requesting that a number of ministers remain behind.

When the other Cabinet members had departed, Begin proceeded to read out the contents of Peres' letter.

The ministers were dumbfounded. They knew that the Cabinet's October 1980 decision to bomb the reactor had been conveyed to Peres by Begin the previous December. But Peres' closing sentence, "I add my voice—and it is not mine alone—to those who tell you not to act . . .," clearly indicated that he was acquainted with other individuals who shared the secret and opposed the operation. Furthermore, the urgency of the letter testified that Peres was aware of the precise time set for the attack.

How did the opposition leader come to share a secret supposedly known to no one but the Prime Minister, the Foreign Minister and the Commander in Chief? Privately, the ministers wondered who was being referred to when Peres mentioned "those who tell you not to act." Did the Labor chairman know details of the soul-searchings and uncertainties which had afflicted the Cabinet and all others concerned until they reached their decision to destroy the reactor? Who else shared the secret?

It soon emerged that there were others. Dr. Burg and Begin's two deputies, Ehrlich and Yadin, reported on Ezer Weizman's approaches and his efforts to convince them to stop the operation. "How did Ezer know he should approach me of all people?" Yadin wondered. Ehrlich cited Weizman's words to his wife. Aside from his talks with the three ministers, it transpired that Weizman had discussed the matter with other individuals.

"Motta Gur knows, too," Ehrlich affirmed. At a reception the previous night he had encountered Gur, a former commander in chief and now a prominent Labor politician. As Ehrlich was to relate: "Motta Gur came up to me and said, 'I want to talk to you on a matter which is military par excellence. . . . I requested a meeting with the Prime Minister, but I have received no reply. . .' Gur presented a series of objections to the reactor attack. I rejected them."

Gur's version is very different. "When I spoke with Ehrlich, I did not know of the plan to attack the reactor [the following day]. What I wanted to discuss with Begin was the subject of Lebanon, where I could see clearly there were plans to go to war. Rafful was keeping three divisions up there [in the north] without justification. Knowing Rafful well, I wished to warn the Prime Minister—but Begin was in no hurry to receive me. I told Ehrlich, 'You don't know what is about to happen.' I asked him to request Begin to receive me. The following day I got a reply from Begin, saying an appointment would be arranged for me."

Ehrlich nevertheless remained convinced that Gur had referred explicitly to the reactor attack. The Deputy Prime Minister was indignant over Gur's familiarity with the secret. "With all due respect to the ex–Commander in Chief," Ehrlich complained to his Cabinet colleagues, "do all the exes have to know all the secrets?"

But the ministers were doubly astounded when Begin mentioned two additional names: a prominent journalist for the daily *Yediot Aharonot*, and Amiram Nir, formerly a military correspondent for Israel television. Government circles suspected that Nir—who was then employed at Labor's election headquarters and was a close confidant of Peres—knew of the projected raid, and this is borne out by Barlev and Gur. As for the journalist, he reportedly told a foreign airline director, "I can't go abroad, because Israel is about to do something which will shake the world." Later the journalist would explain that he was referring to a possible Israeli strike against the Syrian missiles in Lebanon.

But the ministers' consternation stemmed principally from Peres' familiarity—as reflected in his letter—with the precise timing of the raid. True, the Labor leader had been made privy to the decision in principle to launch the strike, but how did he learn that most highly guarded secret, the date, which not even all the Cabinet knew? Peres was a former defense minister, as was Weizman, who had also commanded the Air Force; Gur was a former commander in chief. All three men naturally retained their own sources of information, political as well as military. But how was it that no secret was safe from them?

The ministers suspected a pooling of information between the two former defense ministers, Peres and Weizman, whose joint efforts may have been supported by a Cabinet minister, or by interested parties in the administration or the defense establishment.

Who gave Peres the precise date set for the attack? The source will probably never come to light, though accusing fingers were pointed at Mossad chief Yitzhak Hoffy, who was among the opponents of the operation. A close associate of Ariel Sharon, journalist Uri Dan, voiced the accusation publicly, but refused to divulge his own sources; although forced to resign his job with the daily *Ma'ariv*, he never withdrew his charges. Hoffy denied them outright, and continued to enjoy Begin's unqualified confidence.

But that was not the pressing concern now. Unnerved by the leak, Begin and his ministers nevertheless had no time to consider its source. The planes were preparing for takeoff from Etzion; should the Cabinet instruct the Commander in Chief to press on with the operation?

Yadin argued that the leak now made it imperative to go ahead. He assumed that the Iraqis would eventually learn of Israel's intention; in the interest of preserving the element of surprise, the earlier the attack went off, the better.

Apprehensive that the news had already reached foreign ears—in the West, for example, from where it could filter through to unforeseen quarters—Begin proposed that a new date be considered, in spite of his fear that a postponement till the following month, June, would invite nefarious interpretation "by the evil tongues of vicious men": June 30 was voting day in the Knesset elections.

Sharon, fearful lest the matter be deferred till after the elections, called for an immediate decision. "I do not see a different government with persons possessing broader authority to reach a decision."

In the ensuing discussion, several ministers again voiced their objections to the attack. On the opposing side, Sharon pressed for the operation to go ahead as planned. Begin opted for a postponement. "If Peres and other opposition leaders are acquainted with the secret, who knows where else it could have leaked to?" he mused aloud. It was accordingly left to the "troika"—Begin, Shamir and Eytan—to fix a new date.

At Etzion, the pilots were beside their planes, making their final preparations, when the unexpected stand-down message arrived from the Commander in Chief. Colonel Eliezer Malachi, who headed the strike force's second formation, recalls: "We were in the planes when we were notified: the operation had been postponed. We felt frustrated. Any mission you prepare for, and you're suddenly told you're not going, is frustrating. When the mission is dangerous, disappointment, frustration and anger all get mixed up together. We felt terribly deflated."

Major General Eytan sent off a cable directing that all operational plans and directives be shredded. The cable itself was likewise destroyed.

Peres had achieved his purpose. Later he was to relate: "Mitterrand, the new French President, was aware of my intervention, even though I didn't tell him thereof."

On May 13, Begin was determined to order the reactor attack at the earliest feasible date that same month. He argued that the strike should be as remote as possible from election day, June 30, but foresaw that his adversaries would accuse him of mounting it as an election stunt. "Even if we carry out the bombing in May, they'll claim that we did it because of the elections," the Prime Minister added.

Rafful echoed his words. "Whatever happens, they'll say it's on account of the elections."

Begin summarized: "I am not afraid of being accused that it was done with the elections in mind. All the same, any proximity between the date of the operation and election day should be avoided as far as possible."

The Prime Minister again reviewed and updated information which predicted that the reactor would be hot by mid-July or early September. "The Iraqis," he said, "are exerting heavy pressure on the French to have it active by Revolution Day, July 17. The French claim that they will find that timetable difficult to meet, and request that activation be put back to early September. But if we delay the bombing, we run the risk of Iraqi pressure ultimately inducing the French to get the reactor into operation by mid-July. Aside from that, there is no evading the crucial question: What will be the outcome of the impending elections?

"Perhaps," Begin continued, "this room will soon belong to Shimon Peres. The substance of his letter is known. Can we deduce from it that when he officiates as prime minister he will order the reacor attack?"

It was a purely rhetorical question. Begin assumed that his listeners would share his own conviction that Peres would do no such thing. He resumed: "Can we [members of the present Cabinet] afford to leave the stage and bequeath to our children this dreadful danger, of a gravity unprecedented since the extinction of the ovens at the extermination camps?" With the reactor still cold, Israel had an opportunity which would not recur.

The force of Begin's arguments brought around some ministers who had hesitated previously. One of these was Health Minister Eliezer Shostak, who likewise shared the view that Labor would denounce the attack as an election stunt, but he attached no importance thereto.

Consistent in his views, Ariel Sharon complained of the opportunities missed hitherto. He urged a decision on immediate execution of the raid, and when Begin appeared to have reservations Sharon requested permission for a personal statement.

Was he about to threaten resignation? It is conceivable. But Begin hastened to smooth the Agriculture Minister's ruffled feathers, and no personal statement was forthcoming. The timing of the raid was left to the discretion of the ministerial group.

Several of the experts involved continued to voice vigorous reservations and objections. One of these, Uri Eran, who expressed his dissenting views in closed forums, spent several days composing a personal memorandum explaining his stubborn opposition to military action. The memorandum was sent off on May 11, one day after the original date set for the attack.

Eran rested his case upon Mitterrand's declaration that he would not follow Giscard's policy regarding the agreement with Iraq, because of the blatant military potential of the equipment, material and technology being supplied to Iraq. Eran also recalled Mitterrand's indication that he would halt deliveries of weapons-grade uranium and force the Iraqis to use Caramel.

Additional arguments put forward by Eran: the risk of casualties among the hundreds of foreign experts employed at al-Tuweitha; the attack would constitute a severe blow to French prestige, thus forcing Mitterrand, in defiance of his own secret wishes, to reconstruct the reactor; the world, Eran foresaw, would regard the raid as a barbaric act, thereby providing Iraq with justification for pulling out of the nonproliferation treaty; furthermore, the strike was liable to unite the entire Arab and Moslem world in a joint project for the manufacture of an atom bomb.

Former Commander in Chief Mordechai Gur likewise had vigorous objections to the proposed attack. On May 12 he was received by Begin, Simha Ehrlich having kept his promise to arrange the meeting. Begin recalled: "Motta Gur came to see me and said, 'The entire nation is talking about the operation against the reactor.' Where he got the information, I have no idea. I did not discuss it with him."

Gur's account of the meeting is startlingly different. "In the course of the conversation, I gave my assessment of developments in the region. I warned Begin against his intention of making Sharon defense minister if the Likkud retained power after the elections. I told him, 'All Sharon can guarantee you is all-out war in Lebanon and Syria.'

"Another prolonged portion of our conversation dealt with 'Israel in the nuclear age': How could Israel survive in the Middle East as the region rapidly plunged into the nuclear era? Begin said, 'With the murderer in Iraq [Saddam Hussain] and the madman in Libya [Muammar al-Qaddafi], there's no knowing what will happen in the region when they have nuclear forces.'

"But beyond that," Gur claims, "I proffered no comment either for or against the planned bombing of the Iraqi reactor."

By contrast, Begin's version: "Why did he come to me out of the blue and criticize the reactor operation? How could he have learned it? Through being an ex–commander in chief? What business was it of his? If I were ex-something, would I come along and proffer advice? I was alarmed; this was a life-and-death matter. It could have reached the ears of the Iraqis. I therefore postponed the operation—then planned for May 17—by several weeks, and we silenced the whole matter."

Gur claims to have learned of the operation previously, from none other than his own successor as commander in chief, Major General Eytan. Gur recalls hearing of it at a meeting of "the forum of commanders in chief," an informal body composed of all former heads of Israel's armed forces, who convene from time to time at the invitation of the serving commander in chief. The "forum" held two meetings in 1980—in January and July. The latter included a visit to the Air Force, and that, as Gur remembers, was when the reactor operation appears to have come up.

Gur: "Rafful told us that Iraq was developing a reactor, and we were thinking of bombing it. We were shocked. Rabin took a very poor view of it. None of us took the matter seriously. Someone remarked, 'Rafful thinks [the reactor] is a police fortress'" (a favorite target for Israeli reprisal raids against Jordan during the fifties, when Eytan was a junior combat commander in the paratroops).

Major General Eytan has refused to comment on his predecessor's claim. Other former commanders in chief who attended that meeting—Yadin, Zvi Tzur and Rabin—do not remember the reactor attack coming up.

But it was discussed quite freely at a routine meeting of the *Ha'aretz* daily editorial board early in May. Journalist Yoel Markus related that while he was seated in a Tel Aviv café his neighbor (at Markus' request, the man's identity remains confidential) told him that Israel was about to attack the Iraqi reactor. The man claimed to have drawn his information from "the forum of commanders in chief." Markus: "The man told me that the matter was raised by Rafful, and his guests then proceeded one by one to voice their personal views. Gur went to talk the matter over with the Prime Minister."

Be all that as it may, Begin remained firm in his resolve: the reactor had to go. He read the memorandum from Uri Eran, but remained unconvinced. He saw no distinction between the uranium reaching Iraq in one shipment or in several smaller deliveries. In either case, the reactor would enable Iraq to achieve a weapons potential. Begin did not dismiss Eran's concern over casualties among the foreign technicians: one of the principal reasons for timing the raid on a Sunday was the assumption that the foreigners would be off the site that day. As for the diplomatic risks Israel would face, Begin was constantly aware of them, recalling them specifically whenever the matter came up for discussion. But he viewed destruction of the reactor as a vital necessity for the survival of the state and the Jewish nation, and the diplomatic risk appeared negligible by comparison with the risk of sitting by idly.

In mid-May, updated assessments predicted that the reactor would be ready to go into operation by late September at the latest; Begin knew that the raid must go through before the reactor was hot. It was not only adverse international reactions that Begin worried about: he was truly concerned about preventing Baghdad's civilian population from being exposed to radioactive contamination.

But in view of the elections, postponement beyond June was also out of the question, leaving Begin with a narrow time span. His determination was reinforced by a further development. If he had entertained some faint hope of the new Socialist government in France reviewing its nuclear cooperation with Iraq (as Uri Eran and Peres both hoped), along came the new French Foreign Minister, Claude Cheysson, and dashed all expectations. On May 26, Cheysson declared that France would honor in full all agreements signed by the previous administration. Noting that President Mitterrand regretted that certain agreements were concluded, he nevertheless pledged that they too would be honored.

Mitterrand and Cheysson were both known to be sympathetic toward Israel, in concern for whose welfare they certainly surpassed the men of the former administration. But the new leaders soon learned that, with a munitions industry bound by numerous long-term contracts to Arab states pledged to pay for the arms with oil in large amounts and at stable prices, France had reached the point of no return. The moment Cheysson took office he embarked upon strenuous efforts to convince the Arabs that, Mitterrand's pro-Israel leanings notwithstanding, there would be no change in

France's Mideastern policies, in arms sales to the Arabs, or in cooperation with them—economic, technical or military.

These developments were overt and unconcealed, and teleprinters conveyed the tidings to Israel at lightning speed, fortifying Begin's resolve to attack the reactor. More than ever before, he now feared that, should he lose the elections to Peres, the latter would expend his energies in futile pressure upon his friend Mitterrand, meantime missing a once-only opportunity.

However, in his public stance the Prime Minister remained tightlipped with regard to the Iraqi reactor. Exercising his rhetorical gifts at tempestuous election rallies, Begin whipped his followers into a frenzy with his vigorous declarations—termed "arrogant" by his adversaries—directed against Syria. Time and time again, he pledged that the Syrian missiles would be removed from Lebanon; but he did not so much as mention Iraq. Subsequently, after the attack, Begin was to confess, "My sharply worded statements sought to distract attention from the impending operation over Baghdad. I was dutybound to mislead the enemy."

On May 14, a new directive went out for the reactor raid. In place of its former code name, "Mount Moriah,"* it was now dubbed "Operation."* The date was set for the coming Sunday, May 17. Noting that Tammuz 1 was "coming into operation," the order defined the aim as damaging the reactor seal with the purpose of halting work or, hopefully, causing the site to be abandoned. The attack would be carried out by F-16s.

After the date had been set for May 17, there was a further postponement —the reason this time being operational, not political. Nevertheless, the delay upset the Commander in Chief and the Air Force commander, and their dissatisfaction filtered downward to the Air Force's planning and operational echelons. The sense of frustration prevalent in May found expression in a note that Rafful sent to General Ivry:

DAVID,
The civilians are driving us mad.
There's talk now of next Saturday.
I told him: "It's either or. This can't go on." So don't tell anyone anything. Just make a personal note of next Saturday.
I share your perplexity on the subject.

Ivry naturally found no difficulty in deciphering the code terms:

"The civilians": the cabinet.
"driving us mad": the numerous postponements.
"I told him": the Prime Minister.

*Fictitious name.

"it's either or": either the operation is carried out or it is abandoned.

"Don't tell anyone": because a further postponement remained probable.

"your perplexity": the quandary in which you, as overall commander of the operation, find yourself.

Command procedures in Israel's armed forces outline a clearly defined course for any order emanating from the civilian echelons—whether the Cabinet, the Prime Minister or the Defense Minister; it reaches the Commander in Chief, who transmits it to the appropriate rung of the military hierarchy, in this case the Air Force commander. The latter conveys it to his operational echelons—commanders of squadrons or wings. Fazed by the repeated postponements, Ivry on this occasion withheld the order from his operational echelons; only when convinced that there were good prospects of the operation going ahead did he give the necessary instructions to the colonel who was his gifted head of operations.

Relapsing into pilot's jargon, Ivry recalls: "At times I would tell him, 'Hold it . . . wait . . .'" At the same time, the Commander in Chief repeatedly complained to Begin, "You are driving our Air Force crazy."

As already noted, all the dates set hitherto had fallen on a Sunday, with the aim of avoiding casualties among the French technicians. Now, in view of the short time left for the operation to go ahead, the Commander in Chief requested information on the following points: In Iraq, did Friday, the Moslem holy day, resemble Israel's Saturday, the Jewish Sabbath, when most activity ceases? Did Thursday evening approximate in its level of activity Israel's Friday evening, the Jewish Sabbath eve, when activity outside the home largely comes to a halt?

Intelligence reported as follows: Friday was Iraq's weekly rest day, but it was uncertain whether activity—either in the country at large or at the reactor site in particular—came to a halt as early as Thursday afternoon. The foreigners, who had a free day on Sundays, stopped work at midday Saturday.

Theoretically, therefore, the raid could be fixed for a Saturday or a Friday; but on further consideration the balance tilted back in favor of the original choice: Sunday.

In a personal note, Rafful told Ivry:

For the last time!

The date fixed is May 31, Sunday. Don't say anything to anybody.

I told them [Begin and Shamir, delegated with Eytan to set the attack date] "either or." If it's not this date, they should stop harrying us up and down.

So until further notice, that is the appointed date.

But it was still not final. On May 20, the Commander in Chief was obliged to notify Ivry of a further week's postponement, to June 7. The reason this time: to avoid marring Begin's summit meeting with Egyptian President Sadat, scheduled to be held at Sharm al-Sheikh (in Hebrew, Ophira) on June 4.

Rafful wrote a note to Ivry in his characteristically laconic style: "'Operation' + a week due to next week's summit P.M.–Sadat Ophira."

On May 22, rising Labor politician Moshe Shahal arrived at Ezer Weizman's Caesarea home for a private talk. "He came," Weizman related, "to convince me to take a senior position with the Labor Party—on its Knesset slate or in the government the party would form after the elections; he asked me at least to help Labor in the election campaign. I declined."

Shahal recalls: "Weizman divulged a closely guarded secret. He told me that the government intended to carry out the attack on the nuclear reactor in Iraq close to election day."

Weizman: "I only discussed the possibility of military action against the Syrian missiles in Lebanon. I told him that such an operation would take place close to polling day."

Shahal: "Weizman is ducking the truth. I couldn't even get in additional questions to clarify what he knew of the proposed raid. He inundated me with a flood of descriptions. The way he put it, here as elsewhere Begin was a prisoner of Sharon. Ezer told me, 'I am profoundly concerned about the Prime Minister's overall judgment. It will be a reckless action, and liable to jeopardize the entire peace process.' I was shocked by the vigor of Weizman's description of what went on in the government in which he had so recently served as defense minister."

When Shahal disclosed the gist of his conversation with Weizman, the latter responded with a single word: "Liar!" Be that as it may, Shahal did not keep Weizman's revelations to himself. "Ezer did not authorize me to make use of the information he'd given me," Shahal related later. "But I understood him to be interested in my doing something at my own discretion. I phoned party chairman Shimon Peres and told him I had something of supreme importance to tell him but could not do so by phone.

"Peres immediately invited me to his Tel Aviv home. An hour later I was there, reporting in detail on what I had heard from Weizman. Peres listened intently, but I sensed clearly that he was not surprised."

21 "The alternative is our destruction."

"France has completed construction of Osirak," reported the Parisian *Le Point* on June 1, 1981. "The reactor will commence operation in a few months, after undergoing a number of last-minute tests."

Saddam Hussain was notified that work on the reactor would be completed ahead of schedule. At the presidential palace in Baghdad there was great jubilation.

The new date set for the Israeli raid was June 7. On June 3, Rafful again sent advance notice to Ivry.

"This time," Ivry recalls, "it seemed to be in earnest."

On June 4, the Commander in Chief, accompanied by the commanders of the Air Force and the Navy and by U.S. naval attaché Robert Peterson, was scheduled to fly to Italy to attend the ceremony marking the change of commanders of the Sixth Fleet, the U.S. naval force on permanent duty in the Mediterranean.

The visit to Italy came at an incredibly opportune moment. Anyone, friend or foe, observing developments in Israel could deduce that it was "business as usual." Who could imagine that the Air Force was about to embark upon one of the most complex and perilous operations it had ever mounted, when its own commander, and the Commander in Chief, were on a trip abroad?

Before his departure, General Ivry summoned his head of operations, Colonel Ahiam Tzur* and gave him the following instructions: "You will prepare everything for execution, because I won't be here tomorrow. Activate everything: alerts, stop furloughs, everything."

Tzur directed the base commander to issue the appropriate standby orders to all concerned.

*Fictitious name.

• • •

During the evening of June 4, while Rafful and Ivry were in Italy attending the Sixth Fleet's festive functions, a long-scheduled party was held at an Air Force base. In the course of the revelries, the commanders of the squadrons from which the assault force was drawn were summoned, with a number of other officers, to the office of Wing Commander Yitzhal Melrom.

"The operation is about to go off shortly," Malrom announced. Suddenly he paled. Among the officers was a colonel whom he did not recall as being privy to the secret. Had someone exceeded instructions? Malrom wondered. But the colonel turned out to be substituting for another officer in command of one of the auxiliary services.

The pilots returned to the party, their facial expressions giving no hint of their feelings.

The squadrons designated to take part in the operation were placed on top alert. Initially, only two squadrons were alerted, but for reasons of security the alert was extended to additional squadrons unconnected with the reactor raid. Their commanders were told that a strike into Lebanon might be in the offing. Pilots going on furlough were instructed to remain close to a telephone. Expanded standby crews stayed behind at base.

The following day, June 5—the fourteenth anniversary of the 1967 Six-Day War—the planes designated for the raid carried out various tests to verify the reliability of the bombs to be dropped on the reactor.

As their plane made its way back from Italy, Rafful and Ivry received instructions to come to the Prime Minister's residence immediately upon landing. Without doubt, the summons had to do with the reactor attack; they sincerely hoped they were about to get the green light, not notification of a further postponement.

When their plane landed at Tel Aviv's Sdeh Dov Airport, the two officers found the usual reception party in attendance. Colonel Tzur gave Ivry a handwritten document, classified top secret. Departing from normal military jargon, the text commenced with the words "Thank God!," going on to report that Ivry's absence had not been exploited for "upheavals." The writer added that the operational base was "aware and keeping men within arm's reach." The assault planes, as yet unarmed, were, however, prepared. The officers and the pilots would receive final notification "after you return from Jerusalem," from the meeting with the Prime Minister; having learned from bitter experience that a further postponement remained possible, Tzur held back until Begin gave the final word. The head of operations reported further that there would be a minor modification in the original timetable, with zero hour being put back by twenty minutes.

It remained only to await the final order for everything to be set in motion. Tzur had brought along the commander of the operational base, Colonel Avraham Darom,* to have him available when Ivry brought the final directives. Tzur left home, to await the call from the Air Force commander. Rafful and Ivry headed for Jerusalem.

Arriving at the Prime Minister's residence, they found the head of the Mossad awaiting them, with General Saguy. A day earlier, a dispute had flared when it emerged that the new date set for the operation had somehow failed to reach the Military Intelligence director. Learning of it fortuitously, a highly offended Saguy announced that he was withdrawing from responsibility for the operation "and there'll be no intelligence." Great efforts were required to smooth his ruffled feathers. But he showed up for the meeting at the Prime Minister's residence, where he took an active part in the proceedings.

At this final phase, the most irksome problem was the weather. There was unfortunately no possibility of inducing the Iraqi metereological service to provide an updated forecast. But the weather reports available in Israel turned out to be reasonably accurate.

The Prime Minister announced, "The operation will take place the day after tomorrow, Sunday, June 7."

Ahiam Tzur waited impatiently at his home. The long-expected phone call came through immediately upon conclusion of the meeting at the Prime Minister's residence. The operation, Ivry announced, would go off on the date and at the hour scheduled. Tzur heaved a massive sigh of relief. The Rubicon had been crossed, there was now no way back.

"From here on," Ivry said, "operational decisions are up to us. The Prime Minister was of course unable to help us with regard to the weather." Only a marked deterioration in weather conditions could now impede the departure of the assault force.

Returning to Tel Aviv, Ivry met with Tzur. The two men decided to brief the assault pilots the following day.

At one of the squadrons designated for the operation, the pilots had planned an outing with their families on June 4. In the words of Colonel Eliezer Malachi, "What could be more appropriate to Shavuoth, the Festival of Granting of the Torah, than a drive into Sinai, the reputed scene of that historic event?" But the outing was, of course, called off, upon instructions from the Air Force's head of operations: Colonel Tzur blamed the cancella-

*Fictitious name.

tion on tension in Lebanon. Malachi did not notify his pilots; he waited all day, hoping for the "tension" to dissipate so that the tour could go ahead as planned. Instead, there was a further call from Tzur reiterating the cancellation order. Nevertheless, the following morning, June 6, the pilots arrived at the appointed spot, expecting to clamber into jeeps for the promised tour of Sinai. "Cut your engines!" they were told. "And come on over to the briefing room." Closeted there, the pilots were informed that the reactor strike would be launched the following day.

At one o'clock on Saturday, June 6, the order came through: "Prepare for execution of mission." The F-16 squadrons summoned all technical crews and armorers from their homes; special flights ferried them to the operational base, which they reached that evening. In the coming hours they would test the armament and bomb loads and prepare to receive the planes as they flew in from their home base the following morning, June 7. Forward base commander Colonel Avraham Darom, called from his home in central Israel, also arrived, immediately taking all necessary steps to prevent leaks, mount patrols and guarantee security.

At their home base that Saturday, the pilots, on duty since morning, prepared their planes for takeoff, with a thorough check of all systems and instruments.

In the morning hours of Sunday, June 7, the planes flew down to the forward field. The Commander in Chief and the Air Force Commander also came, arriving by a light plane.

The final briefing was held at ten that morning. The pilots learned everything they needed to know: intelligence, weather, details about the flight to target, attack sequence, as well as directives on how to evade traps, flight formation outward bound and back, report procedures, flight routes and the like.

That morning, ominous reports warned of sandstorms raging along the flight route. "Just as long as we don't run into what the Americans faced in Iran," David Ivry prayed silently. But later reports indicated that the weather was clearing up, with the ground visible from a height of thirty thousand feet, though there was still a possibility of haze. There was a westerly breeze which would affect the planes on their homeward route.

"I felt confident that it would go off well," recalled Rafful. "I didn't know how the operation would end. Some thought one thing, others thought differently. But I was convinced that we had done everything we could to make it a success."

For lead commander of the assault force, Ivry had chosen Colonel Aryeh Ran, the commander of an F-16 squadron. Ivry's head of operations, Colonel Tzur, who had supervised planning, was now placed in command of the advance command group. His assignment would be confined to control functions in the event of unforeseen difficulties during the operation. Direct command would be exercised by Ivry personally.

Before the final briefing, the pilots joined the Air Force commander and the Commander in Chief for a cup of coffee. Then came the briefing, principally concerned with technical details. But it was impossible to overlook the once-in-a-lifetime nature of the operation. "This is a unique national mission," Ivry said in his soft voice. "Not every combatant gets the opportunity to take part in such an undertaking." Right up to the last moment, he dreaded a sudden cancellation. "This isn't the kind of exercise which can be repeated over and over," he reflected later, though he did not share his thoughts with others. As commander, he related, "the responsibility is yours, and you keep your feelings to yourself."

The Commander in Chief also addressed the pilots. Rafful rarely gives away his feelings, but on this occasion his listeners could detect his anxiety over the dangers the fliers faced. The gist of his words was: "If you don't hit the target, or don't reach it, that's a shame. But even in that event," he reassured the pilots, "we can put it to advantage as a warning to the Iraqis."

The way the pilots understood it, Rafful was telling them: Everything would be forgiven, even failure to complete the mission, "just as long as we don't crash."

But Rafful also had something to say about the supreme national importance of the operation. "The alternative is our destruction," he cautioned. Colonel Malachi recalled: "Rafful delivered an impassioned address on the vital necessity of completing the operation. I was convinced that he believed in it with all his heart. It was my impression that he knew that bombing the reactor wouldn't eliminate the Iraqi nuclear threat, merely delay it; but in any case, the operation would give Israel options for creating a new situation."

The pilots listened, silently attentive. "I imagine that, deep inside, they had their fears and doubts," Ivry mused later. "After all, they're human like anyone else. But they were not deterred—on the contrary, all the pilots competed for a place in the assault force. I came under pressure to send additional planes, even escorts, so as to allow the largest possible number of pilots to take part."

The briefing ended. "I'll see you afterward," Ivry cried. "I look forward to seeing you at the debriefing." Rafful personally shook hands with each of the pilots, wishing them all luck.

Each flier was given a bag of dates. The fruit is a staple of the traditional Iraqi diet. "It's just as well to get used to eating Iraqi food," Rafful said with a grin. "Just in case you fall into captivity." One of the pilots made a similarly morbid remark. Ivry offered no comment. As an experienced flier, he knew that such macabre jokes are an integral feature of combat missions. Pilots' thoughts inevitably imagine the worst—and black humor is a good way of working off psychological stress.

Ivry handed final handwritten directives to forward command group commander Colonel Tzur. Then he and Rafful returned to Air Force headquarters, where they stepped down into the control room. Here they were awaited by a distinguished group of eighteen high-ranking officers, all connected in one way or another with the operation.

In the meantime, the technical crews had gone to work on the planes, preparing them for takeoff. They checked on every detail, recalibrating the instruments and feeding the map references into the navigation computers. The technicians are renowned for doing their jobs with unswerving earnestness and responsibility; on this occasion, they seemed determined to outdo themselves. The scene was described by one pilot: "Mechanics and pilots were hastening back and forth, 'with countenances set in grim determination,' to put it in flowery terms. I suppose the maintainence crews were thinking, inwardly, so as not to incur bad luck, Which plane will go missing? Which one will make it back?"

At the last moment, the takeoff direction was changed, due to an unforeseen wind. The fliers were called together for an additional briefing.

In the afternoon, as zero hour approached, the pilots started their engines and taxied to the takeoff positions, to await the thumbs-up signal from squadron technical officer Major Gai. No plane would take off without his okay, which denoted that he took full responsibility for its flightworthiness. The pilots were already immersed heart and soul in the imminent mission; each one shuddered at the thought of Gai discovering some malfunctioning which would cause his particular plane to be grounded. One plane displayed a fault in its fuel supply, but the pilot hotly denied detecting any snag. He would confess to the deception on his return from the mission, when he argued, "How could I have explained that I didn't go out on the raid because of some technical hitch?"

Seated in their cockpits, the pilots started the engines. "We're making history," remarked Major Gai.

At 16:01, the reported time of takeoff, Major Menahem Adiv,* flying third in the second formation ("Ruby"*) said, "The mission has begun."

At his official residence in Jerusalem's Talbia quarter, Menahem Begin paced back and forth, though taking care to remain within arm's reach of the phone which gave him a direct link to the Commander in Chief and the Air

---

*Fictitious name.

Force commander. Begin reflected on the long sleepless nights he had spent weighing up the various options. If we do not act, he thought, what will become of this nation? And its children? If we act, there's every chance of failure. What happens if our planes are shot down on the way, before they even reach the target? And if they make it, but some are shot down? . . .

The ringing of the phone disrupted his train of thought.

"The boys have set out," said Rafful.

"Let's hope for the best," said Begin. "We're relying on them."

"I'll report on the results," the Commander in Chief concluded the brief exchange.

This must have been the moment when King Hussein, on the deck of his yacht *Nur*, heard the thunder of jets and got his first glimpse of the Israeli assault force roaring overhead.

It is unknown whether the pilots spared much time for the blue waters of the Gulf of Aqaba below them, or, if they did, whether they caught sight of the royal yacht. What would they have thought, had they known they were being subjected to the scrutiny of the Jordanian monarch? In all probability, they would not have given it a second thought.

Hussein stared up at the formation, examining the planes with the eyes of an experienced flier. He noted the eight multipurpose F-16s and their six-plane escorting umbrella of F-15s. He made a shrewd estimate of their flight path. As the formation swiftly receded from sight, the King furrowed his brow. He was making some rapid calculations and trying desperately to comprehend the significance of what he had just seen.

Begin was in a reflective mood. Inwardly, he prayed incessantly. He flung a glance at the snapshot of his parents, recalling that they had been murdered by the Nazis at a time when the Jews did not have a state of their own. Then he regarded a picture of his grandchildren. These past months, his heart grieved whenever he saw children at play; he would ask himself, What will happen to them in two or three years' time, when Iraq gets its atom bomb? What are you doing to save them?

With his renowned sensitivity to human life, Begin was also aware of the enormous risks attending the operation. During the forties, when he commanded the Etzel underground, whose resources and manpower were infinitely inferior to those of Israel's mighty army, Begin never approved combat operations before being satisfied beyond any shadow of doubt that everything had been done to avoid casualities or to keep them to an absolute minimum.

• • •

Takeoff having been completed without hitches, the planes cruised at a low altitude, maintaining radio silence. They had several hundred minutes of flying time ahead of them. Everything had been calculated with split-second accuracy. Navigation was entrusted to the most precise and reliable systems ever manufactured.

One of the pilots mused, "We're flying fast, I don't know why exactly—it's a waste of fuel."

It transpired subsequently that Major Adiv dabbled in poetry. Having observed the landscape beneath him on his way to the objective, he later indulged in the following "outpouring":

> *Red earth—beautiful vista.*
> *Not a living soul to be seen—gigantic expanses,*
> *Without so much as a track, a genuine wilderness.*
> *The landscape is monotonously flat, a real desert,*
> *Inclines to dazzle, in spite of being reddish.*

At that precise hour, Mossad head Yitzhak Hoffy was hosting a Shavuoth party. He welcomed his guests with a smile, his expression betraying nothing of what was going on in his mind.

Afterward his friends would complain, "What a wily bastard you are! We never noticed a thing. You didn't even call off the party!" Esther Hoffy alone sensed something. "My wife noticed that people were talking to me and I seemed not to be listening, just looking pensive."

If the Saudi-leased AWACS surveillance planes were in flight at the time, they failed to detect the Israeli assault force. Their attention was directed eastward, to the Persian Gulf and the Iraq–Iran battlefront, not to the west. Later, the Saudis would explain their oversight by alleging that the Israeli planes masqueraded as Jordanians. That was, of course, a fabrication from beginning to end—the uncamouflaged planes clearly displayed their Israeli insignia—and the Iraqis do not appear to have swallowed the story.

At four-thirty that afternoon, shortly before the onset of the Shavuoth festival, an unusual bustle of activity could have been detected in the vicinity of the Prime Minister's residence. Volvo limousines, their rear windows draped, halted a short distance from the two-story house. Security guards, easy to identify by the miniature microphones in their ears, requested the passengers to get out and make their way to the residence on foot.

Returning from a foreign trip, Labor and Welfare Minister Dr. Yisrael Katz had landed one hour previously at Ben Gurion Airport, where he learned that the Prime Minister's military aide was looking for him. Putting in a call, Katz was instructed to come to Begin's residence without delay. "I assumed it was the Syrian missiles," Katz recalled later.

Leaving his father's home, the Prime Minister's son Benyamin Zeev Begin was surprised to see such purposeful activity at such an unusual time. But he asked no questions.

The arriving ministers made themselves comfortable in the reception room, whose furnishings provided momentos of the house's former tenants: Yitzak Rabin (as prime minister) and Abba Eban (as foreign minister). As customary in meetings held at the Prime Minister's residence, the Cabinet members occupied a semicircle of chairs facing a sofa placed at the center of the room. The ministers took their seats, awaiting the prime minister's appearance.

Emerging from his library-cum-study, Begin now made his entrance. A few moments previously, he had spoken with the Commander in Chief, their conversation overheard only by aide Yeshiel Kadishai. As he seated himself in the center of the room, Begin's countenance did not wear its habitual smile.

It was five. Thirty-one minutes to go.

"Welcome, my friends," the Prime Minister commenced. "At this very moment, our planes are approaching Baghdad, and the first one will be over the reactor in a very short time."

"There was a deathly hush in the room," Begin recalled. "All the Cabinet members sensed the burden of responsibility they bore."

The occasion, recalled Dr. Katz, was highly dramatic. The Prime Minister appeared agitated, but he remained purposeful and in control.

Begin spoke at length, reiterating the principal points already familiar to the ministers from earlier discussions. Israel had reliable information that the reactor would be active by July or September. It would then be too late for an attack, which was liable to release large amounts of radioactive material over Baghdad, bringing death to hundreds of thousands of innocent people. No Jew, no Israeli government, would dare perpetrate such a deed. Sunday had been chosen for the operation as a further precaution to prevent casualties.

"A few moments ago," Begin revealed, "my wife asked why I was so jumpy. But I could not tell her, any more than I could tell my son, whom I trust entirely. I told him nothing, in spite of his surprised expression when he was here earlier. I have taken the responsibility, and the anxiety, upon myself, and the decision likewise. My soul-searching extended over many weeks. I knew that if I did not give the order today, that lunatic Saddam

Hussain, who aspires to become the leader of the Arab world, will have two or three atomic bombs. He possesses enormous sums in petrodollars which he received from several Arab states. With that kind of money, the Arabs can buy anything—and indeed they have bought sixty kilograms of enriched uranium, an amount adequate for construction of three Hiroshima-type bombs. Our experts claim that one Iraqi twenty-kiloton bomb could kill fifty thousand Israeli citizens instantly, and cause the deaths of a further one hundred fifty thousand subsequently. Radioactivity victims die; they lose their childbearing faculties, or give birth to children defective in mind and body. With three atomic bombs, the enemy could destroy Jerusalem and its vicinity, Tel Aviv and its suburbs, Haifa and its satellites. About twenty percent of the Israeli population would be annihilated or injured. In the United States, such a ratio would signify forty-six million casualties.

"Consequently," Begin went on, "Iraq's manufacture of atomic bombs constitutes an existential threat to the state of Israel. It is the sacred duty of the Israeli government to act in good time to ward off a danger which threatens, at a single stroke, to destroy everything we have built up here over more than one hundred years. The operation is planned to last no longer than two minutes, and if it succeeds it will take the Iraqis at least four years to repair the reactor and restore it to its present state. What are two minutes in comparison with four years?"

Begin gave a detailed account of the assault force, its bomb load, the dangers accounted for, and similar details. "If all goes well," he said, "the last of our planes will land at its base around seven-thirty this evening.

"We are today carrying out an action without precedent in world history," Begin pointed out, "but it is being done in the full awareness that we are thereby saving our people, and our children, from a terrible danger which is liable to descend upon them in another year, or two, or three."

The Prime Minister concluded by submitting a dilemma for his colleagues to consider: What policy should the government pursue with regard to publicizing the operation? Begin himself was inclined to refrain from announcing it before the Arabs did so. He foresaw that the Iraqis might be too shamefaced to say anything. They might blame the Iranians. In that case, Begin would forgo an Israeli announcement. But if the Iraqis did not remain silent, what should Israel do? The following day being a festival, a decision had to be reached without delay. If the Iraqis made the attack public and threw the whole world into an uproar, should the Israelis say nothing? Everyone would know that it was their work. Should they abandon the global propaganda field to the Arabs?

Simha Ehrlich asked, "Why do we have to admit attacking the reactor?"

Begin: "Because such an operation cannot be concealed, and because we do not operate like thieves in the night. Our silence will be maintained as long as the Iraqis remain silent, but such a secret obviously cannot be preserved for any length of time. An atomic reactor does not vanish as though it had never existed. If the Iraqis do not wish to admit their downfall, someone else will be sure to do so on their behalf." Should Israel get in first with its announcement, Begin feared that Saddam Hussain would feel impelled to mount some insane reprisal action. However, in the event that—God forbid—an Israeli plan was downed on the way there or back, a response had to be prepared ahead of time.

Declaring himself convinced, Ehrlich went a step further; "It might even be profitable," he suggested, "to get in our statement first."

Ariel Sharon thought likewise: "We must tell the world why we did it. Of course, the correct timing has to be found. A state cannot lie. We should go public, but only after we know the response of the other side."

Burg, first beseeching God Almighty to bring the pilots back safely, proposed a moderately worded announcement, without mention of the number of casualties liable to be inflicted should Iraq drop a nuclear bomb on Israel. He also suggested avoiding criticism of France and Italy, so as to give France's new President, Mitterrand, an opportunity to extricate himself from the embroilment.

Hammer: "We should publish if we are attacked by the other side."

Moda'i: "We should make it plain that we did it for lack of any other choice."

Shostak: "As long as the other side is silent, don't publish."

Yadin: "Let us wait till the operation is concluded."

The Israeli planes had disappeared into the haze. From the deck of the royal yacht it must have been evident to King Hussein that they had entered the airspace of his Saudi neighbors. With the vessel's highly sophisticated radio equipment, it would not be not be difficult to warn Riyadh of the approaching Israeli assault force.

But the Saudi King, Khalid, was in Switzerland for medical treatment, and Hussein's message—whatever it was—failed to get through.

The planes entered Iraqi airspace.

Pilot-poet Major Adiv resumed his "outpourings":

We cross [the border] at the correct time and place. Two
Trucks there. A large army camp. All seems well. All
Has worked well. No sweat. We've entered banditland. A plateau
Dry and arid. Every few miles there's some encampment in memory
of some town from
The past, or some skyscraper (Tower of Babel?). Everything

Arid and monotonous, with a populated desert.
We're flying too fast. We're in too much of a straight line—
but that makes no difference.
That is a mighty tower. . . . That mosque is mighty. . . .

"A great sightseeing tour," mused formation leader Colonel Malachi, aware that his assignment made the thought incongruous. He did not have too much time to observe the landscape. It was far more important to concentrate on navigation, altitude, regular functioning of all systems.

Five minutes before the moment he was to release his bombs, Major Adiv, several hundred feet off the ground, contemplated the sights:

See people down below. Waving greetings. I make the gesture of
Shwoyeh.*
Very pretty: a sailing resort for lots of people. There are
Lots of people. Buses.
I see there's a train. All kinds of Arabs looking up, not
comprehending what's going on.
Soon we'll pass over the Euphrates. What a Euphrates! Some
river! Really imposing.
We've passed the Euphrates.
To our left, we should see a field. There it is—a field!
Just what we wanted.

At the head of the leading "Emerald"* formation Colonel Aryeh Ran picked out a potential hazard and hastened to warn his fliers: "Watch out for the antennas and columns! They're very tall."

Heading the second formation, Ruby, the other leader, Colonel Malachi, peered ahead, gazing at the horizon. Suddenly, he fancied he could see his thirteen-year-old daughter and ten-year-old son. Swiftly he pulled himself together; with a wave of the hand, he banished the apparition. But his children—wasn't it for their sakes that he was on this mission?

Near the Tigris, the planes climbed to an altitude of one thousand feet. Becoming aware of sporadic antiaircraft fire, Emerald's leader alerted his colleagues.

Suddenly, the pilots got their first glimpse of the objective. Yitzhal Melrom, flying second in Ruby, cried, "Look at the ramps around the reactor!" He was referring to the earthworks erected after the Iranian raid. Tow-

*Arabic for "Slowly."
*Fictitious name.

ering as high as the reactor dome, they were part of the fortified defensive system, which included antiaircraft cannon and Soviet-made surface-to-air missiles.

"I can see it—the target. Terrific!" enthused Major Adiv. Immediately below them, surrounded by the soaring ramps, they identified the reactor dome. It bore no camouflage paint.

"It looked different," related one of the pilots, "unlike what I had thought or imagined. Even the Tigris is different, not the way it looks on the maps. The whole site looked darker than I had envisaged. The ramps were higher than I had imagined, and so was the reactor dome."

There was no sign of activity from the missile batteries.

The planes attacked precisely according to plan. Diving from several thousand feet, they achieved the correct altitude to release their bombs.

"For a brief moment you sense that—in spiritual terms—you have shrunk to the smallest conceivable size," recalled Colonel Malachi. "You think, I am just a tiny particle in the sky. And then you ignore everything around you—including the pilots under your command—and you concern yourself with just one thing: aiming correctly. The moment you press the bomb button, and the bomb is released, you're free to look out for dangers, and, of course, for those you are leading, to make sure they're okay."

Momentarily, as Malachi prepared to press the bomb button, he recalled his experiences fourteen years earlier, during the Six-Day War, when he was with an armored brigade lunging down the northern edge of the Sinai Desert. As the column pressed ahead, Egyptian MIG 17s suddenly appeared overhead and strafed the vehicles. "We jumped out," Malachi related "I knew there was a risk of getting hit, whether you lie on your back or your belly. I chose to lie on my back. Looking up at those planes as they swooped down upon us, I decided, I should be among those who fire, not those who get fired at."

The reactor attack was completed in a single swoop, with only the briefest of intervals—mere seconds—between one plane and the next. The numerous dummy runs carried out in the preceding months had inspired the pilots with utter self-confidence, each one being thoroughly versed in his role and position. From descent of the first plane in Emerald until the last in Ruby dropped its bombs, the time lapse was unbelievably short.

Only now, after the attack had been accomplished, did the antiaircraft cannon around the reactor go into action. Opening up with dense fire, they blasted away, keeping up their barrage for fifteen minutes or so, by which time the assault force had long vanished into the distance. The last two fliers in Ruby noticed a missile which had been fired off toward them, but it missed.

Most of the pilots sensed the powerful blast released by their bombs.

They thought they had been hit by antiaircraft fire; only later did they learn that they had come out unscathed.

Ruby leader Malachi recalls: "Before releasing my own bombs, I of course saw the planes before me drop theirs. I suppose I can claim to have seen about two thirds of the bombs. I saw them explode, I saw the target collapse. I think I saw the reactor dome crumble. As I passed over the dome, on my way out, I saw my own bombs explode on it.

"I thought, So far, so good; I've done my part. Now I began to worry about my number two, who is superior to me in rank, and my number four, the youngest of our group. I worried about them before the attack, I worried about them immediately afterward. I called them up on the radio. They didn't hear, maybe because they were busy with the bombing, with its analysis, with guiding themselves. Within seconds, I made sure they were with me."

Subsequently there was some controversy over the timing of the strike. The French Foreign Minister claimed that the weekly rest day at the reactor was Friday, as in any Moslem country, and that this also applied to the French experts, for whom Sunday was a regular work day. His charge was refuted by Israeli Military Intelligence chief Saguy: "The timing was meticulous, being selected after careful examination." Such prudence was doubly important in view of the fact that some of the French engineers lived with their families no more than five hundred yards from the reactor.

The hour of the attack was dictated by a number of operational factors, one of which assumed—correctly—that most of the employees, the foreigners in particular, would be off the site by this time of day.

French technician Jacques Rombeau, a fortuitous witness to the bombing, confirmed: "The Israelis chose the most appropriate time for their attack, to avoid casualties." The bombing having been timed for last light, there were indeed almost no casualties at the reactor site. The only foreigner killed was a French technician working at an underground installation which exploded. Later, the Israeli government compensated his family and sent its condolences. Iraqi casualties—dead and injured—came to a total of nine.

The pilots had scored total success.

Under the impact of the bomb blasts, the reactor dome collapsed into the core housing, which filled up with rubble. The cylindrical structure supporting the dome was hurled sideways and its lower section totally destroyed. The building's foundations were also damaged. Water—probably from an underground source—inundated the structure as a result of the tremendous blast. All electric circuits and control systems suffered severe damage.

As Commander in Chief Eytan would put it: Within the space of one minute and twenty seconds, the sole target of the bombing, Tammuz 1, suffered grave damage.

Al-Tuweitha's military potential had been completely destroyed. The smaller Tammuz 2, not having been struck by bombs, was not demolished. But part of its sensitive equipment was damaged by the undermining of the foundations which supported both structures. The offices of the French company and of the Italian project were totally gutted by fire.

Two bombs failed to explode. One fell near Tammuz 2, the other plunged into the devastated structure of Tammuz 1. Additional explosions were reported during the days following the attack, with further damage to the reactor. Foreigners in Iraq reported that the number of bombs which failed to explode came to six; one reportedly penetrated underground to a depth of one hundred feet, while another was located twenty-five feet deep, close to the ravaged core. Three additional bombs, it is claimed, were found at a radius of some seven hundred feet from the reactor dome, and they caused grave damage to the French offices. However, the bombs which did go off caused irreparable damage to the reactor.

As foreseen, the bombing spared the Russian reactor, and the Italian laboratories some eight hundred yards from Tammuz 1. Nor was there any damage to the store of nuclear fuel, thereby precluding potential radioactive contamination.

The bombing attack had been completed.

Colonel Ran, who commanded the assault force and led its first formation, Emerald, now directed all his pilots to radio the squadron code name, their own serial number in their formation, and the anxiously awaited "Charlie," pilots' jargon for "I'm safe." Ran experienced a brief moment of dread when the leader of the other formation radioed: "Ruby Four is out of formation"—suggesting that his number-four flier might have suffered some mishap.

But Major Yaniv Eshkol,* the youngest of the pilots, hastened to reassure his commander with a chirpy "Ruby Four. Charlie." And, in rapid succession, the other pilots also reported present.

Major Menahem Adiv: "Ruby Three. Charlie."
Colonel Yitzhal Melrom: "Ruby Two. Charlie."
Colonel Eliezer Malachi: "Ruby One. Charlie."
Colonel Elad Lev: "Emerald Four. Charlie."
Major Aryeh Naeh: "Emerald Three. Charlie."
Major Micha Avner: "Emerald Two. Charlie."

*All of the following pilots' names are fictitious.

Major Avner complained of having lost visual contact with his leader, but Colonel Ran could see him clearly, and consequently felt free to radio off the message so eagerly awaited at advance operational headquarters: "Ruby and Emerald—Charlie all."

Colonel Ran now queried his colleague, Colonel Malachi: "How did the results look to you?"

"Very good," Malachi radioed back "One of the pilots undershot, but all in all, very good."

The lead formation's commander concluded the brief exchange. "Affirmative. The target seems to have been destroyed according to plan."

At 17:30, within minutes of the attack, Colonel Ran's concluding message was conveyed by way of advance operational headquarters to the Commander in Chief at Air Force headquarters. Now, at long last, Rafful could request Begin's military aide to convey the anxiously awaited tidings to the Prime Minister. "The attack was successful. The target has been destroyed. The boys are on their way back. All are well."

Receiving the news over the direct line in his library, Begin hastened into the reception room, where he confronted the expectant ministers. "I have just received the report that tons of bombs were dropped on the reactor four minutes ago. May the Holy Name be blessed, the target has been utterly destroyed and all our planes are on their way home. Beyond any doubt, these are good tidings for the people of Israel."

Later Begin would recall: "A weight was lifted from our hearts. We did not shake hands, but we were all prepared to embrace one another."

Simha Ehrlich would say, "We sat spellbound. Just as we were almost ready to give up the ghost, the good news arrived."

Yitzhak Shamir conceded only that "there was personal concern over the outcome."

Labor and Welfare Minister Katz walked over to Begin and said, "Prime Minister, I want to shake your hand and say, Well done!"

Begin replied, "See what a splendid people we have. True, there are criminals, rapists and murderers among us, but on the other hand, look—such superb boys!"

Dr. Katz mused: "It's fortunate that I supported the operation. I contemplated the responsibility I would bear a few years ahead, when the Iraqis acquired an atomic bomb and people asked, 'Why didn't you bomb the reactor?' And I'd think, Because I didn't vote with the Prime Minister, they now have a bomb which can destroy us all."

Encountering the French ambassador at a school ceremony a few days later, Katz recalled Begin's account of the anguish he invariably sensed when, seeing children at play, he wondered what would become of them in two or three years' time. "Your Excellency," Katz said to the ambassador, "look at these children, the coming generation of humanity. Aren't they preferable to the construction of reactors?"

At that dramatic moment when the good tidings reached them in the Prime Minister's reception room, some ministers wept, several laughed, others gazed into empty space.

Dr. Burg took his leave to head for the Renanim Synagogue, where he was scheduled to expound upon the significance of the festival of Shavuoth. His lecture included a scriptural quotation which promised that when the festival falls on a clear day "it is a good omen for the entire coming year." Burg explained the passage to his listeners: "If there are no clouds on the day of the festival, it will be a good year. You may understand that as you wish. Tomorrow," he added significantly, "you may understand it even better." He left it at that.

Moshe Nissim went off to pray at the synagogue presided over by his father, a former chief rabbi. The Justice Minister slyly modified one of the festive prayers with a play on the Hebrew words so that, instead of praising God "who strikes the firstborn of Egypt", it read: ". . . who strikes the reactors of Iraq."

The royal yacht *Nur* had turned; in the waning light of late afternoon, it headed for Aqaba harbor. To the powerful transmitters on board the vessel, Baghdad was within easy range. But Field Marshal Saddam Hussain was unavailable: he had left the capital for a tour of the Iranian battlefront. That could perhaps explain why the Iraqis received no forewarning from King Hussein.

Puzzled, the Jordanian monarch listened to the radio, waiting to hear what the Israelis were up to.

At the Prime Minister's residence, the remaining ministers continued to argue about whether or not to issue a public statement.

Finance Minister Aridor called for immediate publication, without waiting for the Arabs to react.

Katz supported Aridor's proposal.

Deputy Defense Minister Zippori remarked, "We should denounce the former French administration for its aid to Iraq."

Seizing on Zippori's words, Begin thundered, "Former French Premier Jacques Chirac is the progenitor of the primordial sin of granting Iraq the instruments for the manufacture of nuclear weapons. He and his President Giscard are both 'foes of Israel' [anti-Semites]."

Yitzhak Shamir reverted to the topic under discussion: "It would be better to publish nothing until we know the final measure of damage to the reactor."

David Levi said, "The moment the pilots return, make it public!"

"The homeward route," Colonel Malachi recalls, "was just as it says in the books: an anticlimax. There is no better definition. Everything was dwarfed in comparison with the assignment we had accomplished. True, there was a problem: we had no reserve fuel, but that was dwarfed, too. It's second nature among us: there's a distinction between an obstacle on the way to completion of a mission and an obstacle on the way home. The fear of failure is greater. The dangers on the flight home are of the variety we can cope with. In such a situation, spare fuel isn't a pressing problem. In effect, it was all behind us, even though we would still be over enemy territory for some time."

The homeward flight, Begin told his ministers, still had a considerable time to run. He went on to say that when the festival came to an end, the following evening, he intended to dispatch personal letters to Presidents Reagan and Sadat, to explain the Israeli action. He did not conceal his unease toward Sadat, with whom he had conferred only three days previously at Sharm al-Sheikh. Even so, Begin did not expect Sadat—who detested Saddam Hussain—to "sit *shiva*" (go into mourning) over the Iraqi reactor.

Yet again, the Prime Minister depicted his feelings in recent months, and his growing conviction of the necessity of bombing the reactor; he reiterated that a government headed by Shimon Peres would be incapable of reaching such a decision. "The attempts to intimidate us into abandoning that decision only reinforced my awareness that it's a question of now or never."

Ariel Sharon: "It will nevertheless be alleged that the raid stemmed from electoral considerations."

Begin responded, "If such demagogues open their mouths, I shall ask them whether the elections are grounds for desisting from our concern for the future of the state. Are fateful decisions to be evaded out of electoral considerations? More than anything else, inaction is the height of irresponsibility. Had the operation failed, heaven forbid, would they say it was a matter of electoral considerations?"

Ruby's leader warned his colleagues that he had detected antiaircraft batteries. But the pilots found little difficulty in bypassing the hazard.

Prior to the operation, there had been some apprehension over enemy planes or surface antiaircraft systems attempting to down the Israeli aircraft on course to target or homeward bound. Pilots of the escort planes which provided a protective umbrella were cautioned to keep a sharp look out. It was learned later that enemy planes took off after the attack in a bid to intercept the departing Israeli assault force; but, failing to make contact, they turned back on their tracks.

At one point on their homeward route, the Israeli fliers detected an unknown aircraft flying below them; but a brief inspection showed it to be a civilian airliner.

The royal yacht was close to its home port when King Hussein again heard the roar of jet engines, this time coming from the opposite direction. Raising his eyes, he got his second glimpse of the Israeli planes as they sped across the sky. This time, there could be no doubt as to their destination: they were evidently preparing to land at Etzion airbase.

Glancing at his watch, Hussein made some rapid calculations. Whatever mission the Israeli planes had pursued, it must have taken them a very long way from home.

At 18:47, as the planes approached base, David Ivry radioed to the pilots to congratulate them on their brilliant performance. But the Air Force commander, apprehensive that, with the tension relieved, some pilot would make a stupid blunder, qualified his congratulations with a warning: "Pay attention when landing!"

It was close on 19:00 when Begin was summoned to the phone.

"They're coming in to land," the Commander in Chief reported. "Everything is in order, sir. Execution was one hundred percent, couldn't be better."

"I congratulate you," said Begin, and requested the Air Force commander: "David, I embrace you. You and your men are unequaled."

One of the kitchen staff brought in a bottle of wine, and the ministers raised their glasses to toast the people of Israel, the armed forces and the Air Force.

The sun was setting when the assault commander's voice resounded over the radio: "We're touching down. We're home."

"We knew they had all come back," recalls Etzion technical officer Major Gai. "But all the same, we counted them, one by one, to make sure they had all made it. The last two planes were late in landing. The second leader's eyes were tearful. To this day, I can't fathom why I chose such a manner of expressing my joy: I punched him in the face."

• • •

Summoning his aide Yehiel Kadishai, Begin dictated the text of the official communiqué to be released in the event of the bombing being attributed to Israel. Mentally, the Prime Minister was already laying plans for the diplomatic onslaught Israel could expect. "We're sure to be condemned," he told himself confidently.

Flying back to their home base in central Israel, the pilots deliberately set off a number of supersonic booms within earshot of a million citizens. With the Shavuoth festival already in full swing, the civilians failed to understand what the noise was all about. It was only the following day that they grasped that the pilots had been indulging in a celebration of their triumph.

The Air Force calculated the cost of the entire operation at $8 million.

Two days after the raid, Cabinet members watched a movie of the operation, shot by the planes' TV cameras and embellished with an appropriate soundtrack.

"Wonder of wonders," Begin marveled.

"Concert in Baghdad," commented David Ivry.

22 "Now I understand . . ."

The reactor had been destroyed. The pilots were all home, safe and sound. Menahem Begin could now focus his attention on the impending diplomatic confrontation.

His first concern was to bring the United States into the picture and reassure the Administration by explaining the reasons behind the Israeli action. The Prime Minister tried to reach the U.S. ambassador, but Sam Lewis and his wife, Sally, had left home. They were on their way to the Tel Aviv Sheraton when the telephone installed in their official limousine alerted Lewis, asking him to contact Begin without delay.

On arrival at the hotel, the Lewises made their way to the suite of Bill Butcher, a prominent American banker who had come for talks with his Israeli colleagues. Also present was Congressman Jack Kemp of New York. After a brief exchange of greetings, Lewis hastened to the bedroom, which was divided from the sitting room by nothing but a curtain.

Lewis dialed the Prime Minister's number. At the other end, Begin's voice was calm and matter-of-fact: "Mr. Ambassador, I request you to convey to the President the message I shall now give you. Two hours ago, planes of our Air Force bombed the atomic reactor near Baghdad. All the planes returned safely."

The ambassador's initial response was a long-drawn-out silence. In the course of a lengthy diplomatic career Lewis had experienced numerous surprises, but even he needed a little time to pull himself together. "Mr. Prime Minister," he said finally, "I shall convey your message to the President without delay."

The ambassador's next call was to the embassy, where he gave instructions to transmit the message to the White House with all dispatch.

Resuming the discharge of their diplomatic duties, the Lewises now headed for the nearby Hilton, for a reception in Butcher's honor. On the

way, the ambassador told his wife why Begin had sought him out this evening, in disregard of the religious festival. Sally Lewis did not need to be
told that she was dutybound to keep the story to herself.

The Hilton reception was attended by a number of ministers who had
come directly from the Cabinet meeting in Jerusalem. It goes without saying
that they made no reference to the raid. Scrutinizing their facial expressions,
Lewis found them all calm and relaxed.

Ariel Sharon seated himself beside Sally Lewis. "Does Sam know?" he
asked.

The ambassador's wife pretended not to understand. "What are you talking about?"

Sharon was taken aback; but Lewis, seated on his wife's far side, had
heard the exchange. He winked at her and she, getting the hint, muttered,
"Yes, Sam knows."

The Prime Minister remained in his study for a long time. He phoned
reports of the raid to State President Yitzhak Navon, to former Foreign
Minister Moshe Dayan and to opposition leader Shimon Peres.

Peres hastened to notify Yitzhak Rabin, only to learn that his Labor colleague had already been informed by Begin (Rabin responded with the traditional Hebrew "All honor!").

Peres was spending the Shavuoth festival at the southern Israeli resort of
Eilat, where he was scheduled to address election rallies. From his hotel
room he contacted Mordechai Gur, likewise visiting Eilat. "The matter we
discussed," Peres told "Motta," "has been accomplished." There was no
room for further discussion. In any case, Gur's own private sources had
alerted him the previous day that the raid was about to go ahead.

Begin also called Knesset Foreign Affairs and Defense Committee Chairman Moshe Arens. Congratulating Begin, Arens went on to draw a parallel
between the Iraqi reactor and the Cuban missile crisis. "Had the Russians
not capitulated over the missiles emplaced in Cuba, the Americans would
ultimately have taken action against them. 'Our' Russians [the Iraqis] did
not capitulate, and we were obliged to act."

That evening, shortly after the return of the planes, Military Intelligence
Director Saguy summoned U.S. military attaché Colonel Peter Hoag, for
the purpose of briefing him on the operation.

With unerring instinct, Hoag zeroed in on the reason for the invitation.
"Do you mean to tell me you've bombed the Syrian missiles in Lebanon?"
he demanded confidently.

Saguy: "Not quite."

Hoag: "What, then?"

Saguy: "An hour back, our planes returned safely from Iraq. The reactor has been destroyed."

The attaché broke into a fit of coughing. Feebly, he requested a glass of water. Then he hastened to report to his superiors in Washington.

At the same time, Saguy sent a message—marked "For your attention only"—to Israel's military attaché in Washington, General Menahem Meron, notifying him of the raid and informing him that the U.S. ambassador in Tel Aviv was already privy to the matter.

Meron was in Canada at the time; the message was accordingly conveyed to his deputy, Brigadier Yoel Ben Porat, who had served for many years in Military Intelligence. Ben Porat immediately called Ambassador Evron and asked to see him without delay.

"Come to my home," Evron replied. A few minutes later, Ben Porat, seated in an armchair facing the ambassador, began to read out the text of Saguy's cable.

A rich diplomatic career had made Evron accustomed to the unexpected, and he remained calm in spite of his unconcealed surprise. "Now I understand," he said slowly, "why Haig has been looking for me these past two hours."

Alexander Haig, learning of the reactor attack from his aide Woody Goldberg, hastened to notify President Reagan. The first question which engaged Haig's thoughts "was the natural one: had radiation been released?" Further, as his memoirs reveal, he wondered: "Would it affect the population of Baghdad and nearby communities? Did we have aircraft available that could detect such radiation? Did we have decontamination teams and other resources available? If so, could we find a way to offer these as a humanitarian gesture to Iraq, with which we had no diplomatic relations?"

While Haig headed for the State Department's operations center, his aides began to prepare answers to his queries. The experts soon reassured him that there was no danger of radiation, either at the reactor site or in its proximity.

Scarcely had Evron shown Ben Porat out than the phone rang. On the line was the Secretary of State. Haig, uncertain whether Evron knew of the raid, began by sounding him out discreetly. When Evron indicated that he did know, Haig said, "I have before me the report from the military attaché in Tel Aviv. It should be clear that we are in for an outcry without precedent, and we should be well prepared for it." The Secretary of State posed three queries: Did the Israelis know whether any radioactivity had been released by the bombing? What were Israel's assessments regarding Iraq's capacity for construction of nuclear weapons? What use had been made of American equipment in the reactor strike? He requested Israel's replies that same evening.

It was 5:20 P.M. Washington time, but in Israel it was past midnight. Nevertheless, Evron phoned Foreign Minister Shamir at his Jerusalem home and transmitted Haig's questions. Shamir decided to consult Begin. The latter replied without delay. Three hours later, Evron already had detailed answers.

Had the bombing released radioactivity?

Begin-Shamir: "The danger of contamination is negligible, because the reactor was not yet hot, though it was due to become so shortly. Israel struck first so as to minimize the danger of radioactive fallout."

What were Israel's assessments regarding Iraq's capacity for construction of nuclear weapons?

Begin-Shamir: "We estimated that it was a matter of a few years—at least two, five at most—until Iraq achieved a nuclear-weapons capability. Without the aid of France and Italy, the Iraqis would have been unable to construct the reactor or operate it, nor plan to use it for military purposes."

What use was made of U.S. equipment in the reactor strike?

Begin-Shamir: "We used U.S.-made F-16s."

"These replies will be of great assistance to me," said Haig. Right from the outset, he was seeking a line of defense for Israel's action.

Haig now conveyed the Israeli answers to the President, noting that Jerusalem accepted responsibility for the raid. The Secretary of State made sure the information he had accumulated was disseminated to congressional leaders and to American's principal allies (the French, having already learned of the raid, were not taken by surprise).

Haig foresaw criticism over Israel's offensive use of U.S. equipment which had been supplied for exclusively defensive purposes. He was also apprehensive about possible Arab charges of U.S.-Israel collusion prior to the operation. Nevertheless, he showed no hesitation in affirming that even though the strike was stunningly audacious, it was not technically an attack by a warmongering state on a peaceloving country, as Iraq and Israel had been belligerents ever since the 1948 War of Independence. Haig predicted that the Arabs would appeal to the Security Council. If the resolution they introduced turned out to be sharply worded, he promised an American veto.

Information reaching the United States indicated that the raid had inflicted grave damage on the reactor; satellite photographs showed accurate hits in the target area. Tests conducted by French experts confirmed American data about the absence of radioactive contamination.

At his office in the State Department, Haig began to issue directives for the response to be published when news of the raid emerged. Israel would not escape U.S. condemnation, but, as he told Evron over the phone the following morning, June 8, such condemnation need not be overly severe. In the midst of their conversation Haig suddenly cried, "Just a moment!" One of his aides had brought in a note stating that Israel radio had just announced the attack on the reactor.

"The storm," Haig told Evron "is about to burst right away—at gale force."

During the night following the attack, information somehow reached the American media about Israeli aerial action over Iraq. Did the leak stem from U.S. intelligence sources, as on past occasions? Be that as it may, a CBS correspondent phoned the State Department, requesting confirmation that Israel had carried out a bombing raid in Iraq. The woman duty officer at State called the Tel Aviv embassy, conveying the journalist's query. The embassy's political adviser William Brown, called Deputy Defense Minister Mordechai Zippori to ask whether Israel intended to make known that its planes had bombed the reactor. Zippori replied that Israel would wait until Iraq published an announcement of its own.

While CBS failed to elicit the desired confirmation, a Pittsburgh radio station did not await confirmation before broadcasting the news of the Israeli strike.

In the morning of June 8, while Israel celebrated Shavuoth, William Brown, accompanied by military attaché Hoag, arrived at the office of Military Intelligence Director Saguy. The two men told Saguy that the American media had already ferreted out the story and would soon have all necessary details for a complete exposé.

While Israeli Cabinet members were careful to reveal nothing to their families, there was no concealing their own eagerness to hear news broadcasts. Some of the Orthodox ministers even departed from their normal custom by leaving radios switched on throughout the festival, in defiance of religious practice.

Justice Minister Nissim found an original way of quenching his curiosity. Declining to drive during the religious festival, he went by foot to the Prime Minister's residence and marched in, to find Begin in the kitchen eating lunch.

"No announcement has been published so far," Begin stated. "But I have conveyed information to Haig. The American reaction hasn't been startling. Haig didn't fall out of his chair when he heard of the bombing."

Shortly afterward, Radio Amman's two-o'clock news bulletin announced that Israeli planes had repeatedly bombed vital targets in Iraq. The report was given as the summary of an address by Jordanian Prime Minister Mudar Badran to the country's National Consultative Council. "There is cooperation and coordination between Iran and Israel," Badran alleged. "Israel is taking advantage of present circumstances to intervene against Iraq, Jordan's sister-state, and Israel has repeatedly sent its planes to take part in the bombing of vital targets in Iraq." The Jordanian Prime Minister laid the blame at the door of the United States. "Without sophisticated long-range American weaponry, such tragedies for the Arab nation could not occur."

Israeli Military Intelligence's twenty-four-hour monitoring service, Hatzav, which keeps constant track of all radio emissions in the region, picked up the broadcast and recognized its importance. The report, classified "top urgency," was swiftly sent out to the regular dissemination list. At the same time, Hatzav personnel made efforts to contact the Prime Minister's deputy military aide, Azriel Nevo, who was spending the festival at his Rishon Letzion home. The aide himself, Brigadier Poren, was at a vacation village in Eliat.

Nevo hastened to notify the Prime Minister of the Amman radio report. Begin decided to release the prepared official statement and have it broadcast on Israel radio's upcoming newscast, at three. The text was dictated by phone to the Prime Minister's media adviser, Uri Porat, who was staying with a relative at an army camp. Porat in turn called the radio station's duty editor, Moshe Negbi, and asked him to place the announcement at the head of the newscast. But Porat having only recently taken up his post, his voice was unfamiliar to Negbi, who suspected that he was being made the victim of an April Fool's Day–type hoax. He asked Porat to contact one of the radio's political correspondents; if the latter confirmed the report, he, Negbi, would immediately order it broadcast. Porat phoned political correspondent Amnon Nadav, who recognized his voice and promptly called Negbi, urging him to clear the report.

Still beset by lingering doubts, a hesitant Negbi contacted news department head Emmanuel Halperin, to seek his advice. Halperin pronounced that the report required checking. This put the ball back into the court of Porat, who flared up at Nadav: "What do they want me to do—bring them the Prime Minister in person?"

Ultimately, that was almost literally what came about. Halperin, still seeking corroboration of the report, hit on the idea of exploiting his family ties—he is the son of Begin's elder sister Rachel. He proceeded to call the Prime Minister's residence, and when he got Begin on the line he asked anxiously, "Uncle, is this story correct?"

Begin, who had switched on his radio at three to hear the announcement and was mystified by its absence, hastened to confirm the veracity of the announcement, while his embarrassed nephew was forced to explain the reasons for the foul-up.

The official statement finally went out on a special three-thirty newscast, though in view of its importance the manner of its publication was less than dignified: it was first broadcast on the radio's third network, which is devoted almost exclusively to pop music. However, the communiqué did head the hourly newscast at four:

On Sunday, June 7, 1981, the Israel Air Force launched a raid on the atomic reactor Osirak near Baghdad. Our pilots carried out their mission fully. The reactor was destroyed. All our aircraft returned safely to base.

The government feels dutybound to explain to enlightened public opinion why it took this decision:

For a long time, we have been watching with growing concern the construction of the atomic-reactor Osirak. From sources whose reliability is beyond any doubt, we learned that this reactor, despite its camouflage, is designed to produce atomic weapons. The target for such bombs would be Israel. This was clearly announced by the ruler of Iraq. After the Iranians had inflicted slight damage to the reactor, Saddam Hussain stressed that the Iranians had attacked the reactor in vain, since it was being constructed against Israel alone.

The atomic bombs which that reactor was capable of producing, whether from enriched uranium or from plutonium, would be of the Hiroshima size. Thus, a mortal danger to the people of Israel progressively arose.

Again from the most reliable sources, we learned of two dates when the reactor would be completed and put into operation: one, the beginning of July 1981; two, the beginning of September 1981. In other words, within a short period of time the Iraqi reactor would be operational and hot. Under such circumstances, no Israeli government could contemplate bombing the reactor. Such an attack would have brought about a massive radioactive lethal fallout over the city of Baghdad, and tens of thousands of its innocent residents would have been hurt. We would have been compelled to passively observe the process of the production of atomic bombs in Iraq, whose ruling tyrant would not hesitate to launch them against Israeli cities and the centers of its population. Therefore, the government of Israel decided to act without further delay, to ensure our people's existence. The planning was exact. The operation was timed for Sunday on the assumption that the one hundred to one hundred fifty foreign experts employed at the reactor would be absent on the Christian day of rest. This assumption proved to have been correct. No foreign experts were hurt.

Two European governments, in return for oil, have assisted the Iraqi tyrant in the construction of atomic weapons. We again call upon them to desist from this horrifying inhuman deed. Under no circumstances will we allow an enemy to develop weapons of mass destruction against our people.

We shall defend the citizens of Israel in time and with all the means at our disposal.

Deputy Prime Minister Yigael Yadin heard the newscast. Infuriated, he stormed out of his Rehavia home and hastened to the Prime Minister's residence only a few blocks away.

"Mr. Begin," Yadin demanded, "why was the statement broadcast on the radio? To the best of my recollection, it was resolved that if the operation was successful we would not publicize it unless the Cabinet decided to do so; and you agreed thereto."

Begin agreed that it had been decided to withhold publication—unless someone else released the report. "My military aide informed me that Jordan radio announced an Israeli bombing raid inside Iraq."

Questions as to Israel's initiative in publicizing the raid would come up again and again. Begin disputed fiercely with his critics, arguing that the initial report came from Jordan, not from Israel. Furthermore, Israel was not ashamed of its action; on the contrary, Israel was proud of the exploit and confident of its vindication, so why trouble to deny it?

"After the boys returned home," Begin recalled, "we began, in the course of the Cabinet meeting at my home, to consider what to tell the world. The Jordanians identified [our planes]. The Saudis identified them. The Iraqis identified them. The planes were ours, bearing Israeli insignia. There was no dissembling. The next day we remained silent. Then I got a call from my military aide about the Jordanian broadcast . . . any child could have grasped the significance of their announcement. . . . We were not the first to go public. Had we not published our statement, matters would have unfolded as follows: the Iraqis would have made it public within a short time. That would have left us without any choice. What would people have said then? True, the Israelis did destroy the reactor, but they didn't even have the minimal iota of courage to tell the world, they're trying to conceal it. . . . What are we, thieves in the night? We set out to destroy the reactor because it was a mortal danger to our people, to our children. There was nothing to apologize for. We were dutybound to proclaim it, particularly when it had already been broadcast by Jordan radio."

Miri Reshef, who is employed at the Israeli Foreign Ministry's information department, heard of the raid from the radio newscast. Having tried in vain to locate her superior, she displayed resourcefulness and initiative: acting on her own discretion, she cabled the government statement to Israeli legations the world over. Colette Avital, a Foreign Ministry section director, personally translated, typed and distributed the official statement, together with a summary of past interviews and explanations about the Iraqi reactor, all backed up with special directives on how the Israeli viewpoint was to be presented.

The Foreign Ministry took two and a half hours to embark upon diplomatic action—an excessively lengthy time in view of the fateful nature of the matter. (A subsequent internal inquiry within the ministry found that it possessed no crisis task force, nor even an Iraqi desk, the whole matter being delegated to a woman clerk employed in a part-time capacity. The inquiry led to formation of a special team for crucial issues, headed by the ministry's director general or his deputy.)

Israel's diplomatic legations were instructed to use the background material on the reactor which Hanan Baron had sent as far back as October 1980. Part authored by outside experts, the Foreign Ministry document comprised a detailed account of developments at Iraq's nuclear center and of Israel's diplomatic efforts to block it, as well as quotes from Iraqi leaders to show that the avowed aim of their nuclear efforts was the annihilation of Israel.

Radio and TV newscasts the world over heralded the destruction of Iraq's reactor, which made headlines in the press of all lands. Israeli diplomats were eagerly sought after; everyone wanted to hear Israel's official position. In a summary she composed on June 11, Colette Avital could justly boast: "The swift action of our legations immediately upon publication of the event gave our version prominence and near exclusivity in the initial reporting, whether radio and television or in the printed press."

That exclusivity was of little avail in the diplomatic arena. Few official voices were raised in Israel's defense. Most governments, Arab, Western and Communist alike, issued fierce condemnations.

23 "Astonishment with Exasperation"

Shortly after learning of the bombing, Haig began to draft an official U.S. statement. Read out on June 8 by State Department spokesman Dean Fischer, a onetime head of *Time*'s Jerusalem bureau, the text was relatively mild, arousing fleeting Israeli hopes that the reactor attack would not prejudice Israel–U.S. relations.

> The government of Israel has informed the United States that the Israeli Air Force attacked the Iraqi nuclear research facility at Tuweitha on June 7. We had no prior knowledge of the raid, and we have no further information. . . . This is clearly a very serious development and a source of utmost concern. We have no firsthand details of the attack or of the overall damage, including casualties. Our initial estimate of potential radiation effects is that they would probably be minimal and limited to the immediate vicinity of the installation. . . . The United States government is ready to respond to any requests for help in monitoring the extent of any nuclear effects and in dealing with any other related problems.

However, only two hours elapsed before Fischer read out a further statement—likewise authored by Haig—with specific condemnation of the Israeli action. From Israel's viewpoint, storm clouds were gathering on the horizon.

> The United States government condemns the reported Israeli air strike on the Iraqi nuclear facility, the unprecedented character of which cannot but seriously add to the already tense situation in the area. Available evidence suggests U.S.-provided equipment was employed in possible violation of the applicable agreement under which it was sold to Israel, and a report to this effect is being prepared for submission to the United States Congress in accordance with the relevant U.S. statute.

The "agreement" referred to was the 1952 mutual-defense assistance agreement the two countries signed in 1952.

The Israeli Embassy in Washington was alarmed. No administration had ever initiated a report to Congress about a "possible violation" of the 1952 agreement. In his memoirs, Haig was to confess: "My feelings were mixed. The suspicion that Iraq intended to produce nuclear weapons was hardly unrealistic. In that context, Begin's action in destroying the plant where they might be made was understandable and might well be judged less severely by history than by the opinion of the day."

But at the time of the operation, Haig's spokesman adopted a tone of gruff hostility: the United States was not convinced of the justification of the Israeli attack; there was no evidence that Iraq had violated its undertakings according to the Nonproliferation Treaty; Iraq had placed itself under IAEA supervision, unlike Israel. The statement contained not one word in defense of Israel, unlike earlier American declarations, which generally condoned Israeli motives even when the actions themselves came in for criticism.

Fuming, Ambassador Evron set out to find Haig. But the Secretary of State had gone to Dulles airport to welcome the President of Mexico and escort him to Camp David. Several hours elapsed before Evron managed to reach Haig by phone and convey Begin's protest over Fischer's second statement. Haig, however, defended the U.S. condemnation as "unavoidable."

The Administration came under heavy anti-Israel pressure from two directions: external, from America's allies and the "moderate" Arab states, Egypt, Saudi Arabia and Jordan; and domestic, from those portions of the Administration that disputed the strategic value of Israel, which they regarded as a burden on U.S. global strategy.

Haig would write:

> Within the Administration, reaction to the Israeli raid combined astonishment with exasperation. Some of the President's advisors urged that he take strong, even punitive, measures against Israel. I argued that, while some action must be taken to show American disapproval, our strategic interests would not be served by policies that humiliated and weakened Israel.

President Reagan's inner circle included a number of persons unsympathetic toward Israel. Prominent among these was Vice-President George Bush. Although not outspoken in his anti-Israel views, Bush always kept his distance. He now urged immediate publication of a sharp reprimand to Israel. A similar course was espoused by presidential counselor Edwin Meese III and by Haig's deputy, William P. Clark, a personal friend of the President and widely rumored to have been appointed to his post to keep an eye on Haig. Another advocate of that view was Defense Secretary Caspar W. Weinberger.

This group now resolved to seize upon the reactor attack so as to procure long-awaited Senate approval for the sale of advanced AWACS surveillance planes to Saudi Arabia—a sale Israel had gone all out to block.

Haig continued his efforts to placate Evron, telling the ambassador he had hoped that the first, more moderate statement would calm the tempest but had soon realized that it had achieved the precise opposite; he had then decided that a further and more sharply worded declaration would silence Israel's critics by taking the wind out of their sails. Even so, the Secretary of State sought to reassure Evron: there would be no further condemnations or "crazy statements"; he himself would step into the breach.

Israel could not expect the United States to approve the raid, Haig pointed out. Even so, he recalled his conversation with Begin in Jerusalem in April, when the two men had agreed that Israel and the United States shared joint strategic objectives. "Tell the Prime Minister," Haig added, "that neither he nor the ideas we discussed in Jerusalem will come to any harm as a result of the reactor raid."

But matters did not unfold according to the scenario Haig had in mind, which—so he claimed—also enjoyed the President's support. Israel found itself in a predicament to which it was unaccustomed: sections of the Administration, including the intelligence agencies, inundated congressional committees—foreign relations, armed services, and intelligence—with voluminous material aimed at proving two points: (1) Iraq possessed no real capacity for constructing atomic bombs—at worst, such a capacity would be achieved "within a few years" or "at the end of the decade," and there was therefore no justification for bombing the reactor at this time; (2) the combination of French supervision with routine IAEA inspection was effective and adequate to forestall any Iraq attempt to subvert the reactor to military uses.

The implied conclusion was plain: Israel had not acted in good faith; the reactor attack had been mounted to serve the domestic political needs of the Begin government.

Anti-Israel elements added a further allegation: the bombing had delivered a fatal blow to the Lebanon mediation efforts of presidential envoy Philip Habib, thereby harming the prestige of Reagan, who had flung all his weight behind the mission.

Referring to these charges, Begin commented: "There were two schools of thought in the State Department. There were some who argued, citing Habib, that I was the source of the trouble in the Middle East. I requested that Habib be contacted and asked if this was correct. Habib replied by letter that it was an outright lie and he had never held such a view; he added that he would never lend a hand to anything which could offend me. The State Department was headed by Haig, whose behavior toward us was exemplary, but it also employed senior officials of long standing, leftovers from previous administrations, who held different views and effectively detracted from Haig's position as master in his own home."

Regrettably, the anti-Israel campaign in Washington drew considerable sustenance from the utterances of Israeli leaders. The first to comment on the bombing was Labor's election propaganda chief, Haim Herzog (later to become state president). Interviewed by CBS correspondent Bob Simon, Herzog characterized the timing of the raid as "very strange," pointing out that it could have been mounted five months earlier or, equally, it could have been left to the new government which would emerge after the elections. Herzog repeated the view that the reactor would not have been hot before September. Herzog's words carried considerable weight: he is a superb speaker and well known to U.S. television viewers, having achieved renown in his former roles as director of Israeli Military Intelligence, ambassador to the UN, and a military commentator of authority.

Israel's Washington embassy had hoped that the U.S. media would endeavor to depict the reactor attack in objective terms, but disappointment was swift. Yet again it became evident that on matters of foreign policy the U.S. Administration, using material carefully selected and edited, can generally manipulate journalists, editors and commentators in the direction it desires.

It soon became plain that the controversy would focus on a matter of crucial importance to Israel: was the use of U.S.-made planes and equipment in the reactor attack a violation of Israel's 1952 agreement with the United States, and if so, did it constitute an infringement of U.S. law, thus calling for punitive action by the Americans?

When Reagan learned of the reactor bombing, he was "shocked," according to national-security adviser Richard V. Allen. It emerged later that Reagan's "shock" stemmed from a grave omission dating back to the period of transition from the Carter Administration. Intelligence files relating to the Iraqi reactor had been relayed to members of the new Administration, but with neither explanation nor adequate stress on their importance. In consequence, the first Reagan heard of the very existence of the Iraqi reactor was when Israel destroyed it.

The President was under the influence of groups eager to exploit the bombing to shape U.S. policy into a new configuration far less sympathetic toward Israel. Not content with their efforts in the White House, these groups made great efforts to sway influential senators. Senate Majority Leader Howard H. Baker, Jr., of Tennessee deplored the destruction of the reactor, and he was soon followed by Senate Foreign Relations Committee

Chairman Charles H. Percy of Illinois, a former friend of Israel who had long since switched to an unfriendly stance. Before his committee could launch any inquiry, Percy flung out accusations closely resembling those voiced by State Department and Pentagon circles critical of the Israeli action.

As prime minister and acting minister of defense—and the moving spirit behind the reactor attack—Menahem Begin now placed himself at the head of Israel's counteroffensive. On June 9, two days after the bombing, the Prime Minister held a press conference in Jerusalem, flanked by Commander in Chief Eytan, Air Force Commander Ivry and Military Intelligence Director Saguy. Speaking vigorously and with profound inner conviction, Begin rejected the censures to which Israel was being subjected from all quarters.

"Israel," he declared, "has nothing to apologize for. Ours is a just cause. We stand by it and it will triumph." He spoke of Saddam Hussain, "who with his own hands killed his best friends in order to become the sole ruler of that country; [Hussain] had an ambition: he wanted to develop nuclear weapons so that he can either bring Israel to her knees on behalf of the Arab world or destroy her menfolk and infrastructure and the great part of her army." Disclosing intelligence information about Iraq's pressure on the French experts to get the reactor active by July, he noted, "If that had happened, if the reactor had become . . . hot, we couldn't do anything further. Because if . . . we would open it . . . a horrifying wave of radioactivity would come out from the reactor and cover the sky over Baghdad. . . . Hundreds of thousands of innocent citizens—residents, men, women and children—would have been hurt." Laying his hand on his breast, Begin proclaimed in dramatic tones, "I for one would have never made a proposal to my colleagues under such circumstances to send our Air Force and bomb the reactor, and I believe with all my heart that none of my colleagues either in the government or in the Army would have ever made a proposal or would have ever accepted such a proposal . . . to send our planes and bomb the reactor—because we wouldn't wish . . . to hurt the residents of Baghdad. They are innocent people; they belong to the enemy's camp, but as people they are untouchable, and these are our ethics."

Therefore, should the reactor become hot, Begin added, "we couldn't do anything whatsoever in order to prevent the Iraqi tyrant from developing at least in the near future between three and five Hiroshima-type nuclear bombs of twenty kilotons . . . During the Second World War a bomb of twenty kilotons caused at least two hundred thousand casualties in killed and in afflicted, the afflictions being for several generations. . . . With three such bombs, which Iraq could have developed in that reactor . . . they could have destroyed completely, utterly, the Dan [Tel Aviv] district, the basis of our industrial, commercial, agricultural and cultural life. Six hundred thousand casualties we would suffer, which would mean, in terms of the United States, forty-six million casualties, in terms of Egypt over eight million casualties. Where is the country which would tolerate such a danger knocking at its door?"

Hundreds of journalists representing the world's largest media networks fell silent as Begin intoned, "We have a special reason to guard our people. A million and a half of our children were poisoned by a gas called Zyklon B. There is no difference between poisons. Radioactivity is also poison, and there was a direct danger that hundreds of thousands of our little children may be poisoned by that radioactivity as a result of using even three Hiroshima-type bombs." In a tone which displayed no trace of contriteness, the Prime Minister added, "For simple logic we decided to act now before it is too late—so that we will not allow a bloodthirsty enemy who marches on Abadan and declares that this is the beginning of his march on Jerusalem and to Jaffa. . . . We chose this moment: now, not later, later may be too late, perhaps forever. And if we had stood by idly, two, three years, at the most four years, and Saddam Hussain would have produced his three, four, five bombs, what should, what could we have done in the face of such a present, direct, horrifying peril? Nothing. Then this country and this people would have been lost, after the Holocaust. Another Holocaust would have happened in the history of the Jewish people. Never again, never again! Tell so your friends, tell anyone you will meet, we shall defend our people with all the means at our disposal. We shall not allow any enemy to develop weapons of mass destruction turned against us."

The line of defense adopted by Begin was marred by two grave mishaps of a most embarrassing nature.

Three days after the reactor attack, the outgoing British ambassador held a garden party at his Ramat Gan villa. The function was attended by the Prime Minister, and the journalists seized the opportunity to pounce on him and seek further details on the reactor attack. Responding to a question from Reuters' Israel correspondent, Begin claimed that bombs had penetrated forty meters (130 feet) underground to destroy a secret installation which constituted a component of the reactor complex. The claim seemed worthy of headlines, and on publication it aroused considerable attention. The U.S. military attaché raised the matter with the director of Military Intelligence, requesting further information; the Americans, he said, had no knowledge of any such installation that depth.

But French media investigations elicited that no such installation had ever existed. It transpired that Begin had fallen victim to his own technical ignorance. One of the intelligence reports depicting the reactor structure specified that it contained an installation at a height of minus four meters (" − 04 meters"). As Begin put it, "When I read it, the zero simply wandered from left to right." The French explained that the installation referred to was a small chamber designed for supervision of neutron-ray tests. As soon as Begin realized his error, he personally called the Reuters correspondent and apologized for having unintentionally misled him.

Another mishap, which likewise left egg on numerous Israeli faces, stemmed from a passage in the official statement Begin had composed. After claiming that the reactor was designed for the production of nuclear bombs, the statement went on: "The target for such bombs would be Israel. This was clearly announced by the ruler of Iraq. After the Iranians had inflicted slight damage to the reactor, Saddam Hussain stressed that the Iranians had attacked the reactor in vain, since it was being constructed against Israel alone."

When the communiqué was released, Israeli legations the world over were inundated with inquiries as to the source of the quote attributed to Saddam Hussain. In the meantime, Begin held his Jerusalem press conference, where he repeated the quotation, which was drawn from the Foreign Ministry background paper dated October 1980. But it soon emerged that there had been a most distressing blunder.

The mixup dated back to September 1980, when Hanan Baron, the Foreign Ministry's deputy director General, decided to draw up a background paper for use in the information campaign Israeli legations were mounting all over the world. He sent a draft of the paper for study by various bodies, one of which drew up a parallel draft with various additions, including six quotes from Iraqi leaders about their country's nuclear program which were grouped under the heading "Declarations of Heads of the Iraqi Regime." The two drafts were unified into a single paper which, over Baron's signature, was then disseminated according to the original plan.

In response to questions at the press conference, Begin specified the source of the quote attributed to Saddam Hussain as the October 4, 1980, issue of the Iraqi *ath-Thawra*.

In view of the questions being posed, a Foreign Ministry official was sent to Jerusalem's Truman Institute to check the accuracy of the quote. He failed to find it in *ath-Thawra*, but he did identify a similar passage in an editorial published by a different Iraqi paper, *al-Jumhuriya*, which however did not attribute the words to Saddam Hussain.

It having become obvious that the quote featured in the official statement, and in Begin's address to the press conference, did not coincide with its alleged source, the Foreign Ministry requested the body which had prepared the parallel paper to specify its source. The reply pointed to one of the newssheets regularly issued by Hatzav, which tracks Arab radio and television broadcasts and press publications. Dr. Moshe Yeger, head of the Foreign Ministry information department, requested the relevant newssheet, which was ultimately tracked down after a lengthy search.

An internal Foreign Ministry inquiry found that the mixup originated with the official body which had submitted the additional quotes, and which had confused the *al-Jumhuriya* editorial published on the date mentioned with a different declaration made by Saddam Hussain in a different context and published by *ath-Thawra* on a different date.

On June 11, the Foreign Ministry directed Israeli legations to make no further use of the quotation which had caused the misunderstanding. But the damage had been done.

Nevertheless, in spite of these two mishaps, Israel's information services did a good job in the adverse circumstances prevailing.

Among Israel's severest critics in the United States was House Foreign Relations Committee Chairman Clement Zablocki. On June 9, Zablocki convened his committee to hear an Administration briefing on the reactor bombing. The speaker, Assistant Secretary of State for Near Eastern and South Asian Affairs Nicholas A. Veliotes, who had served some years in Israel, adopted a moderate tone, arguing that the entire matter called for close inquiry. However, without waiting for any such inquiry, Zablocki hastened to voice fierce criticism of the raid, backed up with a call to the Administration to halt aid to Israel. Committee member Paul Findley of Illinois, the most outspokenly anti-Israeli congressman, could only rub his hands in glee: Israel's foes in the Administration and the Congress seemed to be coming into their own.

But it soon emerged that Israel still had powerful friends in the U.S. establishment. Senator Edward M. Kennedy of Massachusetts urged the Administration to devote its energies to self-criticism instead of attacks on Israel. Senator Alan Cranston warned the Administration against condemning Israel, which had only done what the United States had thought of doing toward Cuba in the 1962 missile crisis.

As always in such situations, American Jewish bodies hastened to Israel's defense. Howard M. Squadron of the umbrella Conference of Presidents of Major American Jewish Organizations initiated a series of meetings with Administration officials, warning them that punitive steps against Israel would be a grave offense to the Jewish community in the United States. Presidents' Conference Director Yehuda Helman flew to Israel for a meeting with Begin, for a detailed briefing on the reasons behind the reactor bombing. "You probably asked yourself why I was so pensive during our many meetings," Begin conjectured in his talk with Helman. "Now you know why. You can imagine the kinds of thoughts which ran through my mind—

the arguments I conducted with myself." Helman returned to the United States persuaded that Begin was in the right. Recalling his meeting with the Prime Minister, Helman stated, "I found a man convinced one hundred percent of the justice of his actions, a statesman combining Hassidic enthusiasm with cold political logic."

Signals from Washington indicated that punitive measures were on the way. A statement by Pentagon spokesman Henry Catto characterizing the Israeli action as "coming out of the blue" added, "No decision has been reached as yet on delaying sale or delivery of military equipment to Israel," but recalled that three days ahead, on June 12, Israel was due to receive four additional F-16s. Hinting at a possible departure from normal procedures attending U.S. arms sales to Israel, the mere mention of "delay" in such a context posed a question mark over the plane delivery. When Evron protested to Haig, the Secretary of State could only promise to pursue the matter with Weinberger. However, said Haig, the Pentagon did not speak for the President, who did not believe that Israel should be penalized; if matters turned out differently, he, Haig, would draw personal conclusions.

The State Department fumed—orally and in writing—over what it regarded as Pentagon intervention in a matter which was diplomatic *par excellence*. But its protests did not represent a fundamentally different view; the State Department too was coming around to the notion that "Israel must be taught a lesson."

On June 9, President Reagan summoned the National Security Council for that same afternoon, at the hour he usually set aside for rest. The urgency of the summons was due in part to Haig's imminent departure for a long tour of the Far East.

Before meeting the council, the President studied two letters. One, from Egyptian President Sadat, adopted a most belligerent tone toward Israel. It was accompanied by a memorandum from the U.S. ambassador to Cairo, who reported on his conversation with Sadat the previous day: the Egyptian President urged the United States to penalize Israel and suspend delivery of the warplanes.

The second letter was from Menahem Begin. Addressed "Dear Ron," it again recalled the one and a half million Jewish children gassed by the Nazis, and the threat of a similar fate, from radioactivity, hanging over the children of Israel. The Iraqi reactor was "a nightmare," wrote Begin; it caused him sleepless nights. He went on to explain that the decision to bomb the reactor had been taken months earlier; it was now or never. Recalling that U.S. intervention in Paris and Rome had borne no fruit, Begin affirmed that Israel was left with no choice but to act without further delay. Expressing the hope that Reagan and his "great people" would understand

Israel's motives, Begin pointed out that an Iraqi nuclear attack on Israel would inflict 600,000 casualties, the equivalent for the United States being 46 million. "It would have been a new Holocaust. It was prevented thanks to the heroism of our pilots, to whom we owe so much."

The National Security Council convened in the White House Cabinet Room. Although no one defended the Israeli action, it soon emerged that the participants represented two schools of thought, one hawkish, the other more moderate.

The spokesman for the first school was Defense Secretary Weinberger, who called for drastic steps, including a temporary halt on all military aid to Israel and a parallel cutback of economic aid. He buttressed his recommendations with these arguments: Refraining from severe punitive action against Israel would implicitly entitle other recipients of American military aid to employ the arms for attacks on neighboring states. To preserve the momentum of the peace process, as reflected in the current Habib mission in Lebanon, and to safeguard the Camp David Accords, the United States must convince the Arabs that Israel had been "put in its place." In its agreements with the United States, Israel had undertaken to use the U.S. military equipment it acquired—including, of course, the F-15s and F-16s—for exclusively defensive purposes; now that Israel had employed those weapons for an unprovoked attack on Iraq, could the United States condone such a flagrant violation of agreements?

Weinberger's arguments were not new to the President, who had earlier received a confidential memorandum from the Defense Secretary specifying his proposals. Weinberger also warned that a U.S. failure to respond was liable to entail grave consequences in relations between the superpowers, in the North Atlantic Treaty Organization and in Latin America.

A milder view, more favorable toward Israel, was voiced by Weinberger's perennial adversary, Secretary of State Haig. Punitive action against Israel, claimed Haig, would help the United States neither in the Mideast nor in its overall global policy. Imposition of sanctions against Israel would be interpreted as an act of weakness on the part of the United States. True, he conceded, Israel had not made the U.S. privy to the planned operation; but on learning of it Washington had immediately issued a protest and announced an investigation. Far-reaching steps now, before any inquiry, would be interpreted as an admission of embarrassment and nervousness in the White House. The only genuine threat to U.S. interests in the Mideast was Soviet expansionism, argued Haig. The only effective way of blocking the Soviets was to lean upon Israel's military might. Consequently, the United States must not take any step—such as a halt in military aid—which would weaken Israel. Furthermore, he added, the Israeli government now faced a severe test: the evacuation of Sinai, in compliance with the peace treaty with Egypt. Why burden Israel with further difficulties?

National-security adviser Richard Allen inclined toward Haig's view, but he did demand some measure of response. "For tactical reasons," he argued, "we must take some action, so as to preserve our foothold in the Arab world. We must also prove that Israel's destruction of a nuclear installation by means of U.S.-made equipment and technology cannot constitute a precedent. But our response should be moderate, and must not inflict genuine harm upon Israel, particularly not on the eve of the Sinai withdrawal."

Allen likewise submitted a confidential memorandum to the President, but his conclusions bore no resemblance to those reached by Weinberger. The national-security adviser claimed that penalizing Israel for an action aimed at preventing nuclear proliferation would encourage such proliferation. Anyone on the threshold of a nuclear capability could claim a United States go-ahead.

President Reagan appears to have inclined toward the view espoused by Haig and Allen, but he could not overlook the vigorous demands for sanctions as voiced by George Bush and Weinberger, and by numerous State Department and Pentagon experts.

In the meantime, ambassadors of the moderate Arab states stepped up their efforts to talk the Administration into penalizing Israel. That same day, the Saudi ambassador visited both the White House and the State Department.

The National Security Council adjourned till the following day, June 10. Meanwhile, Reagan received Senate Majority Leader Howard Baker, who reportedly advised the President to "slap Israel over the wrist, symbolically at least." Such an act would convince Congress that Israel had received its just deserts, defusing pressure for stronger sanctions.

The National Security Council concluded its deliberations on June 10 with the President directing suspension of shipment of the four F-16s due for delivery to Israel two days later. Haig and Allen saw this step as a triumph for their view and a rejection of Weinberger's more far-reaching demands. From the outset, the suspension was seen as temporary, representing no real reduction in U.S. military aid to Israel.

Weinberger disclosed the suspension to the media before the decision had been officially transmitted to the Israeli government. An enraged Haig called Weinberger to protest.

24 "Scandalous"

During the afternoon of June 10, Ambassador Evron was summoned to Haig's office. "In a few hours," the Secretary of State said, "the State Department spokesman will officially announce the President's decision to suspend delivery of the four F-16s." Adopting a reassuring tone, Haig endeavored to convince Evron that the suspension was "the lesser evil."

Profoundly upset, Evron refused to be consoled, reminding the Secretary of State of his promise the previous day that there would be no punitive steps. Haig admitted that the Administration had effectively faced a fait accompli when the Pentagon announced that a suspension was under consideration. "I told the President it was scandalous," said Haig, "but by then it was too late."

"We take a grave view of the suspension," said Evron. "It is offensive and unjust, and it will encourage Israel's enemies. By violating a formally concluded agreement with Israel, the United States will set a dangerous precedent that could affect implementation of the peace treaty with Egypt. Furthermore, such a step will exacerbate the situation in the region as a whole. Syrian inflexibility will grow, and Damascus will be tempted into initiatives harmful equally to Israel and to the standing of the United States. After all, Washington will never match Moscow's enmity in word and deed toward Israel."

But Evron knew well that the die was cast and nothing he could say would change the President's decision. Consequently, he got down to brass tacks: How long, he asked, would the plane delivery be suspended?

The gist of Haig's reply: I don't know. There is an urgent necessity to renew negotiations on Palestinian autonomy. I hope you put forward positive proposals.

Evron seized the bull by the horns. "It should be obvious," he said, "that Israel cannot be expected to exhibit moderation while being subjected to an American embargo, and to pressures the likes of which have not been exerted for many years. Prime Minister Begin plans to come to the United States in September. In the kind of atmosphere you are creating, what do you expect of the visit?"

Haig expressed his conviction that the F-16 suspension would be terminated before the Prime Minister's arrival in Washington. The Secretary of State went on to pledge that in the impending Security Council debate on the reactor raid the United States would veto any proposals for sanctions against Israel. However, should such a resolution contain nothing beyond a condemnation along the lines of the Administration's own statement, the United States would vote for it.

Immediately upon official publication of the aircraft suspension, the Israeli Embassy's media adviser Aviezer Pazner released a statement regretting the Administration decision: "We consider this unjust. Israel acted in self-defense."

The following day, June 11, Haig sent an official letter to Senate Foreign Relations Committee Chairman Charles Percy "providing... information pursuant to section 3 (c)(2) of the Arms Export Control Act." The letter raised the curtain on the congressional inquiry into the reactor raid.

The Department of State has learned that on June 7, 1981, the Government of Israel carried out an air attack against a nuclear reactor under construction in Iraq. Israeli Air Force units taking part in this attack were reportedly equipped with defense articles that have been furnished to Israel by the United States under the Foreign Military Sales program, including F-15 and F-16 aircraft.

Sales to Israel under the Foreign Military Sales program are governed by a Mutual Defense Assistance Agreement of July 23, 1952 (TIAS 2675) which provides in pertinent part:

"The Government of Israel assures the United States Government that such equipment, materials or services as may be acquired from the United States... are required for and will be used solely to maintain its internal security, its legitimate self-defense, or to permit it to participate in the defense of the area of which it is a part, or in the United Nations collective security arrangements and measures, and that it will not undertake any acts of aggression against any other state."

In these circumstances, I must report on behalf of the President that a substantial violation of the 1952 Agreement may have occurred. We are conducting a review of the entire matter and will consider the contention of Israel, that this action was necessary for its defense because the reactor was intended to produce atomic bombs and would become operational very soon and that, once it became operational, an attack would have been impossible because it could not be carried out without exposing the inhabitants of Baghdad to massive radioactive lethal fallout.

Evron hastened to phone Prime Minister Begin and brief him on developments. Having heard the report, Begin told Evron to expect a letter addressed to the President. But Evron requested permission to meet with the President without delay, even before Begin's letter arrived, so as to present the Israeli position in person.

"Permission granted," Begin replied, momentarily considering the idea of coming in person to see the President.

Evron contacted the White House and requested a meeting with the President.

The suspension of plane shipments caused consternation in Israel. Former Prime Minister Yitzhak Rabin—an adversary of the Begin government and a critic of the reactor attack—published an article urging Israel not to remain indifferent to the suspension, which he characterized as "violation of an agreement and a precedent of unparalled gravity."

Begin decided that the time was now ripe for a public settling of accounts with Defense Secretary Weinberger, who spearheaded the demand for punitive action against Israel. Addressing an election rally on June 11, Begin directed a bitter personal attack against Weinberger. Such an onslaught upon a minister of a friendly government is an extraordinary act in international relations, but Begin, knowing that his words would reach the entire world, hoped to stir a response in the United States.

"Defense Secretary Weinberger," proclaimed Begin, "is the man who emphatically demanded withholding from us all economic and military aid." Tens of thousands of listeners responded with angry jeers. Begin resumed, "Who are you coming to punish, Mr. Weinberger? What moral standard do you follow? Did you ever hear of six million Jews who were herded into the gas chambers? Saddam Hussain . . . would ruthlessly drop atomic bombs on Tel Aviv . . . so as to finally annihilate the Jewish people. . . . In the generation of the Holocaust and the national renaissance, we shall permit no enemy to develop weapons of mass destruction."

The attack stung Weinberger into a response in which he denied recommending a halt on all aid to Israel; he had merely proposed suspension of the delivery of the four planes. "I did so in consultation with Haig," Weinberger explained. "I'm sorry that Mr. Begin is proceeding on an erroneous assumption. I've made no such recommendation [for a total halt in aid]."

But Begin was unrelenting. While he was delivering his public challenge to Weinberger, there was a personal letter on its way to the latter "from one colleague to another" (it will be recalled that Begin had been the acting defense minister since Weizman's resignation).

The letter began by recalling the Pentagon press release with its first public reference to suspension of the plane delivery. Begin described the

Pentagon's reaction as out of all proportion to "the lifesaving operation" against the reactor. Addressing Weinberger, the scion of a family of Jewish immigrants, Begin wrote:

> I feel morally bound to ask of you, Mr. Secretary, that in all your judgements and actions please bear in mind that whereas your children and grandchildren live and shall continue to live in the great country of the United States of America, my children and grandchildren live and shall continue to live in this tiny Israel which many cruel enemies would like to see wiped off the map and utterly destroyed. . . . Should Israel, because of this (operation) be 'punished' by the suspension of the supply of arms?

Begin concluded: "Having read this letter, perhaps on looking at the photos of your own children and grandchildren you will ponder the thought that one million like them live in the state of Israel. It is of them I write."

On June 11, Ambassador Evron, accompanied by military attaché Meron, came to Weinberger's office to deliver the letter in person. Reading it there and then, Weinberger hastened to defend himself. In flagrant contrast to the impassioned tone of Begin's letter, the Defense Secretary adopted a dry and factual manner. He pointed out that it was the State Department—"headed by an outspoken friend of yours"—which had officially announced the suspension; he recalled that the planes were being withheld due to the Administration's suspicion that the reactor bombing may have violated the terms of American arms sales to Israel.

"You took the law into your own hands," Weinberger charged. "The Iraqis were far from attaining any real capacity for producing nuclear weapons. True, your people in Israel had a different assessment, but I do not suscribe to the view that such disagreements can be resolved exclusively by use of force. We were consequently bound to condemn the action, even though it was undertaken by a friend."

The Defense Secretary nevertheless expressed his professional admiration for the bombing, "which was carried out with scalpel-like precision." Referring to satellite photographs of the reactor site, he commented that it looked as though a tree had been uprooted.

Evron tried to change the subject by praising the excellence of the American weaponry which had enabled the Israeli pilots to do such a superb job, but Weinberger reverted to the original topic: Israel had violated the terms attending the purchase of U.S. arms. "We Americans sell arms to many states. If we slacken the reins, we shall lose control of the arms we sell."

Evron retorted, "We have been using American weapons for fifteen years, and there have been no particular problems hitherto. This instance was no exception. It should also be recalled that we are talking about Iraq, which, to put it mildly, is no close friend of the United States." Evron listed Israel's efforts, in coordination with the Carter Administration, to induce France and Italy to deny to Iraq the technology for production of nuclear weapons.

Weinberger did not back down: Iraq had no capacity for manufacturing a nuclear bomb, he said.

But Evron stood equally firm: "Throughout the course of this prolonged dialogue, we never heard such a contention from your side. On the contrary: why did the United States attempt to induce France not to supply Iraq with enriched uranium? Was that not precisely for fear that the fuel would serve for construction of an atomic bomb?"

Ignoring the ambassador's arguments, Weinberger remained inflexible. The United States could not overlook the Israeli action, he said, particularly not when some Mideastern states credited Soviet propaganda charges that the United States had prior knowledge of the operation.

Anxious to know when the plane suspension would end, Evron demanded, "Where do we go from here?"

Weinberger: "The ball is in the court of Congress, which will hold hearings, hear testimony and adopt the appropriate resolutions."

Evron: "What position will the Administration adopt?"

Weinberger did not reply. The meeting was at an end. As Evron and Meron took their leave, they were despondent. They had found Weinberger willing neither to listen nor to discuss matters in earnest, making them wonder whether his attitude would have a bearing upon other sensitive topics currently on the Administration's agenda.

"The early part of the conversation was quite relaxed," Evron recalled subsequently. "But later it became very unpleasant, even strident. One of the least cordial exchanges I ever held with a senior Administration figure."

Evron could only hope that his talk with President Reagan, scheduled for a few hours ahead, would sound a more friendly note.

Shortly before his meeting with Evron, Reagan received the ambassadors of five "moderate" Arab states: Saudi Arabia, Sudan, Morocco, Jordan and Bahrein. The President again stressed that "no one was more surprised than me" by the reactor bombing. He ventured to imply that Israel could have pursued other options, but if the ambassadors hoped to hear him censure Israel outright they were disappointed.

Accompanied by the embassy's political adviser, Eytan Bentzur, Ephraim Evron entered the Oval Room. President Reagan was awaiting them, flanked by Vice-President George Bush, White House counselor Edwin Meese and numerous other White House and State Department officials and advisers.

"The Prime Minister of Israel," Evron commenced, "has requested that I express our profound disappointment over the President's unprecedented decision to suspend delivery of the F-16s." Evron reviewed events leading up to the reactor raid. He elaborated on Iraq's enmity toward Israel and the United States, its efforts to foil all Mideast peace efforts, and its prominence among states supporting international terrorism. He also detailed efforts by Israel and the United States to coax France and Italy away from their perilous cooperation with Iraq. "Israel," Evron stressed, "is aware of the gravity of the action it took. But it was done in self-defense. We were dutybound to protect Israel's citizens and the future of the state."

Furthermore, he went on, the reactor bombing buttressed the United States's standing in the region by removing a threat to the peace process. An Israel exposed to threats of annihilation was an asset to no one, other than those wishing to deny peace and stability to the Mideast. In the long run, the reactor's destruction would reinforce the region's moderate elements, who could now argue that those who supported terrorism and the destruction of Israel had failed in their endeavors.

Having contrived throughout to conceal his own impassioned feelings behind a cool diplomatic tone, Evron concluded, "Therefore, Mr. President, please reconsider your decision."

Reagan replied that the United States's response was the bare minimum prescribed by American law. The Congress was now investigating whether there had been any violation of Israel-U.S. arms agreements. Even so, he stressed that the Administration was not reassessing its relations with Israel and had no intention of so doing.

The President went on: "I and my Administration were greatly surprised by the operation. Alternatives to military action should have been explored. Had we known that the reactor constitutes a threat, we would have assisted Israel by appealing for the nondelivery to Iraq of weapon-grade nuclear fuel."

Evron and Bentzur could scarcely believe their ears. They knew that the United States had intervened with France and Italy—in vain, as Haig had admitted in those precise terms during his conversation with Begin in April. Earlier, in December 1980, Ambassador Lewis had delivered to Begin an official American communication summarizing the menace posed by the reactor, in almost total congruity with Israel's own assessments. Had that information failed to reach the President?

Reagan went on to speak of U.S. mediation efforts in Lebanon. He reaffirmed his country's friendship toward Israel and spoke warmly of Begin's personal letter, which he had already studied.

Evron replied, "I hope the situation is soon regularized and supply channels are reopened."

Reagan: "You can depend upon my fundamental position."

At the conclusion of the conversation the President escorted the two Israeli diplomats to the door. The ambassador reiterated his hope that the plane suspension would end soon.

"I hope so, too," replied Reagan.

The White House now delegated the matter to national-security adviser Richard Allen. The latter demanded all the material in Administration files pertaining to the Iraqi reactor. When the date had been assembled, Allen discovered to his astonishment that in the transition from the previous Administration Jimmy Carter had failed to brief Reagan with regard to the reactor; nor was there any briefing at the ministerial or advisory echelons.

Allen reported to the President, who reacted with total consternation, utterly unable to comprehend how such a grave omission could have come about.

In the meantime, Evron, deducing from his conversation with Reagan that neither the President nor his Administration was aware of earlier U.S. endeavors that predated Israel's attack on the reactor, contacted former President Richard M. Nixon and requested a meeting. Nixon responded favorably. While Evron was flying to New York, the ex-President phoned the White House to request information about the reactor bombing. He was put through to Allen, who told him of the failure to inform the new Administration. Nixon likewise did not conceal his astonishment.

Evron met Nixon on June 16. The ambassador began by conveying Begin's good wishes, recalling Nixon's order for a massive airlift of military supplies to Israel at the darkest hours of the 1973 Yom Kippur War. Evron said he now came to solicit Nixon's aid and counsel under the adverse circumstances newly arisen.

Nixon proceeded to confirm what Evron had sensed in the previous day's meeting with the President: Reagan and his aides were totally unaware of the fact that Israel's concern about the Iraqi reactor had been communicated to the United States government—which had endorsed that concern and even made vain efforts to show France and Italy the error of their ways. Only this morning, Nixon said, would Reagan be fully briefed by Allen on the events which had preceded the reactor bombing. The Reagan Administration's ignorance on the subject explained its initial reaction, which Israel had found so incomprehensible.

Nixon advised his guest to be patient, explaining that the United States currently faced anti-Israel pressures from two directions: from Western Europe and from Arab states with pro-American leanings. Reagan was a genuine friend of Israel, Nixon affirmed, illustrating his point with examples predating Reagan's accession to office. The Israelis must show understanding and not attack the Administration—it would do them no good; in any case, plane deliveries would soon be resumed.

Taking his leave of Nixon, Evron returned to Washington, where he briefed Bentzur on what he had heard from the former President. Referring to the breakdown in communications between the Carter and Reagan administrations, Bentzur judged that Carter and his men, being skeptical about possible Israeli military action against the reactor, had consequently not troubled to inform their successors on the subject.

In a quest for further information on this delicate matter, the present writer approached Jimmy Carter with the following query: "During the caretaker period between your Administration and that of President Reagan, what instructions did you or your Administration give the incoming President or his Administration vis à vis this issue [the reactor]?"

Carter's reply: "Reagan only chose his Secretaries of Defense and State at the last moment."

Was Carter trying to claim that there had been no one delegated to receive the information? Was that his excuse for the omission? Be that as it may, there was obviously a grave malfunctioning that disrupted transmission of the information, with harmful results: Reagan's perplexity over the bombing led to a temporary chill which briefly marred his fundamentally sympathetic attitude toward Israel in general and Begin in particular. It should be noted that on becoming acquainted with the full facts Reagan reverted to his traditionally favorable view of Israel.

In the meantime, Begin had opted for a step highly unusual in international relations. On June 14 an open letter from him addressed to the American public was published in the United States. "As a free man to free men," Begin appealed to "my American friends, Christians and Jews," not to permit Israel to be penalized for doing what it was bound to do. Punishment is for those who do evil, he wrote, but those whose cause is just should be helped, and Israel's cause was a just one.

The letter gained considerable publicity—to the embarrassment of the State Department. Israel's own Foreign Ministry was apprehensive about a possible deterioration in relations with the United States as a result of this direct appeal over the heads of the Administration and the Congress, at a time when the latter was debating the issue and the two governments were conducting diplomatic contacts.

Evron and his aides—Minister Yaakov Nehushtan, political adviser Bentzur, scientific adviser Gideon Frank, information adviser Harry Horowitz, media adviser Aviezer Pazner—flung themselves into an energetic campaign to justify the reactor bombing. There were meetings with Cabinet members, senior officials, congressmen of both parties and, of course, representatives of the media. The aim was double: to influence American opinion in Israel's favor and to fend off the anti-Israel hue and cry on Capital Hill.

With the passing of the days, new voices were raised in defense of Israel's action. Senator Larry Pressler of South Dakota, a member of the Foreign Relations Committee, declared that now that the smoke was beginning to clear he could see matters in a different aspect. He predicted that in the long run the Israeli action might serve United States interests. Representative Edward J. Markey of Massachusetts, chairman of the Energy Subcommittee of the House Interior Committee, characterized the bombing as a legitimate act of prevention against Iraq's nuclear program, which was designed for military purposes; while the superpowers pursued a policy of hypocrisy and cynicism with regard to nuclear proliferation, small nations in danger of annihilation, such as Israel, were left with no choice but to do whatever they could to ward off disaster. Representative John E. Porter of Illinois declared that the destruction of the Iraqi reactor had been vital for the protection of Israel and the whole world.

Begin called his friend the Reverend Jerry Falwell. "I did it," the Prime Minister declared, "to save our little children from the danger of annihilation." "I support Israel with all my heart," replied Falwell, and he launched vigorous action to recruit backing for Israel among American church leaders. Having played a prominent role in getting Ronald Reagan into the White House, the Moral Majority leader now wielded considerable political clout. "God's attitude towards the nations is dictated by the nations' attitude towards Israel," Falwell admonished Reagan. The President promised there would be no change in his favorable stance toward Israel. "Everything will work out all right," Richard Allen assured Falwell. In apparent response to White House instructions, the various branches of the Administration began to moderate their tone when referring to Israel.

Right from the outset, Israel enjoyed the support of U.S. Jewry—national leaders as well as ordinary members of the community. When Israel's New York consulate conducted a survey of eleven synagogue congregations with a total membership of 365,000, the findings indicated marked support for Israel, with a majority critical of the Israeli opposition for its objections to the reactor bombing.

To fend off continuing attacks on Israel, Evron now decided to exhibit to a number of friendly senators and congressmen the December 1980 memorandum conveyed to Begin by Ambassador Lewis. Pledged to deny ever having seen the document, the legislators nevertheless acquired useful ammunition for their battles on Israel's behalf. Evron and his aides made frequent references to President John F. Kennedy and his action in 1962 against Cuba—and, indirectly, against the Soviet Union—in defense of U.S. national interests. The reaction of some senior Administration officials was ambiguous. "If I were Israel," said one, "I would probably have acted the way you did. But as an American, I am convinced that the reactor bombing has caused the United States a lot of trouble."

Democratic Senator John H. Glenn, Jr., of Ohio, noted for his coolness toward Israel, attempted to refute the arguments put forward in Israel's defense. The former astronaut—a leading member of the Senate Foreign Relations Committee and considered a good presidential prospect for 1984—claimed that Osirak's capacity was only 40 megawatts, not 70 as Israel alleged. Moreover, he argued that French supervision of the enriched uranium would have sufficed to preclude the production of atomic bombs. Glenn also dismissed the military potential of the Italian hot cells. Representative Jonathan Bingham of New York, chairman of the nuclear subcommittee of the House Foreign Relations Committee, replied that his panel had concluded that Iraq was in the process of developing nuclear weapons.

In anticipation of the projected committee hearings, the congressional research service was asked to draw up comprehensive scientific reports reviewing all aspects of the reactor raid. The two most prominent reports sought to answer the following questions: How long would Iraq have required from the time the research reactor went into operation, to acquire a nuclear bomb? What degree of radioactive fallout could have been anticipated over Baghdad if the reactor had been bombed when hot?

The answers brought Israel little joy. The first report affirmed that "if acquisition of nuclear weapons materials were the only limitation of Iraq's ability to produce a nuclear explosive . . . then Iraq might have had one plutonium device in somewhat less than a year, or one uranium device within a few months." However, the report appended a rider affirming that it would be necessary to assume that the sole restriction upon Iraq's bomb-producing capacity was acquisition of nuclear explosive, and that Iraq would have succeeded in its first attempt to manufacture a sophisticated bomb—both assumptions being dismissed as "implausible."

The second report, authored by Dr. Warren Donnelly, a senior expert at the Environment and National Resources Policy Division of the Congressional Research Service, held it most improbable that an attack with conventional weapons after the activation of the reactor would have exposed Baghdad to lethal radioactivity, though some individuals at the reactor site itself were liable to exposure to a certain measure of radiation.

After scrutinizing the Donnelly report, Israeli scientists drew up a riposte which refuted its conclusions. To Donnelly's credit, he appended the Israeli objections to his own report when it was submitted to Congress, though he still adhered to his own view.

In an interview eighteen months later, Donnelly continued to reject the Israeli claim that the reactor had to be attacked before it became hot. Even so, he conceded that Begin may have genuinely believed in the danger of radioactive contamination. Donnelly added the conjecture (shared by other experts) that Israel attacked the reactor before it was hot for fear that bombing it when it was in operation would have been regarded as "semi-nuclear warfare," whereas the attack on the cold reactor was nothing more than a conventional strike at a structure. Incidentally, Donnelly totally disagreed with Senator Glenn's claim that the reactor's capacity was only 40 megawatts; the scientist endorsed the Israeli assessment of 70 megawatts.

Be that as it may, more and more experts came out in support of Israel. British Colonel Jonathan Elford, a noted researcher at London's International Centre of Strategic Studies, noted numerous indications that the Iraqis would have been capable of producing five nuclear bombs within five years.

A specialist commission appointed by the United Nations Secretary General found that there would have been no great danger of nuclear contamination in the event of the reactor being bombed while hot, though admitting that the Israeli assessment to the contrary was "not unrealistic" even though improbable. (Paragraph 47 in the Secretary General's report to the Thirty-eighth General Assembly).

The June 20, 1981, issue of *The New Republic* carried an editorial entitled "No Option," which dismissed criticism of Israel as "more than routinely hypocritical" and pronounced that, with its survival threatened, Israel was left with no choice other than sending its Air Force to eliminate the threat. This coincided with Begin's argument that the reactor bombing was permissible under international law, being an act of self-defense.

This view was further supported by a man regarded as one of the United States's most brilliant legal minds. In a letter to Begin, former Supreme Court Justice Arthur J. Goldberg, onetime U.S. ambassador to the United Nations, wrote on June 16:

In light of the fact that by its own decision Iraq deems itself to be at war with Israel, the State of Israel, under established rules of international law, has the right to take military action, including bombing, against installations in Iraq which potentially may assist Iraq in its proclaimed war-like designs. It is not necessary, in my understanding of applicable rules of international law, for Israel to prove that the nuclear installation in question is producing nuclear bombs. It is sufficient that this nuclear installation potentially may be of assistance to Iraq in its announced program designed to undermine the security of the State of Israel.

By way of illustration, international law permits the bombing of a non-nuclear electric generating plant of a hostile and belligerent power inasmuch as such a plant may be helpful in the waging of war.

Thus, since Iraq is in a state of war with Israel, military action by Israel against Iraqi installations helpful to its war-like designs, would be regarded in international law as justified acts of self defense by Israel. The Allied Powers, during World War II, bombed, as acts of self defense, installations by Germany, such as oil refineries, steel mills, public utilities, ball bearing plants and other such installations which might contribute to Germany's war efforts against the Allied Powers.

It is my conviction, therefore, that the criticism of Israel for the bombing of the Iraqi nuclear installation has overlooked the basic fact that Iraq, by its own choice, is in a state of war with Israel and that Israel, therefore, had the legal right to seek to destroy such an installation. It is relevant, in this context, that Israel, contrary to Iraq, has expressed its willingness to make peace with Iraq, in accordance with Resolutions 242, 338 and other relevant resolutions of the United Nations Security Council.

There are, in addition to the nuclear installation, other evidences of Iraq's hostile intent, namely, the involvement of Iraqi forces in recent wars against Israel by the front line Arab States and its frequent statements since that its armed forces are available for future deployment and for the same purpose.

Begin answered Goldberg with a warm letter in which he argued that the Israeli action rested equally upon the principles of international law and upon the supreme moral law of national survival.

Experts on international law illuminated fresh sides of the issue. Anthony d'Amato, writing in *The American Journal of International Law*, affirmed:

I suggest that it is open to serious question whether Israel's strike was a use of force against either Iraq territorial integrity or its political independence. No portion of Iraq's territory was taken away from Iraq by the bombardment. A *use* of the territory—namely, to construct a nuclear reactor—was interfered with, but the territory itself remained integral. Nor was Iraq's political independence compromised. Iraq's *power* was undoubtedly lessened. . . . But there has been no evidence of any Israeli purpose beyond the limited one of destroying the nuclear reactor itself. In this respect, Israel's action was analagous to a limited "humanitarian intervention" such as the Entebbe raid, which can be justified along similiar lines. . . .

Entirely supporting Begin's claims, d'Amato went on:

... there is hardly a more fundamentally important value than the preservation of the lives of the inhabitants of the claimant state. If Iraq were to develop a nuclear weapons capability, the existence of a small state such as Israel would be in jeopardy. In other words, Israel may have been justified in attacking a nuclear reactor in Iraq, where it would not have been justified in attacking a plant that manufactured tanks or conventional artillery, because of the enormous destructive potential of nuclear weapons.

... Iraq is a party to the Non-Proliferation Treaty and has had its nuclear installations inspected on a regular basis by the International Atomic Energy Agency. ... The question, of course, is whether IAEA inspection of the facility will continue to be frequent and thorough enough to prevent diversion of fissionable material produced by the reactor to military uses. Clearly, Israel was not convinced. Indeed, is it unreasonable to think that Iraq, or any nation building a nuclear reactor under IAEA safeguards, may at some point bar the inspection team and announce to the world that it has successfully transferred its fissionable material to its weapons program? ... [I]s it not clear there there is at least a substantial basis for Israel's frontal challenge to the NPT-IAEA system?

D'Amato also drew an analogy between the Israeli action and the 1962 U.S. blockade of Cuba. At that time, the United States was accused of violating the United Nations Charter's Article 51, which sanctions military actions solely in response to prior military action. The Americans responded with a series of counterarguments which d'Amato found relevant to the Israeli raid on the reactor.

This viewpoint was further elaborated by the renowned jurist Beth N. Polebaum in a long and comprehensive article published in *The New York University Law Review*. Polebaum pointed out that the threat to Israel was no less immediate or powerful than the threat the United States faced during the Cuban missile crisis. Nevertheless, the U.S. government, while convinced that it had been in the right in 1962, censured Israel for its action in 1981. In her view, the principles of international law all argued for Israel: "Israel's leaders acted reasonably in concluding that the last moment had arrived for effective action in the face of a credible nuclear threat. Israel did not exceed the force necessary to eliminate the danger."

A thorough study of the reactor attack in its constitutional aspects was authored by Colonel Uri Shoham, Israel's chief military prosecutor. Published in the summer 1985 issue of *The U.S. Military Law Review*, Shoham's article, which rested on his personal knowledge, a close study of press publications, expert opinion, U.S. congressional proceedings and various research works, argued: "The Israeli attack was not a result of an arbitrary decision but instead was reasonable under the particular circumstances and was legal under the current rules of self-defence in international law. The Israeli action fulfilled the requirements of necessity and proportionality as well." Shoham characterized the parties in the following terms: on the one side stood Iraq, which continually threatened Israel with annihilation, and which violated international law by supporting anti-Israel terrorism; on the other side, Israel, a small country which, ever since its creation, had faced the tangible threat of destruction, and which had repeatedly demonstrated its desire for peace with all its neighbors, Iraq included. In bombing the reactor, Israel sought to remove the nuclear threat it faced, so as to safeguard its basic physical existence. The necessity of the bombing was vindicated by the enormity of the danger—total destruction—and its immediacy; had the reactor become hot, that would have created an entirely new situation. Furthermore, the raid itself was "surgical," in no way directed against Iraq's territorial integrity and carried through with a "minimal" loss of life.

But all these legal debates and contentions saw light long after the storm had abated. Immediately following upon the reactor bombing, judgment was delegated exclusively to Washington politicians.

25 "Dynamite in Congress"

On June 12, Senate Foreign Relations Committee Chairman Charles Percy met with his House counterpart, Clement Zablocki, in anticipation of the congressional hearings on the reactor bombing. Neither man could be numbered among Israel's friends in Congress, but Ambassador Evron and his aides could reply upon numerous sympathetic members in both committees to block the anti-Israel efforts of their respective chairmen and of Administration officials.

President Reagan displayed no underlying anti-Israel bias in his attitude to the reactor attack. He continued to condemn the action itself, but did so in moderate terms. "I thought that there were other options that might have been considered," he said at a June 16 press conference—his first since his injury in an abortive assassination attempt ten weeks earlier. Reagan added, "On the other hand, I do think that one has to recognize that Israel had reason for concern in view of the past history of Iraq, which has never signed a cease-fire or recognized Israel as a nation, never joined in any peace effort." He noted that "very possibly in conducting that mission Israel may have genuinely believed it was a defensive move." The President withheld judgment on whether Israel had violated its undertakings to the United States. That matter, he stressed, was currently under study by the Congress.

As the two congressional committees prepared to launch their hearings, Washington teemed with rumors planted with the aim of discrediting Israel's case. Officials, named and unnamed alike, continued to seize upon Begin's two slips—his incorrect quotation from Saddam Hussain and the erroneous reference to the underground chamber beneath the reactor—to pour cold water on Israel's other claims. By contrast, Washington granted a high measure of credibility to information from Paris that the uranium supplied to Iraq had been treated to render it unfit for use in nuclear weapons.

In flagrant contradiction of the document submitted by Ambassador Lewis to Begin in December 1980, an Administration expert who briefed the two committees argued that the United States was not entirely convinced of Iraq's intention of developing nuclear weapons; even if such was Baghdad's plan, at least three more years would elapse before such a bomb could be constructed. On the other hand, the expert alleged, Israel had embarrassed Egyptian President Sadat and undermined his efforts toward convincing the Arab world to emulate him in making peace with Israel. Israel had demonstrated that it did not believe in the prospects of peace in the region.

Not all his listeners accepted that view. Under a barrage of questions, the expert was forced to concede that some Arab states were gratified by the reactor bombing. He also admitted that Iraq had intended ultimately to develop nuclear weapons.

That was borne out by Herbert Skoville, a nuclear scientist who had once served as deputy director of the CIA; in a press interview, Skoville declared that Iraq had indeed sought to build up a capacity for acquiring nuclear arms.

The House committee launched its hearings on the reactor raid on June 17, one day before its Senate counterpart. The opening statement by Chairman Clement Zablocki was predictably hostile toward Israel. Quoting an Administration statement, he charged that the Israeli action could not but "add to the already tense situation in the area."

The first witness to testify before the committee was State Department Undersecretary for Political Affairs Walter J. Stoessel, Jr. Stoessel's testimony clearly foreshadowed the line the Administration would adopt in the hearings: it would accuse Israel of "prejudicing peace efforts in the Mideast," though conceding that Iraq had not played a constructive role in those efforts. From Israel's viewpoint, Stoessel's most significant utterance was the acknowledgment—even if understated—of Israel's anxiety, and his admission that this anxiety was known to and shared by the Administration. "We were concerned about the Iraqi nuclear program because of the sensitivity of the region and because it would eventually give Iraq the capability to build an atomic weapon."

Lee H. Hamilton of Indiana, chairman of the subcommittee on Europe and the Middle East, tried to extract a more explicit declaration. In the view of the Administration, he demanded, was Iraq pursuing a nuclear-weapons capability?

Stoessel endeavored to adhere to his original formulation. "We had some concerns . . . we had not made any definitive conclusions . . ."

Hamilton asked whether the Administration disagreed with the Israeli declaration that Osirak was designed for atomic bombs.

Stoessel: ". . . We are not able to make a definitive judgment, ourselves, which would confirm that Israeli position."

Hamilton pressed the official to agree that Iraq sought ultimately to produce nuclear weapons, at some time or other in the future.

Stoessel: "No, we have no definitive confirmation of that."

The Undersecretary's diplomatic shillyshallying did not satisfy committee member Stephen J. Solarz of New York, who proceeded to discard the kid gloves. "Mr. Stoessel," he declared, "I have to say that I am amazed and appalled at your unwillingness to characterize the purpose of the Iraqi nuclear program as being one designed to provide them with the capacity to manufacture nuclear weapons, in view of what we have heard from so many other people associated with the Administration over the course of the last week. What do you think was the Iraq purpose in going forward with this program? Was it to give them the capacity to replace oil as a source of energy in their country?"

Pinned down, Stoessel was forced to admit, ". . . As I have indicated, we have had concerns clearly about the Iraqi nuclear program and what their intentions might have been, and I think it is fair to say if they had continued on the course outlined, they would have had the option to produce nuclear weapons."

As the hearings proceeded, State Department officials were obliged to admit that Israel did have a case. They did so unwillingly, and the pro-Israel members of the committee had their work cut out in extracting admissions to reinforce the Israeli view.

Representative Robert G. Lagomarsino of California demanded, ". . . isn't it beyond argument really that to bomb a nonoperative reactor would cause less threat of nuclear radiation release than one that is operational?"

Assistant Secretary of State Nicholas Veliotes: "There is no question in my mind, but I would ask others to address it." Acting Deputy Assistant Secretary of State for Nuclear Energy John Boright filled in with "Basically, yes." With that, the two officials went to the trouble of pointing out that the congressional research service report upheld a diametrically opposed view.

Representative Jonathan Bingham, a long-standing friend of Israel, could not withhold a sarcastic remark: ". . . the critics of Israel are now arguing that the danger to Baghdad, if the reactor was bombed while operational, was not so great. If Israel had waited until that reactor was hot and had then bombed it, those same critics would have increased the decibels of their criticism by about tenfold, for the heartlessness of Israel in bombing a live, hot reactor."

Representative Robert K. Dornan of California, a decorated former combat pilot, supported the bombing, even if it had been precipitated by Begin's anxiety that the new Israeli government likely to emerge after the approaching elections would not order such an action. Israel's decision to act, Dornan argued, was "moral and patriotic."

When the Senate committee commenced its hearings the next day, Senator Howard Baker declared, "We . . . have been aware and concerned about the development of the reactor in Iraq for a long time." Senator Paul E. Tsongas of Massachusetts, a sometime Begin critic, attempted to see the Israeli perspective. "Were I in Israel's shoes, would I have done the same thing? I am not sure, but I would have been sorely tempted." Jewish Senator Rudy Boschwitz of Minnesota rejected charges that the reactor raid was an election stunt by Begin.

But the star speaker was Alan Cranston, who had long warned publicly from the Senate floor that Iraq was making systematic efforts to acquire nuclear weapons. Cranston now told his colleagues that he had received four confidential IAEA documents from American sources within the agency. "These documents contain an estimate that Iraq could have produced enough plutonium each year in the Osirak reactor for up to three nuclear bombs. Furthermore, these IAEA documents indicate that there is a significant possibility—indeed, probability—that this plutonium production would not have been detected by the IAEA inspectors. Under the terms of Iraq's current agreement with the IAEA, inspections could be limited to three a year. Thus, Iraq could load its reactor between inspections but unload it before each preannounced inspection."

Referring to the declaration of IAEA Director-General Sigvard Eklund, who claimed that agency inspectors would have detected Iraqi attempts to produce plutonium, Cranston pointed out, "This statement is contradicted by a special study conducted for the IAEA earlier this year which concluded that a reactor like Iraq's could produce as much as twenty-four kilograms of plutonium per year, as much as three bombs' worth. In response to this study, an extraordinary meeting of nine senior IAEA technical specialists was convened to consider the dangers presented by the Iraqi program. Their unanimous conclusion was that such 'plutonium diversion paths are technically practicable.'"

The testimony of CIA Director William J. Casey was delivered behind closed doors, but American sources quote him as saying that the Iraqi program ultimately aimed at the manufacture of nuclear bombs. He confirmed that the reactor would have become hot in September 1981, and calculated that Iraq could have achieved a nuclear-weapons capability at earliest by 1983, but more probably by 1984. Casey confirmed that several Arab states —Syria, Saudi Arabia, Kuwait and the oil emirates—felt relieved after the destruction of the reactor, though they could not, of course, admit as much. He also agreed that IAEA supervision is faulty, mainly because it does not include unannounced inspections.

The next witness was Haig adviser and Administration rising star Robert McFarlane, a Marine officer turned diplomat. Committee Chairman Percy drew McFarlane's attention to a report in that day's *New York Times* about a hitherto unpublished provision of the Franco–Iraqi agreement whereby French technicians would remain at the reactor till the end of 1989. Since this implied tight French control, did Israel know of that understanding?

McFarlane: "The United States did." Later he added that "it could not be deduced that Israel too knew of that provision"—thereby supporting allegations that France had been evasive over Israeli inquiries with regard to the reactor.

Another important witness was Dr. Robert Selden, director of the applied theoretical physics department of the Los Alamos National Laboratories. Selden had headed teams of nuclear bomb designers and supervised a wide variety of nuclear-weapons projects. He was one of two American scientists who had been requested many years earlier to design an atomic bomb without access to classified material. The experiment, sponsored by the U.S. Army, was aimed at discovering whether a physicist could design a nuclear explosive in spite of such a handicap as long as he had all the required materials and installations. The conclusion was unequivocal: a good physicist could definitely do it. Selden also contributed to the study entitled "Reactor Materials and Nuclear Explosives." He was therefore an expert of the very highest qualifications on the military exploitation of nuclear reactors not initially designed for that purpose, and, as such, an ideal witness to reveal the facts about the Iraqi reactor.

Commencing his testimony on June 19, Selden pointed out that "a small stockpile of militarily useful weapons . . . could be [built up] clandestinely and . . . without nuclear testing." He went on to tell his listeners that in the design and production of nuclear weapons many of the phases can be completed before the fissionable material itself is acquired. Consequently, if the nonnuclear design and production (principally of the detonation mechanism) have been completed secretly, advance warning of a nuclear-weapons program is likely to be relatively brief. In other words: it is possible to design the bomb and prepare its mechanism while still playing "good boy." The fissionable material is then acquired or rapidly produced and is introduced into the prepared mechanism—and the nuclear bomb is ready!

In the decision to construct nuclear weapons, Dr. Selden explained, the limiting factor is not technological, particularly as that technology is not exceptionally costly in relation to other complex technologies routinely employed in modern society. Such a decision is a function of political and economic factors, a specific concept of defense requirements, and various other considerations; technological progress in itself plays no role therein.

All claims for the efficacy of IAEA supervision would be refuted finally and utterly by the next witness. Roger Richter, up till a month previously an IAEA inspector, was the sole American representative in the agency's department responsible for nuclear installations in Iraq, Israel, Pakistan and India.

A graduate of the metallurgical-engineering faculty at the Polytechnic Institute of New York and with a master's degree in nuclear engineering from the University of Maryland, Richter had been employed by the U.S. Atomic Energy Commission and the Energy Research and Development Administration. In his work he acquired familiarity with almost all technological aspects of nuclear-fuel engineering, reactor irradiations and nuclear-waste disposal.

In February 1978, Richter took up a three-year contract as inspector for the IAEA. In view of his training and skills, he was requested to submit a preliminary feasibility estimate for construction of a safeguards system at the Osirak complex, and an assessment of IAEA procedures governing installation inspections. Being free of political constraints, he experienced no inhibitions in drawing his conclusions, which, he claimed, "caused great consternation in the IAEA bureaucracy." His colleagues concurred with Richter's assessment that Osirak, with its extensive potential for production of weapons-grade material, constituted a terrifying threat.

Judging this to be too grave a matter to be left within the framework of the IAEA, Richter proceeded to present his findings to his former colleagues—senior officials at various Washington agencies and the U.S. delegation to the IAEA. "I was advised that my concerns were shared by the U.S. nuclear nonproliferation establishment, and that they were attempting to work with the IAEA to improve the level of planned safeguards on the Osirak. It was, however, acknowledged privately by those intimately involved in that effort, that no matter what arrangements were negotiated with the government of Iraq, it would be a rather simple matter for their scientists to circumvent IAEA safeguards and clandestinely produce enough plutonium 239 to support a weapons-production program in their nondeclared nonsafeguarded facilities."

Realizing that "prospects were bleak for an honest IAEA determination of the safeguard problems of the Osirak," Richter drafted a number of letters on the matter, to be sent to Senator John Glenn. Ultimately the letters were not dispatched, because members of the U.S. delegation to the IAEA repeatedly assured Richter that many of the problems troubling him were undergoing comprehensive study. Furthermore, they advised Richter to exercise his influence from within, while doing nothing to weaken the IAEA. Consequently, he persisted in his efforts to boost the safeguards program; but meanwhile events unfolded rapidly and the Israeli Air Force bombed the Iraqi reactor.

Senator Cranston prefaced Richter's testimony to the committee with the following tribute: ". . . the witness is performing a remarkable act of conscience. He telephoned me last Friday, one week ago, from Vienna, to express to me his concerns about the inadequacies of the inspection system in which he was involved. We had further discussions, and as a result from that, he resigned from the International Atomic Energy Agency so that he could fly here, at considerable personal sacrifice, to state his views and give us his knowledge as a basis for our deliberations."

Senator Glenn, who exhibited a rigidly anti-Israel position throughout, tried to impute questionable motives to Richter. This sparked off a fierce argument between Glenn and another committee member, Senator Boschwitz. When tempers cooled, Richter commenced his testimony.

He began by inviting committee members to put themselves in the shoes of an IAEA inspector called upon to conduct an inspection of the Iraqi nuclear facility. Such an inspector, the witness stressed, would without doubt be Russian, or from the Soviet bloc, or French: since 1976, all inspections of Iraqi facilities had been conducted by Soviet and Hungarian inspectors, and the sole French inspector authorized by the Iraqis had yet to take part in an inspection. This reflected a most salient fact: countries had the right to veto the choice of IAEA inspectors, and that right was exercised regularly.

An inspector, Richter continued, must remember that if he reaches a conclusion offensive to Iraq, it is liable to have a detrimental effect upon its relations with his own country.

The inspection would come as no surprise. The Iraqi government had to be notified several weeks ahead of time of the intention to hold the inspection, and it could either agree to the proposed date or—as recently—suggest a postponement. Such a "suggestion" could not be disregarded.

Richter went on to relate that preliminary Iraqi information did not include the Italian hot cells. As long as Iraq insisted that these facilities were not used for refining plutonium or reprocessing spent fuel, they were off limits to IAEA inspectors. Furthermore, Iraq's stock of natural uranium in its oxide form (U_3O_8) known to scientists as "yellowcake" was subject to no form of control—in spite of the ease with which it could be converted into raw material for the production of plutonium.

What, then, do inspectors do?

Their duties are limited to verifying the amounts of material declared by

Iraq or France; they have to establish that the balance of the material declared is correct. They have no authority to check on undeclared material. IAEA does not investigate clandestine activity; it merely "keeps the books."

Resuming his colorful account, Richter stated:

You, as an inspector, know that Iraq has in its possession some one hundred tons of uranium oxide. You know well that the fuel-processing equipment supplied by Italy—which is under no safeguard—enables Iraq with relative ease to convert that oxide into uranium metal. You also know that it will be possible subsequently to convert that uranium, by means of neutron bombardment in the reactor core or in its blanket, into plutonium. The mixture produced—uranium with plutonium—is identical with the used fuel which must be declared, and which can be reprocessed in the hot cells. The material accountance balance will not show that material has been withdrawn. And you, as an inspector, have no recourse but to limit your inspection to the declared inventory.

Furthermore, since the current agreement between Iraq and the IAEA permits only three annual inspections, there is no difficulty in rapidly clearing the reactor of any element secretly introduced for irradiation. By the time the inspectors reach the reactor, they will find only those fuel rods which have been declared.

In addition, the agreement does not provide for Osirak to be fitted with photographic or TV surveillance systems to monitor the operation of the reactor. True, even a system of that nature could not prevent clandestine plutonium production, but it could at least detect accelerated withdrawal of specimens from the reactor prior to an inspection, and this point to the possibility of illegal irradiation at the reactor.

A year earlier, Richter revealed, he had written a report, portions of which he now proceeded to read out:

"The available information points to an aggressive, coordinated program by Iraq to develop a nuclear weapons capability during the next five years. As a nuclear safeguards inspector at the IAEA, my concern and complaint is that Iraq will be able to conduct this program under the auspices of the Non-Proliferation Treaty and while violating the provisions of the NPT. The IAEA safeguards are totally incapable of detecting the production of plutonium in large-size material test reactors under the presently constituted safeguards arrangements. Perhaps the most disturbing implication of the Iraqi nuclear program is that the NPT agreement has had the effect of assisting Iraq in acquiring the nuclear technology and nuclear material for its program by absolving the cooperating nations of their moral responsibility by shifting it to the IAEA. These cooperating nations have thwarted concerted international criticism of their actions by pointing to Iraq's signing of NPT, while turning away from the numerous, obvious and compelling evidence which leads to the conclusion that Iraq is embarked on a nuclear weapons program."

Senator Cranston's bold statement, immediately succeeded by Richter's testimony, left committee members dumbfounded. Equally stunned, the State Department that same day drew up a reply whose main thrust was that there were numerous reactors far more suitable than Osirak to the production of plutonium—implying that, were this what Iraq desired, it would not have purchased Osirak. Chairman Charles Percy posed a question along these lines to Dr. Selden and to Dr. Kouts, chairman of the nuclear energy department at the Brookhaven National Laboratories in New York State. Both men confirmed that there were reactors far superior to Osirak in plutonium production. But the "chirade" was disrupted when Richter requested permission to speak, commenting acidly:

I think the Government of Iraq would agree with Dr. Kouts and Dr. Selden. They also wanted a graphite reactor from France, but France recognized that this particular type of reactor, a graphite reactor, had very large capabilities for plutonium production. And France said: "No way are you going to get that reactor." In a typical Middle East bargaining fashion, Iraq said, "Well, if you are not going to give us that reactor, what will you give us?" and they said, "Well, we can give you the Osirak." So it is not that Iraq did not want to get the best system possible. They just could not get it.

Richter's charges were borne out by Dr. Kouts. When Richter put it to him that "given the very small industrial base, the very small research base that the Iraq research establishment has, it [Osirak] may be far beyond the needs of such a small, relatively undeveloped state for doing materials and irradiation testing," Kouts conceded, "Yes, I believe that."

In the course of the hearing, Richter revealed further that indications as to Iraq's ability to use Osirak to produce significant amounts of plutonium caused such concern at the IAEA that the agency's director general sponsored an informal investigation. The investigator, Professor Kazia Almenas of the University of Maryland, reached the conclusion that these fears were indeed well founded.

Richter disclosed further that on March 10, 1981, nine IAEA inspectors sent a memorandum to the agency's deputy director general in which they warned expressly that "under the current IAEA inspection procedures, the limitations under which we operate, the fact that those key facilities are outside the scope of the safeguards, we are going to have a very difficult time guaranteeing that that material has not been diverted."

The impression made by the testimony of Richter and other experts is reflected in the statement by Senator Pressler when the committee concluded its hearings: "I began in these hearings to be somewhat of a critic of Israel. But as time has passed, I have come to believe, based on the information Israel had, it probably did the only thing that a country could do, and probably something our country down the road will do at some point."

On June 25, the House Foreign Relations Committee held an additional hearing. The first witness was Dr. Albert Carnesale, Harvard professor of public policy, who specialized in nuclear-energy policy and was a member of the U.S. delegation to the Geneva nuclear-disarmament talks. In a detailed and complex testimony awash with hypothetical questions and answers, Carnesale argued: ". . . I can understand why Israel would assume the worst of Iraqi intentions . . . Israel had too much at stake to assume that Iraq's intentions were benign and would have remained so. . . . They would foresee the possibilities of Iraq obtaining bomb quantities of highly enriched uranium and plutonium." All the same, he felt that "Israel should have deferred the raid and pressed as hard as possible for an alternative solution to the problem. If these efforts had failed, and if the Iraqi nuclear problem had continued unabated, then and only then might the Israelis be 'justified' in resorting to military force to neutralize the potential threat to their survival." The witness admitted, however, "This, of course, is a subjective judgment and probably reflects my personal values more than anything else."

Carnesale was followed by Richter, who repeated the gist of his testimony before the Senate committee. He added critical comments about the IAEA's lack of earnestness about the Iraqi reactor, whose potential from the viewpoint of nuclear proliferation he accused the agency of ignoring.

The anti-Israel faction within the Administration recognized that Richter's testimony was dynamite. There was even a bid to have it classified as confidential, in spite of its remoteness from U.S. defense interests. There were also attempts to discredit Richter by smear tactics. Congressmen told of calls from a State Department official eager to tell them that Richter's wife was Israeli. The story was repeated by *Time* and the Viennese *Courier*; in both cases, Richter reacted sharply. The matter also came up in a gruff exchange between Ambassador Evron and Undersecretary of State Veliotes and other Administration officials. The IAEA director general announced Richter's dismissal for "conduct unbecoming" his post and status. Richter claims to have resigned voluntarily in protest against "the IAEA publicly stating what it privately knew to be untrue, and wantonly disregarding the facts for political expediency."

That same day, June 25, the Senate committee also held its third hearing. The first witness was Dr. Ben L. Martin, a University of Missouri lecturer specializing in Iraqi affairs. Martin sketched the profile of a man characterized by "boldness, ruthlessness, a contempt for the moral conventions of Western interstate relations, . . . an unhesitating willingness to use violence . . . fanaticism, iron determination, and enormous ambition and self-confidence." Martin believed these to be the qualities of a leader who decided to employ nuclear weapons. "Those are qualities Saddam Hussain has displayed in abundance in his political career." In Martin's view, Hussain would certainly be willing to launch a nuclear onslaught upon Israel. Such an attack would automatically make him the leader of the Arab world and guarantee him a place of heroic honor in the annals of Islam for his success in achieving, with a single blow, what mighty Arab armies had failed to attain over the decades.

> Senator Boschwitz: Do you therefore feel that the reactor that the Iraqis put in was primarily designed to produce a weapon to be used against Israel?
> Dr. Martin: Yes, sir.
> Senator Boschwitz: How do you fit into that the signing of the nuclear non-proliferation treaty and the IAEA inspections?
> Dr. Martin: I think that the Iraqis regard treaties and agreements as pieces of paper important only so long as they continue to be convenient and necessary.

Martin was followed by another expert on Iraq, Dr. Daniel Pipes of the University of Chicago. Pipes analyzed the Iraqi regime's pan-Arab ideology, affirming that in practice it was "little more than implacable anti-Zionism." Pipes stated categorically that "given the low state of Iraqi science and its vast oil reserves, the claim that Iraq would conduct research into nuclear power hardly seems plausible." Furthermore, the Iraqi regime had long called for the annihilation of Israel by violent means; from its viewpoint, dropping an atomic bomb on Tel Aviv would not constitute a far-reaching step. To prove his point, Pipes cited Saddam Hussain's pronouncement that "a better decision would be to destroy Tel Aviv with bombs."

"One cannot dismiss the possibility," Pipes concluded, "that [the Iraqis] will deploy [the atomic bomb] against Israel in an unprovoked manner."

26 "The children of Baghdad are not enemies."

Congressional deliberations dragged on, as did the soul-searching by legislators and Administration officials alike with regard to their purpose. Should Congress rest content with a mere recommendation to the executive branch? Or should the legislators reach an unequivocal verdict as to whether or not Israel had violated the terms of its agreements with the United States? Had Israel's destruction of the reactor been a legitimate act of self-defense?

In the Senate committee, a draft resolution censured Israel, alleging that it was questionable whether Israel had fulfilled its undertaking to consult the United States before employing American-made arms. The Administration, sensing that matters had gone too far, was uneasy over this wording, fearing that such a sharp tone would only harm the United States without bringing any benefit. The Administration therefore initiated frenzied consultations in which the President, Haig and Ambassador Evron all took an active part. In conclusion, it was agreed that Haig adviser McFarlane should approach the Congress and urge the legislators to shelve their proposal, temporarily at least, until the whole matter could be cleared up in direct contacts between the two governments.

McFarlane launched his endeavors on Capitol Hill. Acceding to his pleas, the legislators deferred the vote on the draft resolution without fixing a date for its resubmission.

On July 12, McFarlane left for Jerusalem, where he was awaited with some apprehension. He was unknown to the Israelis, though his name had been featured in reports from the Washington embassy. His utterances at the Senate Foreign Relations Committee hearings had not been noted for their friendly tone toward Israel.

McFarlane was preceded by Ambassador Evron, bearing a paper McFarlane had given him: the draft of a joint U.S.–Israeli statement. Begin read the text and frowned: the wording implied that the destruction of the reactor had not been an act of legitimate self-defense. The Prime Minister set to work on an alternative draft.

On July 13, at nine in the morning, McFarlane entered the Prime Minister's office, accompanied by Ambassador Lewis and his chief aide, William Brown. The Prime Minister awaited them flanked by Foreign Minister Shamir, Ambassador Evron and other aides.

McFarlane, a man of military appearance in spite of his elegantly tailored suit, commenced with the customary greetings from his superiors. "President Reagan," he told Begin, "sends his congratulations on your election victory." He then presented a letter from Haig. Apologizing to his guest, Begin studied the communication before embarking upon the conversation. He read rapidly but intently, before pronouncing it a "very fine letter" and handing it to Shamir.

The letter reflected Haig's determination that the reactor episode must not undermine Israel–U.S. relations. It commenced with congratulations on Begin's reelection and went on to restate U.S. policy toward Israel, reaffirming an unambiguous commitment to Israel's security and welfare in Haig's own name and on behalf of President Reagan. The reactor bombing was not mentioned, but it was plainly the background to the letter. Haig made a commendable effort to present the Administration's demands of Israel in positive terms. A close strategic partnership between the two countries was a necessity if peace was to become an enduring reality in the Mideast, he wrote. The present Administration was keenly aware of the dangers posed by the Soviet Union and its proxies in the region. The United States recognized the gaps in Western military capabilities in the region, and the fundamental strategic value of Israel, the strongest and most stable friend and ally the United States has in the Mideast. Consequently, Haig went on, the two countries must work together "to counter the full range of threats that the Western world faces in the region. While we may not always place the same emphasis on particular threats, we share a fundamental understanding that a strong, secure and vibrant Israel serves Western interests in the Middle East, We shall never deviate from that principle, for the success of our strategy depends thereupon."

In an oblique reference to the reactor bombing, Haig wrote: "Like close friends who disagree or suffer misunderstandings, so have we over the past month had occasion to disagree." The two countries must cooperate, leaving misunderstandings behind them, "and bridge any remaining gaps in our mutual understanding." The United States would not "dwell on transient differences," which must not be allowed "to stand in the way of the urgent task of building up security in this vital region.

"Just as we will work closely with you on regional strategy and on safeguarding your security, so will we work as your friend and strategic partner in the peace process."

McFarlane himself had nothing new to say. His words sounded a note familiar to Begin from the numerous cables he had received from the Washington embassy in recent weeks. The U.S. envoy expressed his country's concern over the reactor bombing and its probable consequences. The operation, he claimed, was liable to disrupt the efforts the Administration was making to relieve tension in the region (a reference to Habib's mediation efforts in Lebanon). McFarlane recalled the President's remark that Israel's action against the reactor "was surely not taken lightly" and that the Israelis "strongly believed [it] was in defense of [their] vital interests."

The President also said, Begin pointed out, that Israel didn't endanger its neighbors but they endangered Israel.

McFarlane went on to depict reactions in the White House, Congress and U.S. public opinion, which, he affirmed had been mixed. "I don't imply judgment of the merits of the criticism," he said. But it was "a de facto problem" which the Administration must handle. The Senate Foreign Relations committee had formulated a draft resolution which the White House "thought was not healthy." The President was eager to resolve the issue "as good friends." The aim of current bilateral talks was to find a way of demonstrating to Congress that its concern had been understood, and to forestall adoption of a resolution of outright censure against Israel.

McFarlane soon got to the crux of the matter: If "we here" reached agreement on an expression that would reflect the differing views of the United States and Israel on the issue, the Administration would be able to tell the Congress unabashedly that there had been "an exchange of views as partners, friends and allies," with the two countries reflecting concern for the interests of each other. That, he stressed, was also the view of the Secretary of State: if the proposal was acceptable to Israel, "we could quickly move on to important issues." McFarlane suggested that it be left to the Foreign Minister or his aides "to work out the details" of the joint statement.

Begin accepted McFarlane's proposal in principle. But, continuing to regard the reactor bombing and its repercussions as a matter he should handle personally, he refused to delegate it to others. "I'll work it out with you now."

Before they set to work, Begin insisted on reading out sections of the document Ambassador Lewis had delivered to him in December 1980. Stressing each word, the Prime Minister intoned the passages which showed beyond any doubt that the United States had fully shared Israel's anxiety over developments at al-Tuweitha. "What can be clearer?" Begin demanded. "That paper was written after your country had exhausted all possibilities of dissuading Iraq from continuing its program . . . I, the Prime Minister of Israel, . . . received information that everything done in that reactor is intended to give Iraq the option to develop nuclear explosives. I repeat—nuclear explosives!" Briefly, a deathly hush descended upon the room.

McFarlane's technical training was probably superior to that of Begin, but the latter, referring to further passages of the 1980 memorandum, seized on the opportunity to recall the distinction between plutonium and enriched uranium. A Hiroshima-type bomb requires 20 kilograms of enriched uranium; but "if you have plutonium, you need only seven kilograms."

McFarlane listened intently, but he obviously had no intention of conceding that Israel was in the right. He was well acquainted with the document from which Begin quoted—as he proved by recalling that it also contained a specific warning that "precipitate action" against the Iraqi nuclear installations would disrupt Mideast peace efforts.

"Sam [Lewis] already drew my attention to this," Begin retorted. "We did not initiate precipitate action!" Begin persisted in his efforts to convince McFarlane that Israel had acted properly with regard to the reactor. The UN Security Council condemnation accused Israel of failing to take diplomatic steps before launching the attack. But that was untrue, Begin said. Had not Foreign Minister Shamir discussed the matter with French President Giscard? Not only had that conversation produced no results, but Giscard had committed the further sin of not telling the truth. France had promised Iraq 70 kilograms of weapons grade uranium, of which 12 kilograms had already been delivered. At the time of the bombing, Saddam Hussain was "short of only seven kilograms" of the amount he needed for a bomb. With the billions of money at his disposal, he would have been able to purchase the amount he required "on the open market."

After the reactor bombing, Begin went on, had Hussain not declared publicly that he would develop atom bombs? Begin referred to his private talk with Haig during the latter's visit to Israel in April 1981. The Secretary of State had reported that Washington had intervened with Paris and Rome in an attempt to induce its allies to curtail their nuclear aid to Iraq, "but in vain," Haig had admitted. "I am prepared to swear on the Bible that Haig said 'in vain,'" Begin declared.

"In the meantime," he related, "we received further information that the reactor would be operational in July or September." With a dramatic gesture, the Prime Minister pointed to himself, to Shamir and the other Israelis. "We here before you—what did you really expect us to do? To sit idly by after the Secretary of State of the United States said that all our efforts were in vain? To let them produce an atomic bomb to drop upon Tel Aviv?" Hussain would not give tuppence for any possible Israeli retaliation "unless we bombed Baghdad, but I don't think I would have agreed to that. Our national poet, Haim Nahman Bialik, wrote: 'Vengeance for the blood of a small child has not been created, not even by Satan!' That is our morality. . . . Hussain would not have minded at all what would happen to Baghdad if he could show he had destroyed Tel Aviv, so long as he could be the leader of the Arab world."

Could responsible Israeli leaders have acted otherwise with the information they received? Begin demanded, adding wryly, "Our opposition said it was an election stunt. That is an outrage. What would have been in the elections if our planes had been shot down? Osirak is a fortress, surrounded by SAM missiles. I'd have endangered the life of our boys for the sake of the elections? What would have been if they had been taken prisoners? It is worse than death. Even the most valiant soldier could not withstand their torture. I needed to send our boys into such danger? The polls were already in our favor, the Likkud already had an edge. Mr. Peres regretted that accusation very much, it was one of the reasons why he lost the elections."

Begin did not overlook McFarlane's imputations against the legality of the Israeli action. "I studied law," the Prime Minister recalled, "including international law. I know very well what is self-defense. I know of no self-defense clearer and more decisive than the subject before us. It is not a matter of territory or just plain defense, but, quite simply, a matter of saving our people—a remnant of our people. Should a tyrant again be permitted to kill our children? Never again!

"Your national history," Begin reminded his guest, "contains the Monroe Doctrine whereby no European power shall intervene in the affairs of the Western Hemisphere, and the United States shall not intervene in the political affairs of Europe. President John Kennedy recalled that doctrine when Soviet missiles threatened your country from Cuba. 'The hour of actual national danger does not start with the actual shooting.' The danger to us would have commenced when Saddam Hussain acquired the option to construct a bomb, not when he already had it. In the most supreme sense, this was legitimate national self-defense." Begin referred to the Camp David conference, and his disagreement with Carter when the latter submitted a document questioning Israeli's right to sovereignty over a united Jerusalem, whereupon Begin had replied, "Let my right hand forget its cunning before I make such a statement."

Begin complained that it was still necessary to prove that Jews do not willingly submit to being killed. "There are enemies who think so. We shall show them that Jews were born to live, not to be killed, whether by Zyklon B or by radioactivity."

McFarlane's draft statement implied that the Israeli action had not been an act of legitimate self-defense. It was obvious that Begin would refuse to sign such a statement. He accordingly advised McFarlane to follow the precedent set during President Nixon's visit to China: when the two governments failed to find an agreed wording for their joint statement, each side expressed its own position. "You write what you wish on your behalf, and we shall write what we want on ours." Begin proposed the following wording:

We had it on the best reliable information that the French-built 70-megawatts reactor near Baghdad was destined to produce atomic bombs to be used against Israel. For the last two years Israel exhausted all possible diplomatic efforts to prevent this new dangerous development in the Middle East from taking place. Our diplomatic interventions were both direct, with the appropriate Governments, and indirect, especially through the good offices of the United States. All those efforts were in vain. Subsequently, we learned again from absolutely reliable sources that the aforementioned reactor would become operational—or, as the experts say, "hot"—either in July or September, 1981. Nobody could have given us any guarantee whatsoever that this would happen in September. We learned, too, that the Iraqis used incessant pressure on the French scientists, experts and technicians to "inaugurate" the atomic-bomb-producing reactor in July and, notably, as our military intelligence chief revealed, on the anniversary of the Iraqi "revolution," July 17. We, therefore, declare that when we decided to destroy the Ossirak plant we did so for the sake of the children of Israel who, even with one atomic bomb directed, for example, at Tel Aviv, would have been wiped out by the thousands. And we carried out the operation on the designated date of June 7, 1981, also for the sake of the Iraqi children, for, as our scientists explained to us—and they are expert on such matters as much as any in the world—that were the reactor to become "hot" its "opening" by a bombing raid would produce an immense radioactive wave which would cover the skies of Baghdad and cause death and horrible infliction upon tens of thousands of children, women and men. The tyrant Saddam Hussain is Israel's implacable enemy as he has declared time and again. The children of Baghdad are not. Ultimately, after the Israel Air Force carried out its now famous operation, Saddam Hussain twice declared that it is his resolve and decision to produce atomic bombs. Consequently, Israel's operation against the Osirak reactor was an act of supreme legitimate self-defense.

Israel has never committed a breath of its agreement with the United States of 1952. All the operations carried out by Isarel's defense forces have been acts of legitimate self-defense. And so it will be in the future.

Begin read out his prepared text to McFarlane. The usually unruffled ex-Marine was evidently moved by the Prime Minister's impassioned delivery. "I respect the depth of your convictions," McFarlane said. "Your words are very moving." He also acknowledged Begin's strong belief in the legitimacy of the Israeli action. The U.S. diplomat did not believe there was anything "incongruous" between the two governments. "Quite apart from whether there is a valid reason for the U.S. to take a legal position, this is a matter which my government believes should be put quickly behind us." McFarlane reiterated Haig's proposal: "We shall state the fact that views have been exchanged," each side explaining the basis of its position and the reasons for its actions. "Both sides reaffirm the importance that each take account of the concern and the interests of the other as friends and allies, as an expression of the close friendship between us."

Begin asked to hear the wording of the U.S. proposal. McFarlane said he had a draft, though he hastened to apologize that, as a former naval officer, he was "not the best drafter." If the sides reached agreement, this text would be submitted to Congress:

> The Governments of Israel and the United States have had extensive discussions concerning the Israeli attack on Iraq's nuclear reactor. These discussions have been conducted with the candor customary between nations with close ties of friendship. The Government of Israel expressed its view that its action was justified and the government of the United States made clear the basis for its condemnation of that action. The two sides reviewed the arrangements under which the United States extends security assistance to Israel and, more broadly, the full scope of the U.S.–Israel security relationship. Both sides are agreed that within the parameters of national sovereignty, the interests of each country should be fully considered by the other and that every effort should be made to consult closely concerning problems affecting these interests in order to resolve them through peaceful means. The two Governments agreed that the discussions and review have increased their understanding and respect for the concerns of the other.

Begin's expression reflected dissatisfaction. He was particularly irked by the phrase "the interests of each country should be fully considered by the other." "Have we not taken U.S. interests into consideration?" he demanded. "We provide you with intelligence which you would never receive otherwise. We help you. Can it be said that, with regard to the bombing of the reactor, we did not consider your defense needs? I won't say that! This reference to condemnation," Begin went on. "What does that mean? In an operation of this kind, could I have confided in the American ambassador? Could I have shared with him a secret upon which our lives depend? Qaddafi wants an atomic bomb," Begin noted. "If we hear that Libya is making efforts to acquire an atomic bomb, we shall do the utmost to prevent it. Qaddafi is insane, he wanted to torpedo the liner *Queen Elizabeth* when she was cruising to Israel, and only Sadat held him back."

Begin concluded by urging McFarlane to study the Israeli proposal. For his part, he would consider McFarlane's draft thoroughly. Even so, Begin again stressed that its "condemnation" of the Israeli action was "a grave mistake."

McFarlane proposed that the statement be completed that same day, since he wished to return to the United States on the morrow. A second meeting was accordingly set for eight that evening, at the Prime Minister's residence.

That evening Begin presented a new text, based upon the envoy's own proposal. It soon became evident that both sides wished to achieve an understanding without further delay. After some give and take, they reached agreement on the clear, succinct text drawn up by Begin.

> The two governments have held extensive talks on the operation against the Iraqi reactor. These talks were conducted with the candor [Begin: "That is a diplomatic term which indicates there were differences of viewpoint."] and friendship customary between friends and allies.
>
> The Israeli government explained the reasons for its action. The United States government clarified the basis for its position toward the action. In these talks, both sides reaffirmed the arrangements made under the 1952 mutual defense agreement, and the broader U.S.–Israel security relationship.
>
> Both governments agreed that these talks have increased the mutual understanding between them.

It was a striking diplomatic triumph for Begin. The final text conveyed everything both governments wished to express, without implying that Israel had disregarded U.S. interests or acted in defiance of them, and without binding Israel to consult the United States before reaching a decision on its own strategic interests.

The following day, after McFarlane's departure with the agreed text, Begin wrote a reply to Haig's letter, which he characterized as "one of the best I have ever received," its contents reflecting "your profound and continuing friendship for Israel." The Prime Minister naturally agreed with Haig's appeal to work together always, in accord; when disagreements arise, "we shall do our best to overcome them." Begin was in an elated mood, sensing that his talk with McFarlane had succeeded beyond all expectations; he depicted it in his habitually flowery style: ". . . the sunshine broke through on our evening discussion which, though not a miracle, was a serious achievement nevertheless . . ."

McFarlane landed in New York on July 15 and immediately met with Haig. The two men then flew on to Washington.

The two congressional foreign-relations committees now reconvened, with McFarlane presenting the text of the joint statement as agreed between the two sides. Senator Percy withdrew his draft resolution with its express condemnation of Israel and endorsed the draft which contained no such censure.

27 "To Rub Our Noses in the Dirt"

It goes without saying that Israel was anxiously awaiting the White House decision revoking the suspension of the F-16 delivery. The four planes constituted part of a deal whereby the United States was to supply seventy-five F-16s—the largest and costliest arms deal in Israel's history. The Administration leaked sporadic reports that the suspension would shortly end. Early in July, "a senior Administration official" announced that the President's decision revoking the suspension would be published on the fifteenth of the month. One day in mid-July, the four "suspended" planes did indeed take off from the General Dynamics plant in Fort Worth, Texas, flying to the U.S. Air Force base in New Hampshire from where they were to make their way to Israel.

At almost precisely the same time, other F-16s returned to their bases in Israel after sowing devastation in Beirut, in reprisal for terrorist bombings and shellings of settlements in northern Israel. The massive Israeli strike destroyed terrorist headquarters, with over two hundred terrorists killed or injured. But civilian casualties were also numerous: some two hundred dead and eight hundred wounded.

News of the raid on Beirut reached Washington shortly before scheduled publication of the official announcement renewing plane deliveries to Israel. An infuriated Reagan promptly decided to extend the suspension without fixing a date for renewal of shipments. The President was in Ottawa at the time, attending a conference of the heads of the major Western industrial countries. He probably heard harsh criticism of Israel from his European colleagues and may have feared that, should he fail to act in response to the Israeli raid, he would appear weak and pliable, a President who permitted Israel to dictate U.S. policy in the Mideast. Reagan had been in office no more than six months, and rumors suggested that he understood next to nothing of foreign affairs. His anxiety was therefore compounded by the urgent need to demolish that image.

Leaks originating from Reagan's entourage credited him with expressions such as "That guy Begin makes it very difficult to help him." National-security adviser Richard Allen would explain later that the President saw the Beirut bombing as "a personal affront"; having been seized upon by Israel's enemies, it led to the plane suspension being extended. Some reactions were even more vitriolic. A personage described as "a senior State Department official" snapped, "Israel decided to attack just on the day Washington was about to release the planes, so as to rub our noses in the dirt." On Capitol Hill, even Israel's closest friends, including some, like Senators Alan Cranston and Richard G. Lugar of Indiana, who had only recently come out in defense of the reactor attack, voiced angry criticism. Begin was personally condemned for indifference to U.S. interests. Israel and its Prime Minister even came in for harsh words from Jewish leaders, though most—like some non-Jewish politicians—stressed that, not living in Israel, they found it hard to sit in judgment on Begin's actions.

Presidential envoy Philip Habib returned to the Mideast. "The bombing did make it more difficult to carry on the mediatory mission," Habib recalled. But after prolonged efforts he managed to work out a cease-fire—albeit unwritten—which came into force on July 24. "So my mission was not 'torpedoed' by the bombing." The Lebanese cease-fire seemed to offer a good opportunity for terminating the plane suspension. But Haig declared that the United States still declined to send the planes. And to make matters worse, Defense Secretary Weinberger unexpectedly declared that the embargo also applied to the F-15s. The planes would be delivered, Weinberger stated, when a combination of circumstances proved that the situation was stabilizing. His words indicated that the cease-fire did not of itself constitute an adequate precondition for revoking the suspension. Weinberger also declared that the Administration, while engaging in a "general assessment" of the Mideast situation, was still considering the facts and reasons which had given rise to the original suspension decision. There were no final decisions meanwhile, and in any case it was unclear how many planes would be delivered to Israel, or when.

One ray of light came from Haig, who summoned Ambassador Evron to a meeting on August 3, endeavoring to moderate the hostile tone adopted by the Defense Secretary. Haig promised that the suspension would not apply to the F-15s, which would be sent off on schedule on August 15. But that date came and went, and the F-15s did not take off. Observers familiar with behind-the-scenes Washington were left in no doubt: the suspension had sparked a confrontation between Haig and Weinberger, and, for the moment at least, the latter had the upper hand.

Israeli indignation flared up when it emerged that Egypt was exerting powerful pressure in Washington for the suspension to be extended. Egyptian defense Minister General Razk Abu Gazala, in conjunction with senior presidential adviser Osama al-Baz, "welcomed" the decision to extend the suspension. Egypt's ambassador to Washington, Ashraf Ghorbal, likewise urged that release of the planes be deferred. They were supported by President Sadat, who apparently took a direct hand in stirring matters up in Washington.

The Israelis were shocked to find that the Egyptians had direct input to such sensitive aspects of Israel–U.S. relations. Ambassador Evron complained about it at his August 13 meeting with Haig, where he cited reports that it was Egyptian pressure which had led the embargo to be extended to the F-15s.

Haig denied these charges, claiming that Egypt had done nothing more than express its concern that release of the planes would draw allegations that Egypt was in collusion with the United States, just as Cairo had been accused of foreknowledge of the reactor attack.

Evron insisted on an answer: When would the planes be released?

Haig: On August 16 or 17. The President, he explained, had decided to release the planes, even though there were those in the Administration (Weinberger, Evron noted silently) who wished to extend the suspension further. On the substance of the matter, Haig stressed, "there is no change in the President's favorable attitude toward Israel."

That favorable attitude was reflected in the Administration's decision against submitting to Congress written documents summarizing official investigations into Israel's use of American weapons against Iraq. As far as is known, several such papers were drawn up, and there would have been no difficulty in composing a document affirming that Israel had violated the terms of its weapons purchases from the United States. Such a document would have inflicted grievous harm upon Israel, whose congressional enemies would have seized upon it to propose extension of the suspension to other forms of U.S. military and economic aid.

On August 17, Haig kept his promise. His statement ran as follows:

On June 7, 1981, Israel conducted an attack on Iraq's nuclear reactor. On June 10, 1981, we reported to the Congress about the Israeli attack and informed the Congress that the scheduled delivery of four F-16 aircraft to Israel was being suspended. That suspension has continued in force and 14 F-16 aircraft and two F-15 aircraft are now affected by it.

The Administration conducted an intensive review of the implications of the Israeli action for the agreement which governs Israeli use of U.S.-supplied military equipment. The review included candid discussions with Prime Minister Begin and Israeli Ambassador Evron.

The Administration in its review has also taken account of events and trends in the Middle East, particularly the events in Lebanon leading to a ceasefire there. The ceasefire is a very positive new element in the region, one which the Administration hopes will continue and which perhaps will make possible other steps toward peace in that troubled region.

Following our discussions with the government of Israel, consultations with the Congress, and completion of the Administration's review, the President has lifted the suspension of military aircraft deliveries to Israel.

Needless to say, Ambassador Evron welcomed the termination of the suspension, which, however, he could not refrain from characterizing as "harmful and unjust."

Predictably, the Arabs criticized the U.S. decision to revoke the suspension. The PLO hastened to declare that the decision encouraged "Israeli aggression" and proved that the United States insisted on supplying Israel with sophisticated weaponry which would serve to murder Palestinian and Lebanese civilians. The Arab League likewise issued a sharply worded statement, which dismissed the suspension as a short-lived U.S. "adventure" aimed at minimizing the Arab reaction.

28 The United Nations: "A Festival of Hypocrisy"

Predictably, Moscow condemned the reactor bombing as "an act of international piracy." But was that what the Soviets really thought of the raid? Twelve days after the attack, a veteran of Israel's diplomatic service met—in the United States—with a Soviet colleague who had attained senior rank though still relatively young. "That was a good thing," said the Soviet diplomat; he had once served in a Moslem capital and was well versed in Israel's relations with its neighbors. The reactor bombing, he went on, was a major event for the future of the Middle East; moreover, it coincided with the Soviet Union's global outlook, which was concerned about the dissemination of nuclear weapons and opposed the transfer of nuclear-weapons technology to other countries. The Russian went so far as to praise Begin: "A strong leader who does not permit anyone to dictate his policy. The Begin regime is a historic process representing a rightward trend in Israel; it is no mere episode." He added that the United States was coming to realize that Israel was neither a client nor a satellite, but a partner.

The Soviet Union, the diplomat specified, would not supply Iraq with a reactor to replace the one Israel had destroyed. But he predicted that France would supply a replacement. He argued that, Israel having again demonstrated its military superiority, this would be a good time to show flexibility in negotiations with its neighbors; but he did not elaborate.

A certain African president likewise exhibited mixed feelings on the matter. "Diplomacy is filled with hypocrisy," he confessed to his Israeli collocutor, "therefore I shall publicly condemn the reactor raid. But you Israelis did a good job."

A very senior minister from another African country sent a secret message to the Israeli government: "Congratulations on the success of your operation. You acted to safeguard the existence of Israel, and you had full justification for doing so."

A French military attaché serving in a European capital—an officer of colonel's rank—whispered to the local Israeli ambassador, "You had no choice. It's the only language your adversaries understand."

This festival of hypocrisy centered about a thirty-seven-story skyscraper on New York's First Avenue: United Nations headquarters.

The Arabs launched their diplomatic offensive. An emergency meeting of the Arab League called upon all countries of the world, the United States in particular, to respond to the reactor raid by severing their ties with Israel and terminating all aid—economic, military or technical. This appeal was to be the basis for the draft resolution submitted to the United Nations Security Council urging severe sanctions against Israel. The onslaught was spearheaded by the so-called "moderate" Arab states, apparently in the hope that this would make it more powerful and persuasive. For their part, the "moderates" may have volunteered their services to convince the hard-liners of their loyalty to the pan-Arab cause.

Saudi Arabia's UN ambassador, Sheikh Feisal al-Hajlan, made a statement carrying a strong whiff of anti-Semitism, pointing out that the reactor raid had no historical precedent, and adding that "even in the time of Hitler" there had been no instance of a state claiming to be democratic and peace-loving which nevertheless committed such an act of "international terrorism." Off the record, however, the Saudi reaction was quite different, as American officials confided to their Israeli colleagues: "They perceive the benefits they can reap from the operation." Indeed, the Saudis had shown consistent concern over Saddam Hussein's ambition of elevating Iraq to the rank of the number-one power in the Middle East.

At the time of the Israeli raid, UN Secretary-General Dr. Kurt Waldheim was in Tokyo. No sooner had he heard of the operation than he hastened, as was his custom, to accuse Israel of an action which, he said, was "in clear contravention of international law and must be condemned."

His charge was rejected outright by Israel's UN ambassador Professor Yehuda Blum, an expert on international law. (Blum had been attending Shavuoth services at a New York synagogue the previous day when one of the worshipers, learning of the reactor raid from a radio newscast, conveyed the news to the rabbi, who stepped to the altar and proclaimed, "Jews, good tidings . . ."; apprised in this unusual manner, Blum concluded his prayers and hastened to his office, where he found countless requests for interviews from media representatives.) Blum now fired off a sharply worded reply to Waldheim, accusing him of exceeding his authority as secretary general of an organization whose members pursue diverging interests. Waldheim, Blum complained, did not even make a pretense of objectivity and independence, having failed to condemn Iraq's invasion of Iran or the call for an anti-Israel jihad voiced by Saudi Arabia and other UN members from the General Assembly rostrum in flagrant violation of the UN Charter.

The Iraqi delegation, headed by Foreign Minister Sa'adun Hammadi, was confident of eliciting a sharp condemnation of Israel from the Security Council. But the Iraqis hoped for more: a resolution to impose concrete sanctions. But these hopes were promptly dashed when the United States declared that it would veto any resolution of a punitive anti-Israel nature. Nevertheless, it was evident that the U.S. would support a condemnation of Israel. When friends of Israel put out feelers at the White House to find out whether the United States would veto such a condemnation or at least abstain, their approaches met with sharp rebuffs from the President's confidants.

Discreet inquiries revealed that Britain was likely to join the United States in vetoing any sanctions resolution, and, astonishingly, there were similar indications from France. In view of the adverse prospects, the Arabs were forced to waive their main objective, sanctions; instead, they now sought the broadest possible Western support for a resolution censuring Israel in harsh terms.

When the Security council began its deliberations on June 12, Iraqi Foreign Minister Hammadi claimed, "There should be very little doubt ... that Israel's real target... was not merely our peaceful nuclear installations. The Zionists and their friends were actually aiming at Iraq's crucial role in rallying the Arab nations against the Camp David conspiracy... and in being the vanguard of the fight against colonialism, racism including Zionism..."

Responding for Israel, Professor Blum did not mince his words: "A threat of nuclear obliteration was being developed against Israel by Iraq, one of Israel's most implacable enemies. Israel tried to have that threat halted by diplomatic means. Our efforts bore no fruit. Ultimately... we were obliged to remove that mortal danger. We did it cleanly and effectively. The Middle East has become a safer place... Several States in the Middle East and beyond are sleeping more easily today in the knowledge that Saddam Hussain's nuclear-arms potential has been smashed.... But all this," Blum added with bitter irony, "will not preclude a hypocritical parade here in the Security Council." Blum knew what he was talking about.

From his Jerusalem office, Menahem Begin closely observed developments in Washington and New York. Rather than pursue formal contacts with officials and ministers motivated primarily by material interests, the Prime Minister preferred to cultivate personal links with the White House.

* * *

Begin's personal letter to Reagan, dated June 16, commenced with a compliment: "Since the two days when President Truman recognised the state of Israel and President Nixon ordered the airlift to Israel, we have never had a more friendly President in the White House as we have now . . . It is to this friend that I respectfully address myself today." Begin referred with great indignation to France: not satisfied with urging the Security Council to condemn Israel, the French insisted on Israel's paying compensation to Iraq. "The France of President Giscard was the main builder of that reactor," providing Iraq with the knowhow, the personnel and also the 12 kilograms of enriched uranium, over half the amount required for a 20-kiloton atomic bomb. But now that Israel had "saved the lives of its citizens and children," France wanted Israel to make reparations to "the would-be mass killer." Ironically Begin demanded to know why the French representative "did not ask for indemnities to be paid to France too." In the same sarcastic tone: "I have not yet heard the Italian representative . . . but I can imagine what he is going to say during that festival of international hypocrisy."

Begin went on to cite the memorandum conveyed to him by Ambassador Lewis in December 1980, whose first three paragraphs bore out information Israel had compiled about the reactor. Begin thanked Reagan for his decision to veto any resolution calling for sanctions against Israel. However, in view of the Lewis document he considered himself entitled to request a U.S. veto on any resolution condemning Israel or demanding compensation for Iraq.

"Mr. President," Begin concluded, "I ask simply for the supremacy of that rule in which we all believe, and to which we have consecrated our lives. *Let justice be done.*"

This direct appeal to the heart might have influenced Reagan. But developments at the United Nations unfolded more quickly than expected.

In the meantime, United States UN Ambassador Jeane Kirkpatrick closeted herself in a back room at UN headquarters for two confidential ninety-minute conversations with Iraqi Foreign Minister Hammadi. Kirkpatrick was following up an initiative by Secretary of State Haig. Immediately after the reactor bombing, Haig sought to establish contact with the Iraqis; but in the absence of diplomatic relations between the two countries, Iraq had no ambassador in Washington. Richard Allen reminded Haig that Dr. Hammadi had recently had a narrow escape from death when an elevator he was riding in a New York skyscraper plunged down the shaft. Seizing on the pretext, the Secretary of State phoned the Iraqi Foreign Minister to congratulate him on his escape, immediately going on to express his country's concern for persons near the site of the reactor bombing and offer "whatever aid might be possible." Haig having taken the first step, the initiative was taken up by Ambassador Kirkpatrick. She was regarded as one of Israel's most fervent champions within the Reagan Administration; consequently, her secret contacts with the Iraqis were perceived in Jerusalem as a grave diplomatic setback. The substance of the U.S.-Iraq talks soon emerged: Kirkpatrick told Hammadi that while the United States continued to oppose any demand for compensation by Israel, she would vote for a resolution which, along with censuring Israel, would recognize Iraq's entitlement to "appropriate redress" for the damage suffered.

Israel regarded this pledge as a violation of Haig's specific pledge that the United States would not so much as enter into negotiations if there were any mention of compensation to Iraq. Angry Israeli diplomats approached Haig adviser Robert McFarlane, who claimed that the State Department knew nothing of Kirkpatrick's meetings with the Iraqi Foreign Minister, which had not been authorized. But Kirkpatrick had acted with the full authority of the President, the Secretary of State and the national-security adviser—a fact of which McFarlane was ignorant because the decision had been reached at the highest levels and no one had troubled to inform him thereof. The decision rested upon the assumption that Iraq might now be open to overtures by the West, a notion advocated by the French and British UN ambassadors, who convinced Kirkpatrick to demonstrate that the United States was not "a slave doing the bidding of his Zionist master."

Israel persisted in its protests, even though there was now no hope of victory in the diplomatic confrontation. National-security adviser Allen, considered a friend of Israel, told Ambassador Evron, "You should take it for granted that the coming days will be turbulent and unfavorable for Israel."

The Kirkpatrick-Hammadi talks—also attended by other personages—produced a draft resolution whose text was transmitted to the relevant Administration officials, including Haig, currently visiting New Zealand. As members of his party told a *New York Times* correspondent, the suggested text angered the Secretary of State, who accused Kirkpatrick of going too far in her concessions to the Iraqis. He hastened to send her a fuming cable in which he demanded immediate modification of the text in Israel's favor, adding unequivocally that the present wording was unacceptable.

Thus, after a week marked by forty speeches all fiercely condemnatory toward Israel, and frenzied behind-the-scenes activity, a seven-point resolution was submitted to the Security Council on June 19. The resolution "strongly condemned" Israel for the reactor bombing, which was characterized as a "clear violation of the UN Charter"; Israel was admonished to refrain in future from similar actions. While defending the right of Iraq—like all developing nations—to nuclear technology for peaceful purposes, the resolution urged Israel to consent to IAEA supervision of its nuclear facilities and concluded by recognizing Iraq's right to "appropriate redress."

After the Security Council approved the resolution, Ambassador Kirkpatrick declared that she felt like a parent forced to rebuke a wayward son. She was dissatisfied with the resolution, which was, however, the lesser evil. Even so, she complimented the Iraqi Foreign Minister, remarking—apparently with no intended irony—that Hammadi's conduct had been "civilized." The United States, Kirkpatrick declared, opted to adhere to a bad resolution rather than remain isolated.

But Senator Edward Kennedy argued that American honor would have been salvaged had the voting gone 14–1 against the United States, rather than ending in 15–0 unanimity. For its part, the State Department was satisfied on the whole: the United States had at long last demonstrated to the Arabs that America did not automatically endorse every Israeli action.

Israel was careful to avoid personal criticism of Ambassador Kirkpatrick. Begin related that the threat of a U.S. veto had led to the resolution's being toned down on several points. With that, he characterized America's support for it as "an act of Sodom and Gomorrah: the guilty is acquitted and the innocent [pronounced] guilty." But when all was said and done, he told an election rally, "better a condemnation and no reactor than a reactor and no condemnation."

When the U.S. National Security Council convened at the White House on June 19, shortly after the UN Security Council vote, President Reagan urged that everything possible be done to reassure Israel; he instructed Undersecretary of State Walter Stoessel to fix a meeting with Ambassador Evron to that end. At their meeting Stoessel told Evron, "The President has asked me to tell you that what happened today does not affect our friendship and commitment toward Israel." He added that Reagan had promised a declaration to that effect in his upcoming press conference.

"We have never had any doubt as to the sincerity of the President's feelings," Evron replied. Even so, he could not refrain from a number of caustic remarks: this was the first time, he noted, that the United States had negotiated with an avowed enemy of Israel—a country which called for its annihilation—the topic of the talks being the wording of an anti-Israel resolution.

Stoessel: "I appreciate Israel's feelings and understand them, but we are convinced that we adopted the most effective course of action. We must preserve our credibility in the Arab world. An American veto would have caused numerous difficulties, for us and for you."

• • •

After their diplomatic victory in the Security Council, the Iraqis now zeroed in on an objective both technical and diplomatic: the International Atomic Energy Agency, where they sought support for Israel's expulsion. But here they ran into an unequivocal U.S. response: in that event, the United States would immediately halt its support to the agency, of whose budget it finances one third.

After fierce diplomatic wrangling, the Iraqis realized they had no hope of a majority for their expulsion proposal, whereupon they watered down their draft, which affirmed in brief that Israel should comply with the Security Council resolution by subjecting its nuclear facilities to international inspection. Should Israel decline to do so, the IAEA conference would consider suspending Israel's membership. The resolution also denied to Israel IAEA study bursaries, annual aid to the tune of $100,000, and participation in IAEA symposiums, these sanctions to be in effect for one year.

In effect, the resolution changed nothing. The Arabs had made frequent efforts in the past to enforce international supervision of Israel's nuclear facilities, and Israel had never put up much of a fight to block such resolutions. To any sober observer, it was obvious that matters would go on as before.

Meantime, Baghdad hastened to invite IAEA inspectors to visit its own reactors, so as to refute Israel's allegations about its plans to produce nuclear weapons. The inspection, held on June 18, did not include the devastated reactor: the Iraqis insisted on the inspectors signing a waiver releasing them from responsibility for any injury incurred in the event of an unexploded bomb going off. The IAEA officials naturally refused, whereupon they were permitted only to inspect the small Soviet research reactor, and the stores of natural uranium (which were not subject to IAEA supervision). The inspectors, it goes without saying, found no evidence of nefarious Iraqi designs. However, they were not permitted to inspect the Italian laboratories which were such an important component of Iraq's nuclear program.

The IAEA lost no time in publishing its report, which affirmed that "the inspection thus revealed no non-compliance with the Safeguards Agreement concluded between Iraq and the IAEA." This finding seemingly refuted the testimony submitted to the congressional hearings by IAEA Chief Inspector Roger Richter, who claimed that the agency could do nothing to hinder Iraq's advance toward construction of an atomic bomb.

On November 10, the UN General Assembly, referring to the IAEA report, approved a resolution harshly critical of Israel's attack on the reactor. One hundred nine states supported the resolution; Israel and the U.S. voted against it, thirty-four states abstained and eleven were absent. In view of the balance of power prevailing at the Assembly, it was a significant diplomatic success for Israel. The abstentions included almost all the states of Western Europe and several Latin-American delegations.

29 France: "Freed from the Nuclear Nightmare"

Three hours after publication of the Israeli announcement about the reactor bombing, French Premier Pierre Mauroy issued a statement of condemnation. It is safe to assume that he did so in consultation with the newly elected President, François Mitterrand. The French Foreign Ministry followed Mauroy's statement with a string of acidly worded announcements which totally rejected Israeli allegations. In particular, the French assailed Israel's claim that the reactor attack fell within the legal definition of self-defense as set out in international law. "We shall condemn any infringement of international law, whatever its origin," declared Mitterrand in his initial statement, though he qualified his words by stressing "the sympathy we sense toward Israel." Such a rider would hardly have been appended by the previous administration.

Foreign Minister Claude Cheysson adopted a similar tone when Arab ambassadors came to complain about the Israeli attack: "Israel is France's friend; it has the right to security; we shall not change our policy toward Israel as a result of the grave action it has committed."

Mitterrand was, however, offended by Begin's failure to send him a personal communication similar to the letters dispatched to Reagan and Sadat. "We hoped you would regard us as a friendly state," Cheysson reproved Israeli Ambassador Meir Rosenne at their meeting on June 9.

Cheysson argued that Israel had violated a sanctioned principle of international law: one state was not entitled to intervene within the territory of another. "Even our friendship toward Israel does not permit us to overlook such a grave violation," he claimed. "If we condone it, where will we stand?"

Cheysson argued further that the new Socialist administration intended, together with other governments concerned (an apparent reference to Italy), to inspect the reactor so as to close off any possible loophole whereby the Iraqis could develop a nuclear-weapons option.

Rosenne listened intently; when it came to his turn to reply, he chose to commence with the principles of international law—a subject on which he is an unchallenged authority. There was no violation of international law, he argued. There could be no clearer case of self-defense. The Iraqi government had repeatedly declared its intention of annihilating Israel, and the Israeli government therefore had a clear duty to protect its citizens. Israel was aware of what the Foreign Minister termed "the gravity of its action," but had undertaken it in the absence of any alternative. Furthermore, the reactor attack had been moved forward purposely so as to preclude any danger of radioactive contamination.

Cheysson's reply was mild: France intended to keep this grave incident "within its bounds."

During the coming days, French reactions fluctuated between loud indignation and a more moderate tone which included declarations of friendship toward Israel. This seesaw appears to have reflected traditional differences within the French administration: at the pro-Arab Quai d'Orsay, most officials insisted that the Arab world must be convinced of the great gravity with which France regarded the Israeli action, whereas President Mitterrand refused to countenance such a response in view of his fundamentally warm friendship toward Israel. In fact, France submitted no written protest to Israel over the reactor bombing, nor was the French ambassador in Israel "recalled for consultations." On the contrary, with the possible aim of demonstrating that it was "business as usual," Mitterrand cancelled a directive issued by his predecessor whereby French companies were permitted to go along with the Arab boycott against Israel; Israel had campaigned for its abolition for four years.

A business meeting had been scheduled for June 12 at the Versailles Palace between representatives of the Israeli Defense Ministry and their French oppposite numbers. Without warning, the Israeli Defense Ministry was notified that the meeting, and a later banquet, had been called off in consequence of the reactor attack. On vigorous protests by Ambassador Rosenne, the French Defense Ministry's director-general, François Bernard, replied that the cancellation reflected the "private initiative" of some senior official, and ordered it rescinded forthwith.

In unattributed private conversations, French officials told their Israeli colleagues, "You have freed us from the Iraqi nuclear nightmare." A man who refused to identify himself called the Israeli Embassy in Paris to declare, "I am a technician just back from al-Tuweitha. Justice is with you. . . ."

One day after his meeting with Rosenne, Cheysson publicly alleged that the reactor bombing had been inspired by "electoral considerations."

A startled French journalist inquired, "Is it not conceivable that the Israeli Prime Minister had other reasons?"

"Are you playing naive, or are you ill-intentioned?" snapped Cheysson. "Don't take me for a fool!"

Meeting Israeli journalists in Paris on July 23, the Foreign Minister voiced grave charges against their government. "After we Socialists won the elections, we notified Israel that we have stepped up supervision of the reactor, but Israel disregarded our announcement and bombed the reactor."

Off the record, officials of the new French administration expressed gratification that the bombing of the reactor had released them from an undertaking with which even Giscard claimed to be dissatisfied. When Cheysson himself was questioned on the future of Franco-Iraqi nuclear cooperation, he noted that it had been disrupted "with a mighty bang." He did not know whether it would be renewed. "To that end, they will have to apply again. As president Mitterrand has made known, any future cooperation will involve stricter control of the reactors. We shall not pursue nuclear cooperation which can be diverted into military channels." He stressed that France would not approach Baghdad to renew cooperation. "We will not be the ones to proffer our wares. If the Iraqis apply to renew cooperation, we shall redouble control twofold, threefold, fourfold."

Saddam Hussain hastened to send Deputy Prime Minister Tarik Aziz to Paris to request reconstruction of the reactor and renewed supplies of enriched uranium. Aziz got a warm welcome; he held talks with the President and with the Ministers of Defense and Foreign Affairs—but the message he got was very plain: "France does not intend to supply Iraq with further deliveries of nuclear fuel which can be diverted to military uses."

In an interview to the *Washington Post* on June 18, Mitterrand expressed regret that prime minister Begin did not "put his trust in the President of the French Republic, whose feelings on the subject [of Israel's security] are well known." Mitterrand recalled his conversations with Peres in November 1980 and January 1981, when he had expressed "disquiet that France could contribute to new tensions in that region through the delivery of nuclear reactors." However, he did not know whether Begin was informed of these conversations, although the Israeli Prime Minister "could not have been uninformed of my position."

(Begin's comment: "Contrasting with Mitterrand's favorable utterances, there was the deplorable announcement by Cheysson prior to the reactor bombing, when he said that his country would not renege on agreements it had signed.")

According to Mitterrand, it was only after the bombing that he had learned—from press revelations—that the agreement with Iraq contained a provision for French control of the reactors to extend until 1989. This fact made him "less severe" in his "judgments about the previous French government's sale to Iraq"; with that, he wished to make it plain that any French reactor sold in future would be subject to tight supervision to preclude possible military use. Questioned on the report by three French scientists (see Chapter 18) who charged that the Franco-Iraqi agreement could endow Iraq with a nuclear-weapons option, Mitterrand noted that these views contradicted those of the French Atomic Energy Commission, and that he himself accepted the AEC's stand that "there was no possibility of imminent physical danger to Israel."

The French AEC indeed hastily launched a counterattack. Its chairman, Michel Pecqueur, convened a press conference to expose alleged inaccuracies in Israeli statements issued after the bombing. Terminating the conspiracy of silence surrounding the 1979 agreement with Iraq, Pecqueur ordered publication of its confidential portions so as to prove that France had done everything to prevent use of the reactor for construction of an atomic bomb. It was also argued that the reactor would remain under French supervision until 1989, and that any suspicious manifestation—such as consumption of large amounts of uranium, or irradiation of amounts exceeding research purposes—would have entailed an immediate halt on uranium shipments. The reactor's operation would have been directed by a Franco-Iraqi joint commission of experts; reinforcing IAEA safeguards, that would have been adequate to prevent military use of the reactor. "If only you knew the contents of the agreement," Pecqueur told an Israeli diplomat, implying that had the man known, he would have been able to reassure his government. The diplomat's response was a direct "In that case, why did you keep the agreement confidential?"

Faithful to French diplomatic tradition, Claude Cheysson persisted in doubletalk. "The declaration of Saddam Hussain" (who called upon the nations of the world to help the Arabs build an atomic bomb) "will make it harder than ever before to maintain future Franco–Iraqi nuclear cooperation." But a few days later, in a July 6 interview to the Lebanese weekly an-Nahar, Cheysson pledged: "If Iraq makes such a request, France will be prepared to reconstruct the reactor, on condition that proper control is guaranteed."

In a meeting with Cheysson in New York, Israeli Foreign Minister Shamir voiced objections to France's rebuilding the devastated reactor or supplying a replacement. "We have come to the conclusion," Shamir stated, "that even use of Caramel fuel will not solve the problem." Such fuel would indeed deny to Iraq the option of building a uranium bomb, but the reactor would still produce an alarming amount of plutonium which could then be extracted by means of the Italian installations. (Indeed, the destruction of Osirak had left Iraq without a plutogenic—plutonium-producing—reactor; but the Italian engineers nevertheless continued to construct the network of installations for chemical separation of irradiated fuel, while all available evidence pointed to renewed Iraqi efforts to acquire a plutogenic reactor.)

Shamir also expressed Israel's concern over developments in Pakistan. Western publications were firm in claiming that that country, having gone a long way toward development of nuclear weapons, was now negotiating with a French company for purchase of the equipment and knowhow required for completion of its nuclear project. Cheysson promised to go into the matter without delay.

In his conversation with Shamir, Cheysson admitted that the Franco–Iraqi agreement lacked concrete guarantees for its full implementation. He also conceded a further grave omission: there was no coordination between France and other countries (i.e., Italy) which were supplying Iraq with nuclear equipment, material and technology. In theory, he acknowledged, the situation could be perilous.

Throughout his meeting with Shamir, Cheysson's tone was factual and friendly—in marked contrast with his earlier accusations that Begin's decision to bomb the reactor stemmed from purely "electoral considerations." Did his statements convey implied criticism of the previous French administration? On the surface, they did. (Reading Shamir's report on the conversation, Begin commented with a weary smile, "Partial confession . . .")

All in all, the period following the reactor bombing witnessed numerous expressions of penitence, in France and elsewhere. One such admission came from no less a personage than former President Valéry Giscard d'Estaing. In a series of conversations with Yeshayahu Ben Porat of the Israeli *Yediot Aharonot*, Giscard, queried on his approval of sales of weapons-grade uranium to Iraq, replied, in brief: He had been the president, true; he was neither able nor willing to remove the responsibility from his own shoulders. But, he said, one should remember that it was not he who had conducted the negotiations with Iraq, nor had he signed the agreement. Jacques Chirac, who was then premier, conducted the negotiations and signed the agreement. At that period, the ex-President recalled, France concluded agreements with several countries for supply of nuclear reactors. The agreement with Iraq was depicted to him, he said, as providing for delivery of a research reactor with no weapons potential. At that time, France had a contract with Pakistan for sale of an installation for enrichment and reprocessing of nuclear fuel; but when the French intelligence services discovered that Pakistan intended to produce nuclear weapons, France called the deal off.

Giscard insisted that no party—"Israelis included"—had brought it to France's attention that the Iraqi reactor was to be used for military purposes.

Ben Porat did not relent: "Did French intelligence, or someone else, deliberately conceal the information from you?"

The ex-President flung up his hands. "I don't know, I don't know."

"It was my impression," Ben Porat observed, "that he did know more; but, for obvious reasons, he preferred to remain silent."

Giscard's defense was astounding. Foreign Minister Shamir discussed the Iraqi reactor with him on two occasions, as did Shimon Peres. France's intelligence services knew perfectly well what was going on at al-Tuweitha, and where Iraq was headed. Did all this evade Giscard's memory? Apart from an uneasy conscience, did he have any specific reason for denying the undeniable?

Giscard's former colleagues in office were in no haste to relieve him of responsibility. Chirac said he had operated within the guidelines laid down by the President, but the agreement was signed by his successor as premier, Raymond Barre. As for Barre, he explained: "True, I did sign the agreement, but I received it complete from my predecessor, Jacques Chirac."

On June 12, shortly after the Rome government issued a sharp condemnation of Israel's attack on the reactor, Israeli Ambassador Moshe Alon met with Italian Foreign Minister Emilio Colombo. The Israeli ambassador did not employ diplomatic niceties. In World War Two, recalled Holocaust survivor Alon, Jewish leaders attempted in vain to persuade the Allies to bomb Auschwitz and other extermination camps. Had the Allies acted as requested, hundreds of thousands of Jews, millions perhaps, would have been saved. Had the United States and Britain acted as the Israelis had just acted, one third of the Jewish people would perhaps have escaped annihilation. "At times," Alon continued impassionedly, "we Jews are accused of operating under the trauma of the Holocaust. That may be true. But that does not contradict the fact that what we did in Iraq was aimed at safeguarding Israel's very existence."

Colombo repeated the familiar charges: Israel had violated the sovereignty of a foreign state; it had committed an act which was liable to exacerbate the threat of war in the region. He refused to consider his guest's claim that Israel had acted in self-defense as understood by international law.

As reports of the Israeli ambassadors' meetings reached his Jerusalem office, Menahem Begin thundered: "It is a shame and a disgrace to two ancient and civilized European countries—countries which directly witnessed what happened to the Jewish people. Those two countries should bear our tragedy in mind. It is a shame and a disgrace to those countries that they should help develop weapons of mass destruction for the bloodthirsty archenemy of the Jewish state. They should be ashamed—instead of summoning our ambassadors and rebuking them."

30 Egypt: "May God forgive you, O Menahem!"

On June 4, three days prior to the reactor bombing, Begin had been host to Egyptian President Sadat at the Sinai port of Sharm al-Sheikh, which was scheduled to revert to Egyptian rule within less than a year. The two leaders conducted their talks in a friendly atmosphere. "We talked about every topic under the sun," Begin related. "Libya, Lebanon, negotiations in Jerusalem, the bilateral cultural agreement which awaited ratification, the future of the Etzion and Itam airfields in Sinai." At the conclusion of their meeting, Sadat invited Begin to come to Alexandria in the first half of July, after the impending Knesset elections.

At the time of the meeting with Sadat, Begin knew, of course, precisely what was due to happen three days ahead. "In my head, I already had the text of the statement to be issued after the operation," Begin recalled subsequently. Begin would be accused of timing his encounter with Sadat in such proximity to the reactor raid with the deliberate intention of diverting attention from Israel's intentions, and of creating an impression of utter tranquility in the region. The truth was quite different: the idea of the Sharm al-Sheikh meeting arose fortuitously, and it was Sadat, not Begin, who proposed the date.

In the course of their conversation, there was one reference to the Iraqi leader: "Saddam Hussain," said Sadat "is even more vicious than Qaddafi." Begin, it goes without saying, did not disagree.

On learning of the reactor bombing, Sadat naturally feared accusations of collusion in the Israeli operation, or prior knowledge thereof. In his heart of hearts Sadat may have rejoiced over the setback inflicted upon Saddam Hussain, though he could not, of course, express glee at the downfall of one of his Arab "brethren." Furthermore, he feared—with justification, from his viewpoint—that the Israeli action would give an additional boost to the Refusal Front states which, with Moscow's blessing, were out for his blood. "I did not expect Menahem to tell me about the operation at Sharm al-

Sheikh," Sadat complained to his intimates. "But who—apart from the Egyptian people— will believe that I was unaware of it? God alone knows how I and my people will surmount this matter."

Begin himself related, "I gave him not the slightest hint of the matter. Had I told him—even if he made no comment at all—the responsibility would have fallen upon him. The fact that he knew of such an extraordinary undertaking would make him into a kind of accomplice, and he would come to bear responsibility. Would I burden him with such a responsibility? Aside from that, would I reveal such a closely guarded secret to anyone outside of those required to know, with all the possible implications? We consulted neither the United States nor Egypt. The entire responsibility is ours."

The Israeli action raised an outcry in Egypt. On June 9 the Egyptian parliament convened for its first meeting after the bombing; there were calls for relations with Israel to be frozen, for the expulsion of Israeli Ambassador Moshe Sasson, and the recall of Egyptian Ambassador Saad Murthada from Tel Aviv. Speaker Muhammed Rashwan called for severance of relations with Israel, and a halt on oil sales. An opposition member openly referred to Begin as "a gangster."

Foreign Minister Kamal Hassan Ali, regarded as a spokesman for Sadat, addressed the deputies, condemning the raid as "an act of international terrorism." The parliament urged the United States "to take steps against Israel and review arms deliveries to Israel, after its use of American-made weapons in its attack."

Initially, Ambassador Sasson applied to attend the parliament's deliberations, but he decided at the last moment to stay away. Sadat later complimented him on his decision, adding that the presence of the Israeli diplomat could have inflamed feelings. Sadat directed that media reports on the parliament's debate be checked—or "cooled," as he put it—so as to forestall harm to the peace process.

Sasson received urgent instructions from Jerusalem to lose no time in arranging a meeting with Sadat for delivery of a personal message from Begin, an unforeseen snag having blocked communications between the two leaders. Begin had intended to notify Sadat of the reactor raid without delay; he relayed his message by way of the U.S. embassies in Tel Aviv and Cairo. But he learned to his astonishment that his communication, instead of being delivered directly to Sadat, was instead handed to another prominent Egyptian personage, who was apparently requested to act as courier. The hitch angered Begin, who did not hesitate to vent his indignation when he met U.S. diplomats Sam Lewis and Philip Habib on June 18.

But prior to that, on June 10, Sasson went to see Sadat at Alexandria's Maamoura Palace, where, after the usual exchange of courtesies, he presented the Prime Minister's letter.

Sadat studied the letter intently. There were moments when he appeared to be reading it again and again.

Moshe Sasson—his father, Eliyahu, had been the liaison between the Jewish leaders and their Arab counterparts before and after the creation of Israel—waited without uttering a sound.

"Saddam Hussein, who is more vicious than Qaddafi," Begin began, recalling Sadat's own recent characterization of the Iraqi ruler, "planned to develop, mainly with the help of France, several atomic bombs of the Hiroshima type. He would then have tried to either bring Israel to her knees or to destroy her menfolk and infrastructure. Three such bombs would have inflicted on us 600,000 casualties. In Egyptian terms it would have meant more than 6 million persons. Could or would Egypt have stood by [in the face of such a threat]?" Begin replied to his own rhetorical question: "Israel likewise could not. We had to act before the reactor became 'hot' which has to have happened . . . either in July or the latest in September . . ." It was the twelfth hour to prevent mortal danger to the people of Israel, Begin went on, pointing out that bombing the reactor when it was hot would have exposed the citizens of Baghdad to radioactive fallout. "I for one would never have taken such a decision, nor do I believe that any of my colleagues would ever have supported such a proposal. Nothing would have been left for us but to sit passively by for a period of between two and four years until Saddam Hussein would have readied his three or four or five nuclear bombs."

"Mr. President," Begin resumed, "this description is simple but factual. We did our duty to defend our people and prevent disaster from taking place in our country, and so we shall in the future when the necessity arises. So help me God."

In view of the heavy cloud overshadowing Israeli-Egyptian relations, Begin made great efforts to preserve a personal note in addressing Sadat. The Prime Minister conveyed regards from his wife, Aliza, who was still hospitalized but felt better. "I was deeply perturbed, the doctors having suspected a stroke of the brain. Now the improvement is great and the terrible anxiety is relieved. With God's help she will soon come home." Begin concluded the letter with regards, from himself and his wife, to Sadat's wife.

With the letter, Begin sent the official Israeli statement defending the reactor bombing.

Sadat completed his perusal of the letter and, after a brief moment of reflection, addressed Sasson in somewhat subdued tones. The reactor attack, he declared, had turned matters back to where they stood prior to the peace process. It recreated the great psychological barrier dividing Jews and Arabs, the barrier he, Sadat, had managed to break down. Now Israel was reverting to the familiar image of "invincible force with a long arm which reached everywhere." ("Oh, yes," Begin commented wryly on reading Sasson's report of the meeting. "A long arm is a very bad thing. An arm should be short and vanquished.")

But in spite of what had happened, Sadat declared, he did not intend to turn his back on peace. With his invariable penchant for personal gesture, Sadat stressed that resolve by referring to Begin by his first name throughout the conversation. Adopting a dramatic tone, he now told Sasson, "tell Menahem for me: May God forgive you, O Menahem!" (reading the report, Begin remarked, "He [the Almighty] will, I'm convinced of that!")

"O Menahem!" Sadat went on. "Why should the Soviets and the Syrians say they are right while Reagan, Begin and Sadat are wrong?" But he hastened to add: "I will not retreat before the Soviet Union and Syria."

Ambassador Sasson knew there was no hope of the Egyptian President voicing support for the Israeli action. But he listened intently, his sole aim being to coax Sadat toward some measure of understanding of Begin's motives, so as to prevent a breakdown in relations between the two countries. The time for verbal explanation having arrived, Sasson began by pointing out that the Prime Minister had sent personal communications to two heads of state, the Presidents of the United States and Egypt, a fact which reflected Begin's profound trust and friendship for Sadat. The ambassador went on to a brief survey of Israel's diplomatic efforts to prevent Iraq's acquisition of nuclear arms; he told of France's cynical response, and of Italy's evasiveness.

Iraq imagined, Sasson declared, that it could pose an alternative to peace: the annihilation of Israel as a state and a people. "As an observer from afar," Sasson concluded his brief address to Sadat, "you will certainly understand that Israel acted solely out of self-defense. Never has Israel faced such a threat to its existence as it would confront should Iraq acquire a nuclear-weapons capability. Accordingly, please do not regard the Israeli action as running counter to the peace process."

Sadat made no effort to conceal his inner feelings. But the fact that he refrained from attacking Israel spoke for itself. "Tell Menahem I am silent . . ." As he had told Begin in the past, he went on, no one could undermine the peace process other than the three parties to the peace treaty: Egypt, Israel and the United States. What had happened, he said, was shocking, but he could do nothing but continue to work for peace and stand firm against the Soviets and the Syrians.

Sasson responded by referring to the Jewish rabbinical tradition, and the compilation of wise precepts known as Pirkey Avot (the Sayings of the Fathers). "One of the greatest and most profound of these offers the counsel 'Do not judge your fellow until you stand in his place.' I do not wish you or your people ever to stand in the place where Prime Minister Begin stood. But I am convinced tha the President, as Egypt's head of state and supreme commander of its armed forces, were he to learn that Qaddafi, for example, was seeking a military nuclear option to employ against Egypt, would act like Prime Minister Begin."

Sadat heard him out in silence; but as the ambassador was taking his leave the Egyptian President made a somewhat cryptic remark: "Between friends treading the same path, it is important that you understand how matters stand." Earlier, Sadat had employed a colorful expression: the Israeli operation against Baghdad, he said, was like "a check which we should swiftly recover and tear up, to prevent the Soviets and the Syrians from using it to harm the peace process."

The policy now pursued by Egypt—apparently on Sadat's personal directives—was clear-cut: total condemnation of the Israeli action as "a vile error" while simultaneously ensuring that it was not exploited to harm or block the peace process.

But if Israel hoped that Egypt would rest content with mere verbal condemnation, that hope was soon to be dashed. As will be recalled, Egyptian diplomats in Washington embarked on strenuous efforts to halt U.S. arms deliveries to Israel. Other Egyptian representatives were active against Israel at the UN General Assembly, in the Security Council and in the IAEA. When the ministerial council of the Organization of African Unity convened in the Kenyan capital, Nairobi, it was Egypt which, in total indifference to its peace treaty with Israel, introduced the most sharply worded anti-Israel resolution.

These actions could hardly have been undertaken without Sadat's knowledge; under the circumstances, the Egyptian President could not have acted differently. Some indication of his thoughts on the matter emerged in August 1981, two months after the reactor attack and the same time span before his own assassination, in his conversation with Richard Nixon. This is how the ex-President recalls the talk in his book:

Two months earlier Israel had made a preemptive strike on a nuclear reactor in Iraq. I told Sadat that I felt Israeli Premier Menahem Begin had acted irresponsibly and erratically. He blurted out, "Yes, he is crazy." But then he added, "He is also probably crazy like a fox." I said that while I understood that Israel had to protect itself against its enemies, I thought it was unwise for Begin to embarrass his friends, such as Sadat and Reagan, in the process. Sadat agreed.

But when I added that more progress could have been made in the Mideast had Begin not been in power, Sadat demurred. "I prefer to deal with him," he said "he is very tough and will be able to make a deal that others may not be able to make. Israel needs a deal, and I am confident that between Begin, Reagan and myself, we will be able to make greater, more lasting progress than was made during the Carter administration."

As shown by Nixon's account, Israeli apprehensions about Sadat's reaction turned out to have been exaggerated. The President's public announcements proved to be less critical than predicted. Even his public debate with Begin, during the latter's visit to Egypt—which Sadat had insisted on holding, as scheduled, on August 25–26—did not exceed the bounds of ordinary disagreement. The Prime Minister again explained why it had been necessary to attack the reactor before it became hot. He tried to show that what Hussain planned to do with his reactors jeopardized not Israel alone but the entire region. For his part, Sadat pointed to the blow to Egypt's credibility and its standing in the Arab world.

Beyond their public exchange, the two leaders also conversed in private, giving Begin an opportunity to expand on his explanations as to Saddam Hussain's intentions. But he also heard Sadat utter one remark which caused him considerable gratification. The precise wording of that remark will probably remain a secret unto eternity.

31 Iraq: "Give us a nuclear bomb!"

Immediately upon the bombing of the reactor, Baghdad was blacked out and its international airport closed down. Learning from the breakdown of Baghdad–Amman–Riyadh communications while the Israeli planes were heading for their target, Iraq now approached Jordan and Saudi Arabia with proposals for promoting cooperation. According to Western sources, the Jordanians and the Saudis were requested to provide instant warning of any hostile planes they detected. Iraq also urged the Saudis to pass on the information picked up by their omniscient AWACS spy planes. (It emerged later that these planes' early warning systems could be "dazzled" to a degree which made them incapable of picking out objects no more than two hundred feet away.)

Foreseeing a possible Iraqi attempt to hit back by way of Jordanian territory, Prime Minister Begin sent an urgent message to King Hussain, warning him that his consent to such an action would endanger the future of the Hashemite kingdom. It was Israel's intention, Begin hinted obliquely, to preserve good-neighborly relations of mutual respect. Hussein is known to have rejected Iraqi requests for a reprisal raid to be launched from Jordan.

With prime responsibility for safeguarding the Baghdad regime, Iraqi Military Intelligence set up a commission of inquiry to investigate the functioning of the antiaircraft network during the Israeli raid. Four days later, the commission directed that a number of officers and soldiers be punished for a grave dereliction of duty. A rumor never officially confirmed claimed that the local antiaircraft commander was executed on personal orders from Saddam Hussain. French technicians employed at the reactor also fell under suspicion of aid to the Israelis.

While Saddam Hussain and his advisers were racking their brains about whether or not to publish an official announcement about the Israeli attack, Jordan, as will be recalled, hastened to publicize Israel's bombing raid on "vital targets near Baghdad." The Jordanian announcement soon evoked the official Israeli statement. Iraq was left with no choice: three hours after release of the Israeli communiqué, an official announcement was issued in Baghdad.

It began by tossing out charges against "the reactionary Iranian regime" which recruited aid for its anti-Iraqi efforts from various quarters, "the Zionist entity" first and foremost. In this context, Iraq charged that "the Zionist enemy" had taken part in two aerial bombings of Baghdad the previous September. The latest raid was likewise carried out "on behalf of the rulers of Iran." The crux of the Iraqi communiqué referred to the strategy behind the bombing—as perceived by Baghdad. "The Zionist entity" sought every means to preserve its technological edge over the Arabs, so as to prevent the latter from attaining a standard which would bring them victory.

The Iraqis must have decided that this was their most promising line. Neither able nor willing to admit that they had attempted to construct an atomic bomb, they did want to seize upon the devastated reactor to prove, to the Arab states and the world at large, that they spearheaded the struggle against Zionism. Official propaganda accordingly pursued this theme: the reactor, though not directly designed for military purposes, was to have given Iraq—and the Arab world—the possibility of exercising Arab scientific and technological potential so as to close the gap between them and Israel. This presentation came to expression in a statement by Propaganda Minister Latif Nasif al-Jasim on June 12: "The economic and human potential of the Arab nation should be augmented by scientific and technological proficiency; together, these will constitute a deathblow to Israel. Therefore, the reactor bombing obliges us to place our trust in nuclear energy . . . and to use all scientific means for the implementation of this strategy and for the liberation of Palestine."

On June 9, Iraqi Foreign Minister Hammadi summoned the Arab ambassadors accredited in Baghdad to a briefing. His address included the following passage: "The Zionist enemy has long conducted a series of actions to foil Iraq's efforts to construct a nuclear program for peaceful purposes, while Israel possesses nuclear weapons, as is well known. Iraq's nuclear installations were constructed for peaceful purposes, and they are under international supervision. The Zionist enemy wishes to deny the Arab states technological development and scientific progress which will enable them to develop their might, with the aim of preserving the Zionist entity's hegemony in the region. The Iraqi government is determined to continue building up its independent might."

On June 14 Hammadi was in New York, where he had come to direct

Iraq's efforts at the Security Council. Interviewed that day for NBC's *Meet the Press*, Hammadi—possessed of a perfect command of English and a close acquaintance with the United States, both acquired while working on his economic thesis at the University of Wisconsin—endeavored to touch on chords pleasing to the ears of his American viewers. The Iraqi nuclear program, he claimed, was "absolutely peaceful. The only commission in the world which is responsible to say whether the program was peaceful or not, which is the International [Atomic Energy] Agency, had said that." Asked why Iraq insisted on weapons-grade uranium, Hammadi replied that the aim of the Iraqi program was "to get into the technology of the atomic energy. Now, I can't see why should we get a very backward type of technology. . . . Your question is just the same as asking us . . . why do we buy 1981 cars and not the Ford type of car? . . . Is it really legal, is it right, to allow Israel to have a free hand to destroy a scientific research center just because they want to keep our country backward?"

Hammadi's interviewers were insufficiently familiar with the topic, otherwise they might have asked him whether his country had fully exhausted all the research openings available at its Soviet reactor and therefore needed the possibilities offered by Osirak and its enriched fuel.

For two weeks after the reactor bombing, Saddam Hussain maintained total silence; during this time, he drew up a carefully worded statement which was then read out to the Iraqi Cabinet and immediately disseminated by the country's official news agency. The statement wasted no time in delineating Iraq's most immediate objective; it appealed to any country "which seeks peace and security" to help the Arabs "in one way or another to obtain the nuclear bomb, in order to confront Israel's existing bombs." Realizing that such an outspoken appeal was liable to draw hostile reactions, Hussain attempted to tone it down: "This is not a justification for the acquisition of nuclear technology for military purposes by the Arabs, but an open appeal to universal human intelligence to deal with the situation now existing in Israel, as confirmed by all experts on nuclear armaments and on the Middle East." Further points in Hussain's statement:

· Israel dreads Iraq's scientific, economic and diplomatic progress far more than it fears the Iraqi nuclear bomb.
· The two superpowers maintain a "balance of terror," with each side constantly replenishing its nuclear arsenal even though neither side wishes to use it. Like the superpowers, the Arabs too need nuclear arms with which to counter the nuclear threat posed by "the Zionist entity."
· The Israeli strike at Iraq's vital installations was aimed at blocking Iraq's

scientific and economic advance. Since early 1979, Iraq had been asking friendly states to supply such weapons which would cause Israel to hesitate before launching a blow of this nature.

· The Arabs need atomic bombs so that the states bordering upon Israel would not be placed in a diplomatic or economic predicament, and so that Iraq, which has no common border with Israel, should not find itself powerless to respond to Israel.

· Even were the Arabs to recognize Israel's "secure borders" as defined by Israel, that country would continue its expansionism at the expense of Arab sovereignty, under the protection of its nuclear might. Israel would even intervene in internal Arab matters such as "changing the siting of a road in Saudi Arabia because it constitutes a threat [to Israel] . . . The Arabs will be forced to omit from their school curriculum subjects like chemistry, physics and mathematics, because they could lead to the accumulation of knowledge in the military sphere . . . [Israel] will demand the dismissal of kings, princes and presidents, and even a grade-school principal, because of the national education he is giving . . . [Israel] will demand that the Arabs change their history and rewrite it, including the history of the war between the Prophet Mohammed and the Jewish tribes in the Arabian Peninsula."

· The Arabs were dutybound to prepare for the struggle on all levels—scientific, technical, diplomatic, economic and social. If they succeeded in doing so, the damage would be partial and temporary. Iraq would continue to learn the lessons. What the enemy destroyed today, Iraq would build tomorrow. No force would prevent Iraq from continuing to engage in the nuclear field and guaranteeing its scientific and technological progress. Implementation of the decisions arising from the lessons learned had already commenced.

Israeli experts who studied the declaration noted that Saddam Hussain avoided an express appeal for aid to Iraq in acquiring nuclear weapons, apparently because his country was still a signatory of the NPT; that may have been why he opted for the term "Arabs." The wording indicated that Iraq was prepared to act on behalf of the Arab states as a "contractor" in the field of nuclear development in general and Arab nuclear deterrence against Israel in particular. In effect, this was the first public declaration by an Arab leader advocating acquisition of nuclear weapons by the Arabs. Predictably, the declaration contained no hint that such weapons would ever be directed against an Israeli target; on the contrary, it stressed throughout that they would serve a deterrent purpose. The Iraqi ruler attempted to make the rules of the superpower "balance of terror" applicable to the Mideastern conflict.

That latter notion was rejected outright by Professor Yuval Ne'eman. "The Arab world harbors regimes such as those of Muammar al-Qaddafi and Saddam Hussain. Can these leaders, to whom human life is without worth, be relied upon to follow rational reasoning like that of the leaders of the superpowers? Furthermore, the global balance of terror is between the

United States and the Soviet Union; what Saddam Hussain seeks is a balance of terror between Israel and twenty-one Arab states which are disunited, engage in uninhibited mutual rivalry and often pursue active warfare with one another."

Hussain's appeal for international aid in acquiring an Arab atom bomb evoked a sharp and pithy response from U.S. Secretary of State Alexander Haig: "Hussain's declaration is disgusting."

Menahem Begin commented, "If the Iraqis again attempt to construct the reactor, Israel will use all the means at its disposal to destroy it." Asked whether that also held true for Libya, the Prime Minister replied, "Let us first deal with that *meshuggener* Saddam Hussain. The second *meshuggener* [Qaddafi] will be dealt with some other time." (The question about Libya arose from Qaddafi's call to the Arab states to destroy the Israeli reactor in Dimona, where, he alleged, atomic bombs were being manufactured. The Libyan leader even dreamed up a plan, which was, however, rejected by Syria. Saddam Hussain pledged; "if Qaddafi is capable of putting his threat into effect, Iraq will support it.")

Before and after the reactor bombing, Iraqi conduct showed up Saddam Hussain as a ruthless, unscrupulous tyrant who, given nuclear arms, would not hesitate to use them for blackmail or for the direct destruction of Israel. The country report on human-rights practices submitted to the U.S. Senate's Foreign Relations Committee in 1982 states: "The [Iraqi] government neither acknowledges human rights violations nor facilitates outside investigations of allegations of human rights violations. Activities which the state considers threats to its security can lead to detention without charge, severe prison sentences, mistreatment, torture or execution. Most of these actions are carried out by a large and feared internal security police force." The report details a long list of fiendish "innovations" employed by the Iraqi regime: thalium poisoning, mass executions, "disappearances," electric shock, beatings with rubber hoses, burns, sexual abuse and so on. All these findings were repeated, with extensive updating, in the 1983 human-rights report.

In September 1982 an Amnesty International representative testified before the UN Human Rights Subcommision, "Some three hundred persons were executed in Iraq in 1981, and we are aware that the executions went on in 1982." In 1981, Iraqi diplomats in Europe and Asia were implicated in acts of violence, including use of firearms.

On March 26, 1984, a report was submitted to the Security Council by an independent UN commission which investigated Iranian charges that Iraq, in defiance of international conventions, was using gas in the war between the two countries. The commission was composed of highly reputable scientists: Dr. Gustav Andersson, chief chemist at the Swedish Army's research center; Dr. Manuel Dominguez, colonel in the Spanish Army, professor of preventive medicine and a specialist in atomic, bacteriological and chemical warfare; Dr. Peter Dunn, head of the materials research laboratories at the Australian Department of Defence research center; and Colonel Ulrich Imobersteg, former chief of nuclear, biological and chemical weapons defense at the Swiss Defense Ministry. The commission's conclusions, adopted unanimously, were clear and unequivocal: Iraq had used chemical weapons, which were dropped from airplanes. The Iraqis used mustard gas and the deadly "tabun" nerve gas, both featuring in the list of weapons banned by numerous international conventions to which Iraq is a signatory, just as it is a party to the IAEA convention with regard to manufacture of nuclear weapons.

According to international media reports, Iraq erected its gigantic complex for the manufacture of gas and chemical weapons with the help of the West German Karl-Kolb company. Tabun gas, it will be recalled, was invented by the Nazis in 1936.

32 Israel: "The Wars of the Jews"

On the evening of Saturday, June 6, someone told Shimon Peres, "It's going to be tomorrow afternoon." Peres was in need of no further elaboration to know what "it" was.

Who revealed Israel's most closely guarded secret to the leader of the labor opposition? Was it Ezer Weizman? Was it a senior official in the defense establishment? Was it someone entrusted with some aspect of the operation? It became evident yet again that Labor, even out of office, has eyes and ears everywhere. It will be recalled that Peres had also been acquainted with the precise date originally fixed for the raid—May 10— two months previously. At that time, having consulted with several confidants and party colleagues, Peres dispatched his personal letter to Begin urging that the raid be called off or deferred. "I don't know," Peres said later, "whether the letter did or did not have its effect. But I was pleased that the matter was not carried out that day."

The "matter" was again imminent. That same Saturday evening, June 6, Peres phoned a select group of Labor leaders and summoned them to a meeting the following day, at twelve-thirty, at his office in Labor's Tel Aviv headquarters.

It was a Sunday, immediately succeeding the Saturday rest day and one day before the onset of the Shavuoth vacation—the sort of opportunity when most Israelis declare a "bridge" to grab an extra day off work. Nevertheless, there were numerous people at the party headquarters, engaged in routine election campaign work. The meeting in Peres' office therefore attracted no undue attention.

The participants included former Prime Minister and onetime Commander in Chief Yitzhak Rabin, at that time on extremely hostile terms with Peres; former Foreign Minister Abba Eban; another former Commander in Chief and also former Trade and Industry Minister, Haim Barlev, then Labor secretary-general and the party's candidate for defense minister; former

Justice Minister Haim Tzadok; Labor senior statesman Yisrael Galili; and former Ambassador to Washington Simha Dinitz. This unofficial group constituted Labor's military-diplomatic "brain trust."

(Others privy to the secret of the projected reactor strike were Eliezer Zhorabin, who directed Labor's information and publicity campaign; and former Military Intelligence Director Shlomo Gazit, who had learned of it the previous day while on vacation in northern Israel, where an army officer he encountered told him, "Tomorrow they're bombing the reactor.")

The decision in principle to bomb the reactor having already come to the attention of most of those seated in Peres' office, he therefore wasted no time in declaring, "To the best of my knowledge, the Air Force will bomb the Iraqi reactor today." Peres briefly reviewed developments with regard to the reactor since he had first heard from Begin late in December 1980 of the government's decision. Labor's chairman now sought counsel from his colleagues. "Would it be profitable to send a delegation to the Prime Minister and advise him to call off the operation or postpone it?"

Eban spoke against a renewed approach to Begin, who had long been aware of Peres' firm opposition to the bombing.

Rabin likewise spoke against an official Labor approach to Begin. "If anyone wishes to meet with the Prime Minister in a private capacity, let him go," Rabin said. Those present construed the remark as a personal barb directed at Peres. Rabin's resentment of Peres went back to the days when the latter served as defense minister in his Cabinet; in his memoirs, Rabin bluntly characterized Peres as "a tireless intriguant." Rabin argued that Peres' information was not entirely above question. "It should be regarded as a rumor—a well-found rumor possibly, but in no way authoritative information."

Rabin was in two minds about his attendance at the consultation. As prime minister he had suffered grievously from leaks; he therefore felt uneasy at taking part in deliberations resting exclusively upon the leaking of a top national secret. As he was to explain later, "Opposition leaders meeting to consider sensitive secret information which came to their attention in an unauthorized manner—that is not a desirable phenomenon," even though "it was an error on the part of the Prime Minister not to share the secret with the leaders of the opposition." Like other participants, Rabin was troubled at this furtive manner of weighing up a life-and-death issue. Furthermore, having been made privy to experts' reports on the reactor, which were conveyed to him by Aharon Yariv on personal instructions from Begin, Rabin probably sensed that he was showing ingratitude toward the Prime Minister by taking part in the secret conclave.

"The information did not reach us from official sources," Barlev confirmed later; but he added, "Even though Labor was then in opposition, its military leadership was not divorced from developments. We have experience and contacts. I don't need to chase anyone to know what is happening in the armed forces. The matter came to our attention, and we could not pass it over."

The exchange proceeded. As Eban recalled the discussion, all participants agreed that there was no point in repeating Peres' earlier advice to Begin to halt the reactor attack. Peres: "I came to the conclusion that a further intervention on my part would not lead to cancellation of the operation."

With that, there was firm and unanimous opposition to the projected raid, and general consensus on the following points: there was no prospect of the reactor going into operation in the months to come; the timing of the operation was linked to the election campaign; and it was irresponsible of the present government to adopt this course of action, particularly in view of the fact that its consequences would be borne by the incoming government.

The meeting resolved to make no further approach to Begin. If the bombing was announced officially, Labor would issue a statement expressing its admiration for those who carried it out; as for the operation itself, the party would withhold comment.

Shortly after the safe return of the planes, Begin personally phoned Peres and Rabin to tell them of the operation's successful outcome. Peres in turn notified Rabin (who had already heard) and Gur. But it was a day later, June 8, before the news reached the other Labor leaders who had attended the consultation at Peres' office: they learned of it from the Israeli radio newscast.

Abba Eban, for example, got the tidings at a reception at Tel Aviv's Dan Hotel in honor of American banker Bill Butcher; Eban immediately called the radio station to request the full text of the news item (another guest, U.S. ambassador Sam Lewis, had been privileged, as the reader will recall, to get the news from Begin in person).

After the official announcement, dozens of journalists, foreign and local, approached Labor leaders for their comments. Peres, Rabin and Gur each responded along the guidelines laid down at their confidential consultation the previous day: they praised the courage and skill of the pilots, offered no comment on the operation itself, and ignored the government.

But other Labor leaders, not privy to the decisions reached at the secret conclave, publicly attacked the reactor bombing. First to do so was Labor information chief Haim Herzog (see Chapter 23). Herzog's statement was featured in a Labor election telecast, whereupon it was promptly transmitted to every part of the world. Drawing upon his position as a military commentator enjoying the respect and confidence of the Israeli public, Herzog implied that his view rested upon information received from experts.

Labor Knesset member Gad Yaakovi was angered by Herzog's comments. He called Peres to urge private consultations before any further public statements, "so as to avoid harmful utterances." Unaware of the decisions reached at the previous day's meeting, Yaakovi nevertheless proposed a line broadly similar: the party should restrict itself to a statement lauding the Air Force for the success of its exploit, while withholding politically controversial assessments.

When Peres flew back to Tel Aviv after his Shavuoth visit to Eilat, he was received by his American image adviser, David Sawyer, and by Labor's information adviser Eliezer Zhorabin. They drove to Peres' north Tel Aviv home, where they discussed the line the party should follow with regard to the raid. They soon realized that their circle needed extension; with Peres himself called away to urgent business, the group that met at Labor headquarters consisted, in addition to Sawyer and Zhorabin, of Galili, Haim Tzadok, Dinitz and Herzog.

Zhorabin now repeated what he had said previously to Peres and Sawyer: Labor had nothing to lose. All credit for the operation would go to Begin and his government. Consequently, Labor must attack Begin personally, accusing him outright of ordering the bombing for purely electoral ends. Zhorabin hoped that, if charged with jeopardizing the pilots for party profit, Begin would be thrown off balance and would come back with an unbridled reaction, highlighting his tough-bogyman image, which would be beneficial to Labor.

While the group continued to debate the propaganda line to adopt, a young man named Yoav Lavi was seated at Labor headquarters, penning an impassioned personal letter to Shimon Peres. Lavi, an adviser to Labor's election staff, recalled that he had been in the United States when Khomeini's Revolutionary guards took over the U.S. Embassy in Teheran and seized fifty American hostages. Even though it was an election year, the Republicans refrained from attacking President Carter on the issue. But Carter did come under fire from Democratic Senator Edward Kennedy, whose image adviser at the time was none other than the selfsame David Sawyer, currently in Israel in a similar capacity for Peres. Fearing that Sawyer would advocate an attack on the Likud government's action against Iraq, Lavi therefore hastened to warn the party leader to disregard such counsel. He drew an American analogy: "Ronald Reagan acted wisely when he refrained from intervening in Carter's handling of the hostage issue, including the abortive rescue mission; Reagan proclaimed that on crucial issues America should stand as one man behind the President. That is the line to adopt." When Reagan declared; "I shall express my view on what should and could have been done about the hostage issue one day after becoming President," U.S. voters grasped that the Republican candidate was critical of Carter; but the

American public appreciated what it perceived as Reagan's restraint in refusing to disrupt the national consensus. The election outcome spoke for
itself.

However, Lavi's warning fell on deaf ears. As the young man had feared,
Peres followed Sawyer's counsel. Sawyer argued that a failure to attack
Begin directly would make Labor appear to endorse the operation, whereas
criticism would awaken doubt in the public mind. In conversation with
intimates and colleagues Peres explained, "A favorable [Labor] response [to
the raid] will give the public the impression it's a phenomenal triumph,
thereby endowing it with a powerfully favorable electoral impact from the
Likkud viewpoint."

Addressing the party's election staff, Peres said, "The reactor bombing
will have [a detrimental] electoral effect upon us. We have congratulated the
armed forces on the successful exploit, but the government should not be
relieved of responsibility [for an operation] which could entail grave com-
plications in the future." He expressed his fear that the government, drawing encouragement from its success against Iraq, was not liable to launch
parallel military action in Lebanon. "I have all kinds of indications," he said
without elaborating. "It is therefore vital to speak out against the government's policy."

Of course, Peres' position rested in part on his original conviction that the
reactor bombing was an error (even though he continued to hold that Israel
must never consent to Iraq or any other irresponsible state coming into
possession of nuclear arms.) The Labor Party leader claimed that most "professional community" experts were not convinced of the reactor's genuine
military potential. Under certain circumstances, it would be feasible to mili-
tarize the reactor, but, he added with barbed irony, "that's like someone
saying that if wings were mounted on a truck, it could fly. . ." Peres argued
that the Iraqi threat stemmed from the French undertaking to supply Baghdad with weapons-grade uranium. But in fact, after the first shipment,
France sent no more; for a uranium bomb, Peres pointed out, Iraq needed 25
kilograms of weapons-grade uranium, but possessed only half that amount.

Peres' arguments, which he claimed to have put forward at the December
1980 meeting when Begin first disclosed his intention of bombing the reactor, failed to convince the Prime Minister, who claimed that the Iraqis could
buy uranium on the open market; whereupon Peres retorted, "Weapons-
grade uranium can't be bought on the open market. Furthermore, if they do
buy it on the open market, they don't need the reactor at all!"

As for the option of producing a plutonium bomb, Peres argued that the
reactor by itself was inadequate without an extraction plant. True, Iraq had
purchased such a plant from Italy, but it was of a research-laboratory type
which could not produce a bomb. In Peres' view, the principal danger lay in

the emergence of a generation of trained Iraqi engineers and scientists; however, training of this nature requires a number of years, and there was thus no call for such perilous action to eliminate so remote a threat. "I deduced that Iraq's path to a nuclear option would be a long one, and it was doubtful whether it was at all feasible. Consequently, there was no need to bomb the reactor."

But a majority of the Israeli public thought otherwise. A Labor-commissioned poll examining trends after the reactor attack showed a clear Likkud edge over Labor for the first time for several months. Peres received the report with a heavy heart. "That was the worst day I experienced during the election campaign."

The morning of June 9, several hours before a scheduled meeting of the Knesset's Foreign Affairs and Defense Committee, Peres summoned a larger forum to his office. The participants in the previous consultation were now joined by other prominent Labor figures, as well as by representatives of the party's Mapam allies. Peres spoke out boldly against the Prime Minister and his conduct of the reactor raid. If Begin sought a national consensus on a matter so vital and grave, he ought to have first consulted the opposition. Peres argued that, the raid having fallen so close to election day, polling should be delayed by three months. However, he was only letting off steam: he knew there was no prospect of any such postponement.

When the Knesset Foreign Affairs and Defense Committee convened that day, its members enjoyed a gratifying half hour as they heard a detailed report on the raid and watched a film taken by the planes' cameras. But shortly afterward "the wars of the Jews" erupted in full ferocity.

The opening shot was fired by Peres, whose praise for the Air Force pointedly omitted any praise for the government's decision. "My congratulations to the armed forces and the Air Force. It was a brilliant exploit, and I endorse the words of the Commander in Chief that it was one hundred percent. There is no doubt that Israel cannot sanction a military nuclear option in an Arab state. On that there is no disagreement. But as to the course of action, the timing, the priorities, I have grave reservations and more."

Begin: "If Peres wishes to draw a distinction between those who made the decision and those who implemented it, I respect that. If he wants to congratulate the armed forces and the Air Force, and not the civilians who deployed them constitutionally, that is permissible."

Peres: "It's not a matter of congratulations. I simply question the decision."

Begin: "I don't think that in days gone by anyone indulged in such a distinction . . . Don't you understand that I see before my eyes my two little nephews who were murdered by the Nazis, and all the children of Israel? [In Europe] there was Zyklon B [poison gas] and here too it's poison—radioactive poison. If we don't stand together on matters like this, on what do we stand together? Did I not extend my hand to Ben Gurion in 1956, before the Sinai war? And did we not join the national unity government in 1967 because of the danger that threatened us? And what about Operation Entebbe? Now, post factum, should the leader of the opposition declare that he disagrees with the operation or its timing? Is that proper?"

But the two men also had substantive disagreements.

Peres: "As a man of experience, I say, if the French said it was impossible to activate the reactor before October, I doubt whether it could have been activated in October. In other words, if there were no other alternatives, we had time to bomb it [after the elections] in July, August or September, not at this particular time. Mitterrand should have been recruited to this cause. It would have been possible to reach agreement with the French on halting delivery of military-grade uranium. Were it not election time, I would have come to request your permission to go and talk to Mitterrand about it. I hesitated to do so because I feared that my words would again be construed as pertaining to the realm of political disagreement entailed by the election campaign. It was possible to wait another week or two and reach an understanding with Mitterrand's France."

Begin: "What has Mitterrand got to do with it? I would not have objected to you going to Mitterrand. For example, you're going to see Sadat; go in peace! You can go and see Mitterrand now. But the question is different: you heard that it is impossible to activate the reactor before October. Military Intelligence chief Saguy never ceased telling me, 'The reactor will be active by July.' Then he came and said, 'There may be time till September.' October was never mentioned. Rafful told me all the time, 'The Iraqis are unrelenting in their pressure on the French experts to get the reactor ready for operation by July.' In other words, three or four weeks from now. The truth is, there was no knowing what would happen between the Iraqis and the French in the interim.

"On that basis, when it's a matter of life and death for the nation, could we afford to wait till October? And meantime talk with Mitterrand? And wouldn't Mitterrand need to consult his ministers? In the meantime, the reactor would have become hot, leaving us openmouthed and helpless to do anything. A hot reactor cannot be bombed, for fear of radioactivity spreading over Baghdad. The Commander in Chief said he would not have consented to bomb the reactor under such circumstances—which could have arisen within a few weeks. Meanwhile, Mitterrand's Foreign Minister says the opposite of his President: 'We shall honor the agreements concluded.' "

Peres: "In choosing the timing, you should have taken account of the mission of U.S. presidential envoy Philip Habib, who was pursuing the removal of the Syrian missiles from the Bekaa Valley in Lebanon. In view of the Arab reaction, the reactor raid endangers his mission to a degree which will make it impossible to solve the problem by diplomatic means [forcing us to resort to] military means. After the reactor bombing, removing the missiles by military means involves a high measure of escalation. Therefore I regard it as more logical had we attacked the missiles first, and then the reactor."

Begin: "When Habib returned from Riyadh [where he sought Saudi support for his mediation efforts] he told me, 'I failed, I achieved nothing.' I had to comfort him and tell him, 'It wasn't you who failed, someone else failed.' But the Syrians announced: 'We won't withdraw a single missile.' What should we have done? Habib isn't even capable of removing half a missile. But we can destroy the missiles within two hours. However, we are in no hurry to do that. Had we relied on Habib, we would have been left openmouthed, because the reactor would meantime have become hot." Begin glared at the leader of the opposition. "Forgive me, Shimon, you were wrong. We did it at the correct and appropriate time. We could not have waited longer."

The fierce verbal duel extended to events preceding the reactor attack, when Peres' intervention prevented the bombing at the earlier date scheduled, May 10.

Peres: "My reservations over the bombing on May 10 arose because elections were held for the French presidency that same say. Had the reactor been bombed then, Israel would have made the worst imaginable mistake."

Begin: "I do not recall our letter mentioning the date May 10. You explained in your letter that such an operation does not always solve the problem, but sometimes spurs [to greater efforts]."

The Prime Minister promised to check the matter. ("I put your letter into my [shirt] pocket, because I feared that someone would read it, and that shirt is now at my home.") Begin's promise carried the rumble of an impending storm.

When deliberations ended, Chairman Moshe Arens proposed that the committee send congratulations on the destruction of the reactor to the Commander in Chief, the heads of the Mossad and Military Intelligence, the Air Force commander and their respective subordinates. At Begin's request, the message was amended to characterize the reactor: ". . . which constituted a grave threat to Israel." Now, on behalf of "the overwhelming majority" of the committee, Arens congratulated the government and the Prime Minister for the vital decision they had adopted. "No small measure of courage was required," Arens said.

• • •

A few hours later, the Labor Party's entire leadership convened in Tel Aviv; present were the party's representatives in the Knesset Foreign Affairs and Defense Committee, its candidates for Cabinet office, heads of the election staff and a number of senior members, as well as Mapam representatives. The meeting worked out guidelines for a propaganda offensive based on outright condemnation of the government for the reactor bombing.

The only reservations from this line came, surprisingly, from Abba Eban, a man renowned for his moderate views. "It was impossible not to be impressed by such resourcefulness," said Eban, recalling the film of the raid. "We heard the pilots' voices. We saw the hits. Let's forget it."

"It was a cynical act," prominent dove Yossi Sarid said of the reactor attack. "Don't they tell the people the truth? Not even on fateful matters?"

"Begin wanted it [the raid] for the elections," argued "Motta" Gur. "His decision reflects a want of national responsibility. His words about critical timing are incorrect. He should have given a chance to the incoming government and talked with France."

"The diplomatic process was not exhausted," pronounced Haim Barlev. "But with regard to our response, I propose we wait. With the nation rejoicing, and in this preelection atmosphere, there's no prospect of convincing people that the reactor bombing was irresponsible and incorrect. [We would] be in the right—but [we would] be harmed in the elections; why, what for?"

"I'm convinced the euphoria will very soon be over," Haim Herzog declared hopefully. "If we stick to our view and show courage, it won't harm us in the elections."

Rabin was far more cautious. "Even if there are queries as to the timing and the diplomatic preparation for the raid, I won't say so today, as the Security Council convenes [to condemn Israel]. Even so, Israel is unanimous in perceiving the threat posed by nuclear weapons in the hands of an Arab state, certainly of a state headed by Saddam Hussain. Unarguably, everything should be done to disrupt such an eventuality, to postpone or prevent it. Today, when, following the strike, [Israel is] in trouble on the regional and diplomatic [plane] and with a potential military confrontation, we [of Labor] must resist the diplomatic onslaught upon the state of Israel, even with regard to an operation over which we did not share in the decision-making." Rabin's conclusion: the party's response had been over-negative.

Aharon Harel disagreed. "No stammering! Let us embark upon a decisive offensive against the Prime Minister, his government and his policy."

Shlomo Hillel counseled prudence. "Now is not the time to say what we have to say." Later Hillel would explain his view: "Even prior to the bombing, Labor's situation was very difficult. Two or three days after the raid, there was a collapse in our public support. What good would it have done us to argue that the government conducted the reactor operation in an ugly manner? It did many things in an ugly manner . . ."

"It will be difficult to convince the public that the operation was indeed launched from electoral considerations," argued Micha Harish. Referring to information he had heard earlier in the Knesset's Foreign Affairs and Defense Committee, Harish held that the timing had not been critical and the bombing could have been delayed till September or October.

Mapam leader Victor Shemtov: "We should say that it was done from electoral motives; that we don't accept responsibility for the operation, and that we are in favor of removing the issue from the electoral campaign."

His colleague Meir Talmi adopted a similar view: "After we voice our criticism, we shall say that the subject must not become an electoral issue."

"Perhaps we should defer our criticism till after the elections?" mused Dani Rosolio, a kibbutz movement leader.

"There should be no hesitation in exhibiting our reservations, publicly and clearly," retorted Mussa Harif, another kibbutz representative.

Haim Tzadok commented: "We should congratulate the armed forces but avoid attacking the government, even if the timing leaves room for suspicion that the order to bomb the reactor was given on electoral grounds. The operation was vital and was executed superbly; but the date should have been deferred. Anyway, we should regard the bombing as water under the bridge and there's no point in occupying ourselves therewith."

Having listened intently to his colleagues' views, Peres now voiced his own: "We must reach a decision. Either we say the operation was vital without relation to the elections or we say it was an electoral operation. I suggest we say what we truly think." The Labor leader reitereated his view that the bombing had caused a diplomatic imbroglio: there were now few prospects for Habib's efforts to remove the Syrian missiles from Lebanon. Peres repeated that there had been no possibility of the reactor going into operation before September. Diplomatic action should have been pursued, to hold Mitterrand to his pledge to deny Iraq French assistance in developing a military nuclear capability.

A team comprising Galili, Sarid, Dinitz and Shemtov was delegated to formulate the Labor Party's press release on the bombing. Rather than a direct accusation that the government had mounted the raid out of electoral motives, the team hit upon a roundabout way of saying the same thing in reverse: "Regrettably," the statement read, "the Likkud government has taken all too many . . . steps in the spheres of defense, economy and diplomacy, with regard to which it was obliged to affirm that they were not guided by considerations arising from the election campaign." Hinting broadly at what Labor saw as governmental irresponsibility, the release stated: "In view of our national responsibility, and the diplomatic predicament and struggle into which we have been propelled as a result of the government's policy, we will not now disclose all the specific reasoning behind the objections voiced today by our representatives in the Knesset Foreign Affairs and Defense Committee."

Gad Yaakovi was dissatisfied with the propaganda line adopted by his party's leaders. On June 10, one day after release of the Labor Party statement, Yaakovi sent a note to Peres expressing his dissent. He urged Peres to brook no delay "in summoning the lead group to lay down the strategy for our public propaganda and election tactics." Meanwhile, Yaakovi did not keep his reservations to himself. Addressing a small meeting in Haifa, he said, "The operation was justified. The problem was the timing. The government should have been careful [to avoid such] timing which was liable to place it under suspicion of service to the elections. But Labor's response was erroneous.'"

A few days later Peres was to tell Yaakovi, "Our response was effectively forced upon us when Begin published the letter I sent him on May 10."

What did Peres mean by his reference to a "forced response"? On June 10, the morning after his fierce disagreement with Peres in the Knesset Foreign Affairs and Defense Committee, Begin came to his office bearing his adversary's letter. To his aide Yehiel Kadishai, Begin said, "Peres claimed yesterday that he expressed no objections in principle to the reactor bombing, but merely opposed the proposed date—May tenth. I recall him objecting in principle to the bombing itself, without reference to the date. A rereading of the letter testifies that I remembered correctly." The Foreign Affairs and Defense Committee having just convened to hear a report from the Foreign Minister, Begin directed Kadishai to convey a photostat of the letter to Chairman Moshe Arens for distribution to committee members. With the photostat Begin also sent a brief letter to Arens.

My friend [he wrote], as you will remember, committee member Shimon Peres said yesterday that he wrote me a letter in which he expressed no objection in principle to the reactor bombing, but conveyed his reservations as to the date, May 10, which was election day in France. You also know that I promised to check the matter by rereading the letter which was handwritten by Knesset member Shimon Peres. This morning, I did so. I found that Mr. Peres' memory failed him.

That ironical note was characteristic of Begin. But his conduct was uncharacteristic: without soliciting Peres' permission, he published the Labor leader's letter, which had been sent to him in utter confidence. Begin was aware of that point, which he went on to justify to Arens:

> The confidential nature of Mr. Peres' letter has expired, because over twenty committee members heard him speak yesterday of the letter's contents. It is not merely my right, it is my duty to place a complete copy of that letter at their disposal. As you will learn from reading it, Mr. Peres urges me altogether "to desist . . . I add my voice . . . to those who tell you not to act, certainly not under the present timing and circumstances."
>
> It is conceivable [Begin conceded] that Peres did indeed mean to desist from launching the operation on May 10 in particular, but the date does not feature in his letter—and it can be deduced from the letter that Peres opposed the operation itself, not any specific timing.

When the committee terminated its discussion of the Foreign Minister's review, Arens read out Begin's letter to him, and the text of Peres' letter to Begin. The committee decided against publishing the letters, but on leaving the meeting its members were astounded to hear both texts broadcast by Israel radio, to which they had been released on Begin's directive.

Peres responded by calling a press conference where he strongly criticised the Prime Minister. Begin had committed "an unpardonable act" in the unsanctioned publication of Peres' highly confidential letter, which he had written by hand to keep even his secretary from learning its contents.

On the substance of the matter Peres explained, "I did oppose the reactor bombing on May 10, but it was not the timing alone. I saw, in the change of government in France, an opportunity for preventing Iraq from developing a military nuclear option by means of the reactor. François Mitterrand told me specifically that if he became President he would do everything he could to excise the reactor of its military potential."

What about Begin's charge that his objections referred to the operation itself, not merely its timing? "The Prime Minister knew the truth, that my calculations were far broader, and he cannot play innocent. . . . He has the effrontery to say that my memory failed me, but his own memory failed him . . ."

Peres accused Begin of "nuclear blabbing" which was liable to precipitate "the nuclear race." "In the past two days," Peres complained, "there's been more talk in Israel of nuclear matters than in all of the preceding twenty years—all because the Prime Minister can't conquer his urge to blab." Peres did not conceal his conviction that Begin's "blabbing" arose from electoral considerations. "During the past three months Begin has begun to conduct the election campaign, and to subordinate the administration of the country . . . to electoral considerations. To improve the Likkud's standing, he shoots down helicopters in Lebanon, holds an election festival with Sadat in Ophira, and now he has attacked the reactor. Had the reactor attack not been launched from electoral motives, it would have been possible to consult the opposition . . ."

"Words of vicious vulgarity," was the comment from the Prime Minister's office on Peres' indictment.

Peres had an additional complaint against the government: Mitterrand's rise to power in France provided an opportunity to renew diplomatic efforts, but nothing was done. The government referred exclusively to the public declaration of the new Foreign Minister, Cheysson, that France would meet all obligations of the Giscard Administration, including its nuclear undertakings to Iraq. That was what the French said in public, Peres argued, "but Mitterrand told me that immediately upon assuming office he had decided to withhold delivery of additional shipments of military uranium."

Peres' accusation drew a sharp response from Foreign Minister Shamir: "Persistence in diplomatic efforts would have been liable to entail the loss of Israel's military option. As a new president, Mitterrand was occupied with the French parliamentary elections. By the time he turned to the issue of nuclear cooperation with Iraq, the reactor would have been hot—precisely the situation Israel sought to forestall."

Begin fumed. He was convinced that his adversaries' charges were providing propaganda fodder to be used by Israel's foes. At a June 11 election rally the Prime Minister alleged, "Messrs. Peres, Herzog and Gur have helped Defense Secretary Weinberger to ram through the decision about suspension" of the airplane shipments to Israel.

"Shame upon you, how dare you!" Begin thundered in response to Labor charges that the raid had been timed for electoral ends. "Would I send Jewish boys to risk death, or captivity which is worse than death? Would I send our boys into such danger for elections? Our Commander in Chief, the Air Force commander, the director of Military Intelligence—have they all become members of Herut overnight? My political career [was] in the balance. Let us imagine, heaven forbid, that the operation had failed and the planes were shot down. They would speak of my frivoliity, about sending men to their deaths, as they would have said of Yitzhak Rabin had the Entebbe operation . . . failed."

Deputy Defense Minister Mordechai Zippori, who had opposed the reactor bombing throughout the preliminary deliberations, also adopted a harsh tone toward the Labor party. "There has to be a prime minister of extraordinary strength to adopt such a difficult decision," he said. "I'm afraid Shimon Peres would have found it hard to adopt such a decision. But with such a 'gallery' of Labor leaders, the future of the state is in grave jeopardy."

Labor's attacks—masterminded by Zhorabin and Sawyer—were profoundly painful to Begin. The Prime Minister must have asked himself, Had a Labor government carried out a similar operation, which I considered misguided, would I behave as Labor leaders are behaving today?

Begin would have found little difficulty in answering with a ringing "No!" Seething, he resolved to seize upon the upcoming Cabinet meeting as an opportunity to hit back.

At that meeting, convened just one week after the reactor raid, Begin began with encouraging accounts of understanding for Israel's action, which was beginning to emerge the world over. From here, he went on to depict his state of mind from the moment the cabinet adopted its decision to approve the raid until the pilots' safe return. "I suffered from sleeplessness for many months. To act, or not? Until I heard the announcement that the target had been destroyed and the boys were on their way home . . . May the Name be praised, today the sun shines, you can see your children at play, the terrible danger hovering over their heads has been removed . . . Without any mysticism, I say, God was our succor." Begin launched into a frontal attack on Labor. Peres, he said, accused him of nuclear blabbing. Was there any nuclear blabbing worse than Labor's election commercials about the reactor at Dimona? "They publish full-page [advertisements claiming] that Dimona is the fruit of Shimon Peres' vision . . . What are they boasting about? 'Vote for Peres for prime minister, because there is Dimona and he constructed it.' All that without conscience, in total cynicism, taking advantage of a thing like that, which is a matter pertaining to the entire nation, for elections; and then they come along and tell us that we destroyed the Iraqi reactor because of elections!" Responding to the latter charge, Begin cried, "That is despicable! I don't hesitate to say so!

"The opposition is quoted abroad as saying that the reactor wasn't dangerous and would have remained cold till early September. I reported candidly what authoritative persons told me: The reactor will be hot early in July or early in September. Can we be sure that the reactor will be hot in September [not July]? Should we wait till September? And if they get in one week ahead of us? . . . Suppose it were August. Do the dates depend upon us? Maybe some scientist will come along and bring [activation] forward by a certain time?"

Begin's passion mounted when he came to charges from Yossi Sarid and Amiram Nir, who accused him of "an act of deceit," denying the Israeli claim that Jordan radio was the first to announce the operation. "The word 'reactor' was not mentioned in the Jordanian communiqué," the two men argued.

Responding to that charge, Begin read out the full text of the Jordanian broadcast. "Is it necessary to 'poke a finger into the mouth' [pull them by the tongue] to know what they meant by 'vital targets in Iraq'? On their way to the target, our planes were [probably] identified by the Jordanians, the Saudis and the Iraqis. Should we have been the sole Don Quixotes, remaining silent and leaving the Iraqis to be the first to publish their statement with their lies? And then we'd have to admit that we were caught like thieves in the night?"

The Prime Minister concluded his impassioned address on a note of unparalleled severity. "You have never heard the word 'treason' cross my lips. Everyone can express an opinion, they can err, and that isn't yet the deed of a traitor. But what the opposition has done is an act of sabotage: they are truly sabotaging Israel's diplomatic effort."

Begin urged his ministers, and the ruling coalition as a whole, "to denounce, before the entire nation, orally and in writing, this conduct by the leader of the opposition!" The Prime Minister set a personal example by an extraordinary directive to Cabinet secretary Aryeh Naor to publish his statement in Cabinet.

The Cabinet concluded its deliberations with a severe condemnation of the opposition. Labor was accused of "consciously misleading propaganda, which is exploited by all those with evil designs against us, in connection with the tremendous exploit of the armed forces." The statement noted that foreign governments critical of Israel expressly cited opposition charges whereby the reactor had posed no threat to Israel. "No responsible opposition in a democratic country has ever conducted itself thus. Let the public note this conduct by the opposition, in face of the arduous diplomatic engagement which has arisen in the wake of the operation of national salvation."

Deputy Prime Minister Yadin was alone in voting against the resolution, even though he characterized the conduct of the opposition as "wanting in responsibility." Yadin objected particularly to the final paragraph commencing "Let the public note . . .," fearing that it would be seen as exploitation of the controversy for electoral ends. Other ministers called for an even tougher wording, though there were Cabinet members who favored a milder formulation.

The Cabinet statement naturally evoked loud reverberations. The Labor Party immediately issued a response, whose wording was foreseeably vitriolic in tone.

The government statement is testimony to the moral and political bankruptcy of the Israeli government. Instead of discussing Israel's pressing problems, arising out of the bombing raid in Iraq, [the Cabinet] prefers to discuss the opposition . . . June 30 [polling day] exclusively occupies the attention of the Likkud government . . . Never has there been a less responsible government . . .

The Likkud government is in quest of culprits. The Prime Minister is seeking a scapegoat now it emerges that no adequate preliminary diplomatic work was done prior to the operation, and the Prime Minister likewise failed to weigh up all the foreseeable implications, even getting himself embroiled in inaccuracies and contradictions. The irresponsible government conducted itself with election frenzy. It was in a hurry, and opted for the shortcut of "one swift sharp blow" which is the most dangerous and harmful of all.

At this stage, some individuals told Peres he should have expressed his support for the government immediately after the operation; had he done so, his popularity would have soared, giving him a chance of winning the elections. "If you didn't do so then," someone told him, "at least keep your mouth shut now."

Peres was indignant. "Was I the one that talked? Did I publicize the operation? I have no doubt that the commmotion, the noise and the fuss which the Prime Minister generated after the bombing were for electoral purposes. Had Israel remained silent after the operation, the harm would have been kept to a minimum."

Moshe Dayan—a years-long Peres associate before becoming foreign minister in Begin's 1977 Cabinet and going on to head an independent party—argued that Peres and his colleagues erred in attacking the government after the bombing. "Were I in Labor's place," Dayan explained, "I would have acted like Rabin, who declared that, in view of the national interest, he does not wish to express an opinion as long as the matter is being debated in the Security Council. That is the way to behave. When the whole world flings brickbats at us, I wouldn't provide it with ammunition."

Labor sensed that public opinion was turning away. "Spies" sent to observe Begin's election rallies reported that "prolonged cheers" erupted when the Prime Minister mentioned the reactor bombing, followed by resounding jeers against Labor when Begin referred to the opposition's criticism of the operation, and the effect that criticism had abroad.

After Labor's defeat in the elections, when the party leadership considered the lessons of the campaign, Peres declared, "The reactor bombing made a great impact upon public opinion, causing it to shift. I question what lessons we can draw therefrom."

Some held that Labor's adverse comments on the bombing were justified, even in the retrospect of an electoral setback. Election director Aharon

Harel argued, "Without stressing our differences with the ruling party, we would have lost voters. If the labor leaders considered the bombing misguided, they were bound to oppose it unhesitatingly."

A different view was taken by newly elected Knesset member Dr. Michael Bar Zohar, the biographer of Ben-Gurion. "Our response to the reactor bombing caused us great harm," he said. Asked what response he would have proposed, Bar Zohar replied, "To rest content with congratulations to the armed forces."

Most experts inclined to the view that Labor's criticism of the raid rebounded against the critics themselves. Election staff adviser Yoav Lavi declared:

> The unbridled attacks ... inflicted inestimable harm upon Labor and Peres, and halted a slight improvement in Labor's standing which was beginning to emerge in opinion polls for the first time in five months, after a constantly declining trend from the February peak. After the criticism, not only did support for the Likkud grow, but a considerable portion of the undecided voters rallied to the Likkud, while Labor support fell to a record low. The surveys at that time showed Labor receiving no more than 37 or 38 Knesset seats. Only the impact of ... electoral violence, which was on the rise at that time, and a slight change in Labor propaganda, induced voters who were undecided between Labor and the [left-wing] fringe parties to revert to Labor. With that, the surveys showed a majority of the public persisting in clear support for the reactor bombing.

Surveys conducted for Labor reflected these swings. Between June 1 and June 5, prior to the reactor bombing, polls showed the two major parties neck and neck, with a possible one-seat edge to Labor. After the bombing, the ratio changed sharply: between June 14 and June 16 the Likkud held a twelve-to-fourteen-seat lead. When violence that was attributed to Likkud supporters erupted, the odds again swung against the Likkud, whose lead shrank to six seats in a June 23 poll. On June 26, after a televised Begin–Peres debate, and a leadership reshuffle which made Rabin Labor's candidate for defense minister, the balance tilted in favor of Labor, with an estimated three-seat lead. On June 29, the Likkud again drew level after a powerful address by Begin in Tel Aviv's main square, where he responded to remarks against Oriental Jews uttered at a previous Labor rally held in the selfsame square.

Be all that as it may, Labor failed utterly in its attempts to convince the Israeli public that the Likkud government had erred in deciding to bomb the reactor.

Begin was embittered over Labor's vicious personal attacks, which characterized his speeches as "barking." "That I, like Hitler, do not orate, merely 'bark'? While my words reflected the national consensus . . ."

Another aspect of the reactor issue which troubled Begin was the problem of leaks.

On June 9, two days after the reactor bombing, Israel radio began to cite the views expressed by various ministers in the deliberations which had preceded the raid, listing supporters and opponents, specifying those who had voiced threats or exerted pressure.

The matter came up in a question to Begin during a meeting of the Knesset's Foreign Affairs and Defense Committee. "*Rechiless*," Begin replied disdainfully. "Gossip! Do you know what I mean? I purposely used the juicy Yiddish term in place of the Hebrew word."

Veteran Knesset member Zerah Wahrhaftig remarked, "The radio reported today that the entire operation belongs to Agriculture Minister Ariel Sharon, and that it was only his letter threatening resignation that forced the decision upon the Cabinet, otherwise the ministers would have been against the operation."

Begin replied offhandedly, "Yoram Aridor never opposed the bombing, and Ariel Sharon never sent me a letter of resignation. There are two books which prove that someone else made peace with Egypt, and we forgave that." (The Prime Minister was referring to the memoirs of former ministers Moshe Dayan and Ezer Weizman, both men playing down Begin's role in attaining peace with Egypt, while each credited himself with the main achievement. By implication, Begin was drawing an analogy with Sharon: even without the latter, Begin insinuated, the Cabinet would have reached the correct decision. Even so, Begin did not consider this the time or the place to list his numerous grievances against Sharon or to mention his frequent rebukes to the Agriculture Minister with regard to leaks.)

Wahrhaftig did not relent: "One may forgive when insulted, but not when one insults others . . ."

Begin: "Whoever provided that report—whether journalist or politician —will be shown up by our denial as a liar."

Wahrhaftig: "There is nothing more despicable. A few hours after the successful conclusion of the operation, someone publicizes how the ministers voted."

Begin: "I admit and agree. It is scandalous."

The issue of leaks came up again in the Cabinet on June 21. Simha Ehrlich complained that the raid's date had leaked out, recalling the Labor conclave presided over by Peres on June 7, a few hours before the bombing. "It is a matter of the greatest gravity," said the Deputy Prime Minister. "Such a closely guarded secret, upon which human lives depend, leaks out.

And it's a matter of the utmost gravity that people who knew the secret did not keep their mouths shut; instead, they acted against the government, or told their friends in private." Ehrlich argued that this grave blabbing called for thorough investigation, in view of the fact that just three men—Begin, Shamir and Eytan—had set the timing. He demanded a probe to discover who, apart from them, was in the know, in the political and military echelons and in the various ministries.

When the matter rose again on June 22 at a meeting of the Knesset Foreign Affairs and Defense Committee, Begin reported his deputy's complaints. "This is truly improper," he argued. "We were involved in a matter of life and death. The Iraqis could have laid an ambush for our boys."

A committee member asked the Prime Minister whether he would order an investigation, in view of the fact that persons like Ezer Weizman, not required to know of the operation, were nevertheless aware of it.

Begin: "An investigation will do no good. We shall not attach lie detectors to the chests of ministers and generals."

But the most intriguing revelation came from an ultra-Orthodox committee member: he related that, prior to the bombing, someone came to the renowned rabbinical sage Rabbi Moshe Yehoshua Hagger and confided, "There is going to be a great action," and that the rabbi replied, "I already know."

"What can you do?" sighed Begin. "That's the way we live. . . ."

33 "The Opera of Baghdad"

When General Ivry took his leave of his fliers as they set out to Baghdad, his parting words were: "See you after—at the debriefing!"

The debriefing was held immediately upon their return. Ivry and Commander in Chief Eytan were eager for firsthand testimony about the bombing. Prior to that, each of the pilots was requested to complete a special form, as is customary in such instances. Eliezer Malachi, who led the second formation of bombers, was renowned throughout the Air Force for his artistic gifts. He proceeded to take the form and, using no words, sketched the formations of planes, tracing their entry paths into the target area and their departure course. Later Malachi gave Ivry a personal present: a sketch of his F-16, with the anxiously awaited code message "Emerald and Ruby —Charlie all."

The debriefing room teemed with top brass. "I'm unaccustomed to debriefings of that nature," Malachi related later. "Everyone was waiting to hear tales of heroism, but when we got up on the stage there wasn't that much to tell."

Colonel Yitzhal Melrom, the most senior pilot to fly with the assault force, furrowed his brow. "How come the planes didn't suffer any technical failure? The F-16 is a very good plane, that's true, but even good planes have their failures . . . I don't get it—not a single hitch. . . . It's probably the hand of fate . . . a phenomenon unknown in aviation. . . . They're planes with soul."

Someone remarked: "It's from heaven. The hand of God."

Colonel Malachi offered a more rational explanation. "A lot of thought went into that operation, a lot of discussion and a lot of time [training] in the squadrons . . . There were lots of soul-searchings about assault tactics."

Assault group leader Colonel Aryeh Ran attributed its success to "an extraordinary sense of responsibility. [It was] an operation of enormous national significance, in which failure was just out of the question. It's too good to be true. We should rejoice in our lot for being chosen, and for the operation terminating safely with us all here."

Rafful spoke with his customary brevity. "The distinction between brilliant success and painful failure is a very fine one. In this instance, success was brilliant, and that's why the pilots have nothing to tell in the debriefing."

Ivry added, "The exploit was so superb that the debriefing was a bore . . ." His tone was even. "Yes, there are many who have a share [in the operation], but only a few bear direct responsibility. Throughout the process of planning and decision-making, I sensed your full backing, your full confidence in those who bore the responsibility, your faith in your ability to accomplish the mission. I find it hard to weigh up those feelings, but they were very important. Throughout those months prior to the operation, and certainly during its course, you vindicated my expectations of you when I put you in charge of the F-16s." Ivry raised his voice slightly. "Take what I have said as a mark of my high personal esteem."

The Commander in Chief now read out his personal address to the Air Force commander: "Please accept my esteem, which could not be higher, over perfect execution of the destruction of the nuclear reactor. It was a fateful and historic operation, and that is good reason for you to earn praise for your courage and competence. We all sense gratitude and respect which could not be higher."

Then and there, Ivry recommended a citation for Colonel Aryeh Ran, "who prepared and led the operation coolly, exhibiting leadership, a high professional standard, and daring." It goes without saying that the Commander in Chief approved the recommendation on the spot.

Asked later whether he was moved when the pilots returned, or during the initial debriefing, Rafful replied simply, "No. I saw that this was the Air Force's standard of performance, I was sure the Force would accomplish it without any difficulty, and I therefore sensed no particular elation."

On June 9, Ivry came to see Begin, to receive the Prime Minister's personal expression of gratitude. At the conclusion of the meeting Ivry expressed a wish: he asked Begin to receive the fliers who had taken part in the operation.

Begin replied, "They are deserving that I come to them."

One week later, the Prime Minister and Cabinet colleagues arrived at the Air Force base. Ivry greeted the distinguished visitors; just this once, he permitted himself somewhat flowery language: "The operation was a sonata for brass and percussion. The instruments gleamed; they were tuned like those of a superb orchestra. The services of the ground technicians, intelligence which prepared the 'notes,' control, operations—together, they performed the melody like an orchestra with reechoing chords, making the hearer's ears reverberate. I thank the Prime Minister, who permitted us to perform, at Carnegie Hall, the opera of Baghdad. We in the Air Force are constrained to be better and more effective. Our Air Force is important to us all. Let us ring down the curtain on the Baghdad operation, because many missions still lie ahead."

The Commander in Chief spoke with the brevity of habit. "In the annals of the state of Israel, we never had any military operation whose success was so fateful for the generations to come. It would be hard to imagine the fate of the state in another two or three years without that operation."

All eyes now turned to the Prime Minister. Begin declared, "On behalf of the nation, and its democratically elected government, I have come to say, Thank you. We have come here because we wished to inhale the atmosphere in which you fly. . . . Everything said here may perhaps be forgotten, but what you did shall be remembered by the generations to come. Thanks to you, we have been freed of a nightmare which has pursued us for two whole years. . . ."

During the ceremony, veteran flier Yitzhal Melrom sent a note to the leader of the second formation, Eliezer Malachi: "It was a pleasure to fly under your personal command . . ." Malrom sent an additional note to assault group commander Colonel Ran: "You had every good reason to get agitated (we saw that even "Rafful the tough" softened up), but your hands did not shake. As planner, director, leader, commander and pilot, you were a model. Congratulations!"

Later Begin was to add: "If one were to seek some historical analogy, our operation resembles the Allied action during World War Two, when a commando unit raided a Norwegian township where the Germans were producing heavy water in preparation for an atomic bomb. It was one of the miracles of Divine Providence that America got in first before Germany. Humanity stood on the brink of the chasm. That is one of the reasons why a man should believe in Divine Providence."

34 "A Dog with Teeth"

The reactor bombing led to some rethinking on the part of certain Israeli personages who had earlier opposed the operation.

Shimon Peres—meanwhile elevated to the office of prime minister—appears to adhere to the view that the reactor bombing was misguided, arguing that the assumption of the presidential office by François Mitterrand would have finally eliminated the threat posed to Israel.

By contrast, former Mossad chief Hoffy admits: "I was in the wrong. Begin was right. The fact is that the reactor bombing did not incur [the adverse effects] we expected it to bring."

The man who was then director of Military Intelligence, Yeshua Saguy, says, "I admit to having been wrong with respect to the diplomatic fallout I foresaw on the part of the United States. But it's the prolonged war with Iran which has blocked renewal of work on the Iraqi reactor."

Aharon Yariv, who, as will be recalled, drew up a memorandum specifying the detrimental effects to be awaited from the raid, affirms, "Our unfavorable views were not borne out." Two months after the bombing, Yariv predicted that the Iraqis would have a new reactor in operation within three or four years. That forecast, like a similar prediction by David Ivry, has proved incorrect.

Mordechai Gur, who foresaw somber results to the raid, declared, "Up to this point in time, the fact is that I was not right."

Abba Eban showed no hesitation in pronouncing, "It was a triumph, no diplomatic harm was caused, and Israeli deterrence was reinforced."

Ezer Weizman, however, has his reservations: "The bombing merely deferred the issue. The problem is, how is the matter to be dealt with quietly? In a military sense, it was a fine operation, but it did not resolve any problem."

Indeed?

The late Deputy Prime Minister Simha Ehrlich, one of the most enthusiastic advocates of the bombing, was convinced. "After the bombing, no Western state will repeat what Giscard's France did in Iraq. Just as one must never entrust a loaded pistol to a small child, it was dangerous to humanity to entrust nuclear weapons to the rulers of the Arab states."

Then Foreign Ministser Yitzhak Sharmir (meanwhile elected leader of the Likkud and prime minister) drew his own conclusions: "In the Mideast, there's no maintaining a balance of terror along the formula which prevails between the two great blocs, because the rational judgment of some Arab leaders cannot be relied upon. The reactor bombing highlighted Israel's resolve and showed that in anything to do with safeguarding its existence there are no physical frontiers."

Former Commander in Chief Raphael Eytan explained: "The state of Israel has no capacity for defending itself against nuclear arms. It has no absorptive capacity; any nuclear strike is liable to be a deathblow. Consequently, should Israel ever face a similar situation, I would urge a repetition of the action. The operation in Iraq was performed at the last moment, and I hope fervently that developed countries possessing nuclear knowhow will have many second thoughts before helping any Arab state to construct a nuclear reactor."

Rafful's view was disputed by Mordechai Zippori, who was defense minister at the time of the bombing and is very knowledgeable on the subject. Zippori, who was halfhearted about the raid, argued that a standing policy based on Eytan's principles would be "a great dream" which, however, would be incapable of fulfillment. Israel was, and would remain, powerless "to change the world order."

But Professor Yuval Ne'eman affirmed, "It is Israeli policy to delay as long as possible the day when the Arabs have nuclear weapons. The bombing in Iraq postponed that situation by a number of years."

Moshe Dayan, in the last interview he ever gave (it was published posthumously), said, "Not one Arab would shed a tear were Israel to vanish off the face of the map. The Arabs should know that Israel is not a dog which barks, but a dog with teeth. To me, [the reactor bombing] was a positive action. Iraq was producing nuclear weapons against Israel, and we were obliged to defend ourselves. Consequently, the operation was justified, without going into the question of its timing—i.e., whether or not it was an election stunt."

Menahem Begin foresaw that renewal of Iraq's nuclear capacity would require five years, "and I won't be prime minister then. Resting upon the precedent we set, I am sure that every prime minister, and every government in Israel, will destroy the reactor before it becomes operational."

• • •

After the reactor bombing, the Iraqis sought to renew their ties with France. On October 4, 1981, French Foreign Trade Minister Michel Jobert arrived in Baghdad, where he proclaimed his government's willingness in principle to rebuild the shattered reactor. As proof of the earnestness of French intentions, a delegation of nuclear engineers arrived in Iraq for the purpose of pinpointing a new site for construction of the reactor. This time, it would be built in an isolated mountainous area, facilitating erection of a comprehensive defensive system to protect it from any future attack.

However, France also announced that the rebuilt Osirak would not operate on uranium enriched to a grade of 93 percent; instead, the fuel delivered would be Caramel, which the Iraqis had refused in the past and which French scientists had now shown to be adequate for almost all the scientific experiments calling for highly enriched uranium. The French also requested return of the 12 kilograms of enriched uranium in Iraq's possession, should the renewed negotiations break down.

The truth is that even Caramel does not entirely eliminate the danger of Iraq exploiting the reactor for military purposes. Georges Amsel, director of France's national scientific research center, warned President Mitterrand: "True, Caramel is not regarded as suitable raw material for the production of [uranium] bombs, but it will give the Iraqis the opportunity to produce plutonium."

Be that as it may, Saddam Hussain demanded a new reactor without delay, and on the same terms as before. He also wanted the promised weapons-grade fuel. But France did not give in. In reply to a question by Senator Pierre-Christian Taittinger, Claude Cheysson announced that France would supply nothing but Caramel; under no circumstances would there be further deliveries of military-grade uranium. For further stress, Louis Amigues, a senior French Foreign Ministry official, informed Yuval Ne'eman in September 1981: "The team now in power is not one which Israel can argue is not pro-Israeli. On this team you can rely."

Ne'eman retorted: "It is better to rely postfactum."

About a year later, the French approached Ne'eman—now minister of science and development—with an offer to sell a nuclear reactor to Israel. Paris made the sale conditional upon an Israeli undertaking to refrain from attacking the Iraqi reactor, should France rebuild it. Ne'eman rejected the condition.

In April 1985, it was reported that Prime Minister Shimon Peres, while negotiating the purchase of French nuclear reactors, pledged that Israel would not repeat the attack on the Iraqi reactor if it should be rebuilt. The disclosure, originating from French sources, was denied by the Prime Minister's office.

Just one year later, in April 1986, Peres met with Jacques Chirac—who, as premier, had signed France's framework agreement with Iraq—now restored to his previous office under Socialist President Mitterrand. Chirac again denied that it was he who had made the decision to sell the reactor to Iraq, insisting that the responsibility rested upon President Giscard and his intimate the then Industry Minister, Michel d'Ornano. With that, Chirac strenuously criticized the reactor bombing, claiming that France had adopted all suitable safeguards to prevent its use in production of nuclear bombs. Chirac said that the Iraqis were examining the feasibility of reconstructing the reactor and had approached the Soviet Union to that end.

Peres responded: "The question is, to whom is such a reactor entrusted? There is no comparison between sale of a reactor to Israel and a similar sale to Iraq. It has already been demonstrated that the Iraqi reactor generates trouble, not energy."

In fact there has been no progress in Franco-Iraqi contacts since the reactor raid. Iraq has held contacts with interested parties in West Germany and has even gone abegging to the Soviet Union, but experience shows that Moscow never supplied a nuclear-weapons capability to any country, not even its Soviet-bloc allies.

There has been no change in Israel's basic position that it will not be the first country to introduce nuclear weapons into the Mideast. Prime Minister Begin even proclaimed Israel's willingness to sign the Non-Proliferation Treaty, on condition that the neighboring Arab states make peace. "If they refuse to recognize Israel, and also decline to make peace with Israel, what is the point of signing such a treaty?"

A postscript: Sometime after the reactor bombing, Iraq employed chemical weapons in action against the Iranian forces. Many observers who had earlier condemned Israel for attacking the reactor now deduced that if Saddam Hussain had acquired a nuclear bomb he would have used it against Iran.

And after that, it would, in all probability, have been the turn of Israel.

Principal Sources and Bibliography

Books

Arian, Asher (ed.), *The Elections in Israel 1981*. Ramot, Tel Aviv, 1983.

Eban, Abba, *The New Diplomacy*. Random House, New York.

Eytan, Raphael, (with Dov Goldstein), *Raful, the Story of a Soldier*. Ma'ariv, Tel Aviv, 1985 (Hebrew).

Feuerstein, Dr. Emil, *The Twentieth Century Lexicon*. Defence Ministry publications, Tel Aviv, 1982 (Hebrew).

Golan, Matti, *Peres*. Schoken, Jerusalem and Tel Aviv, 1982 (Hebrew).

Haig, Alexander M., *Caveat*. Macmillan, New York, 1984.

Heller, Mark, Tamari, Dov, and Eytan, Ze'ev (eds.), *The Middle East Military Balance 1983*. Jaffee Center for Strategic Studies, Tel Aviv University, 1983.

Herzog, Haim, *Who Stands Accused?* Bronfman, 1978 (Hebrew).

Jabber, Fuad, *Israel and Nuclear Weapons*. International Institute for Strategic Studies, Los Angeles, 1971.

Kissinger, Henry, *Nuclear Weapons and Foreign Policy*. Norton, New York, 1969.

Krosney, Herbert and Steve Weissman, *The Islamic Bomb*. New York Times Book Co., Inc., New York.

Lavi, Yoav, *Missed Opportunity*. Revivim, Tel Aviv, 1981 (Hebrew).

Nixon, Richard, *Leaders*. Warner Books, New York, 1982.

Segev, Shmuel, *The Iranian Triangle*. Ma'ariv, Tel Aviv, 1981 (Hebrew).

Shiff, Ze'ev, *The Airforce* (Encyclopedia on Army and Security, vol. 3), Revivim, Ma'ariv publications, Tel Aviv, 1981 (Hebrew).

Shiff, Ze'ev, and Haber, Eytan (eds.), *Israel, Army and Defence*. Zmora, Modan, Beytan, "Davar" publications, Tel Aviv, 1976 (Hebrew).

Shiff, Ze'ev and Ya'ari, Ehud, *The War of Deceit*. Schoken, Jerusalem and Tel Aviv, 1984 (Hebrew).

Shimoni, Ya'akov, *The Arab States*. Am Oved, Tel Aviv, 1977 (Hebrew).

Shimoni, Ya'akov and Levin, Avitar, *A Political Lexicon of the Middle East in the 20th Century*. Jerusalem Publishing House, 1974 (Hebrew).

Weizman, Ezer, *The Battle for Peace*. Edanim Publishers, Jerusalem (Hebrew).

Newspapers and Journals

(various dates, before and after the bombing)

Israel

Airforce Journal

Al Hamishmar

Bamahaneh (IDF journal)

Davar

Ha'aretz

Jerusalem Post

Ma'ariv

Monitin

Yediot Aharonot

United States
Boston Globe
New Republic
Newsweek
New York Times
Time
Washington Post

Britain
Daily Mail
Daily Telegraph
8 Days
Nuclear Fuel
New Engineering International
New Scientist
Times

West Germany
Der Spiegel

France
L'Arche
L'Express
Le Monde
Liberation

Switzerland
International Defence Review

Interviews
  Abba Eban, Shlomo Aharonson,
Raphael Eytan, Simcha Ehrlich, Yosef
Burg, Eytan Bentzur, Haim Barlev,
Mordechai Gur, Warren H. Donnelly
(Congressional research service,
interviewed by Rami Tal), Aharon Harel,
Shlomo Gazit, Ezer Weizman, Avraham
Tamir, Yigael Yadin, Yisrael Katz, Naftali
Lavi, Yuval Ne'eman, Ephraim Evron,
David Ivry, Uri Porat, Shimon Peres,
Haim Zadok, Mordechai Zippori, Yehiel
Kadishai, Amnon Kapeliuk, Yitzhak
Rabin, Yehoshua Saguy, Yitzhak Shamir.
  Col. Eliezer Malachi (pseud.), leader of
the second foursome of bombers; Maj.
(reserve) Gai, technical officer
  Persons from the Israeli
establishment—political, military and
security—who requested anonymity.
  A senior American diplomat—
anonymously; a member of the United

States National Security Council—
anonymously.

Written Testimony
  Raymond Barre, Jonathan Bingham,
Philip C. Habib, Guy Méry, Richard
Stone, Jimmy Carter, Roger Richter,
Jacques Chirac

Documents and Studies

International
Amnesty International reports, 1975 to
  1984
International Atomic Energy Agency
  (IAEA), Vienna, Austria: text of
  agreement between the IAEA and Iraq
Record of the United Nations General
  Assembly and Security Council

United States
Congressional Record, Senate and House
  of Representatives, prior to the bombing
Congressional Research Service: Possible
  Contamination of Baghdad from
  Bombing of the Iraqi Reactor, Warren
  H. Donnelly, Library of Congress,
  18.6.1981
Congressional Research Service: Western
  European Reactions, Joseph Pilat,
  19.8.81
Correspondence between Arthur Goldberg
  (16.6.1981) and Menahem Begin
  (22.6.81)
Department of State Bulletin, June 1981
Discover, August 1981, Bruce Schechter
Extracts from the U.S. press, disseminated
  by the United States International
  Agency
I.D.F. Spokesman: Anticipatory Self-
  Defence in the Atomic Age, 22.6.1981
Israel and the Iraqi Bomb, Lewis A.
  Dunn, Hudson Institute paper, June
  1981
Middle East Enterprise, 15.12.1975
The Middle East Journal, Autumn 1983,
  vol. 37 no. 4, Ted C. Snyder
Middle East Review, Winter 1980–1981,
  Ben Martin
Report for the Arms Control Association,
  Charles N. Van Doren, 25.6.1981

Reports collated from the written and electronic media in the Middle East by the United States Foreign Broadcast Information Service (F.B.I.S.)

Senate and House of Representatives, Committees on Foreign Affairs, Hearings, June 1981

Britain

The U.S.S.R. and the Arabs, Joan Renvar, C. Hurst, London

Israel

"A Documentary Study of Soviet Policy in the Middle East 1945–1973," by Yaacov Ro'i, John Wiley, New York, Toronto, Israel Universities Press, Jerusalem

Hatzav (daily collation of reports from the written and electronic media in the Arab states) before and after the bombing

Knesset record, before and after the bombing

Middle East Backgrounder, Media Analysis Dept., Government Information Center, Jerusalem

"Middle East Contemporary Survey," vol. 51 1980–1981, by Haim Shaked, Shiloah Center, Tel Aviv University, Holmes and Meier, New York and London

"Nuclear Aspects of the Arab-Israeli Conflict," final paper for masters degree in social sciences, by Oded Brosh, under guidance of Prof. Shlomo Aharonson, Hebrew University, Social Science Faculty, Political Science Dept., Jerusalem 1985 (Hebrew)

Notes and minutes of various meetings, at different levels, before and after the bombing—likewise not yet cleared for full publication

Papers drawn up at various governmental and security echelons, which have not been cleared for full publication

"Report on Saddam Hussain," March 1981, source classified

"Sadam Husayn's Quest for Power and Survival," Ofra Bengiu, Asian and African Studies, Haifa, November 1981

"Soviet-Iraqi Relations (July 1968–March 1973)" by Aryeh Yodfat, in *The New East,* quarterly of the Israeli Orientalist Society, 1984 (Hebrew)

"The Raid on Osiraq," Shai Feldman, Memorandum no. 5, August 1981, Tel Aviv University

"The Saddam Hussain Regime in Iraq—Continuity and Change," Ofra Bengiu, in the monthly review published by the I.D.F. chief education officer January 1981 (Hebrew)

"The Stabilisation of the Ba'ath Regime in Iraq," Ofra Bengiu, monthly review of the I.D.F. chief education officer, Nov. 1976 (Hebrew)

Arab Publications

"Arab Perspectives," July 1981

"Before and After," Iraq Publications

Legal Studies

"The American Journal of International Law," July 1983; by Anthony d'Amato

"Military Law Review," Summer 1985; by Uri Shoham

"New York University Law Review," April 1984; by Bett M. Plebaum

Index

ABOUT THE AUTHOR

Born in Israel in 1936, Shlomo Nakdimon has been a political affairs reporter for *Yediot Aharonot*, Israel's top-circulation daily, for more than thirty
years. The author of six books on contemporary events and political history,
he served as media adviser and press attaché to Prime Minister Begin from
1978 to 1980.